YEARBOOK

1995-1996

ISSN 0074-445X
ISBN 92-1-170073-6

Sales number
Nº de vente: **689**

INTERNATIONAL COURT OF JUSTICE

Yearbook 1995-1996

No. 50

I.C.J. - THE HAGUE - 1996

PRINTED IN THE NETHERLANDS

In March 1947 the International Court of Justice instructed the Registrar to publish a *Yearbook* providing general information concerning its organization, jurisdiction, activities and administration.

The *Yearbook* appears in the second half of each year. The present volume – fiftieth of the series – covers the period from 1 August 1995 to 31 July 1996.

The *Yearbook* is prepared by the Registry and in no way involves the responsibility of the Court; in particular, the summaries of judgments, advisory opinions and orders contained in Chapter VI cannot be quoted against the actual texts of those judgments, advisory opinions and orders and do not constitute an interpretation of them.

Eduardo VALENCIA-OSPINA,
Registrar of the Court.

TABLE OF CONTENTS

Page

INTRODUCTION

The *International Court of Justice*, which has its seat in The Hague, is the principal judicial organ of the United Nations.

It had as its predecessor the *Permanent Court of International Justice*, which was instituted by the League of Nations in 1920 and was dissolved in 1946.

I. Basic Texts

The constitutional texts of the Court are the Charter of the United Nations and the Statute of the Court. Other basic texts are the Rules of Court and the resolution concerning the internal judicial practice of the Court.

1. Charter of the United Nations

The International Court of Justice was brought into being by the Charter of the United Nations, signed at San Francisco on 26 June 1945. The Charter deals with the Court in Article 7, paragraph 1, Article 36, paragraph 3, and Articles 92-96, which form Chapter XIV.

2. Statute of the International Court of Justice

(a) *Text of the Statute*

By virtue of Article 92 of the Charter of the United Nations, the Statute of the Court is annexed to the Charter, of which it forms an integral part. The text of the Statute, which also was signed at San Francisco on 26 June 1945, is published by the Court in the volume *I.C.J. Acts and Documents No. 5*, pages 60-89.

The above-mentioned Article indicates that the Statute is based upon that of the *Permanent Court of International Justice*. The modifications are few in number, most of them being formal adaptations designed to take account of the replacement of the League of Nations by the United Nations. The *I.C.J. Yearbook 1946-1947*, pages 101-102, gives a list of the articles modified.

(b) *States parties to the Statute*

Article 93 of the Charter provides:

> "1. All Members of the United Nations are *ipso facto* parties to the Statute of the International Court of Justice.
>
> 2. A State which is not a Member of the United Nations may become a party to the Statute of the International Court of Justice

on conditions to be determined in each case by the General Assembly upon the recommendation of the Security Council."

The States parties to the Statute are listed in Chapter III, pages 62-68, of this *Yearbook*.

(c) *Amendments to the Statute*

According to Article 69 of the Statute, amendments to that instrument may be effected by the same procedure as is provided for amendments to the Charter. This procedure is set out in Chapter XVIII of the Charter (Arts. 108-109). Article 108 provides that amendments to the Charter "shall come into force for all Members of the United Nations when they have been adopted by a vote of two-thirds of the members of the General Assembly and ratified in accordance with their respective constitutional processes by two-thirds of the Members of the United Nations, including all the permanent members of the Security Council".

Article 69 of the Statute also specifies that provisions concerning the participation in the amendment procedure of States which are parties to the Statute but are not members of the United Nations may be adopted by the General Assembly upon recommendation of the Security Council (see Chap. III, pp. 67-68, below).

Furthermore, Article 70 of the Statute empowers the Court to propose of its own accord such amendments to the Statute as it may deem necessary.

No amendments have so far been made to the Statute.

3. *Rules of Court*

Article 30 of the Statute provides that "the Court shall frame rules for carrying out its functions. In particular, it shall lay down rules of procedure."

Rules of Court were adopted on 6 May 1946, and were published by the Court in the volume *I.C.J. Acts and Documents No. 1*, second edition, pages 54-83. They were based on the latest text of the Rules of the *Permanent Court*, that of 11 March 1936, with certain changes, formal and substantive, a list of which was given in *I.C.J. Yearbook 1946-1947*, pages 102-103.

From 1946 to 1972 the Rules remained unchanged, although from time to time the Court, which keeps its procedure under constant review, considered their modification. In 1967 a revision was undertaken (see *I.C.J. Yearbook 1967-1968*, p. 87; *I.C.J. Yearbook 1969-1970*, p. 114; *I.C.J. Yearbook 1970-1971*, pp. 109-110) and on 10 May 1972 the Court adopted some partial amendments of immediate interest. Amended and partly renumbered Rules of Court (see *I.C.J. Acts and Documents No. 3*, pp. 92-149) thus came into force on 1 September 1972. A Note by the Registry (*Background Note IV*, or see *I.C.J. Yearbook 1971-1972*, pp. 3-11) indicates the changes and gives a table of concordance between the 1946 Rules and those of 1972.

The work of revision was subsequently resumed, and culminated on 14 April 1978 in the adoption of a new set of Rules. These Rules of Court came into force on 1 July 1978 and as from that date replaced the 1972 amended version of those adopted in 1946. They were first published in *I.C.J. Acts and Documents No. 4* concurrently with the issue of *I.C.J. Background Note V*, entitled "Note by the Registry on the Revised Rules of Court (1978)", which includes a table of concordance as between the respective articles of the new set and its predecessor. For a rather more detailed account of the background the reader is referred to pages 111-119 of *I.C.J. Yearbook 1977-1978*, which feature an analytical table enabling the structure of the new set of Rules to be compared with that of the 1946 and 1972 sets, and a table of concordance as between the specific articles of the 1978, 1972 and 1946 Rules of Court. The current publication containing the 1978 Rules of Court is *I.C.J. Acts and Documents No. 5* (pp. 91-161).

II. Chronological Survey

The Charter of the United Nations and the Statute of the Court entered into force on 24 October 1945.

After the election of its Members, on 6 February 1946, the Court met for the first time in The Hague on 1 April of the same year.

The first case entered in the General List of the Court *(Corfu Channel (United Kingdom* v. *Albania))* was submitted on 22 May 1947.

Between then and 31 July 1996 the Court has had to deal with a total of 97 cases, i.e., 75 contentious cases and 22 advisory cases, as listed below[1]. In those cases it gave 61 judgments, of which 39 were on the merits, and 23 advisory opinions. Of the 295 orders made therein, 224 related solely to the fixing or extending of time-limits, while 263 orders related to contentious cases and 32 to advisory cases.

Title	*Dates*
(a) Contentious[2]	
Corfu Channel (United Kingdom v. *Albania)*	1947-1949
Fisheries (United Kingdom v. *Norway)*	1949-1951
Protection of French Nationals and Protected Persons in Egypt (France v. *Egypt)*	1949-1950
Asylum (Colombia/Peru)	1949-1950
Rights of Nationals of the United States of America in Morocco (France v. *United States of America)*	1950-1952

[1] Factual information (dates, etc.) regarding the course of the proceedings in each case is given in *Background Notes II* and *II bis: Synopsis of cases referred to the International Court of Justice* (see p. 147, below).

[2] In the case of proceedings instituted by means of a special agreement the names of the parties are separated by an oblique stroke.

Title	*Dates*
Request for Interpretation of the Judgment of 20 November 1950 in the Asylum case (Colombia v. *Peru)*	1950
Haya de la Torre (Colombia v. *Peru)*	1950-1951
Ambatielos (Greece v. *United Kingdom)*	1951-1953
Anglo-Iranian Oil Co. (United Kingdom v. *Iran)*	1951-1952
Minquiers and Ecrehos (France/United Kingdom)	1951-1953
Nottebohm (Liechtenstein v. *Guatemala)*	1951-1955
Monetary Gold Removed from Rome in 1943 (Italy v. *France, United Kingdom and United States of America)*	1953-1954
Electricité de Beyrouth Company (France v. *Lebanon)*	1953-1954
Treatment in Hungary of Aircraft and Crew of United States of America (United States of America v. *Hungary)*	1954
Treatment in Hungary of Aircraft and Crew of United States of America (United States of America v. *USSR)*	1954
Aerial Incident of 10 March 1953 (United States of America v. *Czechoslovakia)*	1955-1956
Antarctica (United Kingdom v. *Argentina)*	1955-1956
Antarctica (United Kingdom v. *Chile)*	1955-1956
Aerial Incident of 7 October 1952 (United States of America v. *USSR)*	1955-1956
Certain Norwegian Loans (France v. *Norway)*	1955-1957
Right of Passage over Indian Territory (Portugal v. *India)*	1955-1960
Application of the Convention of 1902 Governing the Guardianship of Infants (Netherlands v. *Sweden)*	1957-1958
Interhandel (Switzerland v. *United States of America)*	1957-1959
Aerial Incident of 27 July 1955 (Israel v. *Bulgaria)*	1957-1959
Aerial Incident of 27 July 1955 (United States of America v. *Bulgaria)*	1957-1960
Aerial Incident of 27 July 1955 (United Kingdom v. *Bulgaria)*	1957-1959
Sovereignty over Certain Frontier Land (Belgium/Netherlands)	1957-1959
Arbitral Award Made by the King of Spain on 23 December 1906 (Honduras v. *Nicaragua)*	1958-1960
Aerial Incident of 4 September 1954 (United States of America v. *USSR)*	1958
Barcelona Traction, Light and Power Company, Limited (Belgium v. *Spain)*	1958-1961

Title	*Dates*
Compagnie du Port, des Quais et des Entrepôts de Beyrouth and Société Radio-Orient (France v. *Lebanon)*	1959-1960
Aerial Incident of 7 November 1954 (United States of America v. *USSR)*	1959
Temple of Preah Vihear (Cambodia v. *Thailand)*	1959-1962
South West Africa (Ethiopia v. *South Africa; Liberia* v. *South Africa)*	1960-1966
Northern Cameroons (Cameroon v. *United Kingdom)*	1961-1963
Barcelona Traction, Light and Power Company, Limited (New Application: 1962) (Belgium v. *Spain)*	1962-1970
North Sea Continental Shelf (Federal Republic of Germany/Denmark; Federal Republic of Germany/Netherlands)	1967-1969
Appeal Relating to the Jurisdiction of the ICAO Council (India v. *Pakistan)*	1971-1972
Fisheries Jurisdiction (United Kingdom v. *Iceland)*	1972-1974
Fisheries Jurisdiction (Federal Republic of Germany v. *Iceland)*	1972-1974
Nuclear Tests (Australia v. *France)*	1973-1974
Nuclear Tests (New Zealand v. *France)*	1973-1974
Trial of Pakistani Prisoners of War (Pakistan v. *India)*	1973
Aegean Sea Continental Shelf (Greece v. *Turkey)*	1976-1978
Continental Shelf (Tunisia/Libyan Arab Jamahiriya)	1978-1982
United States Diplomatic and Consular Staff in Tehran (United States of America v. *Iran)*	1979-1981
Delimitation of the Maritime Boundary in the Gulf of Maine Area (Canada/United States of America) [case referred to a Chamber]	1981-1984
Continental Shelf (Libyan Arab Jamahiriya/Malta)	1982-1985
Frontier Dispute (Burkina Faso/Republic of Mali) [case referred to a Chamber]	1983-1986
Military and Paramilitary Activities in and against Nicaragua (Nicaragua v. *United States of America)*	1984-1991
Application for Revision and Interpretation of the Judgment of 24 February 1982 in the Case concerning the Continental Shelf (Tunisia/Libyan Arab Jamahiriya) *(Tunisia* v. *Libyan Arab Jamahiriya)*	1984-1985
Border and Transborder Armed Actions (Nicaragua v. *Costa Rica)*	1986-1987
Border and Transborder Armed Actions (Nicaragua v. *Honduras)*	1986-1992

Title	*Dates*
Land, Island and Maritime Frontier Dispute (El Salvador/Honduras: Nicaragua intervening) [case referred to a Chamber][1]	1986-1992
Elettronica Sicula S.p.A. (ELSI) (United States of America v. *Italy)* [case referred to a Chamber]	1987-1989
Maritime Delimitation in the Area between Greenland and Jan Mayen (Denmark v. *Norway)*	1988-1993
Aerial Incident of 3 July 1988 (Islamic Republic of Iran v. *United States of America)*	1989-1996
Certain Phosphate Lands in Nauru (Nauru v. *Australia)*	1989-1993
Arbitral Award of 31 July 1989 (Guinea-Bissau v. *Senegal)*	1989-1991
Territorial Dispute (Libyan Arab Jamahiriya/Chad)	1990-1994
East Timor (Portugal v. *Australia)*	1991-1995
Maritime Delimitation between Guinea-Bissau and Senegal (Guinea-Bissau v. *Senegal)*	1991-1995
Passage through the Great Belt (Finland v. *Denmark)*	1991-1992
Maritime Delimitation and Territorial Questions between Qatar and Bahrain (Qatar v. *Bahrain)*	1991-
Questions of Interpretation and Application of the 1971 Montreal Convention arising from the Aerial Incident at Lockerbie (Libyan Arab Jamahiriya v. *United Kingdom)*	1992-
Questions of Interpretation and Application of the 1971 Montreal Convention arising from the Aerial Incident at Lockerbie (Libyan Arab Jamahiriya v. *United States of America)*	1992-
Oil Platforms (Islamic Republic of Iran v. *United States of America)*	1992-
Application of the Convention on the Prevention and Punishment of the Crime of Genocide (Bosnia and Herzegovina v. *Yugoslavia)*	1993-
Gabčíkovo-Nagymaros Project (Hungary/Slovakia)	1993-
Land and Maritime Boundary between Cameroon and Nigeria (Cameroon v. *Nigeria)*	1994-
Fisheries Jurisdiction (Spain v. *Canada)*	1995-
Request for an Examination of the Situation in Accordance with Paragraph 63 of the Court's Judgment of 20 December 1974 in the Nuclear Tests (New Zealand *v.* France) *Case*	1995
Kasikili/Sedudu Island (Botswana/Namibia)	1996-

[1] The intervention of Nicaragua was admitted on 13 September 1990 (see *I.C.J. Yearbook 1990-1991*, pp. 160-174).

Title	*Dates*
(*b*) Advisory	
Conditions of Admission of a State to Membership in the United Nations (Article 4 of Charter)	1947-1948
Reparation for Injuries Suffered in the Service of the United Nations	1948-1949
Interpretation of Peace Treaties with Bulgaria, Hungary and Romania	1949-1950
Competence of the General Assembly for the Admission of a State to the United Nations	1949-1950
International Status of South West Africa	1949-1950
Reservations to the Convention on the Prevention and Punishment of the Crime of Genocide	1950-1951
Effect of Awards of Compensation Made by the United Nations Administrative Tribunal	1953-1954
Voting Procedure on Questions relating to Reports and Petitions concerning the Territory of South West Africa	1954-1955
Judgments of the Administrative Tribunal of the ILO upon Complaints Made against Unesco	1955-1956
Admissibility of Hearings of Petitioners by the Committee on South West Africa	1955-1956
Constitution of the Maritime Safety Committee of the Inter-Governmental Maritime Consultative Organization	1959-1960
Certain Expenses of the United Nations (Article 17, paragraph 2, of the Charter)	1961-1962
Legal Consequences for States of the Continued Presence of South Africa in Namibia (South West Africa) notwithstanding Security Council Resolution 276 (1970)	1970-1971
Application for Review of Judgement No. 158 of the United Nations Administrative Tribunal	1972-1973
Western Sahara	1974-1975
Interpretation of the Agreement of 25 March 1951 between the WHO and Egypt	1980
Application for Review of Judgement No. 273 of the United Nations Administrative Tribunal	1981-1982
Application for Review of Judgement No. 333 of the United Nations Administrative Tribunal	1984-1987
Applicability of the Obligation to Arbitrate under Section 21 of the United Nations Headquarters Agreement of 26 June 1947	1988
Applicability of Article VI, Section 22, of the Convention on the Privileges and Immunities of the United Nations	1989
Legality of the Use by a State of Nuclear Weapons in Armed Conflict	1993-1996
Legality of the Threat or Use of Nuclear Weapons	1994-1996

CHAPTER I

ORGANIZATION OF THE COURT

The organization of the International Court of Justice is governed by Articles 2-33 of the Statute of the Court and by Articles 1-18 and 32-37 of the Rules of Court.

I. Members of the Court

1. Composition of the Court[1]

The Court consists of 15 Members (Statute, Art. 3, para. 1).

On 31 July 1996 the composition of the Court was as follows:

Order of precedence	*Country*	*Date of expiry of term of office*
President M. Bedjaoui	Algeria	5 February 1997[2]
Vice-President S. M. Schwebel	United States	5 February 1997[2]
Judges S. Oda	Japan	5 February 2003
G. Guillaume	France	5 February 2000
M. Shahabuddeen	Guyana	5 February 1997
C. G. Weeramantry	Sri Lanka	5 February 2000
R. Ranjeva	Madagascar	5 February 2000
G. Herczegh	Hungary	5 February 2003
Shi Jiuyong	China	5 February 2003
C.-A. Fleischhauer	Germany	5 February 2003
A. G. Koroma	Sierra Leone	5 February 2003
V. S. Vereshchetin	Russian Federation	5 February 1997
L. Ferrari Bravo	Italy	5 February 1997
R. Higgins	United Kingdom	5 February 2000
G. Parra-Aranguren	Venezuela	5 February 2000[3]

The Members of the Court are elected for nine years, one-third of the total number of judges being elected every three years; they may be re-elected (Statute, Art. 13). In the event of a vacancy, an election is

[1] For the composition of chambers, see pp. 16-18, below.

[2] The terms of office of Judges Bedjaoui and Schwebel as President and Vice-President respectively expire in 1997.

[3] Judge Parra-Aranguren was elected to fill the vacancy caused by the death, on 24 October 1995, of Judge Aguilar-Mawdsley (see p. 9, below).

held and the new judge holds office for the remainder of his predecessor's term (Statute, Arts. 14 and 15). Though replaced, Members of the Court finish any cases they have begun (Statute, Art. 13, para. 3).

As required by Article 7 of the Statute, the Secretary-General of the United Nations prepares for each election a list of the persons nominated in accordance with Articles 5 and 6. The election is held by the General Assembly and the Security Council of the United Nations, proceeding independently of each other and simultaneously (Statute, Arts. 8-12). The States parties to the Statute of the Court which are not members of the United Nations take part in the election by the General Assembly in the same manner as Members of the United Nations (General Assembly resolution 264 (III) of 8 October 1948; see Chap. III, p. 67, below).

Members of the Court elected during the same session of the General Assembly whose terms of office begin on the same date take precedence according to seniority of age; Members elected at a previous session take precedence; in the event of immediate re-election a Member retains his former precedence (Rules, Art. 3, paras. 2-4).

The Court elects its President and Vice-President; they are both elected for three years and take precedence over the other judges (Statute, Art. 21, para. 1; Rules, Art. 3, para. 5, Arts. 10-14, Art. 18, para. 2, and Art. 32).

2. Changes in the Composition of the Court in 1995-1996

On 24 October 1995, Judge Andrés Aguilar-Mawdsley, who had been a Member of the Court since 1991, died. On 28 February 1996, the General Assembly and the Security Council of the United Nations elected Mr. Gonzalo Parra-Aranguren to fill the resulting vacancy. His term of office thus extends to 5 February 2000. The following had also been candidates in the elections: Messrs. J. A. Barberis and F. Villagran Kramer.

3. Former Presidents and Vice-Presidents and Former Members of the Court

The following judges served as President or Vice-President before the present holders of those offices:

1946-1949, J. G. Guerrero and J. Basdevant;

1949-1952, J. Basdevant and J. G. Guerrero[1];

1952-1955, Sir Arnold McNair and J. G. Guerrero[1];

---

[1] While he was Vice-President of the Court, Judge Guerrero acted as President, by virtue of Article 13, paragraphs 1 and 2, of the 1946 Rules, in the following cases: *Corfu Channel (United Kingdom* v. *Albania); Protection of French Nationals and Protected Persons in Egypt (France* v. *Egypt); Rights of Nationals of the United States of America in Morocco (France* v. *United States of America); Ambatielos (Greece* v. *United Kingdom); Anglo-Iranian Oil Co. (United Kingdom* v. *Iran); Minquiers and Ecrehos (France/United Kingdom); Monetary Gold Removed from Rome in 1943 (Italy* v. *France, United Kingdom and United States of America).*

1955-1958, G. H. Hackworth and A. H. Badawi[1];

1958-1961, H. Klaestad and Sir Muhammad Zafrulla Khan;

1961-1964, B. Winiarski and R. J. Alfaro;

1964-1967, Sir Percy Spender and V. K. Wellington Koo;

1967-1970, J. L. Bustamante y Rivero and V. M. Koretsky;

1970-1973, Sir Muhammad Zafrulla Khan and F. Ammoun;

1973-1976, M. Lachs and F. Ammoun[2];

1976-1979, E. Jiménez de Aréchaga and Nagendra Singh;

1979-1982, Sir Humphrey Waldock[3] and T. O. Elias[4];

1982-1985, T. O. Elias[5] and J. Sette-Camara;

1985-1988, Nagendra Singh and G. Ladreit de Lacharrière[6];

1988-1991, J. M. Ruda and K. Mbaye;

1991-1994, Sir Robert Jennings[7] and S. Oda[7].

Apart from the present judges, the following have been Members of the Court (the names of those who have died are preceded by an asterisk):

---

[1] While he was Vice-President of the Court, Judge Badawi acted as President, by virtue of Article 13, paragraph 1, of the 1946 Rules, in the cases concerning *Interhandel (Switzerland* v. *United States of America), Interim Protection*, and *Aerial Incident of 27 July 1955 (United States of America* v. *Bulgaria)*.

[2] While he was Vice-President of the Court, Judge Ammoun acted as President, by virtue of Article 11 and Article 13, paragraph 1, of the then Rules of Court, in *Appeal Relating to the Jurisdiction of the ICAO Council, Nuclear Tests (Australia* v. *France), Interim Protection*, and *Nuclear Tests (New Zealand* v. *France), Interim Protection*.

[3] Sir Humphrey Waldock died on 15 August 1981. The functions of the Presidency were thereafter exercised by T. O. Elias as Acting President, by virtue of Article 13, paragraph 1, and Article 14 of the 1978 Rules of Court.

[4] Vice-President Elias was for a time Acting President in *Continental Shelf (Tunisia/Libyan Arab Jamahiriya)* and in the proceedings relating to the Orders made on 20 January and 1 February 1982 in *Delimitation of the Maritime Boundary in the Gulf of Maine Area (Canada/United States of America)*.

[5] Judge Elias continued to act as President in *Continental Shelf (Libyan Arab Jamahiriya/Malta)* after 5 February 1985, by virtue of Article 32, paragraph 2, of the 1978 Rules of Court.

[6] Judge Ladreit de Lacharrière died on 10 March 1987. On 6 May 1987 the Court elected Judge Mbaye to be its Vice-President for the remainder of his predecessor's term.

[7] While he was President of the Court, Sir Robert Jennings, being a national of one of the Parties, did not, in accordance with Article 32 of the Rules of Court, preside in the case concerning *Questions of Interpretation and Application of the 1971 Montreal Convention arising from the Aerial Incident at Lockerbie (Libyan Arab Jamahiriya* v. *United Kingdom)*. Vice-President Oda exercised the functions of the Presidency in that case, as well as in the case concerning *Questions of Interpretation and Application of the 1971 Montreal Convention arising from the Aerial Incident at Lockerbie (Libyan Arab Jamahiriya* v. *United States of America)*. (See *I.C.J. Yearbook 1991-1992*, p. 198.)

	Country	Period of Office
* R. Ago	Italy	1979-1995
* A. Aguilar-Mawdsley	Venezuela	1991-1995
Prince B. A. Ajibola	Nigeria	1991-1994
* R. J. Alfaro	Panama	1959-1964
* A. Alvarez	Chile	1946-1955
* F. Ammoun	Lebanon	1965-1976
* E. C. Armand-Ugon	Uruguay	1952-1961
* Ph. Azevedo	Brazil	1946-1951
* A. H. Badawi	Egypt	1946-1965
* J. Basdevant	France	1946-1964
* R. R. Baxter	United States	1979-1980
* C. Bengzon	Philippines	1967-1976
* J. L. Bustamante y Rivero	Peru	1961-1970
* L. F. Carneiro	Brazil	1951-1955
* F. de Castro	Spain	1970-1979
* R. Córdova	Mexico	1955-1964
* Ch. De Visscher	Belgium	1946-1952
* H. C. Dillard	United States	1970-1979
* A. El-Erian	Egypt	1979-1981
A. El-Khani	Syria	1981-1985
* T. O. Elias	Nigeria	1976-1991
J. Evensen	Norway	1985-1994
* I. Fabela	Mexico	1946-1952
* Sir Gerald Fitzmaurice	United Kingdom	1960-1973
* I. Forster	Senegal	1964-1982
* S. A. Golunsky	USSR	1952-1953
A. Gros	France	1964-1984
* J. G. Guerrero	El Salvador	1946-1958
* G. H. Hackworth	United States	1946-1961
* Hsu Mo	China	1946-1956
* L. Ignacio-Pinto	Benin	1970-1979
Sir Robert Yewdall Jennings	United Kingdom	1982-1995
* P. C. Jessup	United States	1961-1970
* E. Jiménez de Aréchaga	Uruguay	1970-1979
* H. Klaestad	Norway	1946-1961
F. I. Kojevnikov	USSR	1953-1961
* V. M. Koretsky	USSR	1961-1970
* S. B. Krylov	USSR	1946-1952
* M. Lachs	Poland	1967-1993

* G. Ladreit de Lacharrière	France	1982-1987
* Sir Hersch Lauterpacht	United Kingdom	1955-1960
* Sir Arnold McNair	United Kingdom	1946-1955
K. Mbaye	Senegal	1982-1991
* G. Morelli	Italy	1961-1970
* L. M. Moreno Quintana	Argentina	1955-1964
* P. D. Morozov	USSR	1970-1985
H. Mosler	Fed. Rep. of Germany	1976-1985
* Nagendra Singh	India	1973-1988
Ni Zhengyu	China	1985-1994
C. D. Onyeama	Nigeria	1967-1976
* L. Padilla Nervo	Mexico	1964-1973
R. S. Pathak	India	1989-1991
* S. Petrén	Sweden	1967-1976
* Sir Benegal Rau	India	1952-1953
* J. E. Read	Canada	1946-1958
* J. M. Ruda	Argentina	1973-1991
J. Sette-Camara	Brazil	1979-1988
* Sir Percy C. Spender	Australia	1958-1967
* J. Spiropoulos	Greece	1958-1967
* K. Tanaka	Japan	1961-1970
* N. K. Tarassov	Russian Federation	1985-1995
* S. Tarazi	Syria	1976-1980
* Sir Humphrey Waldock	United Kingdom	1973-1981
* V. K. Wellington Koo	China	1957-1967
* B. Winiarski	Poland	1946-1967
* Sir Muhammad Zafrulla Khan	Pakistan	1954-1961 and 1964-1973
* M. Zoričić	Yugoslavia	1946-1958

II. Judges *Ad Hoc*

If in a case the Court, or a chamber of the Court, includes upon the Bench a judge of the nationality of one of the parties, any other party may choose a person to sit as judge; similarly, if the Court or the chamber includes upon the Bench no judge of the nationality of the parties, each of these parties may choose a judge (Statute, Art. 31; Rules, Arts. 7-8, Art. 17, para. 2, Arts. 35-37, Art. 91, para. 2, and Art. 102, para. 3). Should there be several parties in the same interest they are reckoned for this purpose as one party only (Statute, Art. 31, para. 5; Rules, Art. 36 and Art. 37, para. 2).

Since the institution of the Court, judges *ad hoc* have been chosen in the following cases (unless otherwise indicated, they held the nationality of the appointing party):

Corfu Channel (United Kingdom v. *Albania)*. Albania chose Mr. I. Daxner (Czechoslovakia), who sat upon the Bench when the preliminary objection was heard, and Mr. B. Ečer (Czechoslovakia), who sat when the case was heard on the merits and also for the assessment of amount of compensation.

Asylum (Colombia/Peru), Request for Interpretation of the Judgment of 20 November 1950 in the Asylum Case (Colombia v. *Peru)* and *Haya de la Torre (Colombia* v. *Peru)*. Mr. J. J. Caicedo Castilla was chosen by Colombia and Mr. L. Alayza y Paz Soldán by Peru.

Ambatielos (Greece v. *United Kingdom)*. Mr. J. Spiropoulos was chosen by Greece.

Anglo-Iranian Oil Co. (United Kingdom v. *Iran)*. Mr. K. Sandjabi was chosen by Iran.

Nottebohm (Liechtenstein v. *Guatemala)*. Mr. C. García Bauer[1] was chosen by Guatemala and Mr. P. Guggenheim (Switzerland) by Liechtenstein.

Monetary Gold Removed from Rome in 1943 (Italy v. *France, United Kingdom and United States of America)*. Mr. G. Morelli was chosen by Italy.

Right of Passage over Indian Territory (Portugal v. *India)*. Mr. M. Fernandes was chosen by Portugal and the Hon. M. A. C. Chagla by India.

Application of the Convention of 1902 Governing the Guardianship of Infants (Netherlands v. *Sweden)*. Mr. J. Offerhaus was chosen by the Netherlands and Mr. F. J. C. Sterzel by Sweden.

Interhandel (Switzerland v. *United States of America)*. Mr. P. Carry was chosen by Switzerland.

Aerial Incident of 27 July 1955 (Israel v. *Bulgaria)*. Mr. Justice Goitein was chosen by Israel and Mr. J. Žourek (Czechoslovakia) by Bulgaria.

Aerial Incident of 27 July 1955 (United States of America v. *Bulgaria)*[2]. Mr. J. Žourek (Czechoslovakia) was chosen by Bulgaria.

Arbitral Award Made by the King of Spain on 23 December 1906 (Honduras v. *Nicaragua)*. Mr. R. Ago (Italy) was chosen by Honduras and Mr. F. Urrutia Holguín (Colombia) by Nicaragua.

---

[1] The Government of Guatemala had first chosen as judge *ad hoc* Mr. J. C. Herrera and subsequently Mr. J. Matos, before choosing Mr. García Bauer.

[2] Case removed from the list before the Court had occasion to sit.

Barcelona Traction, Light and Power Company, Limited (Belgium v. *Spain)*[1]. Mr. W. J. Ganshof van der Meersch was chosen by Belgium and Mr. F. de Castro by Spain.

South West Africa (Ethiopia v. *South Africa; Liberia* v. *South Africa).* Sir Louis Mbanefo (Nigeria)[2] was chosen by Ethiopia and Liberia and the Hon. J. T. van Wyk by South Africa.

Northern Cameroons (Cameroon v. *United Kingdom).* Mr. P. Beb a Don was chosen by Cameroon.

Barcelona Traction, Light and Power Company, Limited (New Application: 1962) (Belgium v. *Spain).* Belgium chose Mr. W. J. Ganshof van der Meersch, who sat upon the Bench when the preliminary objections were heard, and Mr. W. Riphagen (Netherlands), who sat in the second phase. Spain chose Mr. E. C. Armand-Ugon (Uruguay).

North Sea Continental Shelf (Federal Republic of Germany/Denmark; Federal Republic of Germany/Netherlands). Mr. H. Mosler was chosen by the Federal Republic of Germany and Mr. M. Sørensen (Denmark) by Denmark and the Netherlands.

Appeal Relating to the Jurisdiction of the ICAO Council (India v. *Pakistan).* Mr. Nagendra Singh was chosen by India.

Nuclear Tests (Australia v. *France).* Sir Garfield Barwick was chosen by Australia.

Nuclear Tests (New Zealand v. *France).* Sir Garfield Barwick (Australia) was chosen by New Zealand.

Trial of Pakistani Prisoners of War (Pakistan v. *India).* Pakistan chose Sir Muhammad Zafrulla Khan, who sat in the proceedings on the request for interim measures up to 2 July 1973, and Mr. Muhammad Yaqub Ali Khan[3].

Western Sahara. Mr. A. Boni (Ivory Coast) was chosen by Morocco.

Aegean Sea Continental Shelf (Greece v. *Turkey).* Mr. M. Stassinopoulos was chosen by Greece.

Continental Shelf (Tunisia/Libyan Arab Jamahiriya). Mr. E. Jiménez de Aréchaga (Uruguay) was chosen by the Libyan Arab Jamahiriya and Mr. J. Evensen (Norway) by Tunisia.

Delimitation of the Maritime Boundary in the Gulf of Maine Area (Canada/United States of America) (case referred to a Chamber). Mr. M. Cohen was chosen by Canada.

---

[1] Case removed from the list before the Court had occasion to sit.

[2] The Governments of Ethiopia and Liberia had first chosen as judge *ad hoc* the Hon. J. Chesson, subsequently Sir Muhammad Zafrulla Khan and then Sir Adetokunboh A. Ademola, before choosing Sir Louis Mbanefo.

[3] This case was removed from the list before the Court had occasion to hear argument on the question of its jurisdiction.

Continental Shelf (Libyan Arab Jamahiriya/Malta). Mr. E. Jiménez de Aréchaga (Uruguay) was chosen by the Libyan Arab Jamahiriya. Mr. J. Castañeda (Mexico) was chosen by Malta and sat in the proceedings culminating in the Judgment on Italy's application for permission to intervene. Mr. N. Valticos (Greece) was chosen by Malta to sit when the case was heard on the merits.

Frontier Dispute (Burkina Faso/Republic of Mali) (case referred to a Chamber). Mr. F. Luchaire (France) was chosen by Burkina Faso and Mr. G. Abi-Saab (Egypt) by the Republic of Mali.

Military and Paramilitary Activities in and against Nicaragua (Nicaragua v. *United States of America).* Mr. C.-A. Colliard (France) was chosen by Nicaragua.

Application for Revision and Interpretation of the Judgment of 24 February 1982 in the Case concerning the Continental Shelf (Tunisia/Libyan Arab Jamahiriya) *(Tunisia* v. *Libyan Arab Jamahiriya).* Mrs. S. Bastid (France) was chosen by Tunisia and Mr. E. Jiménez de Aréchaga (Uruguay) by the Libyan Arab Jamahiriya.

Land, Island and Maritime Frontier Dispute (El Salvador/Honduras: Nicaragua intervening) (case referred to a Chamber). Mr. N. Valticos (Greece) was chosen by El Salvador and Mr. M. Virally (France) was chosen by Honduras. Following the death of Mr. Virally, Mr. S. Torres Bernárdez (Spain) was chosen by Honduras.

Maritime Delimitation in the Area between Greenland and Jan Mayen (Denmark v. *Norway).* Mr. P. H. Fischer was chosen by Denmark.

Aerial Incident of 3 July 1988 (Islamic Republic of Iran v. *United States of America).* Mr. M. Aghahosseini was chosen by the Islamic Republic of Iran.

Arbitral Award of 31 July 1989 (Guinea-Bissau v. *Senegal).* Mr. H. Thierry (France) was chosen by Guinea-Bissau. Following the expiry of Judge Mbaye's term of office on 5 February 1991 Senegal no longer had a judge of its nationality on the bench. It therefore chose Mr. K. Mbaye to sit as judge *ad hoc.*

Territorial Dispute (Libyan Arab Jamahiriya/Chad). Mr. J. Sette-Camara (Brazil) was chosen by the Libyan Arab Jamahiriya and Mr. G. M. Abi-Saab (Egypt) by Chad.

East Timor (Portugal v. *Australia).* Mr. A. de Arruda Ferrer-Correia was chosen by Portugal. Following his resignation, on 14 July 1994, Mr. K. J. Skubiszewski (Poland) was chosen by Portugal. Sir Ninian Stephen was chosen by Australia.

Passage through the Great Belt (Finland v. *Denmark).* Mr. B. Broms was chosen by Finland and Mr. P. H. Fischer by Denmark.

Maritime Delimitation and Territorial Questions between Qatar and Bahrain (Qatar v. *Bahrain)*. Mr. J. M. Ruda (Argentina) was chosen by Qatar. Following the death of Mr. Ruda, Mr. S. Torres Bernárdez (Spain) was chosen by Qatar. Mr. N. Valticos (Greece) was chosen by Bahrain. He resigned for health reasons as from the end of the jurisdiction and admissibility phase of the case.

Questions of Interpretation and Application of the 1971 Montreal Convention arising from the Aerial Incident at Lockerbie (Libyan Arab Jamahiriya v. *United Kingdom)*. Mr. A. S. El-Kosheri (Egypt) was chosen by the Libyan Arab Jamahiriya.

Questions of Interpretation and Application of the 1971 Montreal Convention arising from the Aerial Incident at Lockerbie (Libyan Arab Jamahiriya v. *United States of America)*. Mr. A. S. El-Kosheri (Egypt) was chosen by the Libyan Arab Jamahiriya.

Oil Platforms (Islamic Republic of Iran v. *United States of America)*. Mr. F. Rigaux (Belgium) was chosen by the Islamic Republic of Iran.

Application of the Convention on the Prevention and Punishment of the Crime of Genocide (Bosnia and Herzegovina v. *Yugoslavia)*. Mr. E. Lauterpacht (United Kingdom) was chosen by Bosnia and Herzegovina and Mr. M. Kreća by Yugoslavia.

Gabčíkovo-Nagymaros Project (Hungary/Slovakia). Mr. K. J. Skubiszewski (Poland) was chosen by Slovakia.

Land and Maritime Boundary between Cameroon and Nigeria (Cameroon v. *Nigeria)*. Mr. K. Mbaye (Senegal) was chosen by Cameroon and Prince B. A. Ajibola by Nigeria.

Fisheries Jurisdiction (Spain v. *Canada)*. Mr. S. Torres Bernárdez was chosen by Spain and Mr. M. Lalonde by Canada.

Request for an Examination of the Situation in Accordance with Paragraph 63 of the Court's Judgment of 20 December 1974 in the Nuclear Tests (New Zealand *v.* France) *Case*. Sir Geoffrey Palmer was chosen by New Zealand.

III. Chambers

1. Chamber of Summary Procedure

The Statute (Art. 29) provides that, with a view to the speedy despatch of business, the Court shall form annually a Chamber composed of five judges which, at the request of the parties, may hear and determine cases by summary procedure. The Court also selects two judges for this Chamber for the purpose of replacing judges who find it impossible to sit. Under Article 15 of the Rules of Court, the President and Vice-

President are members of this Chamber ex officio, the other members and the substitutes being elected. The Chamber of Summary Procedure has never as yet been called upon to meet.

The Chamber of Summary Procedure is at present composed as follows: President Bedjaoui; Vice-President Schwebel; Judges Shahabuddeen, Shi and Vereshchetin, members; Judges Koroma and Higgins, substitute members.

2. Chambers Provided for in Article 26, Paragraph 1, of the Statute

The Statute (Art. 26, para. 1) provides also that the Court may from time to time form one or more chambers, composed of three or more judges, as the Court may determine, for dealing with particular categories of cases: for example, labour cases and cases relating to transit and communications. Cases are heard and determined by these chambers if the parties so request.

In the past the Court has considered the question of the possible formation of a chamber to deal with environmental matters. On those occasions it took the view that it was not yet necessary to set up a standing special chamber, emphasizing that it was able to respond rapidly to requests for the constitution of a so-called *"ad hoc"* chamber (pursuant to Article 26, paragraph 2, of the Statute) which could deal also with any environmental case.

In view of the developments in the field of environmental law and protection which have taken place in the last few years, and considering that it should be prepared to the fullest possible extent to deal with any environmental case falling within its jurisdiction, the Court, in July 1993, deemed it appropriate to establish a seven-member Chamber for Environmental Matters. The Chamber is at present composed as follows: Judge Bedjaoui, President of the Court; Judge Schwebel, Vice-President of the Court; and Judges Shahabuddeen, Weeramantry, Ranjeva, Herczegh and Fleischhauer.

The term of office of the members of the Chamber has been extended by the Court until 5 February 1997.

3. Chambers Formed under Article 26, Paragraph 2, of the Statute

The Statute (Art. 26, para. 2) provides that the Court may form a chamber for dealing with a particular case, the number of judges constituting such a chamber being determined by the Court with the approval of the parties.

Chambers of this kind have been formed at the joint request of the parties to deal with four cases. They are listed below with an indication of the date on which the respective Chamber was constituted and the names of its members.

Delimitation of the Maritime Boundary in the Gulf of Maine Area (Canada/United States of America): constituted on 20 January 1982; Judges Ago *(President)*, Gros, Mosler, Schwebel; Judge *ad hoc* Cohen.

Frontier Dispute (Burkina Faso/Republic of Mali): constituted on 3 April 1985; Judges Bedjaoui *(President)*, Lachs, Ruda; Judges *ad hoc* Luchaire, Abi-Saab.

Elettronica Sicula S.p.A. (ELSI) (United States of America v. *Italy)*: constituted on 2 March 1987 with the following composition – Judges Nagendra Singh *(President)*, Oda, Ago, Schwebel, Sir Robert Jennings. Following the death of Judge Nagendra Singh the Court, on 20 December 1988, elected President Ruda to succeed him as member and (ex officio) President of the Chamber.

Land, Island and Maritime Frontier Dispute (El Salvador/Honduras: Nicaragua [as from 13 September 1990] *intervening)*: constituted on 8 May 1987 with the following composition – Judges Oda, Sette-Camara, Sir Robert Jennings; Judges *ad hoc* Valticos, Virally. The Chamber elected Judge Sette-Camara to be its President. After the death of Judge Virally, Mr. Torres Bernárdez was chosen to sit as judge *ad hoc* in his place, and on 13 December 1989 the Court declared the Chamber to be composed as follows: Judges Sette-Camara *(President)*, Oda, Sir Robert Jennings; Judges *ad hoc* Valticos, Torres Bernárdez. On 7 February 1991 Judges Sir Robert Jennings and Oda exchanged places in the order of precedence within the Chamber owing to their election to be, respectively, the Court's President and Vice-President.

4. Provisions in the Rules relating to Chambers

Articles 15-18 and 90-93 of the Rules of Court contain the provisions relating to chambers.

IV. Assessors

Article 30, paragraph 2, of the Statute and Article 9 of the Rules of Court provide that the Court may, either *proprio motu* or upon a request made not later than the closure of the written proceedings, decide, for the purpose of a contentious case or request for advisory opinion, to appoint assessors to sit with it, without the right to vote. The chambers also have the power to appoint assessors.

These provisions have not been applied up to the present.

V. The Registrar

The Court appoints its Registrar (Statute, Art. 21, para. 2; Rules, Art. 22).

The present Registrar is Mr. Eduardo Valencia-Ospina (see Chap. V, p. 142, below).

VI. Privileges and Immunities

Article 19 of the Statute provides: "The Members of the Court, when engaged on the business of the Court, shall enjoy diplomatic privileges and immunities."

In the Netherlands, pursuant to an exchange of correspondence between the President of the Court and the Minister for Foreign Affairs, dated 26 June 1946, they enjoy, in a general way, the same privileges, immunities, facilities and prerogatives as Heads of Diplomatic Missions accredited to Her Majesty the Queen of the Netherlands (*I.C.J. Acts and Documents No. 5*, pp. 200-207). In addition, in accordance with the terms of a letter dated 26 February 1971 from the Minister for Foreign Affairs of the Netherlands, the President of the Court takes precedence over the Heads of Mission, including the Dean of the Diplomatic Corps, who is immediately followed by the Vice-President of the Court and thereafter the precedence proceeds alternately between Heads of Mission and the Members of the Court (*ibid.*, pp. 210-213).

By resolution 90 (1) of 11 December 1946 (*ibid.*, pp. 206-211), the General Assembly of the United Nations approved the agreement concluded with the Government of the Netherlands in June 1946 and recommended that ". . . if a judge, for the purpose of holding himself permanently at the disposal of the Court, resides in some country other than his own, he should be accorded diplomatic privileges and immunities during the period of his residence there" and that "... judges should be accorded every facility for leaving the country where they may happen to be, for entering the country where the Court is sitting, and again for leaving it. On journeys in connection with the exercise of their functions, they should, in all countries through which they may have to pass, enjoy all the privileges, immunities and facilities granted by these countries to diplomatic envoys."

The same resolution contains also a recommendation calling upon Members of the United Nations to recognize and accept United Nations laissez-passer issued to the judges by the Court. Such laissez-passer have been issued since 1950. They are similar in form to those issued by the Secretary-General of the United Nations.

Furthermore, Article 32, paragraph 8, of the Statute provides that the "salaries, allowances and compensation" received by judges "shall be free of all taxation".

CHAPTER II

BIOGRAPHIES OF JUDGES

Biographies of judges who held office in the period 1 August 1995 to 31 July 1996 will be found below.

I. Members of the Court on 31 July 1996

President Mohammed Bedjaoui

(Member of the Court since 19 March 1982; re-elected as from 6 February 1988; President of the Chamber formed to deal with the case concerning the *Frontier Dispute (Burkina Faso/Republic of Mali)*, 1983-1987; President of the Court since February 1994)

Born in Sidi-Bel-Abbes, Algeria, on 21 September 1929.
Doctor of Law (1955).
Doctor *honoris causa* of the Universities of Hyderabad, Aix-en-Provence, Brussels and Kuwait.
Diploma of the Institute of Political Studies, University of Grenoble (1952).
"Avocat stagiaire" at the Court of Appeal of Grenoble (1951-1953).
Research Assistant at the Centre national de la recherche scientifique (CNRS), France (1956-1958).
Legal Adviser to the Provisional Government of the Republic of Algeria (1958-1961).
Expert adviser to the Algerian delegation in the independence negotiations at Evian and Lugrin (1961).
Executive Secretary to the President of the National Constituent Assembly at Algiers (1962).
Secretary-General of the Government (1962-1964).
Dean of the Faculty of Law and Economics of the University of Algiers (1964-1965).
Minister of Justice and Keeper of the Seals (1964-1970).
Algerian Ambassador to France (1970-1979).
Permanent delegate of Algeria to Unesco (1971-1979).
Ambassador and Permanent Representative of Algeria to the United Nations in New York (1979-1982).
Co-President of the United Nations Commission of Enquiry to Iran (February-March 1980).
Vice-President of the United Nations Council for Namibia (1979-1982).
Chairman of the Group of 77 (1981-1982).

Chairman of the Committee on the Drafting of an International Convention against the Recruitment, Use, Financing and Training of Mercenaries (1981-1982).

Member of the Arbitration Tribunal for the determination of the maritime boundary between Guinea and Guinea-Bissau (1983-1985).

Member of the Arbitration Tribunal for the determination of the maritime boundary between Guinea-Bissau and Senegal (1985-1989).

Arbitrator or President in several international commercial arbitrations.

Participated in various sessions of the United Nations General Assembly as member, deputy-head or head of the Algerian delegation.

Head of the Algerian delegations to the United Nations Conferences on Succession of States in Respect of Treaties (1977) and the Law of the Sea (1976-1980).

Took part in various sessions of the OAU Council of Ministers and OAU Summit Meetings, and in various ministerial meetings or conferences of heads of State and government of the non-aligned countries, as member, deputy-head or head of the Algerian delegation.

United Nations Consultant Expert at the Vienna Conference on Succession of States in respect of State Property, Archives and Debts (1983).

Member of the International Law Commission (1965-1982).

Member of the Institute of International Law (since 1977).

Member of the French Society for International Law.

Member of the Scientific Council of the Institut du droit économique de la mer of the Principality of Monaco.

Member of the Governing Board of the Foundation for International Studies of the University of Malta, Valletta.

Member of the Independent Commission on International Humanitarian Issues (co-chaired by Prince Hassan bin Talal of Jordan and Prince Sadruddin Agha Khan) (1982-1987).

Member of several award panels for international prizes, including that of the Albert Schweitzer Prize (United States of America).

Member of the Jury for the Félix Houphouët-Boigny Peace Prize (Unesco).

Member of the Unesco *Ad Hoc* Forum for Reflection (1992).

Member of the Unesco International Consultative Committee on Bioethics.

Member of the International Committee of Advisers of the Chinese International Law Institute, Beijing.

Member of the International Council for Global Health Progress (since 1994).

Member of the Independent World Commission on the Oceans (President: Mr. Mario Soarès) (since its establishment in 1995).

Recipient of various prizes and honours.

Holder of decorations of several States.

Author of eight books and over 150 articles.

Vice-President Stephen M. SCHWEBEL

(Member of the Court since 15 January 1981; re-elected as from 6 February 1988; member of the Chamber formed to deal with the case concerning *Delimitation of the Maritime Boundary in the Gulf of Maine Area (Canada/United States of America)*, 1981-1984, and of the Chamber formed to deal with the case concerning *Elettronica Sicula S.p.A. (ELSI)*, 1987-1989; Vice-President of the Court since February 1994)

Born in New York City, on 10 March 1929.

Harvard University, B.A. *magna cum laude* with highest honours in government (1950); Cambridge University, studies in international law (1951); LL.B., Yale Law School (1954). Doctor *honoris causa*, Bhopal University, India (1982).

Admitted to the Bar of the State of New York (1955); of the Supreme Court of the United States (1965); and of the District of Columbia (1976).

Attorney, White & Case, New York (1954-1959).

Assistant Professor of Law, Harvard University (1959-1961).

Professor of International Law and subsequently Edward B. Burling Professor of International Law and Organization, the School of Advanced International Studies, The Johns Hopkins University, Washington, D.C. (1967-1981). Visiting lecturer or professor at Cambridge University (1957, 1983); the Australian National University (1969); the Hague Academy of International Law (1972); the Graduate Institute of International Studies, Geneva (1980); and at other universities or institutes in the United States and elsewhere.

Assistant Legal Adviser, Department of State (1961-1966); Special Assistant to the Assistant Secretary of State for International Organization Affairs (1966-1967); Consultant to the Department of State (1967-1973). Counselor on International Law, Department of State (1973-1974); Deputy Legal Adviser, Department of State (1974-1981).

Legal Adviser to the United States delegation, and Alternate Representative in the Sixth Committee, during sessions of the United Nations General Assembly (1961-1965). United States representative and chairman of the United States delegation to various committees of the United Nations, including the Special Committee on Principles of International Law concerning Friendly Relations and Co-operation among States (1964); the Special Committee on the Question of Defining Aggression (1971); and the UNCTAD Working Group on a Charter of Economic Rights and Duties of States (1973-1974).

Member of the International Law Commission of the United Nations (1977-1981). Chairman of the Drafting Committee (1978); Special Rapporteur on the Law of the Non-Navigational Uses of International Watercourses (1977-1981).

Participated as Associate Representative, Representative, Counsel or Deputy Agent of the United States in various cases before the International Court of Justice (between 1962 and 1980). Member of the Board of Arbitration in *British Petroleum Company* v. *Iran and the National*

Iranian Oil Company (1982-1985) and arbitrator or president in other international commercial arbitrations (since 1988).

Executive Vice-President and Executive Director of the American Society of International Law (1967-1973). Honorary Vice-President (since 1983). Honorary President (since 1996). President of the Administrative Tribunal of the International Monetary Fund (since January 1994).

Member of the Board of Editors, *American Journal of International Law* (1967-1981); Honorary Editor (since 1996). Chairman of the Editorial Advisory Committee, *International Legal Materials* (1967-1973).

Member of the Institute of International Law; the American Society of International Law; the American Branch of the International Law Association; the American Bar Association; and the Council on Foreign Relations. Honorary Member of the Indian Society of International Law. Member of the International Advisory Committee of the Cambridge University Research Centre in International Law; the Board of Electors of the Whewell Professorship of International Law of Cambridge University; and the Board of Overseers' Committee to Visit the Harvard Law School. Chairman of the Supervisory Board of the Telders International Law Moot Court Competition.

Author of *The Secretary-General of the United Nations: His Political Powers and Practice*, 1952; *The Effectiveness of International Decisions*, 1971 (as editor); "Aggression, Intervention and Self-Defence in Modern International Law", *Recueil des cours*, Hague Academy of International Law, 1972; reports to the International Law Commission on the law of the non-navigational uses of international watercourses; *International Arbitration: Three Salient Problems* (1987); *Justice in International Law* (1994); and some one hundred articles, notes and book reviews in legal and other publications. Research and drafting assistant to United Nations Secretary-General Trygve Lie in the writing of *In the Cause of Peace*, 1954.

Judge Shigeru ODA

(Member of the Court since 6 February 1976; re-elected as from 6 February 1985 and from 6 February 1994; member of the Chamber formed to deal with the case concerning the *Land, Island and Maritime Frontier Dispute (El Salvador/Honduras: Nicaragua intervening)*, 1986-1992, and of the Chamber formed to deal with the case concerning *Elettronica Sicula S.p.A. (ELSI),* 1987-1989; Vice-President of the Court from 1991 to 1994; Acting President in the cases concerning *Questions of Interpretation and Application of the 1971 Montreal Convention arising from the Aerial Incident at Lockerbie (Libyan Arab Jamahiriya* v. *United Kingdom)* and *Questions of Interpretation and Application of the 1971 Montreal Convention arising from the Aerial Incident at Lockerbie (Libyan Arab Jamahiriya* v. *United States of America)*)

Born on 22 October 1924.

Law degree, University of Tokyo (1947). Doctor of Law (JSD), Yale University (1953). Doctor of Law, University of Tôhoku (1962). Doctor *honoris causa* of the Bhopal University, India (1980), and of the New York Law School (1981).

Presently Professor Emeritus of the Tôhoku University (since 1985) and Member of the Japan Academy (since 1994).

Research Fellow in international law, University of Tokyo (1947-1949). Lecturer (1950-1953), Associate Professor (1953-1959) and Professor (1959-1976) at Tôhoku University. Technical Adviser to the Atomic Energy Commission (1961-1964) and to the Council for Marine Science and Technology in the Prime Minister's Office (1968-1971). Special Assistant to the Minister for Foreign Affairs (1973-1976). Member of the Science Council of the Ministry of Education (1969-1976), of the Council for Ocean Development in the Prime Minister's Office (1971-1976), and of the Advisory Committee for Co-operation with the United Nations University (1971-1976).

Delegate to the United Nations Conferences on the Law of the Sea (1958, 1960 and 1973-1975); member of the United Nations Group of Experts on Marine Science and Technology (1967-1968); Alternate Representative of Japan on the United Nations Committee on the Peaceful Uses of the Sea-bed and Ocean Floor (1968-1973); Legal Consultant to the ESCAP Committee for Co-ordination of Joint Prospecting for Mineral Resources in Asian Offshore Areas (1969, 1972 and 1975). Member of the panel of the International Atomic Energy Agency on the Legal Implications of the Disposal of Radio-active Waste into the Sea (1961-1963) and of the Agency's group of experts for the Study of the Character and Purpose of Appropriate Observation of Peaceful Nuclear Explosions (1970). Representative of Japan at the sixth General Conference of the Inter-Governmental Oceanographic Commission (1969); Chairman of the Working Group on Legal Questions related to Scientific Investigations of the Ocean (1968-1975). Alternate Member of the Asian-African Legal Consultative Committee (1971-1975).

Counsel for the Federal Republic of Germany before the International Court of Justice in the *North Sea Continental Shelf (Federal Republic of Germany/Denmark; Federal Republic of Germany/Netherlands)* cases (1968).

Member of the Executive Councils of the Japanese Society of International Law and of the Japanese branch of the International Law Association. Associate (1969) and Member (1979) of the Institute of International Law. Honorary life Member of the American Society of International Law (1975). Honorary Member of the Indian Society of International Law. Member of the Curatorium of the Hague Academy of International Law (since 1987); Member of the Curatorium of the Institute of International Public Law and International Relations (Thessaloniki).

Editor-in-chief of the *Japanese Annual of International Law* (1973-1977). General editor for *Publications on Ocean Development* and *International Law in Japanese Perspective* of Martinus Nijhoff Publications.

Lecturer on the "International Law of the Resources of the Sea" and on "The International Court of Justice Viewed from the Bench (1976-1993)" at the Hague Academy of International Law (*Recueil des cours*, Vol. 127, 1969, and Vol. 244, 1993).

Publications: in English – *International Control of Sea Resources*, reprinted edition with a new introduction, 1989; *The International Law of the Ocean Development* (4 vols.), 1972-1979; *The Law of the Sea in Our Time* (2 vols.), 1977; *International Law of the Resources of the Sea*, reprinted edition with supplement (1979); *The Practice of Japan in International Law 1961-1970* (edited with H. Owada), 1982; in Japanese – *International Law of the Sea* (1956, revised ed. 1969); *International Law of Marine Resources* (3 vols.), 1971-1975; *Judicial Decisions of the Japanese Courts involving International Law* (edited with T. Sogawa), 1978, revised and updated edition, 1991; *The Law of the Sea*, Vol. I, 1979; *The Law of the Sea: 25 Years of Recollections*, 1981; *Treaties and Conventions* (edited with Y. Ishimoto), 1983, revised ed., 1992; *Commentary on the United Nations Convention on the Law of the Sea*, Vol. I, 1985; *The International Court of Justice*, 1987; *A Collection of Essays on the Law of the Sea*, 1989; and various articles on international law in English and in Japanese.

Judge Gilbert Guillaume

(Member of the Court since 14 September 1987; re-elected as from 6 February 1991)

Born in Bois-Colombes, France, on 4 December 1930.

Licence (Bachelor's degree) in law, University of Paris. Diplôme from the Paris Institute of Political Studies; Diplôme d'études supérieures d'économie politique et de science économique (Diploma of Advanced Studies in Political Economy and Economic Science), University of Paris.

Alumnus of the Ecole nationale d'administration.

Member of the Council of State, as Auditeur (1957), then Maître des Requêtes (1963), and most recently Councillor of State (1981).

Legal Adviser to the State Secretariat for Civil Aviation (1968-1979); French Representative on the Legal Committee of the International Civil Aviation Organization (ICAO) (1968-1979) and Chairman of the Committee (1971-1975); delegate to the diplomatic conferences on the suppression of the unlawful seizure of aircraft (The Hague, 1970), the suppression of unlawful acts against the safety of civil aircraft (Montreal, 1971) and air safety (Rome, 1973); President of the Diplomatic Conference on the Liability of the Carrier (Montreal, 1975); Head of the French delegations to the diplomatic conferences on the liability of the carrier vis-à-vis third parties (Montreal, 1978) and the non-use of force against civil aircraft (Montreal, 1984).

Chairman of the Conciliation Commission, Organisation for Economic Co-operation and Development (1973-1978); Member of the European Space Agency Appeals Board (1975-1978); Director of Legal Affairs, Organisation for Economic Co-operation and Development (1979).

Director of Legal Affairs, Ministry of Foreign Affairs (1979-1987).

Counsel for France in the arbitration proceedings between France and the United States over the Franco-American air agreement (1978); Agent for France in the arbitration proceedings between France and Canada over the Franco-Canadian fisheries agreement (1986); Agent for France in numerous cases before the Court of Justice of the European Communities and the European Commission and Court of Human Rights. French Representative on the Central Commission for the Navigation of the Rhine (1979-1987); Chairman of the Commission (1981-1982); French Representative on the Asian-African Legal Consultative Committee (1980-1987).

French delegate to the General Assembly of the United Nations (Sixth Committee) (1982-1987); Head of the French delegation to the Third United Nations Conference on the Law of the Sea (1982), the United Nations Conference on Succession of States in respect of State Property, Archives and Debts (Vienna, 1983) and the United Nations Conference on the Law of Treaties between States and International Organizations or between International Organizations (Vienna, 1986).

Member of the Permanent Court of Arbitration (since 1980). Member of the Court of Arbitration of the Organization for Security and Co-operation in Europe (OSCE). Designated arbitrator by the International Telecommunications Satellite Organization and by the International Civil Aviation Organization, the International Chamber of Commerce and the International Centre for the Settlement of Investment Disputes (ICSID).

President of the French branch of the International Law Association (ILA). Associate Member of the Institute of International Law. Vice-President of the French Society for International Law. Honorary Chairman of the French Society for Air and Space Law. Member of the International Institute of Law of the French-speaking Countries (IDEF). Member of the Académie de marine. Member of the Académie de l'air et de l'espace. Member of the International Academy of Comparative Law. Member of the Scientific Board of the *Revue générale de droit international public* and of the Board of Directors of the *Annuaire français de droit international*. Chairman of the Board of Directors of the *Revue française de droit aérien et spatial*.

Author of numerous works and articles. Has given a course on "Terrorism and International Law" at the Hague Academy of International Law ("Terrorisme et droit international", *Recueil des cours*, Vol. 215, 1989). Author of a work on *Les grandes crises internationales et le droit* (1994).

Judge Mohamed SHAHABUDDEEN

(Member of the Court since 6 February 1988)

Born in Vreed-en-Hoop, Demerara, Guyana, on 7 October 1931.

Bar Finals, London Inns of Court (1952). Called to the Bar, Middle Temple, London (1954). Queen's Counsel (1966). London University degrees – LL.B., B.Sc. (Econ.), LL.M., Ph.D., LL.D. Also LL.D. *honoris causa* of the University of the West Indies.

Private practice (1954-1959) followed by public legal service. Magistrate (1959). Crown Counsel (1959-1962). Solicitor General (1962-1973). Attorney General (1973-1987). Minister of Justice (1978-1987). Other ministerial appointments, including Acting Foreign Minister from time to time (1980-1987).

Member of various Guyana delegations on bilateral missions to other countries (1962-1987). Also member of various Guyana delegations to other international meetings, including: United Nations General Assembly (1972); United Nations Conference on Succession of States in respect of Treaties, Vienna (1977); Commonwealth Heads of Government Meetings, Lusaka (1979), Melbourne (1981), New Delhi (1983), Nassau (1985) and Vancouver (1987); the Cancun North/South Summit (1981); the General Assembly of the Organization of American States, St. Lucia (1981); Meetings of Ministers of Foreign Affairs of Non-Aligned Countries, Georgetown (1972) and New Delhi (1981); Meeting of the Co-ordinating Bureau of the Movement of Non-Aligned Countries, Algiers (1981); the Conference of Heads of State or Government of Non-Aligned Countries, New Delhi (1983); the Commonwealth Caribbean Heads of Government Meetings, Ocho Rios (1982), Port of Spain (1983), Nassau (1984), Georgetown (1986) and St. Lucia (1987); the Commonwealth Law Ministers Meetings at Lagos (1975), Barbados (1980), Sri Lanka (1983) and Harare (1986); and the Commonwealth Law Conference, Hong Kong (1983).

Member of the Board of Governors of the University of Guyana (1963-1965). Member of the Council of Legal Education of the Commonwealth Caribbean (1973-1987). Member of the Commonwealth Association of Legislative Counsel (1983).

Associate Member of the Institute of International Law. Headquarters Member of the International Law Association. Member of the Société française pour le droit international. Member of the American Society of International Law. Honorary Life Member of the Indian Society of International Law. Member of the Advisory Board of the African Society of International and Comparative Law. Associate Member of the International Academy of Comparative Law. Member of the Advisory Board, *European Journal of International Law.* Member of the Board of Electors of the Whewell Professorship of International Law of Cambridge University.

Cacique's Crown of Honour (CCH) (1970); Order of Roraima (OR) (1980); Order of Excellence (OE) (1988).

Author of various books and articles.

Judge Christopher Gregory WEERAMANTRY

(Member of the Court since 6 February 1991)

Born in Colombo, Sri Lanka, on 17 November 1926.

B.A.; LL.B.; LL.D. (University of London); LL.D. *(honoris causa)* (University of Colombo).

Advocate, Supreme Court of Sri Lanka (1948-1965). Lecturer and Examiner, Council of Legal Education, Sri Lanka (1951-1956). Commissioner of Assize, Supreme Court of Sri Lanka (1965-1967). Justice of the Supreme Court of Sri Lanka (1967-1972). Member, Council of Legal Education, Sri Lanka (1967-1972). Honorary Visiting Professor, University of Colombo (since 1984). Honorary Life Member, Bar Association of Sri Lanka.

Sir Hayden Starke Professor of Law, Monash University, Melbourne, Australia (1972-1991). Emeritus Professor of Law, Monash University (since 1991). Chairman, Commission of Inquiry into International Responsibility for Phosphate Mining on Nauru (1987-1988).

Panellist, Unesco Seminar on Teaching of Human Rights, Canberra (1980); Member, United Nations University Task Force on Human Rights (1982); Vice-Chairman, United Nations Centre against *Apartheid*/Government of Nigeria Conference on Legal Status of *Apartheid* Régime, Lagos (1984); Panellist, SCOPE/ENUWAR/UNU (Scientists' Committee on Problems of the Environment/Environmental Consequences of Nuclear War/United Nations University), International Conference on Nuclear Danger, Tokyo (1985); Lecturer, United Nations Human Rights Commission Seminar commemorating 40th anniversary of Universal Declaration of Human Rights, Palais des Nations, Geneva (1988); Editor, United Nations University/United Nations Human Rights Commission's two-volume study on Science, Technology and Human Rights (1988-1990); Co-ordinator, United Nations University/Netherlands Institute of Human Rights Workshop on Science, Technology and Human Rights, Utrecht (1989).

Visiting Professorships and Academic Appointments: University of Tokyo (1978); University of Stellenbosch (1979); University of Papua New Guinea (1981); University of Florida (1984); Lafayette College, Pennsylvania (1985); University of Hong Kong (1989).

Member, Editorial Board: *Sri Lankan Journal of International Law; Human Rights Quarterly*, Johns Hopkins University; *Interdisciplinary Peace Research*, La Trobe University; *Journal of Ceylon Law*; Advisory Board, *China Law Reports.*

Associate Academician, International Academy of Comparative Law, Paris; Vice-President, International Commission of Jurists, Victoria; Past President, World Federation of Overseas Sri Lankan Organizations; Vice-Patron, United Nations Association of Sri Lanka; Member, Club of Rome (Australia); Commonwealth Lawyers Association; Society of Public Teachers of Law; World Association of Law Professors; Lawasia; World Association on the Philosophy of Law and Legal Philosophy.

Books: *The Law of Contracts, being a Comparative Study of the Roman-Dutch, English and Customary Laws of Contract in Ceylon* (2 vols.), 1965; *The Law in Crisis: Bridges of Understanding*, 1975; *Equality and Freedom: Some Third World Perspectives*, 1976; *Human Rights in Japan*, 1979; *Apartheid: The Closing Phases?*, 1980; *An Invitation to the Law*, 1980; *The Slumbering Sentinels: Law and Human Rights in the Wake of Technology*, 1983; *Law: The Threatened Peripheries*, 1984; *Nuclear Weapons and Scientific Responsibility*, 1987 (translated into Japanese); *Islamic Jurisprudence: Some International Perspectives*, 1988; *Human Rights and Scientific and Technological Development*, ed., 1990; *Nauru: Environmental Damage under International Trusteeship*, 1992; *The Impact of Technology on Human Rights: Global Case-Studies*, ed., 1993.

Reports: *Report of the Nauru Commission of Inquiry* (10 vols.), 1988 (joint author).

Articles in law journals in Asia, Africa, Australasia, Europe and North America.

Published lectures include: "Fundamental Perspectives on Equality and Freedom", World Congress on Equality and Freedom, St. Louis, Missouri (1976), an official event marking the American Bicentennial; "National and Transnational Systems as Denigrators of Human Rights", Unesco Seminar on Teaching of Human Rights, Canberra (1981); "The Right to Development", Lawasia Seminar on Establishment of a Regional Human Rights Framework for the Pacific, Suva (1985); "Cultural and Ideological Pluralism in Contemporary Public International Law", World Congress of International Academy of Comparative Law, Sydney and Melbourne (1986); "Traffic in Armaments: A Blind Spot in Human Rights and International Law", Joint Soviet/US International Conference on Nuclear Weapons and International Law, New York (1987); "Emerging Dimensions of Sovereignty in International Law", International Seminar on the Coming Global Civilization, Moscow (1988); "The Teaching of Human Rights", United Nations Seminar commemorating 40th anniversary of Universal Declaration of Human Rights, Geneva (1988); "The Law, Nuclear Weapons and the Real World", First World Convention of Lawyers against Nuclear Arms, The Hague (1989); "International Arbitration under the UNCITRAL Rules", Regional Seminar on International Arbitration, Kuala Lumpur (1989); "Judicial Reasoning under the Common Law", Commonwealth Law Conference, Auckland (1990); "The Importance of Philosophical Perspectives to the Judicial Process", 6 *Connecticut Journal of International Law* (1991); "Does International Law Matter?", *Inaugural Tun Hussein Onn Memorial Lecture*, Kuala Lumpur (1991); "The Right to Know: Freedom of Information as a Human Right", Commonwealth Law Conference, Cyprus (1993); "Introducing Human Rights to the Younger Generation", Unesco, Netherlands (1993); "The Constancy of the Judicial Obligation", Inaugural Fernando Memorial Lecture, Colombo (1994); "The World Court: Its Conception, Constitution and

Contribution", *Inaugural Governor's Forum*, Melbourne, Victoria, Australia (1994); 1995 Martin Luther King Lecture, "On Earth as It Is in Heaven: A Vision of World Order for the 21st Century", *Tulsa Journal of Comparative and International Law*, 1995.

Order of *Deshamanya* (Sri Lanka); Mohamed Sahabdeen Award for International Understanding in the SAARC Region, 1993.

Judge Raymond Ranjeva

(Member of the Court since 6 February 1991)

Born in Antananarivo, Madagascar, on 31 August 1942.

Bachelor's degree in law (1965), University of Madagascar, Antananarivo. *Diplôme* from the Madagascar National School of Administration (1966). Trainee in the Judicial Division of the Conseil d'Etat, Paris (1965-1966). *Diplôme* d'études supérieures de sciences politiques, University of Paris, Faculty of Law and Economic Science (1966). *Diplôme* d'études supérieures de droit public, University of Madagascar (1967). Doctorate of Law, University of Paris II (thesis: "La succession d'organisations internationales en Afrique"). *Agrégé* of the Faculties of Law and Economics, Public Law and Political Science section, Paris (1972).

Laureate of the University of Madagascar. Laureate of the National Association of Doctors of Law. Laureate of the Madagascar National School of Administration.

Civil Administrator (1966). Assistant (1966-1972), Lecturer (1972) and Professor (1981-1991) at the University of Madagascar. Professor at the Madagascar Military Academy and at the Madagascar National School of Administration. Director of the Public Law and Political Science Study Centre. Director of the Legal and Political Science Department of the University of Madagascar. Dean of the Faculty of Law, Economics, Management and Social Sciences (1982-1986); reappointed in 1986. First Rector of the University of Antananarivo (1988-1990). Associate or visiting lecturer at several universities abroad: University of Aix-Marseille III, Bordeaux I, Paris I (Panthéon-Sorbonne), Paris II (Panthéon-Assas) and the Institute of Advanced International Studies, La Réunion and Burundi. Director of the French-speaking research seminar at the Hague Academy of International Law (1987). Member (Ouagadougou, 1988) and President (Cotonou, 1992) of the Board of *Agrégation* Examiners of the African and Malagasy Council on Higher Education.

Conciliator at the World Bank International Centre for Settlement of Investment Disputes since 1970. Member of Malagasy delegations to several international conferences: Third United Nations Conference on the Law of the Sea; Preparatory Commission for the International Seabed Authority and the Law of the Sea Tribunal; United Nations General Assembly (1979-1990); Non-Aligned Countries (1979); Conference of States which use French (1987); Head of the Malagasy delegation to the United Nations Conference on Succession of States in respect of Treaties,

Vienna (1976-1977); Member of the Malagasy delegation responsible for negotiating the revision of the co-operation agreements with France (1973); First Vice-Chairman of the First African Seminar on International Humanitarian Law, Yaoundé (1977). Vice-President for Africa of the International Conference of French-Speaking Faculties of Law and Political Science (1987-1991).

Counsel to the Republic of Mali in the case concerning the *Frontier Dispute (Burkina Faso/Republic of Mali)*. Consultant for Madagascar on the amicable settlement of the transfer to the State of the activities of Eau-Electricité de Madagascar and Electricité de France (1973).

Member and Vice-President of the Malagasy Academy (1974); President of the ethics and political science section (1975-1991). Managing Director of JURECO: legal, economic and financial databank – research and advisory bodies (1986-1990). Editor of the periodical *Lettre mensuelle de Jureco* (1986-1988). Member of the French Society of International Law. Member of the Quebec Society of International Law. Member of the Governing Body of the African Society of International and Comparative Law.

Member of the National Constitutional Committee (1975). Founding Member of the Malagasy Human Rights Committee (1971). Legal adviser to the Catholic Bishops Conference, Madagascar. Secretary-General of the Malagasy Legal Studies Society.

Commandeur of the National Order of Madagascar. Chevalier of the Madagascar Order of Merit. Officer of the National Order of Mali. Six Honours.

Author of numerous books, essays and articles and has given lectures at a number of seminars.

Judge Géza Herczegh

(Member of the Court since 10 May 1993; re-elected as from 6 February 1994)

Born in Nagykapos, on 17 October 1928.

Educated at French Grammar School in Gödöllö, Hungary.

Bachelor's degree in law, University of Szeged (1951); Candidate in Jurisprudence (Ph.D.) (1965); Doctor *honoris causa* at the Law Faculty of the University of Marburg, Germany (1990); Corresponding Member (1985), and Member of the Hungarian Academy of Sciences (1990); Vice-President of the Department of Legal and Economic Sciences of the Hungarian Academy of Sciences (1990-1993).

Research Fellow in public international law at the Institute of Political Sciences, Budapest (1951-1967); studies as Senior Fellow at various institutes, e.g. in Paris (1966), Salzburg (1970); Professor of Law, Head of the International Law Department of the Law Faculty of the University of Pécs (1967-1990); Dean of the Law Faculty of the University of Pécs

(1981-1987); lectured in international humanitarian law at several universities (e.g., Bayreuth, Bratislava, Cambridge, Cracow, Exeter, Graz, Marburg, Moscow, Osijek, Novi Sad, Vienna) (1970-1985); lecturer in seminars for the implementation and dissemination of international humanitarian law, Warsaw (1985), Vegimont (1989).

Judge and Vice-President of the Constitutional Court of the Republic of Hungary (1990-1993).

Represented the Hungarian Red Cross Society as expert on international humanitarian law at the conferences of The Hague (1971), Vienna (1972), Tehran (1973), Monaco (1984); governmental expert on international humanitarian law at the conferences of Geneva (1971 and 1972); member of the Hungarian delegation at the Diplomatic Conference of Geneva on the protection of victims of armed conflicts (1974-1977); served as Vice-President of the Third Commission of the same Conference; member of the Hungarian delegation at the Unesco Conference in Sophia (1977); Rapporteur at the Third Conference on Parliamentary Democracy organized by the Council of Europe on the topic "Problems of Transition from an Authoritarian or Totalitarian Régime to a Genuinely Democratic System", Strasbourg (1991); member of the expert working group ("Badinter Group") preparing the draft convention on peaceful settlement of disputes within the framework of the Conference on Security and Co-operation in Europe, Paris (1992).

Author of the following works: *The Colonial Question and International Law* (in Hungarian), 1962; *General Principles of Law and the International Legal Order*, Series in Foreign Languages, 1969; *Development of International Humanitarian Law*, 1984; *Foreign Policy of Hungary, 896-1919* (in Hungarian), 1987; and of numerous articles in international law and relations, especially in international humanitarian law.

Judge Shi Jiuyong

(Member of the Court since 6 February 1994)

Born in Zhejiang, China, on 9 October 1926.

B.A. in Government and Public Law, St. John's University, Shanghai (1948); M.A. in International Law, Columbia University, New York, United States of America (1951); research in international law at Columbia University, New York (1951-1954).

Assistant Research Fellow in International Law, Institute of International Relations, Beijing, China (1956-1958). Senior Lecturer, Associate Professor of International Law, Foreign Affairs College, Beijing (1958-1964). Research Fellow in International Law, Institute of International Law, Beijing (1964-1973). Research Fellow in International Law, Institute of International Studies, Beijing (1973-1980). Professor of International Law, Foreign Affairs College, Beijing (1984-1993).

Professor of Law, Foreign Economic Law Training Centre, Ministry of Justice of the People's Republic of China, Beijing (1987-1988).

Adviser, Chinese Society of International Law, Beijing. Council member, Institute of Hong Kong Law of the Chinese Law Society, Beijing.

Legal Adviser, Office of the Chinese Senior Representative, Sino-British Joint Liaison Group (on the question of Hong Kong) (1985-1993). Legal Adviser, Chinese Centre of Legal Consultancy, Beijing (1989-1993). Member, Standing Committee, Beijing Committee (1988-1993), and member, Eighth National Committee (1993), Chinese People's Political Consultative Conference. Legal Adviser, Ministry of Foreign Affairs, People's Republic of China (1980-1993).

Legal Adviser, Chinese delegation to the 1980 Annual Meeting of the Boards of Governors of the International Monetary Fund and the International Bank for Reconstruction and Development. Legal Adviser, delegation of the Ministry of Finance of the People's Republic of China for the formal visit to the International Bank for Reconstruction and Development (1980). Adviser, Chinese delegation to the thirty-fifth session of the General Assembly of the United Nations and China's Alternate Representative to the Sixth Committee at that session. Adviser, Chinese delegation to the thirty-sixth, thirty-seventh and thirty-eighth sessions of the United Nations General Assembly and China's delegate to the Sixth Committee at the same sessions (1981-1983). Delegate, Chinese delegation to the sessions of the Asian-African Legal Consultative Committee in 1981, 1985 and 1993. Legal Adviser, Chinese delegation to the talks between the Government of China and the Asian Development Bank on the question of China's membership in the Bank (1986). Legal Adviser of the Chinese side, Working Group of the Sino-British Negotiations on the question of Hong Kong (1984). Legal Adviser of the Chinese side, Sino-British Joint Liaison Group (on Hong Kong), plenary sessions (1985-1993). Delegate, Chinese delegation, legal consultations between the Ministry of Foreign Affairs of the People's Republic of China and the Department of State of the United States of America (1983 and 1984). Delegate, Chinese delegation, negotiations between the Government of the People's Republic of China and the Government of the United States of America on Mutual Promotion and Protection of Investment Agreement (1983 and 1984). Representative of the International Law Commission to the forty-fifth session of the United Nations General Assembly (1990). Expert from China, Senior Legal Experts Meetings on Review of Montevideo Programme, United Nations Environment Programme, 5-6 July 1991 at Geneva and 5-7 September 1991 at Nairobi. Representative of the International Law Commission to the thirtieth meeting of the Asian-African Legal Consultative Conference, Cairo, 22-27 April 1991. Legal Adviser to the Chinese delegation, Disarmament Conference, November 1991 to August 1992.

Member (1987-1993), Rapporteur (1988) and Chairman (1990) of the International Law Commission.

Member, Foreign Economic and Trade Arbitration Commission, China Council for the Promotion of International Trade (1984-1988). Member of the Steering Committee on revision of the Hague Convention of 1907 on Pacific Settlement of International Disputes of the Permanent Court of Arbitration (since 1994).

Taught general course of international law, Foreign Affairs College, Beijing (1958-1963). Taught general course of international economic law, Department of Law, Peking University (1980-1985). Taught general course of international economic law, Foreign Economic Law Training Centre, Ministry of Justice of the People's Republic of China (1988).

Lectures on international financial institutions, National Bureau of Oceanography, the People's Republic of China (1986). Lectures on principles of international law relating to the new international economic order, Department of Law, Peking University (1988). Lectures on protection of private foreign investment (in English), the Hague Academy of International Law, Regional Programme, Beijing (1987). Lecture on the Sino-British Joint Declaration on the question of Hong Kong (in English), Graduate Institute of International Studies, Geneva (1988). Lecture on autonomy in international law and the case of the future Hong Kong Special Administrative Region (in English), International Law Seminar, United Nations Office at Geneva (1988). Lecture on "Nationality of Hong Kong Residents: Present and Future", Graduate Studies, Foreign Affairs College (1988). Lecture on certain issues relating to the legal status of the future Hong Kong Special Administrative Region, Graduate Studies, Department of Law, Peking University (1989). Lectures on international trade regulation, Foreign Service Training Programme of the Ministry of Foreign Affairs of the People's Republic of China (1985 and 1986). Lectures on problems of international economic law, Department of Law, Chinese People's University, Beijing (1987). Chairman, panel discussions on the new international economic order, Beijing Conference on the Law of the World, World Peace through Law (1990). Participant, Symposium on the International Law of Arms Control and Disarmament, held at Geneva (February 1991). Lectures on the International Law Commission, Graduate Studies, Department of Law, Peking University (March 1991). Lectures on selected topics of international economic law, Graduate Studies, Foreign Affairs College (September/October 1991). Participant in the Seminar on the Draft Code of Crimes and International Criminal Jurisdiction, sponsored by the Foundation for the Establishment of an International Criminal Court and International Criminal Law Commission, Talloires, France (May 1991). Lectures on bilateral investment protection agreements (in English), International Law Seminar, United Nations Office at Geneva (June 1992). Participant, Symposium on Teaching, Dissemination and Research of International Law in Developing Countries, Beijing, 1992.

Author of numerous publications on international law.

Judge Carl-August FLEISCHHAUER

(Member of the Court since 6 February 1994)

Born in Düsseldorf, Germany, on 9 December 1930.

Studied at the Universities of Heidelberg, Grenoble and Paris. First State Examination (Law), Heidelberg (1954). Fulbright Scholar, University of Chicago Law School (1954-1955). Junior Barrister Düsseldorf/Heidelberg (1955-1959). Dr. jur., Heidelberg. Second State Examination (Law), Stuttgart (1960). Hague Academy of International Law (1960).

Research Fellow at the Max Planck Institute for International and Foreign Public Law, Heidelberg (1960-1962).

Entered the diplomatic service of the Federal Republic of Germany in 1962. Foreign assignments to Tehran (1962-1963) and Montevideo (1969-1971). Official (1964-1969), Deputy Head (1971) and Head (1972), International Law Section, Legal Department, Federal Foreign Office. Legal Adviser to the Federal Foreign Office and Director-General of the Legal Department (1976-1983).

Member of the Committee of Experts on Human Rights, Council of Europe, Strasbourg (1964-1967). Member of the delegation of the Federal Republic of Germany to the United Nations Conference on the Law of Treaties, Vienna (1968-1969). Observed Sixth Committee during parts of the twenty-third and twenty-fourth sessions of the General Assembly for the then Observer Mission of the Federal Republic of Germany (1968 and 1969). Member of the delegation of the Federal Republic of Germany to the United Nations General Assembly (twenty-eighth to thirty-third sessions as Adviser and Special Adviser, thirty-fourth to thirty-seventh sessions as Alternate Representative) (1973-1982). Alternate Representative and Representative of the Federal Republic of Germany in the Sixth Committee. Representative of the Federal Republic of Germany (1978-1979), on the *Ad Hoc* Committee of the Sixth Committee on the elaboration of the International Convention against the Taking of Hostages. Member of the delegation of the Federal Republic of Germany to the CSCE (Geneva Phase, Helsinki Final Phase) (1974-1975). Member (Vice-Chairman) of the delegation of the Federal Republic of Germany to the Diplomatic Conference on Humanitarian Law applicable in Armed Conflicts, Geneva (1974-1977). Head of the delegation of the Federal Republic of Germany to the United Nations Conference on State Succession in relation to Treaties, Vienna (1977-1978). Member (from 1977 Vice-Chairman) of the delegation of the Federal Republic of Germany to the Third United Nations Conference on the Law of the Sea (1974-1982). Has participated in numerous bilateral meetings and negotiations.

Under-Secretary-General for Legal Affairs, the Legal Counsel of the United Nations (1983-1994).

Was actively engaged, on the side of the Federal Republic of Germany, in the following cases before the Court: *North Sea Continental Shelf (Federal Republic of Germany/Denmark; Federal Republic of Germany/ Netherlands)* (1967-1969); and *Fisheries Jurisdiction (Federal Republic of Germany* v. *Iceland)* (1972-1974). Was actively engaged, on the side of the United Nations, in the advisory cases on the: *Application for Review of Judgement No. 333 of the United Nations Administrative Tribunal* (1984-1987); *Applicability of the Obligation to Arbitrate under Section 21 of the United Nations Headquarters Agreement of 26 June 1947* (1988); and *Applicability of Article VI, Section 22, of the Convention on the Privileges and Immunities of the United Nations* (1989).

Honorary member of the Indian Society of International Law (since 1985). Member of the German Society of International Law and, since 1977, of the Council of the Society. Member of the American Society of International Law. Member of the Curatorium of the Max Planck Institute for International and Foreign Public Law, Heidelberg (since 1975). Member of the Heidelberg Society for International and Foreign Public Law. Member of the Association française pour le droit international.

Awarded the German Cross of Merit, First Class, and several foreign decorations (all before 1983).

Author of numerous publications on international law.

Judge Abdul G. Koroma

(Member of the Court since 6 February 1994)

Born in Freetown, Sierra Leone, on 29 September 1943.

LL.M. (Honours), University of Kiev. Master of Philosophy (International Law), King's College, University of London; Barrister-at-Law, and Honorary Bencher, Honourable Society of Lincoln's Inn, London.

Joined the Government service of Sierra Leone in 1964 and the Ministry of Foreign Affairs in 1969. As a Barrister and Legal Practitioner of the High Court of Sierra Leone, was appointed State Counsel and Special Adviser to the Attorney-General and Minister of Justice. Served as Legal Adviser to the Permanent Mission of Sierra Leone to the United Nations. Served as Ambassador Extraordinary and Plenipotentiary of Sierra Leone to the United Nations, New York, while concurrently accredited as High Commissioner of Sierra Leone to Jamaica and Trinidad and Tobago, and Ambassador to the Republic of Korea (Seoul) and Cuba (1981-1985). Served as Ambassador Extraordinary and Plenipotentiary to Belgium, France, Luxembourg and the Netherlands while concurrently accredited to the European Communities and to the United Nations Educational, Scientific and Cultural Organization (Unesco) (1985-1988). Served as Ambassador Extraordinary and Plenipotentiary of Sierra Leone to the Organization of African Unity (OAU) with concurrent accreditation to Ethiopia, Kenya, the United Republic of Tanzania and Zambia (1988-1992).

Played an active role in and contributed to the elaboration of many contemporary international legal instruments. As delegate to the General Assembly, served on the Sixth Committee (Legal) from 1977 to 1994 and was elected Chairman. Also served as delegate of Sierra Leone to the following United Nations bodies: the Special Committee on the Review of the Charter and on the Strengthening of the Role of the Organization; the United Nations Commission on International Trade Law (UNCITRAL); the United Nations Committee on the Peaceful Uses of Outer Space; the United Nations Programme of Assistance in the Teaching, Study, Dissemination and Wider Appreciation of International Law; served as Chairman of the United Nations Special Committee on the granting of independence to colonial countries and peoples (Committee of 24); headed various United Nations missions on the observance of the exercise of the right of self-determination in various non-self-governing territories.

Represented Sierra Leone at many plenipotentiary conferences, including the United Nations Conference on the Succession of States in respect of Property, Debts and Archives, and was a signatory of the Convention; the Third United Nations Conference on the Law of the Sea (UNCLOS III) and Chairman of the African Group at the Conference. In that capacity, was closely associated with the elaboration of some of the key provisions of the resulting Convention. Was a signatory of the Convention.

Ambassador Extraordinary and Plenipotentiary, Permanent Representative of the Republic of Sierra Leone to the United Nations, New York.

Member of the International Law Commission (since January 1982), and Chairman of the Commission during its forty-third session (1991). Former Chairman of the Committee mandated to elaborate a Draft Statute for an International Criminal Court. As a member of the International Law Commission, was an active participant and contributor to the codification and progressive development of such important international legal instruments as the Draft Code of Crimes against Peace and Security of Mankind; Treaties between States and International Organizations and between International Organizations; the Jurisdictional Immunities of States and their Property; the Law of State Responsibility; the proposed Statute of an International Criminal Court; and the Law of the Non-Navigational Uses of International Watercourses; the draft articles on most-favoured-nation clauses; the draft articles on the status of the diplomatic courier and the diplomatic bag not accompanied by diplomatic courier, and of the optional protocols thereto.

Contributions to other major areas of international law, including the law of self-determination, human rights law, international humanitarian law, and the peaceful settlement of disputes; has written and lectured on these subjects. Serves as an expert on the International Committee of the Red Cross (ICRC) at Geneva on the implementation of and respect for international humanitarian law. Has delivered lectures on all of these topics in many countries, including Cameroon, Canada, China, Ethiopia, Germany, India, Japan, Malta, Norway, Sweden, the United Republic of Tanzania and the United States of America.

Participated in conferences, symposiums and seminars on international law, including those held by the International Ocean Institute (Malta and Halifax, Nova Scotia); the International Law Institute (Hawaii); the International Criminal Jurisdiction (Talloires); the International Institute of Higher Studies in Criminal Sciences; Centre for International Studies, New York University School of Law; the Asian-African Legal Consultative Committee. Also served as external examiner in international law for Ph.D. candidates at the University of Dalhousie, Halifax, Nova Scotia, Canada.

Member of the American Society of International Law and of the Planning Council of the International Ocean Institute (Halifax and Malta).

Member and Vice-President of the African Association of International Law, and an expert consultant on the implementation of international humanitarian law with the International Committee of the Red Cross.

The Order of Commander of Rokel was awarded by the Government of Sierra Leone for outstanding professional service (1991).

Author of a thesis on the *Settlement of Territorial and Boundary Disputes in Africa* (University of London). Has also published articles on the law of the sea, the exclusive economic zone, Antarctica, mercenaries, human rights, international humanitarian law, and the law of humanitarian intervention.

Judge Vladlen Stepanovich VERESHCHETIN

(Member of the Court since 26 January 1995)

Born in Briansk, Russian Federation, on 8 January 1932.

Graduated from the International Law Faculty of the Moscow Institute of International Relations (1954). Post-graduate studies in international law at the same Institute (1955-1958). Candidate of Juridical Sciences (1959). Doctor of Juridical Sciences (1976). Professor of International Law (1982).

Staff member of the Presidium of the USSR Academy of Sciences (1958-1967). First Vice-Chairman and Legal Counsel, Intercosmos, USSR Academy of Sciences (1967-1981). Deputy Director and Head of International Law Department of the Institute of State and Law, Russian Academy of Sciences, Moscow (1981-1995).

Member of the United Nations International Law Commission

(1992-1995); Chairman of the Commission (1994-1995). Member of the USSR delegations to the United Nations Committee on the Peaceful Uses of Outer Space and its Legal Sub-committee (1979-1990).

Member of the Permanent Court of Arbitration (1984-1995).

Has given lecture courses and individual lectures on the theory of international law, the peaceful settlement of international disputes, the law of the sea, the law of outer space and the law of international organizations at the Institute of International Relations, the Diplomatic Academy and the University of Friendship of Peoples (Moscow), the Sverdlovsk Juridical Institute, the Institute of International Public Law and International Relations (Thessaloniki), the European University Institute (Florence), the Universities of Akron and Mississippi (United States) and the Institute of International Private and Public Law (The Hague). Has presented papers on different international law subjects at many international congresses and conferences.

Vice-President of the Russian (formerly Soviet) Association of International Law (since 1985). Chairman of the Scientific Council on International and Comparative Law at the Institute of State and Law, Russian Academy of Sciences (1981-1995). Vice-President, Honorary Director of the International Institute of Space Law (since 1978). Member of the Policy and Finance Committee of the International Law Association (since 1990). Vice-President of the Russian (formerly Soviet) United Nations Association (since 1984).

Member of the editorial and advisory boards of the *Russian Law Journal*, the *European Journal of International Law* (Italy) and the *Journal of Space Law* (United States).

National orders: "Badge of Honour" (1967), "Friendship of Peoples" (1975), "October Revolution" (1981). Honorary Awards of the German Academy of Sciences at Berlin (1978), the Bulgarian Academy of Sciences (1979), the International Academy of Astronautics (1987, 1994), the Russian Association of International Law (1995).

Author of numerous works and articles on international law published in Russia and abroad, including seven-volume *Course of International Law*, Moscow, 1989-1993 (Deputy Editor-in-Chief of the course and co-author).

Judge Luigi Ferrari Bravo

(Member of the Court since 21 June 1995)

Born in Naples, Italy, on 5 August 1933.

Graduated *magna cum laude* in law, University of Naples, 1956.

Assistant Professor of International Law, University of Naples (1956-1961); "Libero docente" of Public and Private International Law

(1961); Professor of International Organization, on an annual term, University of Bari (1961-1965); Professor of International Law, on an annual term, University of Bari (1965-1968); Professor of International Law, on an annual term, Istituto Universitario Orientale, Naples (1962-1968); Full Professor of International Law, Law Faculty, University of Bari; Director of the Institute of International Law, same Faculty (1968-1974); Full Professor of International Organization, Istituto Universitario Orientale, Naples (1974-1979); Dean of the Department of Political Science, same University (1975-1976); Professor of European Community Law, High School of Public Administration, Rome (1965-1979); Full Professor of European Community Law, Faculty of Political Science, University of Rome (1979-1982); Full Professor of Public International Law, same Faculty (1982-1991); Full Professor of European Community Law, Law Faculty, University of Rome (since 1991).

Lecturer on International Law, National University of Somalia, Mogadishu (1971); Lecturer, Hague Academy of International Law (1975 and 1982); on various occasions has given courses on international law at the Training Institute for Diplomats at the Italian Ministry of Foreign Affairs; has lectured at universities and scientific institutions in Argentina, Belgium, Canada, Germany, Peru, Switzerland, United States of America.

Member of the Italian Bar, with the right to plead before the Supreme Court; Head of the Legal Service of the Italian Ministry of Foreign Affairs (1985-1994).

Member of the Governing Council of the International Institute for the Unification of Private Law (UNIDROIT) (1990-1994); President of UNIDROIT (since 1 January 1995).

Member of the Italian delegation to the United Nations Seminar on Economic and Social Rights (Warsaw, 1967); Italian Expert at the World Conference on Human Rights (Tehran, 1968); Italian representative to the preparatory committees for the First to Fourth European Conferences of Law Faculties (Strasbourg, 1968, 1971, 1974, 1976); Chairman of a Committee at the Second and Third Conferences. Member of the United Nations Special Committee on the Question of Defining Aggression (1973-1974). Member of the Italian delegation to the Geneva Diplomatic Conference on Humanitarian Law (1975-1977); Head of the delegation to the Committee on the Charter of the United Nations and the Strengthening of the Role of the Organization (1975-1983); Member of the *Ad Hoc* Working Group on corrupt practices of multinational corporations (1976-1979); of the Special Committee on Enhancing the Effectiveness of the Principle of Non-Use of Force in International Relations (1978-1983); Chairman of the Sixth Committee of the General Assembly (1978-1979); Member of the *Ad Hoc* Committee on the Drafting of a Convention against the Taking of Hostages (1979); Member of the *Ad Hoc* Committee on the Drafting of a Convention against the Recruitment, Use, Training and Financing of Mercenaries (1982 and

1983), Vice-Chairman; Chairman of one of the working groups of the same Committee. Member and Chairman (1982, 1983) of the Working Group of the Sixth Committee on the Protection of Persons Submitted to Any Form of Detention or Imprisonment; Member of the Italian delegation to the Conferences for the Review of the Treaty on the Denuclearization of the Sea-bed and Ocean Floor in Geneva (1977, 1983); Member of the Intergovernmental Group for the Drafting of a Code of Conduct for Transnational Corporations, eighth to seventeenth sessions (1980-1982); Member of the Commission on Transnational Corporations (1980-1993); Member of the United Nations Commission on International Trade Law, thirteenth and fifteenth sessions (1980, 1982); appointed by the Italian Government as Conciliator (provided for in Annex to Article 66, Vienna Convention on the Law of Treaties of 1969; Legal Adviser at the Permanent Mission to the United Nations (New York, 1981-1984); Legal Adviser to the Permanent Mission in Geneva (1984-1985); Head of the Italian delegation to the Codification Conference on the Law of Treaties between States and International Organizations (Vienna, 1986); Member of the *Ad Hoc* Committee on Unlawful Acts against the Safety of Maritime Navigation (1987), Head of the Italian delegation to the IMO Conference (Rome, March 1988), President of the Conference. Member of the Court of Arbitration for Sport.

Agent of the Italian Government before the Court of Justice of the European Communities (1985-1994); Agent of the Italian Government before the European Commission and the European Court on Human Rights (1985-1994); Agent of the Italian Government before the International Court of Justice in the case concerning *Elettronica Sicula S.p.A. (ELSI) (United States of America* v. *Italy)*.

Secretary-General of the Siena Forum on International Law of the Environment (1990), convened under the recommendation of the Summit of the Seven Most Industrialized Countries; Member of the Italian Group of the Permanent Court of Arbitration; Head of the Italian delegation to the Conference on Security and Co-operation in Europe (Valletta Meeting, 1991) on Peaceful Settlement of Disputes, Member of the mechanism created by such meeting; Member of Conciliators' Panel, CSCE Mechanism of the Human Dimension, Moscow Declaration (1991).

Member of the Institute of International Law; Member of Board of Directors of the Italian Society for International Organization; Member, International Law Association, American Society of International Law, Italian Association for Comparative Law, Italian-German Association of Jurists, Institute for International Affairs (Rome), Italian Association for Arbitration, Société française de droit international (Paris).

General co-ordinator (1965-1981) of the Italian National Research Council Team (Italian Society for International Organization – Ministry of Foreign Affairs) on "Il contributo dell'Italia alla formazione delle consuetudini internazionali"; Member, editorial board, Commentaries on the EEC Treaty and ECSC Treaty (1965 and 1970);

Member, editorial board, *Cahiers de droit européen*, Brussels; Member, scientific board, *Rivista di diritto internazionale*; General Editor, *Italian Yearbook of International Law*; Member, editorial board, *German Yearbook of International Law*; Editor-in-Chief, *La Comunità Internazionale*.

Major publications: *La prova nel processo internazionale*, 1958; *Diritto internazionale e diritto interno nella stipulazione dei trattati*, 1964; "Le operazioni finanziarie degli enti internazionali (Banca Mondiale, SFI, IDA)", *Annuario di diritto internazionale*, 1965; "Problemi interpretativi dell'art. 177 del trattato CEE", *Comunicazioni e studi dell'Istituto di diritto internazionale e straniero dell'Università di Milano*, Vol. XII, 1966; *Responsabilità civile e diritto internazionale privato*, 1973; "Les rapports entre contrats et obligations délictuelles en droit international privé", *Recueil des cours,* Hague Academy of International Law, Vol. 146, 1975; "Méthodes de recherche de la coutume internationale dans la pratique des Etats", *Recueil des cours,* Hague Academy of International Law, Vol. 192, 1985; *Codice dell'Unione Europea* (with V. Rizzo), 1994; *Lezioni di diritto internazionale I*, 4th ed., 1994; *Lezioni di Diritto Comunitario* (with M. E. Moavero Milanesi), 1995.

Author also of more than 50 articles and notes, on both public and private international law, as well as on the law of the European Communities.

Judge Rosalyn Higgins

(Member of the Court since 12 July 1995)

Born in London on 2 June 1937.

Dame Commander of the British Empire (1995).

B.A. (Cantab) 1st Class (1959); LL.B. (Cantab) 1st Class (1962); J.S.D. (Yale) (1962); M.A. (Cantab) (1962); Honorary Doctorates of the Universities of Paris XI (1980), Dundee (1992), Durham and London (1995), Cambridge, Kent and Sussex (1996).

Minor Scholar, Girton College, Cambridge (1957); Major Scholar, Girton College, Cambridge (1958); Campbell Scholarship for Professional Studies (1957); Montefiore Award for academic and general distinction (1958); Bryce-Tebbs Scholar, Cambridge (1958); Commonwealth Fund (Harkness) Fellowship (1959-1961); Graduate Fellow, Yale Law School (1959-1961).

United Kingdom Interne, Office of Legal Affairs, United Nations (1958); Visiting Fellow, Brookings Institution, Washington, DC (1960); Junior Fellow in international studies, London School of Economics (1961-1963); Staff specialist in international law, Royal Institute of International Affairs (1963-1974); Visiting Fellow, London School of Economics (1974-1978); Professor of International Law, University of Kent at Canterbury (1978-1981); Professor of International Law, University of London (1981-1995).

Queen's Counsel (1986); Bencher of the Inner Temple (1989).

Queen's Counsel and Bencher of the Inner Temple, practising in public international law and petroleum law. Practice in the English courts and before various international tribunals, including the International Court of Justice, the European Court of Human Rights and the Court of the European Communities.

Counsel for the International Tin Council in a series of cases in the United Kingdom.

Counsel in the following cases in the International Court of Justice: *Territorial Dispute (Libyan Arab Jamahiriya/Chad); East Timor (Portugal* v. *Australia); Questions of Interpretation and Application of the 1971 Montreal Convention arising from the Aerial Incident at Lockerbie (Libyan Arab Jamahiriya* v. *United Kingdom); Gabčíkovo-Nagymaros Project (Hungary/Slovakia).*

President, Tribunal of the International Centre for Settlement of Investment Disputes *(Amco* v. *Indonesia).*

Member of the Committee on Human Rights under the International Covenant on Civil and Political Rights (1984-1995); Special Rapporteur for new cases (1989-1991).

Associé of the Institut de droit international (1987), Member (1991); Chairman, Public International Law Advisory Board, British Institute for International and Comparative Law (since 1992); Hon. Vice-President of the American Society of International Law (1993).

Rockefeller Foundation Fellowship (1961); British Academy Award (1977-1978); Volumes I and II of *United Nations Peacekeeping* received the 1971 Certificate of Merit of the American Society of International Law; *Problems and Process* received the 1995 Certificate of Merit of the American Society of International Law; Wolfgang Friedman Medal for services to International Law, Columbia University (1985); Harold Weil Medal, New York University (1995); Ordre des Palmes Académiques (1988); Honorary Life Membership Award, American Society of International Law (1992).

Member of the Board of Editors of the *American Journal of International Law* (1975-1985), the *British Year Book of International Law* and of the *Journal of Energy and Natural Resources Law.*

Delivered general course on international law at the Hague Academy of International Law (1991).

Author of *The Development of International Law through the Political Organs of the United Nations*, 1963; *Conflict of Interests: International Law in a Divided World*, 1965; *The Administration of the United Kingdom Foreign Policy through the United Nations*, 1966; *UN Peacekeeping: Documents and Commentary*, Vol. I, *Middle East*, 1969, Vol. II, *Asia*, 1970, Vol. III, *Africa*, 1980, Vol. IV, *Europe*, 1981; *Law in Movement – Essays in Memory of John McMahon* (joint editor with James Fawcett), 1974; "The Taking of Property by the State: Recent Developments in

International Law", *Recueil des cours*, Hague Academy of International Law, Vol. 176, 1982; *Liberté de circulation des personnes en droit international* (joint editor with Maurice Flory), 1988; "International Law and the Avoidance, Containment and Resolution of Disputes (General Course on Public International Law)", *Recueil des cours,* Vol. 230, 1991; *Problems and Process: International Law and How We Use It*, 1994; and of various works and articles on international legal theory, United Nations law, the use of force, State and diplomatic immunities, human rights and international petroleum law.

Judge Gonzalo Parra-Aranguren

(Member of the Court since 28 February 1996)

Born in Caracas, Venezuela, on 5 December 1928.

Degree in political science *(summa cum laude)* at the Central University of Venezuela (1950); postgraduate course in comparative law and jurisprudence (LL.M.) at the Inter-American Law Institute, New York University (1951-1952); Doctor of Law *("doktor iuris") (cum laude)* at the Ludwig-Maximileans University, Munich (1955).

Professor at the Central University of Venezuela, Caracas, teaching private international law (1956-1996); has taught that same course at Andrés Bello Catholic University in Caracas (1957-1996).

Judge in the Second Course of First Instance (commercial matters), federal district and state of Miranda, Caracas (1958-1971); first associate judge (1988-1992) in the Chamber of Cassation (civil, commercial and labour matters) of the Supreme Court of Justice; elected alternate judge of the same Chamber in 1992. Has acted as arbitrator, both in Venezuela and abroad, in the latter case regarding international commercial matters of a private nature; on several occasions has testified in foreign courts as an expert on Venezuelan law.

Member of the commission of enquiry appointed in 1985 by the Governing Body of the International Labour Office to consider the implementation by the Federal Republic of Germany of the ILO Discrimination (Employment and Occupation) Convention (1958, No. 111); the report was submitted in 1986, but he did not endorse its recommendations.

Member of the Permanent Court of Arbitration (since 1985).

Member of the legislative committees that drafted the section on Venezuelan nationality in connection with the Constitution that was approved in 1961; the draft law on private international law (1963) and its subsequent revision in 1965; and the revised draft sections of the Code of Commerce dealing with credit instruments and bankruptcy respectively (1963-1965).

Member of the legal advisory committee of the Ministry of Foreign

Affairs (1984-1996) and of the legal advisory council of the National Congress (designated in 1990).

Member of the Institut de droit international (elected in 1979).

Member of the Academy of Political and Social Sciences of Caracas (since 1966) and its President (1993-1995). Corresponding Member of the Uruguayan International Law Association (1978); Corresponding Member of the Argentine International Law Association (1981); Corresponding Member of the National Academy of Law and Social Sciences of Córdoba, Argentine Republic (1982); Honorary Fellow of the Royal Academy of Jurisprudence and Legislation of Granada, Spain (1994); Corresponding Member of the Mexican Academy of Jurisprudence and Legislation corresponding to that of Spain (1994); and Honorary Fellow of the Royal Academy of Jurisprudence and Legislation, Madrid (1994).

Member of the Governing Council of the International Institute for the Unification of Private Law (UNIDROIT) (1982-1993).

Member of the editorial board of the *Revista del Colegio de Abogados del Distrito Federal*, Caracas; the editorial board of the *Revista de la Facultad de Derecho de la Universidad Católica Andrés Bello*, Caracas (since its establishment). Correspondent for the *Netherlands International Law Review* (since 1987).

Taught the General Course on Private International Law at the Hague Academy of International Law (1988), and has given lectures in various countries: in Curaçao, at the commemoration of the centenary of the introduction of codification and establishment of the Court of Justice (1969); at the course on international law (Rio de Janeiro, 1978, 1979, 1982, 1988 and 1992), organized by the Inter-American Juridical Committee and the Fundación Gétulio Vargas; at the Hague Academy of International Law, on "Recent Developments of Conflict of Laws Conventions in Latin America" (1979); at the International Law Colloquium in Salamanca, Spain (November 1992); at the seminar on the UNIDROIT principles for international commercial contracts (Rome, December 1993); at the study encounter on law journals and books to promote unity of the Latin American legal system (Rome, December 1993); at the Eighth World Conference of the International Society of Family Law (Cardiff, Wales, June 1994); at the Congress on Children on the Move, organized by the Dutch committee of the International Year of the Family in collaboration with the Hague Conference on Private International Law (The Hague, October 1994); and at the International Seminar on Adoption, an Act of Love, organized by the Instituto Colombiano de Bienestar Familiar (Bogotá, June 1995).

Co-Chairman of the Committee on Private International Law at the sixteenth meeting of the Inter-American Bar Association (Caracas, 1969). Submitted a paper at the first Latin American International Law Seminar at the Andrés Bello Catholic University (Caracas, 1979) and at the twelfth congress of the Instituto Hispano-Luso-Americano de Derecho Internacional (Mérida, Venezuela, 1980).

Representative for Venezuela at the International Association of Legal Science and the German Society for Comparative Law (Treveris, Federal Republic of Germany, 1961); and at the third meeting of the Joint Venezuelan-Spanish Commission (Madrid, 1974).

Representative for Venezuela at the first Inter-American Specialized Conference on Private International Law (CIDIP-I, Panama, 1975), being Vice-Chairman of the Second Committee; at the second such Conference (CIDIP-II, Montevideo, 1979), being Chairman of the Second Committee; at the third and fourth such Conferences (held, respectively, CIDIP-III in La Paz, Bolivia, 1984, and CIDIP-IV in Montevideo, 1989), being Chairman of the Second Committee; and at the fifth such Conference (CIDIP-V, Mexico City, 1994), being Chairman of the First Committee.

Member of the Committees of Experts that met in Washington, D.C., in 1980 in preparation for the Third Inter-American Specialized Conference on Private International Law (CIDIP-III); in Tucson, Arizona, 1993, in preparation for the Fifth Inter-American Specialized Conference on Private International Law (CIDIP-V); and in Washington, D.C. (1995, 1996) to prepare the Inter-American Convention against Corruption.

Representative of Venezuela at the Hague Conference on Private International Law: thirteenth session (1976-1977); fourteenth session (1980); fifteenth session (1984); special session (1985); sixteenth session (1988); and the seventeenth session (1993); member of the special working group and Special Commission (April and October 1994, respectively) to study the application of the Convention of 1993 to minors who are refugees; and of the Special Commission (second meeting, June 1995) on the protection of minors and incompetent adults. Elected one of the five Vice-Chairmen at the fifteenth and sixteenth sessions.

Rapporteur of the Special Commission of the seventeenth session of the Hague Conference on Private International Law and, in pursuance of these functions, prepared the preliminary report (1992) and the explanatory report on the Convention on Protection of Children and Co-operation in respect of Intercountry Adoption on 29 May 1993.

Author of the following books: *Die Regel "Locus Regit Actum" und die Formen der Testamente*, 1955; *La Nacionalidad Venezolana Originaria*, Vols. I and II, 1964; *La Constitución de 1830 v los Venezolanos por Naturalizacion*, 1969; *Codificacion del Derecho Internacional Privado en América*, 1982; *La Nacionalidad Venezolana: I. Antecedentes Históricos*, 1983; *La Influencia del Matrimonio sobre la Nacionalidad de la Mujer en la Legislación Venezolana*, 1983; *La Ńacionalidad Venezolana: II. Problemas Actuales*, 1983; *Monografias Selectas de Derecho Internacional Privado*, 1984; *Ensayos de Derecho Procesal Civil Internacional*, 1986: *Curso General de Derecho Internacional Privado (Problemas Selectos)*, 1991; *Curso General de Derecho Internacional Privado. Problemas Selectos v Otros Estudios*, 1992.

Has published numerous articles on the law of nationality, private international law and international civil procedural law in Venezuelan and foreign journals.

II. Judges *Ad Hoc*

Article 7, paragraph 3, of the Rules of Court provides that judges *ad hoc* are to take precedence after the Members of the Court and in order of seniority of age.

Judge *ad hoc* Kéba Mbaye

(Judge *ad hoc* in the case concerning the *Land and Maritime Boundary between Cameroon and Nigeria (Cameroon* v. *Nigeria)*)

Holder of the diploma of advanced studies in private law (Paris); holder of the certificate of the Ecole nationale de la France d'outre-mer (Magistrature Department).

Honorary First President of the Supreme Court.

Former President of the Constitutional Council of Senegal.

Former lecturer at the Faculty of Law of the University of Dakar and at the Ecole nationale d'administration of Senegal (1967-1978).

Doctor *honoris causa* of the Universities of Lille II, Savoie (France), Bhopal (India) and Emory (United States of America).

Member of the International Court of Justice (6 February 1982 to 5 February 1991); Vice-President of the Court (1987 to 1991); formerly judge *ad hoc* in the case concerning the *Arbitral Award of 31 July 1989 (Guinea-Bissau* v. *Senegal)*.

Has been a member of various United Nations bodies and has in particular participated as member and chairman in the work of the Commission on Human Rights, the Commission responsible for seeking the settlement of any dispute between States Parties to the Convention against Discrimination in Education, the Special Committee to investigate Israeli Practices Affecting the Human Rights of the Population of the Occupied Territories, and of the *Ad Hoc* Working Group of Experts to investigate violations of human rights in southern Africa; former member of the ILO Committee of Experts.

Vice-Chairman of the Executive Committee of the International Institute of Human Rights (René Cassin Foundation); Honorary Member of the International Institute of Humanitarian Law; former Chairman of the International Commission of Jurists; Honorary President of the World Federation of United Nations Associations; former President of the International Academy of Human Rights; Member of the Société française pour le droit international; Vice-President of the Institut international de droit d'expression française; was General Rapporteur at the Organization of African Unity Conference which adopted the African Charter on Human and Peoples' Rights.

Honorary Member of the Belgian Académie royale des sciences d'outre-mer; Member of the International Academy of Comparative Law, of the

International Law Association, of the Académie française des sciences d'outre-mer and of the Curatorium of the Hague Academy of International Law; Honorary Member of the Institute of International Law; Vice-Chairman of the ICC International Court of Arbitration; President of the Court of Arbitration for Sport and of the International Council of Arbitration for Sport.

Author of numerous publications concerning the law of Senegal, the law of sub-Saharan Africa, human rights in general, and in particular the right to development, the law of sport. Gave a lecture on "'Interest to Act' before the International Court of Justice" at the Hague Academy of International Law (1988).

Judge *ad hoc* François Ernest Robert RIGAUX

(Judge *ad hoc* in the case concerning *Oil Platforms (Islamic Republic of Iran* v. *United States of America)*)

Born in Ixelles, Belgium, on 26 March 1926.

Bachelier of Philosophy (1945); Doctor of Law (1947); Licencié in Criminal Science (1948); Agrégé in Law (1956); Doctor *honoris causa* of the University of Dijon (1981).

Senior Lecturer (1955), Assistant Professor (1959) and Professor (1961) in the Faculty of Law of the Université catholique de Louvain. Subjects taught: civil law (persons and property); private international law; protection of the individual and of privacy. Dean of the Faculty of Law (1980-1984), and President of the International Law Department of the Université catholique de Louvain. Professor emeritus at the Université catholique de Louvain (1991) and Visiting Professor, Faculty of Law (1991-1992; 1992-1993). Visiting Professor, Catholic University, Brussels (1993-1994 and 1994-1995) and University Faculties at Saint Louis, Brussels (1995-1996).

As well as courses and lectures at various foreign universities, particularly in Florence, Bremen, Barcelona, Caracas, Caceres, Geneva, Hamburg, Milan, Munich, Nancy, Regensburg, Rio de Janeiro and Baton Rouge, gave courses as follows: a course at the Hague Academy of International Law on change of connecting factors in private international law (1966), published in the collection *Reuceil des cours*; the General Course on Private International Law in 1989 on "Les situations juridiques individuelles dans un système de relativité générale", also published in the *Recueil des cours*; Visiting Professor at the Université Lovanium, Kinshasa (1970); holder of the Francqui Professorship at the Université libre de Bruxelles (1975-1976 academic year), where he taught a course entitled "Droit public et droit privé dans les relations internationales" (published in 1977); course at the Institut des hautes études internationales (Paris,

1978-1979 academic year) on the new international economic order (published in the Institute's "collection des cours et travaux"); Director of Studies of the 1979 summer programme of the Institut universitaire de Luxembourg on the impact of the EEC on the private international law of its member States (work published in 1980). Holder of the Francqui Professorship in the Faculty of Law of the Katholieke Universiteit Leuven (Catholic University of Louvain) (1980-1981 academic year), where he taught a course on "Le pluralisme juridique". Holder of the Francqui Professorship at the Facultés universitaires Notre-Dame de la Paix, Namur (1991-1992 academic year), where he taught a course on "La liberté de la vie privée". Invited to give lectures at the Tunis Faculty of Law (1988 and 1989), the Florence Faculty of Political Science (1988), the Faculty of Law of the Université d'Aix-Marseille (1991-1992) and the Faculty of Law of Louisiana State University, Baton Rouge (1994-1995).

Served on Ph.D. examining boards at the Universities of Antwerp, Dijon, Ghent, Lyons, Nice, Paris, Reims and Tunis.

Member of the Bar of Brussels (1947-1954). Deputy Royal Procurator (1954-1963). At present, Honorary Deputy Royal Procurator. Assessor, Legislation Section of the Conseil d'Etat (1966-1991), authorized by Royal Order to bear the honorary title of that function.

Member of the Constitutional Court of the Federation of Bosnia and Herzegovina.

Member of the Institute of International Law (and Third Vice-President from 1983 to 1985). Member of the Institut belge de droit comparé. Former President of the Société belge de droit international. Member of the governing board of the Société des amis d'Henri Rolin. Former President of the scientific council of the *Revue belge de droit international.* (Corresponding) Member of the Section des sciences morales et politiques, classe des lettres of the Académie royale de Belgique (January 1988). (Associate) Member of the International Academy of Comparative Law.

Winner of the Prix des Anciens Présidents et du *Journal des tribunaux* awarded to a first-year trainee (1947-1948 judicial year). Winner of the Emile van Dievoet Prize (period 1951-1955) for his work entitled: *La théorie des qualifications en droit international privé.* Winner of the "Legatum Visserianum" Prize awarded in January 1962 by the College of Curators of Leiden University for a dissertation on Representation in Comparative Private International Law, submitted on 1 March 1959. Winner of the José A. Negri Prize awarded by the Federal Council of Argentine Notaries for the collective work "Les régimes matrimoniaux et les successions en droit international privé", edited by him in 1961 on the occasion of the Seventh International Congress of Latin Notaries.

Officer of the Order of Leopold (1968), Commander of the Order of the Crown (1977), Grand Officer of the Order of Leopold II (1988).

Principal publications: *La théorie des qualifications en droit international privé*, 1956; *Le statut de la représentation en droit international privé*, 1959; *La nature du contrôle de la Cour de cassation*, 1966; *Précis de droit international privé*, 1968; *Précis de droit des personnes*, Vol. I: *Les relations familiales*, 1971, updated with the collaboration of M. T. Meulders-Klein, 1978; *Introduction à la science du droit*, 1974; *Droit public et droit privé dans les relations internationales* (publication of the *Revue générale de droit international public*, No. 26), 1977; *Droit international privé*, Vol. I: *Théorie générale*, 1977, revised 2nd ed., 1987; Vol. II: *Droit positif belge*, 1979, revised 2nd ed. with the collaboration of Marc Fallon, 1973; *Pour un autre ordre international*, Droit économique 2, Institut des hautes études internationales de Paris, 1979-1980; *Derecho internacional privado, parte general*, translation and adaptation to Spanish law of Volume I of *Droit international privé*, by Mrs. A. Borras Rodríguez, 1985; *La Carta di Algieri*, translated by Anna Lo Monaco, 1988; "Les situations juridiques individuelles dans un système de relativité générale (Cours général de droit international privé)", *Recueil des cours*, Hague Academy of International Law, Vol. 213, 1989; *Pour une déclaration universelle des droits des peuples*, 1990; *La protection de la vie privée et des autres biens de la personnalité*, 1990; *La vie privé, un liberté parmi les autres?*, 1992.

Judge *ad hoc* Krzysztof SKUBISZEWSKI

(Judge *ad hoc* in the case concerning *Gabčíkovo-Nagymaros Project (Hungary/Slovakia)*)

Born in Poznań, Poland, on 8 October 1926.

Faculty of Law and Economic Sciences, University of Poznań *(magister juris)* (1945-1949); Doctor *juris* (1950); European University Centre (Diploma of European Higher Studies), University of Nancy, France (1957); Harvard School of Law (Master of Law) (1957-1958); "Habilitation" in International Law at the Adam Mickiewicz University in Poznań (1960); Doctor *honoris causa* of the Universities of Ghent, Liège, Turin, Mainz and Geneva.

Assistant teacher and lecturer, Faculty of Law, Adam Mickiewicz University in Poznań (1948-1960); Dozent, Faculty of Law, Adam Mickiewicz University in Poznań (1961-1973), Pro-Dean at that Faculty (1961-1963); Visiting Scholar, School of International Affairs, Columbia University, New York (1963-1964); Visiting Professor at the Law Faculty, University of Geneva (1971 and 1979); Visiting Fellow, All Souls College, Oxford (1971-1972); Professor, Institute of Law, Polish Academy of Sciences, Warsaw (1973-1996); Honorary Professor, University of Bucharest.

Lectures at the Universities of Nottingham and London; International Faculty of Comparative Law in Strasbourg; Graduate Institute of

International Studies at Geneva; College of Europe at Bruges, Belgium, and also the Clubs of International Law of Harvard, Duke and Oxford Universities; Max-Planck Institute in Heidelberg; Universities of Vienna and Graz; Faculty of Law, University of Paris II; Royal Institute of International Affairs, Chatham House; All Souls College, Oxford; Institut d'Etudes Politiques de Paris; Free University, Berlin (1963-1995); also Hersch Lauterpacht Lectures, Cambridge (1985); Cyril Foster Lecture, Oxford (1990); Lord Wilberforce Lecture (1990); Hugh Gaitskell Lecture (1991); and numerous other lectures in European, American, Australian and Asian Societies of Political and Legal Sciences or International Relations (1989-1995).

Member of "Solidarity" (since 1980); Member of the Primate of Poland Social Council (1981-1984); Member of the Co-ordinating Committee of the Poland-Federal Republic of Germany Forum, representing the secretariat of the Polish Episcopate (1984-1989); Member of the Consultative Council to the Chairman of the Council of State of the Polish People's Republic (1986-1989); Minister for Foreign Affairs (1989-1993).

Member (since 4 December 1993) and President (since 16 February 1994) of the Iran-United States Claims Tribunal.

Judge *ad hoc* in the International Court of Justice in the case concerning *East Timor (Portugal* v. *Australia).*

Co-founder and first Chairman of the Council on Foreign Policy (Warsaw, 1996).

Member of the Academies of Sciences of Warsaw and of Cracow; Correspondent, Institut de France; Member of the Society of Arts and Sciences, Poznań; Western Institute, Poznań; International Law Association (Polish branch); Institut de droit international (First Vice-President, 1995-1997); American Society of International Law (Honorary Member, 1991); Société française pour le droit international; Deutsche Gesellschaft für Völkerrecht; Oxford Society; Codrington Club; Honorary Bencher, Gray's Inn. Curator, United Nations Student Association, Poznań (1960-1973).

Gold Cross of Merit (1977); Knight's Cross of the Order of Polonia Restituta (1986); Cavaliere di Gran Croce, Ordine Piano (Holy See, 1991); Grand Officier de la Legion d'honneur (1991); Grosskreuz des Verdienstordens der Bundesrepublik Deutschland (1991); Order of Diplomatic Merit of the Republic of Korea (1991); Cross of Merit of the Republic of Hungary (1994).

Alexander von Humboldt Foundation research prize (1984); Wartburg Prize, Germany (1992).

Author of four books and some 100 articles in law journals or collections of studies, also chapters in collective books and reports, on legal aspects of Polish-German relations, in particular the border between the two countries; use of force by States and law of armed conflicts; law of international organizations; theory of international law, including its sources; rights of individuals.

Judge *ad hoc* Elihu LAUTERPACHT

(Judge *ad hoc* in the case concerning the *Application of the Convention on the Prevention and Punishment of the Crime of Genocide (Bosnia and Herzegovina* v. *Yugoslavia))*

Born in London, United Kingdom, on 13 July 1928.

Cambridge University, B.A. (1949); L.L.M. (1950); Whewell Scholar in International Law (1950).

Director of the Research Centre for International Law and Honorary Professor of International Law, University of Cambridge (1983-1995).

Fellow of Trinity College, Cambridge.

Barrister (1950); Queen's Counsel (1970); Bencher of Gray's Inn.

Commander of the British Empire (C.B.E.) (1989).

Legal Adviser of the Australian Department of Foreign Affairs (1975-1977); deputy leader of the Australian delegation to the United Nations General Assembly (1975-1977); deputy leader of the Australian delegation to the United Nations Law of the Sea Conference (1975-1977).

Counsel or advocate in numerous cases before the International Court of Justice, the European Commission of Human Rights, the Iran-United States Claims Tribunal, various international arbitral tribunals and national courts; counsel and adviser to many Governments and corporations.

Member of the Panel of Arbitrators of the International Centre for the Settlement of Investment Disputes (since 1974); Member of the Panel of Arbitrators of the Dispute Settlement Centre of the International Energy Agency (since 1980).

Chairman of the East African Common Market Tribunal (1972-1975); Member (since 1979) and President (since 1996) of the World Bank Administrative Tribunal; Chairman of the Asian Development Bank Administrative Tribunal (1992-1995); Chairman of the Dispute Settlement Panel under the North American Free Trade Agreement (1996).

Member of the Institute of International Law; Honorary Member of the American Society of International Law.

Director, English-speaking Section, Research Centre of the Hague Academy of International Law (1959 and 1960); delivered course of lectures at the Hague Academy of International Law (1976), on "The Development of the Law of International Organization by the Decisions of International Tribunals".

Editor of the *International Law Reports* (since 1960) and founder editor of *British Practice in International Law.*

Publications include *Aspects of the Administration of International Justice* (1991); "The Development of the Law of International Organization by the Decisions of International Tribunals", Hague Academy of International Law, *Recueil des cours* (1976); *Jerusalem and the Holy Places* (1968); and many articles.

Judge *ad hoc* Marc Lalonde

(Judge *ad hoc* in the case concerning *Fisheries Jurisdiction (Spain* v. *Canada)*)

Born in Ile Perrot, Quebec, Canada, on 26 July 1929.

B.A., St. Laurent College, Montreal (1950); LL.L., University of Montreal (1954); M.A. (Law), University of Montreal (1955); M.A. (Oxon.) (Economics and Political Science), Oxford University (1957); Diploma of Superior Studies in Law, University of Ottawa (1960); LL.D. *honoris causa*, Limburg University, Netherlands (1993).

Called to the Bar of Quebec (1955).

Professor of Commercial Law and Economics, University of Montreal (1957-1959); Special Assistant to the Canadian Minister of Justice (1959-1960); Partner, Gélinas, Bourque, Lalonde & Benoit, Montreal (1960-1967); Lecturer in Administrative Law for Doctoral Students, University of Ottawa and University of Montreal (1961-1962); Policy Adviser to Lester B. Pearson, Prime Minister of Canada (1967-1968); Principal Secretary to Pierre E. Trudeau, Prime Minister of Canada (1968-1972); Member of Parliament (1972-1984); Minister of Health and Welfare (1972-1977); Minister Responsible for the Status of Women (1974-1979); Minister of State Responsible for Federal-Provincial Relations (1977-1978); Minister of Justice and Attorney General for Canada (1978-1979); Minister of Energy, Mines and Resources (1980-1982); Minister of Finance (1982-1984); Partner, Stikeman, Elliott, Montreal, Quebec (since 1984).

Member of the Board of Directors of Citibank Canada, Orléans Resources Inc., and Camdev Corporation Inc.

Member of the International Advisory Council to the Presidium of Ukraine (since 1990); the Advisory Committee on Constitutional Matters in Czechoslovakia (1989-1991); the International Advisory Council of Air France (1991-1994).

Chairman of the Council of Governors, Canada-Chile Board of Trade (since 1995). Chairman of Hôtel-Dieu Hospital, Montreal, Quebec (since 1984).

Member of the Quebec Bar; the Law Society of Upper Canada (Ontario Bar); the American Bar Association (associate member); the International Bar Association; the Canadian Bar Association; the Chambre de Commerce de Montréal; the Chambre de Commerce France-Canada; the International Council on Commercial Arbitration; the Corporate Counsel Committee, American Arbitration Association; the Board of Directors and Executive Committee of the American Arbitration Association; the Board of Directors of the Arbitrators Institute of Quebec; Corresponding Member of the Institute of International Business Law and Practice of the International Chamber of Commerce; the Advisory Board of the Asia/Pacific Centre for the Resolution of the International Business Disputes; the Canadian Arbitration Committee of the International

Chamber of Commerce; Member of the Council of the Royal College of Physicians and Surgeons of Canada (lay member).

Has written a number of articles and delivered lectures in Canada and abroad on arbitration. Has also been a frequent speaker to national and international conferences in the Canada-United States Free Trade Agreement and the North American Free Trade Agreement.

Queen's Counsel (1971); Member of the Privy Council of Canada (1972); Order of Canada (1989).

Judge *ad hoc* Santiago Torres Bernárdez

(Judge *ad hoc* in the cases concerning *Maritime Delimitation and Territorial Questions between Qatar and Bahrain (Qatar* v. *Bahrain)* and *Fisheries Jurisdiction (Spain* v. *Canada)*)

Born in Vigo, Spain, on 18 November 1929.

Licenciado (1952) and Doctor of Law (1959) of the University of Valladolid, Spain. *Diplomé d'études supérieures européennes* (1955) and Doctor of Law (1957) of the University of Saar, Germany. Doctor *Honoris Causa* of Law (1993) of the University of Alcalá de Henares, Spain.

Member of the Madrid Bar Association. Legal consultant and counsel or advocate in international cases.

Member of the Permanent Court of Arbitration; Member of the Humanitarian Fact-Finding Commission; Member of the Institute of International Law; Member of the International Law Association; Honorary Member of the Spanish Association of International Law Professors; Member of the Société française pour le droit international; Member of the American Society of International Law; Associate Member of the Hispano-Luso-American Institute of International Law.

Member of the Spanish National Committee for the 50th Anniversary of the United Nations; Vice-president of the NGO "Spain with the UNHCR".

Judge *ad hoc* in the International Court of Justice in the case concerning the *Land, Island and Maritime Frontier Dispute (El Salvador/Honduras: Nicaragua intervening)* (1989-1992).

Former Registrar of the International Court of Justice (1980-1986). Former Member of the Office of Legal Affairs of the Secretariat of the United Nations (1959-1980) being, since 1975, Deputy Director of the Codification Division and Deputy Secretary of the International Law Commission. During that period served continually United Nations legal bodies (Sixth Committee of the General Assembly; International Law Commission; special or *ad hoc* committees), participating also in all the United Nations diplomatic conferences convened between 1960 and 1980 for the purpose of the progressive development of international law and its codification.

Expert of the United Nations in the Committee established by the International Committee of the Red Cross for the study of a prohibition of specific conventional weapons, including those which may be deemed to be excessively injurious or have indiscriminate effects (1973); Member of the United Nations delegation in the Diplomatic Conference on the reaffirmation and development of international humanitarian law applicable in armed conflicts (1974-1977); Member of the observer mission sent to Panama by the United Nations Secretary-General to monitor the constitutional referendum on the ratification of the Treaties on the Panama Canal (1977).

Professor in the Instituto Universitario Ortega y Gasset, Madrid. Has given many lectures at various universities and societies in Spain and abroad.

Addressed, in 1995, the United Nations Congress on Public International Law on the topic "La función de la Corte Internacional de Justicia en el sistema de la Carta de las Naciones Unidas".

Director (1970) of the French-speaking Section of the Research Centre of the Hague Academy of International Law (subject: interpretation of treaties) and delivered in 1995 course of lectures at the Hague Academy of International Law on "L'intervention dans la procédure de la Cour internationale de Justice".

Author of various published studies and articles on questions of international law and international organizations and procedures, including: *À propos de l'interprétation et de la revision des arrêts de la Cour internationale de Justice*, 1987; *Resignations at the World Court*, 1988; *La reciprocidad en el sistema de jurisdicción obligatoria establecido en el Artículo 36, párrafo 2, del Estatuto de la Corte Internacional de Justicia*, 1988; "Subsidiary Organs of International Organizations", in *A Handbook on International Organizations,* published by the Hague Academy of International Law, 1988; "Problems and Issues Raised by 'Crimes of States': An Overview", *International Crimes of States. A Critical Analysis of the ILC's Draft Article 19 on State Responsibility*, 1989; "L'arbitrage interétatique. Avec des références particulières à la Convention européenne pour le règlement des différends du 20 avril 1957", in *The Peaceful Settlement of International Disputes in Europe: Future Prospects*, Workshop of the Hague Academy of International Law, 1990; "Observations on 'Non-Appearance' before the International Court of Justice", *Annuaire de l'Institut de droit international*, session de Bâle, Vol. 64–I, 1991; "Succession d'Etats", in Unesco, *Droit international. Bilan et perspectives*, 1991; *Reciprocity in the System of Compulsory Jurisdiction and in Other Modalities of Contentious Jurisdiction Exercised by the International Court of Justice*, 1992; *Perspectivas en la contribución de las Naciones Unidas al mantenimiento de la paz y la seguridad internacionales: Comentarios y observaciones sobre la Declaración de los Miembros del Consejo de Seguridad de 31 de enero de 1992*, 1993; "Spain and the Jurisdiction of the International Court of Justice: From Past to Present", *Archiv des Völkerrechts*, 1994; *The* Uti Possidetis Juris *Principle in*

Historical Perspective, 1994; "Some Considerations on the Respective Roles of the Security Council and the International Court of Justice with Respect to 'the Prevention of Aggravation of Disputes' in the Domain of the Pacific Settlement of International Disputes or Situations", in *Proceedings of the Qatar International Law Conference '94* (United Nations Decade of International Law), 1995.

Awarded the Spanish Great Cross of Civil Merit (1987) and other foreign decorations (all after 1987).

Judge *ad hoc* Ahmed Sadek EL-KOSHERI

(Judge *ad hoc* in the cases concerning *Questions of Interpretation and Application of the 1971 Montreal Convention arising from the Aerial Incident at Lockerbie (Libyan Arab Jamahiriya* v. *United Kingdom)* and *Questions of Interpretation and Application of the 1971 Montreal Convention arising from the Aerial Incident at Lockerbie (Libyan Arab Jamahiriya* v. *United States of America))*

Born at Cairo, Egypt, on 4 April 1932.

Licencié en Droit, Faculté de Droit (1952), D.E.S. Droit Musulman (1954), D.E.S. Droit Privé (1955), D.E.S. Droit Public (1956), Cairo University. D.E.S. en Sciences Politiques (1957), Diplôme de Droit Comparé (1959), Paris University. D.E.S. en Histoire et Philosophie de Droit (1960), Doctorat d'Etat en Droit (1962), Rennes University.

Faculty Member of the Law School, Ain Shams University, Cairo (1958-1974). Visiting Professor, Beirut Arab University (1963-1964) and Nanterre University (Paris X) (1987-1988). Professor of International Economic Law and Vice-President of Senghor University, Alexandria.

Partner of Kosheri, Rashed and Riad law firm, Cairo.

Member of the Egyptian Conseil d'Etat (1952-1958). Legal Adviser of the Ministry of Oil and Finance, Kuwait (1968-1969). Founding General Counsel of the Arab Fund for Economic and Social Development, Kuwait (1973-1974). Secretary-General of the Islamic Development Bank, Jeddah (1978).

Member of the Institut de droit international. Member of the Council for International Commercial Arbitration (ICCA). Member of the Conseil d'Arbitrage Franco-Arabe. Member of the Scientific Council of the International Business Law Institute, International Chamber of Commerce, Paris.

Author of numerous books and articles on general public international law, international commercial law and on international arbitration.

Prince Bola Adesumbo Ajibola

(Judge *ad hoc* in the case concerning the *Land and Maritime Boundary between Cameroon and Nigeria (Cameroon* v. *Nigeria)*)

Born to the Royal Family of Gbdaela II, on 22 March 1934, in Ago-Owu, Abeokuta, Ogun State, Nigeria.

Called to the Bar, Lincoln's Inn, 1962 (Barrister-at-Law); holds Bachelor of Laws Degree of London University; LL.D. *(honoris causa)* of the University of Buckingham (Chancellor the Rt. Hon. Baroness Margaret Thatcher) (1996).

Legal practitioner for 23 years, mostly in Lagos and also in all other parts of Nigeria; Principal Partner of Bola Ajibola and Co., with offices in Lagos, Ikeja, Abeokuta and Kaduna (specialization: commercial law practice with particular bias for international arbitration).

Attorney-General and Minister of Justice of the Federal Republic of Nigeria (1985-1991); President of the Association of Arbitrators of Nigeria; President of the Nigerian Bar Association (1984-1985); conferment of an Award of Senior Advocate of Nigeria (1986); Chairman of the Body of Senior Advocates of Nigeria (1985-1991); Chairman of the Disciplinary Committee of the Bar (1985-1991); Chairman of the General Council of the Bar (1985-1991); Chairman of the Advisory Committee on the Prerogative of Mercy (1985-1991); Member of the Advisory Judicial Committee (1985-1991); Member of the Judicial Service Committee (Abuja) (1987-1991); Vice-Chairman of the Body of Benchers (1989-1990); Chairman of the Body of Benchers (1990-1991); Member of the Nigeria Police Council (1989-1991); Chairman of the Task Force for the Revision of the Laws of the Federation (1990).

Leader of the Nigerian Delegation to the United States of America to Initial an Executive Agreement on Procedure for Mutual Assistance on Law Enforcement Matters (1987) and of the Delegation to conclude a Treaty on Mutual Assistance in Criminal Matters (1989), of the Delegation to the United Kingdom to conclude a Treaty concerning the Investigation and Prosecution of Crime and the Confiscation of the Proceeds of Crime (1989), and of the Delegation to the Islamic Republic of Iran and to Algeria, for bilateral talks on Technical and Legal Co-operation (1991).

Member of the Nigerian Delegation to the United Nations General Assembly and Nigerian representative to the Sixth Committee (1986); temporary President of the United Nations General Assembly at its seventeenth special session on narcotic drugs (1990); Member of the International Law Commission (1986-1991).

Member of the International Court of Justice from 5 December 1991 to 5 February 1994.

Member of the World Bank Administrative Tribunal; Member of the Constitutional Court of the Federation of Bosnia and Herzegovina (since 1995); Member of the United Nations Compensation Commission.

Member of the Permanent Court of Arbitration (The Hague) and Member of the Board of Trustees of its Financial Assistance Fund; Member of the International Chamber of Commerce Court of Arbitration, Paris; Member of the International Maritime Arbitration Commission, Paris; Member of the Board of the London Court of International Arbitration; President of the Pan-African Council of the London Court of International Arbitration.

Initiated the first ever African Law Ministers Conference, Abuja (1989) (attended by 32 African countries); Chairman of Meeting of ECOWAS Council of Law Ministers, Lagos, Nigeria (1990), where the Treaty Establishing the Court for the Economic Community of West African States was drafted and agreed to by ECOWAS law ministers; leader of the Nigerian Delegation to the Ethiopian All-Party Conference on Peaceful and Democratic Transition (1991); Chairman of the First Meeting of the Working Committee, All-Africa Law Ministers Conference, Cairo (1991); Member of the Nigerian Delegation to the World Peace through Law Conferences in Seoul, South Korea (1987), and Beijing, China (1990); leader of the Nigerian Delegation to the World Conference on the Reform of Criminal Law, Canada (1987), to the Commonwealth Law Conference in Auckland, New Zealand (1990) and the Commonwealth Law Ministers Conference in Christchurch, New Zealand (1990); leader of the Nigerian Delegation to the World Ministerial Drugs Summit on Action to Reduce the Demand for Drugs and to Combat Cocaine Threat, London (1990), and to the 17th Session of the Asian African Legal Consultative Committee in Cairo (1991). President of the World Association of Judges; Vice-President of the International Contractual Relations Commission of the International Chamber of Commerce (1976-1980); Vice-President of the Institute of International Business Law and Practice, Paris; represented Africa in the demonstration trial on the law of the sea at the World Peace through Law Conference (Manila, 1977); Fellow of the Chartered Institute of Arbitrators; Fellow of the Nigerian Institute of Advanced Legal Studies; Friend of the Institute of Advanced Legal Studies, London.

Member of the International Bar Association and the Association of World Lawyers.

Member of the Governing Board of the International Maritime Law Institute of the International Maritime Organization (IMO); Member of the Board of Directors of the International Development Law Institute, Rome.

President and Founder of "African Concern" (a non-political, non-religious, non-profit-making, non-governmental organization), Lusaka, Zambia (1995).

Editor, *Nigeria's Treaties in Force*, 1970-1990; Editor, *All Nigeria Law Reports*, 1961-1990; Editor-in-Chief, *Justice* (a monthly journal of contemporary legal problems); General Editor of the *Federal Ministry of Justice Law Review Series (FMJLRS)*; Member of the Editorial Advisory Board of the University of Buckingham.

Publications include: *Principles of Arbitration*, 1980; *New Concepts in the Resolution of Disputes in International Construction Contracts*, 1981; *Work Paper on International Commercial Arbitration*, 1982; *Arbitration and State Enterprises – Case Study of Nigerian Cement Transactions*, 1983; *Modernization of National Arbitration Laws in Aid of International Commercial Arbitration*, 1984; *The Law and Settlement of Commercial Disputes*, 1984; *Law Development and Administration in Nigeria*, 1987; *Towards a Better Administration of Justice System in Nigeria*, 1988; *Integration of the African Continent through Law*, 1988; *Narcotics: Law and Policy in Nigeria*, 1989; *Compensation and Remedies for Victims of Crime*, 1989; *Banking Frauds and Other Financial Malpractices in Nigeria*, 1989; *Women and Children under Nigerian Law*, 1990; *Scheme relating to Mutual Assistance in Criminal Matters and the Control of Criminal Activities within Africa*, 1990; "Human Rights under Military Rule in Africa: The Nigerian Experience" in *Essays in Honour of Judge Taslim Olawale Elias*, 1991. Gave a series of lectures on human rights in Accra, Ghana, under the auspices of the Ghana Bar Association, entitled: "Human Rights Agenda for a Stable 21st Century". Author of numerous articles and conference papers.

1987 World Jurist Award (under the auspices of World Peace through Law at Seoul); Senior Advocate of Nigeria; Recipient of 1986 Ogun State of Nigeria Outstanding Citizen Merit Award; Life Member, Nigerian Institute of International Affairs; Life Member, Body of Benchers, Nigeria; Knight of the Order of the British Empire; Patron of the Nigerian Society of International Law.

Judge *ad hoc* Geoffrey PALMER

(Judge *ad hoc* in the *Request for an Examination of the Situation in Accordance with Paragraph 63 of the Court's Judgment of 20 December 1974 in the* Nuclear Tests (New Zealand *v.* France) *Case*)

Born in Nelson, New Zealand, on 21 April 1942.

B.A. Political Science, Victoria University of Wellington (1964); LL.B., Victoria University of Wellington (1966); Doctor of Law (JD) *cum laude*, University of Chicago (1967); Doctor of Humane Letters *Honoris Causa*, Hofstra University, New York (1991).

Law clerk then barrister and solicitor with O'Flynn and Christie (1964-1966); Lecturer in Political Science, Victoria University of Wellington (1968-1969); Law Professor, University of Iowa (three years) and University of Virginia (one year) (1969-1973); Professor of Law, Victoria University of Wellington (1974-1979); Visiting Professor University of Iowa (1977); Visiting Fellow Wolfson College, Oxford (1978).

Retained to draft official commentary of Woodhouse Report prepared by the New Zealand Government (1969); Principal Assistant to the Australian National Committee of Inquiry on Rehabilitation and Compensation (1973-1974); Consultant to the Australian Government on implementation of the National Compensation Scheme (1974-1975); Chairman of the Committee on Flammable Fabrics which reported to the Minister of Trade and Industry (1975); Member of the Law Reform Committee on Defamation which reported to the Minister of Justice (1977); Adviser on Accident Compensation to the Governments of Sri Lanka and of Cyprus under the auspices of the Commonwealth Secretariat (1979-1980).

Laureate of the United Nations Environment Programmes to "Global 500 Roll of Honour" (1991); International Advisory Council Member of the World Wide Fund for Nature; Global Environmental Group Member of the University of Iowa; Executive Advisory Board Member of the Earth Trust.

Member of Parliament, Christchurch Central (1979-1990); Deputy Leader of the Opposition (1983-1984); Leader of the House of Representatives (1984-1987); Deputy Prime Minister (1984-1989); Attorney-General (1984-1989); Minister of Justice (1984-1989); Minister for the Environment (1987-1990); Prime Minister (August 1989-September 1990).

Principal publications: *Tort in Transition: A New Zealand Collection of Cases and Materials on Tort in the Accident Compensation Era* (with R. S. Clark and P. D. McKenzie), 1976; *The Welfare State Today* (edited and contributed), 1977; *Compensation for Incapacity: A Study of Law and Social Change in New Zealand and Australia*, 1979; *Unbridled Power, An Interpretation of New Zealand's Constitution and Government*, 1987; *Environmental Politics: A Greenprint for New Zealand*, 1990; *New Zealand's Constitution in Crisis: Reforming our Political System*, 1992; *Public Law in New Zealand: Cases, Materials, Commentary and Questions* (with Mai Chen), 1993; *International Environmental Law and World Order* (with Lakshman Guruswamy and Burns Weston), 1994; *Environment — The International Challenge*, 1995. Author of numerous review articles.

Judge *ad hoc* Milenko Kreća

(Judge *ad hoc* in the case concerning the *Application of the Convention on the Prevention and Punishment of the Crime of Genocide (Bosnia and Herzegovina* v. *Yugoslavia)*)

Born in Sisak, Croatia, on 19 August 1947.

Received M.A. and Ph.D. (LL.D.) degrees *cum laude* from the School of Law, Belgrade University.

Upon graduation, practised law as an attorney (1973-1974).

Assistant Professor (1975), Docent (1978) and Associate Professor (1985) at the Belgrade School of Law. Full-time Professor of International Public Law (1990) and Associate Dean (1989-1991) at the Belgrade School of Law.

Was on several occasions legal adviser to the Ministry of Foreign Affairs and Government of the Federal Republic of Yugoslavia and to other organs of the Republic of Serbia and the Federal Republic of Yugoslavia.

Papers and books: *Practical Course in International Law* (co-author), 1980; *International Public Law* (co-author), 1983, 1986, 1989, 1990, 1991, 1993, 1996; *Sources of International Public Law,* 1979, 1985; *Treaty-making Power of the State in International Law, with a Special Review of Federal States,* 1988; *Absolutely Binding Norms (Ius Cogens) in International Public Law,* 1989; *Material for International Public Law,* I-III (co-author), 1988-1989; *Law of the Sea – Scientific Research of the Sea and Transfer of Marine Technology,* 1990; *Treaty-making Power of the State in International Law*, 1991. Author of over 70 articles and papers in Serbian and foreign languages, including: "Some General Reflections on Main Features of *Ius Cogens* as a Notion of International Public Law", in *New Directions in International Law, Essays in Honour of W. Abendroth,* 1982; "Quelques observations sur le problème de la hiérarchie des règles de droit dans le droit international public", in *Yugoslav Review of International Law,* No. 1, 1980; "Constitutional Provisions Regulating Activity of Federal Units in International Relations", in *Yugoslav Review of International Law,* No. 1, 1992.

CHAPTER III

JURISDICTION OF THE COURT

I. JURISDICTION IN CONTENTIOUS CASES

It is the function of the International Court of Justice to decide in accordance with international law such disputes as are submitted to it (Statute, Art. 38, para. 1). Its jurisdiction in this respect is defined in Article 93 of the Charter of the United Nations and in Articles 34-37 of the Statute of the Court.

1. States Entitled to Appear before the Court

Article 34, paragraph 1, of the Statute provides that: "Only States may be parties in cases before the Court." International organizations, other collectivities and private persons are therefore not entitled to institute proceedings before the Court.

A State entitled to appear before the Court may fall into one of three categories:

(a) *States Members of the United Nations*

Article 35, paragraph 1, of the Statute provides that the Court shall be open to the States parties to the Statute, and Article 93, paragraph 1, of the Charter of the United Nations provides that all Members of the United Nations are *ipso facto* parties to the Statute.

On 31 July 1996 the following 185 States were Members of the United Nations:

State	*Date of Admission*
Afghanistan	19 November 1946
Albania	14 December 1955
Algeria	8 October 1962
Andorra	28 July 1993
Angola	1 December 1976
Antigua and Barbuda	11 November 1981
Argentina	Original Member
Armenia	2 March 1992
Australia	Original Member
Austria	14 December 1955
Azerbaijan	2 March 1992
Bahamas	18 September 1973
Bahrain	21 September 1971
Bangladesh	17 September 1974
Barbados	9 December 1966

State	*Date of Admission*
Belarus	Original Member
Belgium	,, ,,
Belize	25 September 1981
Benin	20 September 1960
Bhutan	21 September 1971
Bolivia	Original Member
Bosnia and Herzegovina	22 May 1992
Botswana	17 October 1966
Brazil	Original Member
Brunei Darussalam	21 September 1984
Bulgaria	14 December 1955
Burkina Faso	20 September 1960
Burundi	18 September 1962
Cambodia	14 December 1955
Cameroon	20 September 1960
Canada	Original Member
Cape Verde	16 September 1975
Central African Republic	20 September 1960
Chad	,, ,,
Chile	Original Member
China	,, ,,
Colombia	,, ,,
Comoros	12 November 1975
Congo	20 September 1960
Costa Rica	Original Member
Côte d'Ivoire	20 September 1960
Croatia	22 May 1992
Cuba	Original Member
Cyprus	20 September 1960
Czech Republic	19 January 1993
Democratic People's Republic of Korea	17 September 1991
Denmark	Original Member
Djibouti	20 September 1977
Dominica	18 December 1978
Dominican Republic	Original Member
Ecuador	,, ,,
Egypt	,, ,,
El Salvador	,, ,,
Equatorial Guinea	12 November 1968
Eritrea	28 May 1993
Estonia	17 September 1991
Ethiopia	Original Member
Federated States of Micronesia	17 September 1991
Fiji	13 October 1970
Finland	14 December 1955
France	Original Member

State	*Date of Admission*
Gabon	20 September 1960
Gambia	21 September 1965
Georgia	31 July 1992
Germany	18 September 1973
Ghana	8 March 1957
Greece	Original Member
Grenada	17 September 1974
Guatemala	Original Member
Guinea	12 December 1958
Guinea-Bissau	17 September 1974
Guyana	20 September 1966
Haiti	Original Member
Honduras	" "
Hungary	14 December 1955
Iceland	19 November 1946
India	Original Member
Indonesia	28 September 1950
Iran (Islamic Republic of)	Original Member
Iraq	" "
Ireland	14 December 1955
Israel	11 May 1949
Italy	14 December 1955
Jamaica	18 September 1962
Japan	18 December 1956
Jordan	14 December 1955
Kazakhstan	2 March 1992
Kenya	16 December 1963
Kuwait	14 May 1963
Kyrgyzstan	2 March 1992
Lao People's Democratic Republic	14 December 1955
Latvia	17 September 1991
Lebanon	Original Member
Lesotho	17 October 1966
Liberia	Original Member
Libyan Arab Jamahiriya	14 December 1955
Liechtenstein	18 September 1990
Lithuania	17 September 1991
Luxembourg	Original Member
Madagascar	20 September 1960
Malawi	1 December 1964
Malaysia	17 September 1957
Maldives	21 September 1965
Mali	28 September 1960
Malta	1 December 1964
Marshall Islands	17 September 1991
Mauritania	27 October 1961

State	*Date of Admission*
Mauritius	24 April 1968
Mexico	Original Member
Moldova	2 March 1992
Monaco	28 May 1993
Mongolia	27 October 1961
Morocco	12 November 1956
Mozambique	16 September 1975
Myanmar	19 April 1948
Namibia	23 April 1990
Nepal	14 December 1955
Netherlands	Original Member
New Zealand	„ „
Nicaragua	„ „
Niger	20 September 1960
Nigeria	7 October 1960
Norway	Original Member
Oman	7 October 1971
Pakistan	30 September 1947
Palau	15 December 1994
Panama	Original Member
Papua New Guinea	10 October 1975
Paraguay	Original Member
Peru	„ „
Philippines	„ „
Poland	„ „
Portugal	14 December 1955
Qatar	21 September 1971
Republic of Korea	17 September 1991
Romania	14 December 1955
Russian Federation	Original Member
Rwanda	18 September 1962
St. Kitts and Nevis	23 September 1983
St. Lucia	18 September 1979
St. Vincent and the Grenadines	16 September 1980
Samoa	15 December 1976
San Marino	2 March 1992
Sao Tome and Principe	16 September 1975
Saudi Arabia	Original Member
Senegal	28 September 1960
Seychelles	21 September 1976
Sierra Leone	27 September 1961
Singapore	21 September 1965
Slovakia	19 January 1993
Slovenia	22 May 1992
Solomon Islands	19 September 1978
Somalia	20 September 1960

State	Date of Admission
South Africa	Original Member
Spain	14 December 1955
Sri Lanka	" "
Sudan	12 November 1956
Suriname	4 December 1975
Swaziland	24 September 1968
Sweden	19 November 1946
Syrian Arab Republic	Original Member
Tajikistan	2 March 1992
Thailand	16 December 1946
The former Yugoslav Republic of Macedonia	8 April 1993
Togo	20 September 1960
Trinidad and Tobago	18 September 1962
Tunisia	12 November 1956
Turkey	Original Member
Turkmenistan	2 March 1992
Uganda	25 October 1962
Ukraine	Original Member
United Arab Emirates	9 December 1971
United Kingdom of Great Britain and Northern Ireland	Original Member
United Republic of Tanzania	14 December 1961
United States of America	Original Member
Uruguay	" "
Uzbekistan	2 March 1992
Vanuatu	15 September 1981
Venezuela	Original Member
Viet Nam	20 September 1977
Yemen	30 September 1947
Yugoslavia	Original Member
Zaire	20 September 1960
Zambia	1 December 1964
Zimbabwe	25 August 1980

(b) *States, not members of the United Nations, parties to the Statute*[1]

Article 93, paragraph 2, of the Charter of the United Nations provides that States which are not members of the United Nations may become parties to the Statute of the Court on conditions to be determined in each case by the General Assembly upon the recommendation of the Security Council.

The conditions laid down have hitherto been the same in each case. They were laid down for the first time as a result of a request by the Swiss

[1] The full text of the resolutions referred to in this section is given on pages 175-183 of *I.C.J. Acts and Documents No. 5.*

Federal Council; on that occasion the General Assembly, on 11 December 1946, adopted resolution 91 (I) which prescribed the following conditions:

> "*(a)* Acceptance of the provisions of the Statute of the International Court of Justice;
>
> *(b)* Acceptance of all the obligations of a Member of the United Nations under Article 94 of the Charter;
>
> *(c)* An undertaking to contribute to the expenses of the Court such equitable amount as the General Assembly shall assess from time to time after consultation with the Swiss Government."[1]

The date on which the State concerned becomes a party to the Statute is that of the deposit with the Secretary-General of the United Nations of the instrument of acceptance of the conditions.

Pursuant to Article 4, paragraph 3, of the Statute, the conditions on which such a State may participate in the election of Members of the Court were laid down in resolution 264 (III) adopted by the General Assembly, upon the recommendation of the Security Council, on 8 October 1948. The operative part of this resolution lays down that:

> "1. Such a State shall be on an equal footing with the Members of the United Nations in respect to those provisions of the Statute which regulate the nominations of candidates for election by the General Assembly.
>
> 2. Such a State shall participate, in the General Assembly, in electing the members of the Court in the same manner as the Members of the United Nations.
>
> 3. Such a State, when in arrears in the payment of its contribution to the expenses of the Court, shall not participate in electing the members of the Court in the General Assembly if the amount of its arrears equals or exceeds the amount of the contribution due from it for the preceding two full years. The General Assembly may, nevertheless, permit such a State to participate in the elections if it is satisfied that the failure to pay is due to conditions beyond the control of that State (see Charter, Article 19)."

The participation of such States in the procedure for amending the Statute of the Court (Charter, Art. 108; Statute, Art. 69) is governed by the following provisions of resolution 2520 (XXIV) adopted by the General Assembly, upon the recommendation of the Security Council, on 4 December 1969:

> "*(a)* A State which is a party to the Statute of the International Court of Justice, but is not a Member of the United Nations, may participate in the General Assembly in regard to amendments to the Statute in the same manner as the Members of the United Nations;
>
> *(b)* Amendments to the Statute of the International Court of Jus-

---

[1] See below, Chap. VIII, p. 317.

tice shall come into force for all States which are parties to the Statute when they have been adopted by a vote of two-thirds of the States which are parties to the Statute and ratified in accordance with their respective constitutional processes by two-thirds of the States which are parties to the Statute and in accordance with the provisions of Article 69 of the Statute and Article 108 of the Charter of the United Nations."

The following States not members of the United Nations are at present parties to the Statute[1]:

State	*Resolution of the General Assembly*	*Deposit of the instrument of acceptance*
Nauru	42/21, 18 November 1987	29 January 1988
Switzerland	91 (I), 11 December 1946	28 July 1948

(c) *States, not parties to the Statute, to which the Court may be open*

The Court, which is open to States parties to the Statute, is also open to other States, in accordance with Article 35, paragraph 2, of the Statute[2]. This Article provides that the conditions upon which the Court shall be open to such States shall, subject to the special provisions contained in treaties in force, be laid down by the Security Council, but in no case shall such conditions place the parties in a position of inequality before the Court.

On 15 October 1946, the Security Council adopted resolution 9 (1946) which reads as follows:

"The Security Council

In virtue of the powers conferred upon it by Article 35, paragraph 2, of the Statute of the International Court of Justice and subject to the provisions of that Article,

Resolves that:

1. The International Court of Justice shall be open to a State which is not a party to the Statute of the International Court of Justice, upon the following condition, namely, that such State shall previously have deposited with the Registrar of the Court a declaration by which it accepts the jurisdiction of the Court, in accordance with the Charter of the United Nations and with the terms and subject to the conditions of the Statute and Rules of the Court, and undertakes to comply in good faith with the decision or decisions of the Court and to accept all the obligations of a Member of the United Nations under Article 94 of the Charter;

---

[1] Before becoming Members of the United Nations, Japan, Liechtenstein and San Marino were parties to the Statute of the Court, as from 2 April 1954, 29 March 1950 and 18 February 1954 respectively.

[2] See also Rules, Art. 26, para. 1 *(c)*, and Art. 41, and below, Chap. VIII, p. 317.

2. Such declaration may be either particular or general. A particular declaration is one accepting the jurisdiction of the Court in respect only of a particular dispute or disputes which have already arisen. A general declaration is one accepting the jurisdiction generally in respect of all disputes or of a particular class or classes of disputes which have already arisen or which may arise in the future. A State, in making such a general declaration, may, in accordance with Article 36, paragraph 2, of the Statute, recognize as compulsory, *ipso facto* and without special agreement, the jurisdiction of the Court, provided, however, that such acceptance may not, without explicit agreement, be relied upon vis-à-vis States parties to the Statute which have made the declaration in conformity with Article 36, paragraph 2, of the Statute of the International Court of Justice;

3. The original declarations made under the terms of this resolution shall be kept in the custody of the Registrar of the Court, in accordance with the practice of the Court. Certified true copies thereof shall be transmitted, in accordance with the practice of the Court, to all States parties to the Statute of the International Court of Justice, and to such other States as shall have deposited a declaration under the terms of this resolution, and to the Secretary-General of the United Nations;

4. The Security Council reserves the right to rescind or amend this resolution by a resolution which shall be communicated to the Court, and on the receipt of such communication and to the extent determined by the new resolution, existing declarations shall cease to be effective except in regard to disputes which are already before the Court;

5. All questions as to the validity or the effect of a declaration made under the terms of this resolution shall be decided by the Court."

In the past, particular declarations have been filed by Albania (1947) and by Italy (1953), and general declarations by Cambodia (1952), Ceylon (1952), the Federal Republic of Germany (1955, 1956, 1961, 1965 and 1971), Finland (1953 and 1954), Italy (1955), Japan (1951), Laos (1952), and the Republic of Viet Nam (1952).

2. *Basis of the Court's Jurisdiction*

The jurisdiction of the Court in contentious proceedings is based on the consent of the States to which it is open[1]. The form in which this consent

[1] In the following eight cases, the Court found that it could take no further steps upon an Application in which it was admitted that the opposing party did not accept its jurisdiction: *Treatment in Hungary of Aircraft and Crew of United States of America (United States of America* v. *Hungary) (United States of America* v. *USSR); Aerial Incident of 10 March 1953 (United States of America* v. *Czechoslovakia); Antarctica (United Kingdom* v. *Argentina) (United Kingdom* v. *Chile); Aerial Incident of 7 October 1952 (United States of America* v. *USSR); Aerial Incident of 4 September 1954 (United States of America* v. *USSR); Aerial Incident of 7 November 1954 (United States of America* v. *USSR).*

is expressed determines the manner in which a case may be brought before the Court.

(a) *Special agreement*

Article 36, paragraph 1, of the Statute provides that the jurisdiction of the Court comprises all cases which the parties refer to it. Such cases normally come before the Court by notification to the Registry of an agreement known as a *special agreement* and concluded by the parties specially for this purpose[1]. The subject of the dispute and the parties must be indicated (Statute, Art. 40, para. 1; Rules, Art. 39).

(b) *Cases provided for in treaties and conventions*

Article 36, paragraph 1, of the Statute provides also that the jurisdiction of the Court comprises all matters specially provided for in treaties and conventions in force. In such cases a matter is normally brought before the Court by means of a written *application instituting proceedings*; this is a unilateral document which must indicate the subject of the dispute and the parties (Statute, Art. 40, para. 1) and, as far as possible, specify the provision on which the applicant founds the jurisdiction of the Court (Rules, Art. 38).

A list of treaties and conventions governing the jurisdiction of the International Court of Justice in contentious cases is given in Chapter IV (Sec. III) of the present *Yearbook* (pp. 122-139). Furthermore, some of the agreements and conventions mentioned in Section I of Chapter IV (pp. 75-81) relate, in particular, to the jurisdiction of the Court in contentious proceedings.

To these instruments must be added other treaties and conventions concluded earlier and conferring jurisdiction upon the *Permanent Court of International Justice*, for Article 37 of the Statute of the International Court of Justice stipulates that whenever a treaty or convention in force

[1] The following 13 cases were submitted to the Court by means of special agreements: *Asylum (Colombia/Peru); Minquiers and Ecrehos (France/United Kingdom); Sovereignty over Certain Frontier Land (Belgium/Netherlands); North Sea Continental Shelf (Federal Republic of Germany/Denmark; Federal Republic of Germany/Netherlands); Continental Shelf (Tunisia/Libyan Arab Jamahiriya); Delimitation of the Maritime Boundary in the Gulf of Maine Area (Canada/United States of America)* (case referred to a Chamber); *Continental Shelf (Libyan Arab Jamahiriya/Malta); Frontier Dispute (Burkina Faso/Republic of Mali)* (case referred to a Chamber); *Land, Island and Maritime Frontier Dispute (El Salvador/Honduras)* (case referred to a Chamber); *Territorial Dispute (Libyan Arab Jamahiriya/Chad); Gabčíkovo-Nagymaros Project (Hungary/Slovakia); Kasikili/Sedudu Island (Botswana/Namibia)*. In the *Corfu Channel (United Kingdom* v. *Albania)* case the Parties made a special agreement after delivery of the Judgment on the Preliminary Objection. The case concerning the *Arbitral Award Made by the King of Spain on 23 December 1906 (Honduras* v. *Nicaragua)* was submitted by means of an application, but the Parties had previously concluded an agreement on the procedure to be followed in submitting the dispute to the Court.

provides for reference of a matter to a tribunal to have been instituted by the League of Nations, or to the *Permanent Court of International Justice*, the matter shall, as between the parties to the Statute, be referred to the International Court of Justice. The *Permanent Court* reproduced, in 1932, in its *Collection of Texts governing the Jurisdiction of the Court* (*P.C.I.J., Series D, No. 6*, fourth edition) and subsequently in Chapter X of its *Annual Reports (P.C.I.J., Series E, Nos. 8-16)* the relevant provisions of the instruments governing its jurisdiction. By virtue of the Article referred to above, some of these provisions now govern the jurisdiction of the International Court of Justice.

(c) *Compulsory jurisdiction in legal disputes*

The Statute provides that a State may recognize as compulsory, in relation to any other State accepting the same obligation, the jurisdiction of the Court in legal disputes. These cases are brought before the Court by means of written applications. The conditions on which such compulsory jurisdiction may be recognized are stated in paragraphs 2-5 of Article 36 of the Statute, which read as follows:

> "2. The States parties to the present Statute may at any time declare that they recognize as compulsory *ipso facto* and without special agreement, in relation to any other State accepting the same obligation, the jurisdiction of the Court in all legal disputes concerning:
>
> *(a)* the interpretation of a treaty;
> *(b)* any question of international law;
> *(c)* the existence of any fact which, if established, would constitute a breach of an international obligation;
> *(d)* the nature or extent of the reparation to be made for the breach of an international obligation.
>
> 3. The declarations referred to above may be made unconditionally or on condition of reciprocity on the part of several or certain States, or for a certain time.
> 4. Such declarations shall be deposited with the Secretary-General of the United Nations, who shall transmit copies thereof to the parties to the Statute and to the Registrar of the Court.
> 5. Declarations made under Article 36 of the Statute of the Permanent Court of International Justice and which are still in force shall be deemed, as between the parties to the present Statute, to be acceptances of the compulsory jurisdiction of the International Court of Justice for the period which they still have to run and in accordance with their terms."

Texts of declarations accepting the compulsory jurisdiction of the Court are given in Section II of Chapter IV below (pp. 82-121).

(d) *The Court itself decides any question as to its jurisdiction*

Article 36, paragraph 6, of the Statute provides that in the event of a dispute as to whether the Court has jurisdiction, the matter shall be settled by the decision of the Court. Article 79 of the Rules lays down the conditions which govern the filing of preliminary objections[1].

(e) *Interpretation of a judgment*

Article 60 of the Statute provides that in the event of dispute as to the meaning or scope of a judgment, the Court shall construe it upon the request of any party. The request for interpretation may be made either by means of a special agreement between the parties or of an application by one or more of the parties (Rules, Art. 98)[2].

(f) *Revision of a judgment*

An application for revision of a judgment may be made only when it is based upon the discovery of some fact of such a nature as to be a deci-

---

[1] Preliminary objections were raised in the following 26 cases: *Corfu Channel (United Kingdom* v. *Albania); Rights of Nationals of the United States of America in Morocco (France* v. *United States of America); Ambatielos (Greece* v. *United Kingdom); Anglo-Iranian Oil Co. (United Kingdom* v. *Iran); Nottebohm (Liechtenstein* v. *Guatemala); Monetary Gold Removed from Rome in 1943 (Italy* v. *France, United Kingdom and United States of America); Certain Norwegian Loans (France* v. *Norway); Right of Passage over Indian Territory (Portugal* v. *India); Interhandel (Switzerland* v. *United States of America); Aerial Incident of 27 July 1955 (Israel* v. *Bulgaria) (United States of America* v. *Bulgaria); Barcelona Traction, Light and Power Company, Limited (Belgium* v. *Spain); Compagnie du Port, des Quais et des Entrepôts de Beyrouth and Société Radio-Orient (France* v. *Lebanon); Temple of Preah Vihear (Cambodia* v. *Thailand); South West Africa (Ethiopia* v. *South Africa; Liberia* v. *South Africa); Northern Cameroons (Cameroon* v. *United Kingdom); Barcelona Traction, Light and Power Company, Limited (New Application: 1962) (Belgium* v. *Spain); Elettronica Sicula S.p.A. (ELSI) (United States of America* v. *Italy); Aerial Incident of 3 July 1988 (Islamic Republic of Iran* v. *United States of America); Certain Phosphate Lands in Nauru (Nauru* v. *Australia); Oil Platforms (Islamic Republic of Iran* v. *United States of America); Questions of Interpretation and Application of the 1971 Montreal Convention arising out of the Aerial Incident at Lockerbie (Libyan Arab Jamahiriya* v. *United Kingdom) (Libyan Arab Jamahiriya* v. *United States of America); Application of the Convention on the Prevention and Punishment of the Crime of Genocide (Bosnia and Herzegovina* v. *Yugoslavia); Land and Maritime Boundary between Cameroon and Nigeria (Cameroon* v. *Nigeria).* Questions of jurisdiction or admissibility have also been raised in the following 13 cases: *Appeal Relating to the Jurisdiction of the ICAO Council (India* v. *Pakistan); Fisheries Jurisdiction (United Kingdom* v. *Iceland; Federal Republic of Germany* v. *Iceland); Nuclear Tests (Australia* v. *France) (New Zealand* v. *France); Trial of Pakistani Prisoners of War (Pakistan* v. *India); Aegean Sea Continental Shelf (Greece* v. *Turkey); United States Diplomatic and Consular Staff in Tehran (United States of America* v. *Iran); Military and Paramilitary Activities in and against Nicaragua (Nicaragua* v. *United States of America); Border and Transborder Armed Actions (Nicaragua* v. *Honduras); Maritime Delimitation and Territorial Questions between Qatar and Bahrain (Qatar* v. *Bahrain); East Timor (Portugal* v. *Australia); Fisheries Jurisdiction (Spain* v. *Canada).*

[2] An application for interpretation of the Judgment was made by Colombia in respect of the *Asylum (Colombia/Peru)* case. Cf. note 1, p. 73, below.

sive factor, which fact was, when the judgment was given, unknown to the Court and also to the party claiming revision, always provided that such party's ignorance was not due to negligence (Statute, Art. 61, para. 1). A request for revision is made by means of an application (Rules, Art. 99)[1].

II. Advisory Jurisdiction

The advisory jurisdiction of the Court is governed by Article 65 of the Statute and Article 96 of the Charter of the United Nations.

By virtue of Article 65 of the Statute, the Court may give an advisory opinion on any legal question at the request of whatever body may be authorized by or in accordance with the Charter of the United Nations to make such a request. An exact statement of the questions upon which the advisory opinion is asked must be contained in a *request for an advisory opinion.*

Article 96, paragraph 1, of the Charter provides that advisory opinions may be asked of the Court by the General Assembly or the Security Council on any legal question. Paragraph 2 of this Article adds:

> "Other organs of the United Nations and specialized agencies, which may at any time be so authorized by the General Assembly, may also request advisory opinions of the Court on legal questions arising within the scope of their activities."

The following organs and agencies are at present authorized to request advisory opinions[2]:

United Nations:

General Assembly[3],

---

[1] An application for revision and interpretation of the Judgment was filed by Tunisia in respect of the case concerning the *Continental Shelf (Tunisia/Libyan Arab Jamahiriya).*

[2] The International Refugee Organization, which had been authorized to request advisory opinions of the Court, ceased to exist in 1952. The Havana Charter for an International Trade Organization, which provides for the jurisdiction of the Court in proceedings in regard to advisory opinions, has not entered into force.

[3] The General Assembly has requested 14 advisory opinions of the Court in the following 13 cases: *Conditions of Admission of a State to Membership in the United Nations (Article 4 of Charter); Reparation for Injuries Suffered in the Service of the United Nations; Interpretation of Peace Treaties with Bulgaria, Hungary and Romania, First Phase;* id., *Second Phase; Competence of the General Assembly for the Admission of a State to the United Nations; International Status of South West Africa; Reservations to the Convention on the Prevention and Punishment of the Crime of Genocide; Effect of Awards of Compensation Made by the United Nations Administrative Tribunal; Voting Procedure on Questions Relating to Reports and Petitions concerning the Territory of South West Africa; Admissibility of Hearings of Petitioners by the Committee on South West Africa; Certain Expenses of the United Nations (Article 17, Paragraph 2, of the Charter); Western Sahara; Applicability of the Obligation to Arbitrate under Section 21 of the United Nations Headquarters Agreement of 26 June 1947; Legality of the Threat or Use of Nuclear Weapons.*

Security Council[1],
Economic and Social Council[2],
Trusteeship Council,
Interim Committee of the General Assembly,
Committee on Applications for Review of Administrative Tribunal Judgements (for judgements rendered before 1 January 1996)[3];

International Labour Organisation;
Food and Agriculture Organization of the United Nations;
United Nations Educational, Scientific and Cultural Organization[4];
World Health Organization[5];
International Bank for Reconstruction and Development;
International Finance Corporation;
International Development Association;
International Monetary Fund;
International Civil Aviation Organization;
International Telecommunication Union;
International Fund for Agricultural Development;
World Meteorological Organization;
International Maritime Organization[6];
World Intellectual Property Organization;
United Nations Industrial Development Organization;
International Atomic Energy Agency.

In Section I of Chapter IV of the present *Yearbook* (pp. 75-81) will be found references to the instruments by virtue of which such requests may be submitted by the above organs and agencies.

---

[1] The Security Council requested an advisory opinion of the Court concerning the *Legal Consequences for States of the Continued Presence of South Africa in Namibia (South West Africa) notwithstanding Security Council Resolution 276 (1970)*.

[2] The Economic and Social Council requested an advisory opinion of the Court in the case concerning the *Applicability of Article VI, Section 22, of the Convention on the Privileges and Immunities of the United Nations*.

[3] The Committee on Applications for Review of Administrative Tribunal Judgements requested an advisory opinion in the following three cases: *Application for Review of Judgement No. 158 of the United Nations Administrative Tribunal; Application for Review of Judgement No. 273 of the United Nations Administrative Tribunal; Application for Review of Judgement No. 333 of the United Nations Administrative Tribunal.* For judgements rendered after 31 December 1995, see footnote 3, p. 76, below.

[4] The Executive Board of Unesco requested an advisory opinion of the Court concerning *Judgments of the Administrative Tribunal of the ILO upon Complaints Made against Unesco*.

[5] The World Health Assembly requested an advisory opinion of the Court in two cases: *Interpretation of the Agreement of 25 March 1951 between the WHO and Egypt* and *Legality of the Use by a State of Nuclear Weapons in Armed Conflict*.

[6] The Assembly of this organization requested an advisory opinion of the Court concerning the *Constitution of the Maritime Safety Committee of the Inter-Governmental Maritime Consultative Organization*.

CHAPTER IV

TEXTS GOVERNING THE JURISDICTION OF THE COURT

The present chapter, which is compiled from the information available to the Registry, presents a compendium of instruments governing the jurisdiction of the Court. It takes into account, so far as the Registry is informed of them, any amendments to those instruments which have affected their provisions concerning the jurisdiction of the Court. The inclusion or omission of any instrument should not be regarded as an indication of any view entertained by the Registry, or *a fortiori* by the Court, regarding the nature, scope or validity of the instrument in question.

I. Instruments Governing the Relationship of Organs of the United Nations and International Organizations with the Court

This section lists provisions for the contentious or advisory jurisdiction of the Court in the following categories of instruments: constitutional texts of public international organizations; agreements concluded between the United Nations and other international organizations; authorizations accorded by the General Assembly of the United Nations to other organs of the United Nations or to international organizations by virtue of Article 96, paragraph 2, of the Charter; multilateral conventions relating to the privileges and immunities of world-wide international organizations; agreements concluded by international organizations with States.

1. United Nations

Authorization to the *General Assembly* and the *Security Council* to request advisory opinions of the International Court of Justice: Charter, Article 96, paragraph 1.

Authorization to the *Economic and Social Council* to request advisory opinions of the International Court of Justice: resolution 89 (I) of the General Assembly, 11 December 1946.

Authorization to the *Trusteeship Council* to request advisory opinions of the International Court of Justice: resolution 171 (II) of the General Assembly, 14 November 1947, paragraph B.

Authorization to the *Interim Committee of the General Assembly* to request advisory opinions of the International Court of Justice: resolution 196 (III) of the General Assembly, 3 December 1948, paragraph 3[1].

Authorization to the *Committee on Applications for Review of Judgements of the United Nations Administrative Tribunal* to request advisory opinions of the International Court of Justice: Statute of the United Nations Administrative Tribunal, as amended by resolution 957 (X) of the General Assembly, 8 November 1955, Article 11[2,3].

Convention on the privileges and immunities of the United Nations, adopted by the General Assembly on 13 February 1946, Article VIII, Section 30 (United Nations, *Treaty Series*, I, No. 4, Vol. 1).

Agreement between the United Nations and the United States of America regarding the Headquarters of the United Nations, 26 June 1947, Article VIII, Section 21 (United Nations, *Treaty Series*, I, No. 147, Vol. 11).

Agreement between Chile and the United Nations Economic Commission for Latin America regulating conditions for the operation, in Chile, of the Headquarters of the Commission, 16 February 1953, Article XI, Section 21 (United Nations, *Treaty Series*, I, No. 4541, Vol. 314).

Agreement between the United Nations and Thailand relating to the Headquarters of the Economic Commission for Asia and the Far East in Thailand, 26 May 1954, Article XIII, Section 26 (United Nations, *Treaty Series*, I, No. 3703, Vol. 260).

Agreement between the United Nations and Ethiopia regarding the Headquarters of the United Nations Economic Commission for Africa, 18 June 1958, Article IX (United Nations, *Treaty Series*, I, No. 4597, Vol. 317).

Agreement between the United Nations and Japan regarding the Headquarters of the United Nations University, 14 May 1976, Section 22 (United Nations, *Treaty Series*, I, No. 14839, Vol. 1009).

Agreement between the United Nations and Greece regarding the headquarters of the Co-ordinating Unit for the Mediterranean Action Plan, 11 February 1982, Section 26 (United Nations, *Treaty Series*, I, No. 20736, Vol. 1261).

---

[1] The mandate of the Interim Committee was extended indefinitely by resolution 295 (IV) of the General Assembly of 21 November 1949, paragraph 3 of which preserved its authority to request advisory opinions of the Court.

[2] Article not applicable to Judgements concerning the staff of the International Civil Aviation Organization or Inter-Governmental Maritime Consultative Organization (now International Maritime Organization), which have both, however, accepted the jurisdiction of the United Nations Administrative Tribunal.

[3] By resolution 50/54 of 11 December 1995 the General Assembly amended the statute of the Tribunal again, with respect to Judgements rendered after 31 December 1995, *inter alia* deleting Article 11; it also decided "that, with respect to judgements rendered by the Tribunal before 1 January 1996, the statute of the Tribunal shall continue to apply as if the amendments . . . had not been made".

2. All Specialized Agencies

Convention on the privileges and immunities of the specialized agencies, approved by the General Assembly of the United Nations on 21 November 1947, Article VII, Section 24, and Article IX, Section 32 (United Nations, *Treaty Series*, I, No. 521, Vol. 33).

3. International Labour Organisation

Instrument for the amendment of the Constitution of the International Labour Organisation, 9 October 1946, Articles 29, 31-34 and 37 (United Nations, *Treaty Series*, I, No. 229, Vol. 15).

Agreement between the United Nations and the International Labour Organisation, approved by the General Assembly of the United Nations on 14 December 1946, Article IX (United Nations, *Treaty Series*, II, No. 9, Vol. 1).

Statute of the Administrative Tribunal of the International Labour Organisation, adopted by the International Labour Conference on 9 October 1946 and modified by the Conference on 29 June 1949, Article XII[1].

4. Food and Agriculture Organization of the United Nations

Constitution of the Food and Agriculture Organization of the United Nations, 16 October 1945, as amended in 1957, Article XVII (Food and Agriculture Organization of the United Nations, *Basic Texts*, Vol. I, 1968).

Agreement between the United Nations and the Food and Agriculture Organization of the United Nations, approved by the General Assembly of the United Nations on 14 December 1946, Article IX (United Nations, *Treaty Series*, II, No. 10, Vol. 1).

Terms of appointment of the Director-General of the Food and Agriculture Organization of the United Nations: recommendation by the Conference of the Organization, 27 October 1945, paragraph 3 (Food and Agriculture Organization of the United Nations, *Report of the First Session of the Conference*, 16 October-1 November 1945).

---

[1] The jurisdiction of this Tribunal, which is open to officials of the International Labour Organisation or other persons claiming under the terms of appointment of an official, has been recognized also by the following international organizations, which are authorized to request advisory opinions: Food and Agriculture Organization of the United Nations; United Nations Educational, Scientific and Cultural Organization; World Health Organization; International Telecommunication Union; World Meteorological Organization; World Intellectual Property Organization; International Atomic Energy Agency.

5. *United Nations Educational, Scientific and Cultural Organization*

Constitution of the United Nations Educational, Scientific and Cultural Organization, 16 November 1945, Articles V, paragraph 11 (adopted in 1952), and XIV, paragraph 2 (United Nations, *Treaty Series*, I, No. 52, Vol. 4)[1].

Agreement between the United Nations and the United Nations Educational, Scientific and Cultural Organization, approved by the General Assembly of the United Nations on 14 December 1946, as revised and approved by the General Assembly of the United Nations on 8 December 1962, Article X[2] (United Nations, *Treaty Series*, II, No. 11, Vol. 1; *ibid.*, General Assembly, resolution 1786 (XVII)).

Agreement between the United Nations Educational, Scientific and Cultural Organization and France regarding the Headquarters of Unesco and the privileges and immunities of the Organization on French territory, 2 July 1954, Article 29 (United Nations, *Treaty Series*, I, No. 5103, Vol. 357).

6. *World Health Organization*

Constitution of the World Health Organization, 22 July 1946, Articles 75-77 (United Nations, *Treaty Series*, I, No. 221, Vol. 14).

Agreement between the United Nations and the World Health Organization, approved by the General Assembly of the United Nations on 15 November 1947, Article X (United Nations, *Treaty Series*, II, No. 115, Vol. 19).

7. *International Bank for Reconstruction and Development, International Finance Corporation and International Development Association*

Agreement between the United Nations and the International Bank for Reconstruction and Development, approved by the General Assembly of the United Nations on 15 November 1947, Article VIII (United Nations, *Treaty Series*, II, No. 109, Vol. 16).

Agreement on relationship between the United Nations and the International Finance Corporation, approved by the General Assembly of the United Nations on 20 February 1957, paragraph 1 (United Nations, *Treaty Series*, II, No. 546, Vol. 265).

Agreement on relationship between the United Nations and the Inter-

---

[1] See also Rules of Procedure of the General Conference of Unesco, Rule 33, and the Protocol of 10 December 1962 instituting a Conciliation and Good Offices Commission to be responsible for seeking the settlement of any disputes which may arise between States parties to the Convention against Discrimination in Education, Article 18 (Unesco document 12C/Resolutions).

[2] Article XI before the revision of 1962.

national Development Association, approved by the General Assembly of the United Nations on 27 March 1961, Article I (United Nations, *Treaty Series*, II, No. 582, Vol. 394).

8. International Monetary Fund

Agreement between the United Nations and the International Monetary Fund, approved by the General Assembly of the United Nations on 15 November 1947, Article VIII (United Nations, *Treaty Series*, II, No. 108, Vol. 16).

9. International Civil Aviation Organization

Convention on International Civil Aviation, 7 December 1944, Articles 84-86 (United Nations, *Treaty Series*, I, No. 10612, Vol. 740; ICAO, *Convention on International Civil Aviation*, 1969).

Agreement between the United Nations and the International Civil Aviation Organization, approved by the General Assembly of the United Nations on 14 December 1946, Article X (United Nations, *Treaty Series*, II, No. 45, Vol. 8).

Agreement between the International Civil Aviation Organization and Canada regarding the Headquarters of the Organization, 14 April 1951, Article VII, Section 31 (United Nations, *Treaty Series*, I, No. 1335, Vol. 96).

10. International Telecommunication Union

Agreement between the United Nations and the International Telecommunication Union, approved by the General Assembly of the United Nations on 15 November 1947, Article VII (United Nations, *Treaty Series*, II, No. 175, Vol. 30).

11. World Meteorological Organization

Agreement between the United Nations and the World Meteorological Organization, approved by the General Assembly of the United Nations on 20 December 1951, Article VII (United Nations, *Treaty Series*, II, No. 415, Vol. 123).

12. International Maritime Organization

Convention on the Inter-Governmental Maritime Consultative Organization, 6 March 1948, entered into force on 17 March 1958, Articles 55 and 56 (United Nations, *Treaty Series*, I, No. 4214, Vol. 289)[1].

---

[1] As from 22 May 1982 the Inter-Governmental Maritime Consultative Organization (IMCO) became the International Maritime Organization (IMO); the name of the organization was changed in the title of the 1948 Convention and the relevant Articles of the Convention were re-numbered 69 and 70.

Agreement between the United Nations and the Inter-Governmental Maritime Consultative Organization, approved by the General Assembly of the United Nations on 18 November 1948, entered into force on 13 January 1959, Article IX (United Nations, *Treaty Series*, II, No. 553, Vol. 324).

13. World Intellectual Property Organization

Agreement between the United Nations and the World Intellectual Property Organization, approved by the General Assembly of the United Nations on 17 December 1974, Article 12 (United Nations, *Treaty Series*, II, No. 729).

14. International Fund for Agricultural Development

Agreement between the United Nations and the International Fund for Agricultural Development, approved by the General Assembly of the United Nations on 15 December 1977, Article XIII (United Nations, *Treaty Series*, II, No. 806, Vol. 1080).

15. United Nations Industrial Development Organization

Constitution of the United Nations Industrial Development Organization, 8 April 1979, Article 22 (United Nations, *Treaty Series*, I, No. 23432, Vol. 1401).

Agreement between the United Nations Organization and the United Nations Industrial Development Organization, approved by the General Assembly of the United Nations on 17 December 1985, Article 12.

16. International Atomic Energy Agency

Statute of the International Atomic Energy Agency, 26 October 1956, Article XVII (United Nations, *Treaty Series*, I, No. 3988, Vol. 276).

Agreement concerning the relationship between the United Nations and the International Atomic Energy Agency, approved by the General Assembly of the United Nations on 14 November 1957, Article X (United Nations, *Treaty Series*, II, No. 548, Vol. 281).

Authorization to the International Atomic Energy Agency to request advisory opinions of the International Court of Justice: resolution 1146 (XII) of the General Assembly of the United Nations, 14 November 1957.

Agreement on the privileges and immunities of the International Atomic Energy Agency, approved by the Board of Governors of the Agency on 1 July 1959, Article X, Section 34 (United Nations, *Treaty Series*, I, No. 5334, Vol. 374).

Agreement between the International Atomic Energy Agency and Iraq, Lebanon, Libya, Tunisia, United Arab Republic, etc., for the establishment in Cairo of a Middle Eastern regional radio-isotope centre for the Arab countries, approved by the Board of Governors of the Agency on 14 September 1962, Article XVI (United Nations, *Treaty Series*, I, No. 7236, Vol. 494).

Nordic Mutual Emergency Assistance Agreement in connection with radiation accidents, signed on 17 October 1963 by the International Atomic Energy Agency, Denmark, Finland, Norway and Sweden, Article IX (United Nations, *Treaty Series*, I, No. 7585, Vol. 525).

II. Declarations Recognizing as Compulsory the Jurisdiction of the Court

The texts of declarations under Article 36, paragraph 2, of the Statute, which had not expired by effluxion of time, or whose withdrawal or replacement had not been notified by 31 July 1996 will be found below. The fact that a declaration is or is not included in this section, is without prejudice to its possible application by the Court in a particular case.

During the 12 months under review, Poland, on 25 March 1996, deposited with the Secretary-General of the United Nations a new declaration, withdrawing its previous declaration, deposited on 25 September 1990. On 25 June 1996, Norway deposited a declaration amending its previous declaration deposited on 2 April 1976.

In view of the provisions of Article 36, paragraph 5, of the Statute of the International Court of Justice, the present section also contains the texts of declarations made under the Statute of the *Permanent Court of International Justice* which have not lapsed or been withdrawn. There are now seven such declarations.

The declarations, deposited by a total of 59 States[1], are given here in English[2]. Where this is not the original language of the declaration, the translations used, except where otherwise indicated, are by the Secretariat of the United Nations or of the League of Nations.

The date shown after the name of the State is that on which the declaration was deposited.

---

[1] Since 1951, twelve other declarations relating to the jurisdiction of the International Court of Justice, either expressly or by virtue of Article 36, paragraph 5, of the Statute, have expired, been withdrawn or been terminated without being subsequently replaced. These were the declarations of the following States: Bolivia, Brazil, China, El Salvador, France, Guatemala, Iran, Israel, South Africa, Thailand, Turkey and the United States (United Nations, *Treaty Series*, I, No. 261, Vol. 16; I, No. 237, Vol. 15; I, No. 5, Vol. 1; *I.C.J. Yearbook 1987-1988*, pp. 70-72; United Nations, *Treaty Series*, I, No. 8196, Vol. 562; I, No. 12, Vol. 1; *I.C.J. Yearbook 1946-1947*, p. 211; *I.C.J. Yearbook 1984-1985*, pp. 79-80; United Nations, *Treaty Series*, I, No. 2935, Vol. 216; I, No. 844, Vol. 65; I, No. 50, Vol. 4; *I.C.J. Yearbook 1984-1985*, pp. 99-100).

[2] French texts of the declarations are given in the French counterpart of the *I.C.J. Yearbook*, the *C.I.J. Annuaire*.

Australia

17 III 75.

Whereas on the first day of November one thousand nine hundred and forty-five Australia ratified the Charter of the United Nations of which the Statute of the International Court of Justice is an integral part; and

Whereas Australia made a declaration under paragraph 2 of Article 36, of the said Statute on the sixth day of February, one thousand nine hundred and fifty-four[1]; and

Whereas Australia desires to withdraw the said declaration;

The Government of Australia hereby withdraws the said declaration and declares for and on behalf of Australia that it recognizes as compulsory *ipso facto* and without special agreement, in relation to any other State accepting the same obligation, the jurisdiction of the International Court of Justice, in conformity with paragraph 2 of Article 36 of the Statute of the Court, until such time as notice may be given to withdraw this declaration.

The Government of Australia further declares that this declaration does not apply to any dispute in regard to which the parties thereto have agreed or shall agree to have recourse to some other method of peaceful settlement.

In witness whereof, I, Edward Gough Whitlam, Prime Minister acting for and on behalf of the Minister of State for Foreign Affairs of Australia, have hereunto set my hand and affixed the seal of the Minister of State for Foreign Affairs.

Dated this thirteenth day of March, one thousand nine hundred and seventy-five.

(Signed) E. G. Whitlam,
Prime Minister acting for and on behalf of the Minister of State for Foreign Affairs of Australia.

Austria

19 V 71.

I hereby declare that the Republic of Austria recognizes as compulsory *ipso facto* and without special agreement, in relation to any other State which accepts or has accepted the same obligation, the jurisdiction of the International Court of Justice in all legal disputes referred to in paragraph 2 of Article 36 of the Statute of the International Court of Justice.

This Declaration does not apply to any dispute in respect of which the

[1] United Nations, *Treaty Series*, I, No. 2484, Vol. 186.

parties thereto have agreed or shall agree to have recourse to other means of peaceful settlement for its final and binding decision.

This Declaration shall remain in force for a period of five years and thereafter until it will be terminated or modified by a written declaration.

Done at Vienna on 28 April 1971.

(Signed) JONAS,
The Federal President.

In witness whereof the present declaration has been countersigned by the Federal Chancellor and the Minister for Foreign Affairs and the national seal of the Republic of Austria has been affixed thereto.

(Signed) Bruno KREISKY,
The Federal Chancellor.

(Signed) Rudolf KIRCHSCHLAEGER,
The Federal Minister for Foreign Affairs.

BARBADOS

1 VIII 80.

I have the honour to declare on behalf of the Government of Barbados that:

The Government of Barbados accepts as compulsory, *ipso facto*, and without special agreement, on condition of reciprocity, the jurisdiction of the International Court of Justice in conformity with paragraph 2 of Article 36 of the Court until such time as notice might be given to terminate the acceptance, over all disputes arising after the declaration is made, other than:

(a) disputes in regard to which parties have agreed or shall agree to have recourse to some other method of peaceful settlement,
(b) disputes with the government of any other country which is a Member of the Commonwealth of Nations, all of which disputes shall be settled in such manner as the parties have agreed or shall agree,
(c) disputes with regard to questions which by international law fall exclusively within the jurisdiction of Barbados,
(d) disputes arising out of or concerning jurisdiction or rights claimed or exercised by Barbados in respect of the conservation, management or exploitation of the living resources of the sea, or in respect of the prevention or control of pollution or contamination of the marine environment in marine areas adjacent to the coast of Barbados.

24 July 1980.

(Signed) H. de B. FORDE,
Minister of External Affairs.

Belgium[1]

[Translation from the French] 17 VI 58.

I declare on behalf of the Belgian Government that I recognize as compulsory *ipso facto* and without special agreement, in relation to any other State accepting the same obligation, the jurisdiction of the International Court of Justice, in conformity with Article 36, paragraph 2, of the Statute of the Court, in legal disputes arising after 13 July 1948 concerning situations or facts subsequent to that date, except those in regard to which the parties have agreed or may agree to have recourse to another method of pacific settlement.

This declaration is made subject to ratification[2]. It shall take effect on the day of deposit of the instrument of ratification for a period of five years. Upon the expiry of that period, it shall continue to have effect until notice of its termination is given.

Brussels, 3 April 1958.

(Signed) V. Larock,
Minister
for Foreign Affairs.

Botswana

16 III 70.

I, Sir Seretse Khama, President of the Republic of Botswana, have the honour to declare on behalf of the Government of the Republic of Botswana, that it recognizes as compulsory *ipso facto* and without special agreement, on condition of reciprocity, the jurisdiction of the International Court of Justice, in accordance with paragraph 2 of Article 36 of the Statute of the Court.

This Declaration does not extend:

(a) to disputes in respect of which the parties have agreed or shall agree to have recourse to another means of peaceful settlement; or

(b) to disputes relating to matters which, by international law, are essentially within the domestic jurisdiction of the Republic of Botswana.

The Government of the Republic of Botswana also reserves the right at any time, by means of a notification addressed to the Secretary-General

---

[1] Belgium had deposited in 1948 a declaration valid for five years (United Nations, *Treaty Series*, I, No. 260, Vol. 16).

[2] The instrument of ratification was deposited on 17 June 1958.

of the United Nations, and with effect as from the moment of such notification, either to add to, amend or withdraw any of the foregoing reservations, or any that may hereafter be added.

Done at Gaborone this 14th day of January in the year of our Lord one thousand nine hundred and seventy.

(Signed) Seretse M. KHAMA,
President.

BULGARIA

[Translation from the Bulgarian] 24 VI 1992.

On behalf of the Government of the Republic of Bulgaria, I have the honour to declare that in conformity with Article 36, paragraph 2, of the Statute of the International Court of Justice the Republic of Bulgaria recognizes as compulsory *ipso facto* and without special agreement, in relation to any other State accepting the same obligation, the jurisdiction of the Court in all legal disputes arising out of facts and situations subsequent to or continuing to exist after the entry into force of the present Declaration, concerning:

1. the interpretation of a treaty;
2. any question of international law;
3. the existence of any fact which, if established, would constitute a breach of an international obligation;
4. the nature or extent of the reparation to be made for the breach of an international obligation,

except for disputes with any State which has accepted the compulsory jurisdiction of the International Court of Justice under Article 36, paragraph 2, of the Statute less than twelve months prior to filing an application bringing the dispute before the Court or where such acceptance has been made only for the purpose of a particular dispute.

The Republic of Bulgaria also reserves the right at any time to modify the present Declaration, the modifications taking effect six months after the deposit of the notification thereof.

The present Declaration shall be in force for a period of five years from the date of its deposit with the Secretary-General of the United Nations. It shall continue in force thereafter until six months after a notice of its denunciation is given to the Secretary-General of the United Nations.

Sofia, 26 May 1992.

(Signed) S. GANEV,
Minister of Foreign Affairs
of the Republic of Bulgaria.

Cambodia

[Translation from the French] 19 IX 57.

On behalf of the Royal Government of Cambodia I have the honour to declare that, in accordance with Article 36, paragraph 2, of the Statute of the International Court of Justice, I recognize as compulsory *ipso facto* and without special agreement, in relation to any other State Member of the United Nations accepting the same obligation, that is to say on condition of reciprocity, the jurisdiction of the said Court in all legal disputes, other than:

(1) disputes in regard to which the parties to the dispute have agreed or shall agree to have recourse to some other method of peaceful settlement;
(2) disputes with regard to questions which by international law fall exclusively within the jurisdiction of the Kingdom of Cambodia;
(3) disputes relating to any matter excluded from judicial settlement or compulsory arbitration by virtue of any treaty, convention or other international agreement or instrument to which the Kingdom of Cambodia is a party.

This declaration is valid for ten years from the date of its deposit. It shall remain in force thereafter until notice to the contrary has been given by the Royal Government of Cambodia.

Phnom-Penh, 9 September 1957.

(Signed) Sim Var.

Cameroon

[Translation from the French by the Registry] 3 III 94.

On behalf of the Government of the Republic of Cameroon, I have the honour to declare that:

The Government of the Republic of Cameroon, in accordance with Article 36, paragraph 2, of the Statute of the Court, recognizes as compulsory *ipso facto* and without special agreement, in relation to any other State accepting the same obligation, the jurisdiction of the Court in all legal disputes.

This declaration shall remain in force for a period of five years. It shall subsequently continue to produce effect until contrary notification or written amendment by the Government of the Republic of Cameroon.

(Signed) Ferdinand Léopold Oyono,
Minister for Foreign Affairs.

Canada

10 V 94.

On behalf of the Government of Canada,

(1) I give notice that I hereby terminate the acceptance by Canada of the compulsory jurisdiction of the International Court of Justice hitherto effective by virtue of the declaration made on 10 September 1985[1] in conformity with paragraph 2 of Article 36 of the Statute of the Court.

(2) I declare that the Government of Canada accepts as compulsory *ipso facto* and without special convention, on condition of reciprocity, the jurisdiction of the International Court of Justice, in conformity with paragraph 2 of Article 36 of the Statute of the Court, until such time as notice may be given to terminate the acceptance, over all disputes arising after the present declaration with regard to situations or facts subsequent to this declaration, other than:

(a) disputes in regard to which the parties have agreed or shall agree to have recourse to some other method of peaceful settlement;

(b) disputes with the Government of any other country which is a member of the Commonwealth, all of which disputes shall be settled in such manner as the parties have agreed or shall agree;

(c) disputes with regard to questions which by international law fall exclusively within the jurisdiction of Canada; and

(d) disputes arising out of or concerning conservation and management measures taken by Canada with respect to vessels fishing in the NAFO Regulatory Area, as defined in the Convention on Future Multilateral Co-operation in the Northwest Atlantic Fisheries, 1978, and the enforcement of such measures.

(3) The Government of Canada also reserves the right at any time, by means of a notification addressed to the Secretary-General of the United Nations, and with effect as from the moment of such notification, either to add to, amend or withdraw any of the foregoing reservations, or any that may hereafter be added.

It is requested that this notification be communicated to the Governments of all the States that have accepted the Optional Clause and to the Registrar of the International Court of Justice.

New York, 10 May 1994.

(Signed) Louise Fréchette,
Ambassador and
Permanent Representative.

[1] *I.C.J. Yearbook 1992-1993*, pp. 79-80.

COLOMBIA[1]

[Translation from the French] 30 X 37.

The Republic of Colombia recognizes as compulsory, *ipso facto* and without special agreement, on condition of reciprocity, in relation to any other State accepting the same obligation, the jurisdiction of the Permanent Court of International Justice, in accordance with Article 36 of the Statute.

The present declaration applies only to disputes arising out of facts subsequent to 6 January 1932.

Geneva, 30 October 1937.

(Signed) J. M. YEPES,
Legal Adviser of the Permanent Delegation
of Colombia to the League of Nations.

COSTA RICA

[Translation from the Spanish] 20 II 73.

The Government of Costa Rica recognizes as compulsory *ipso facto* and without special agreement, in relation to any other State accepting the same obligation, the jurisdiction of the International Court of Justice in all legal disputes of the kinds referred to in Article 36, paragraph 2, of the Statute of the International Court of Justice. This Declaration shall be valid for a period of five years and shall be understood to be tacitly renewed for like periods, unless denounced before the expiration of the said period.

San José, 5 February 1973.

(Signed) Gonzalo J. FACIO,
Minister for Foreign Affairs.

CYPRUS

29 IV 88.

I have the honour on behalf of the Government of the Republic of Cyprus to declare, in conformity with paragraph 2 of Article 36 of the Statute of the International Court of Justice, that the Republic of Cyprus accepts as compulsory *ipso facto* and without special agreement, on condition of reciprocity, the jurisdiction of the Court, in relation to any

[1] An instrument of ratification was deposited on 30 October 1937. Ratification was not required under the terms of the Optional Clause, the act of signature itself sufficing to make the undertaking binding, except where the declaration has been made expressly subject to ratification. Nevertheless, certain States, which had signed without any such reservation, subsequently ratified their declarations.

other State accepting the same obligation, over all legal disputes concerning:

(a) the interpretation of any treaty –

I. to which the Republic of Cyprus became a Party on or after 16 August 1960 or

II. which the Republic of Cyprus recognizes as binding on it by succession;

(b) any question of international law;

(c) the existence of any fact which, if established, would constitute a breach of an international obligation;

(d) the nature or extent of the reparation to be made for the breach of an international obligation.

Provided that this declaration shall not apply:

(a) to disputes relating to questions which fall within the domestic jurisdiction of the Republic of Cyprus;

(b) where the declaration recognizing the compulsory jurisdiction of the International Court of Justice on behalf of any other Party to the dispute was deposited with the Secretary-General of the United Nations less than six months prior to the filing of the application bringing the dispute before the Court.

The Government of the Republic of Cyprus reserves the right at any time, by means of a notification addressed to the Secretary-General of the United Nations, and with effect as from the moment of such notification, either to add to, amend or withdraw this declaration or any of the foregoing reservations or any that may hereafter be added.

Nicosia, 19 April 1988.

(Signed) George IACOVOU,
Minister of Foreign Affairs.

DENMARK[1]

[Translation from the French] 10 XII 56.

In conformity with the Royal Decree of 3 December 1956, I have the honour, on behalf of the Danish Government, to make the following declaration:

Pursuant to Article 36, paragraph 2, of the Statute of the International Court of Justice, the Kingdom of Denmark recognizes as compulsory *ipso facto* and without special agreement the jurisdiction of the Court in relation to any other State accepting the same obligation, that is to say on condition of reciprocity, for a period of five years from 10 December 1956

[1] This declaration replaced that of 10 December 1946, which had been made for a period of ten years as from that date (United Nations, *Treaty Series*, I, No. 10, Vol. 1).

and thereafter for further periods of five years, if this declaration is not denounced by notice of not less than six months before the expiration of any five-year period.

New York, 10 December 1956.

(Signed) Karl I. ESKELUND,
Ambassador Extraordinary and Plenipotentiary,
Permanent Representative
to the United Nations.

DOMINICAN REPUBLIC

[Translation from the French] 30 IX 24.

On behalf of the Government of the Dominican Republic and subject to ratification[1], I recognize, in relation to any other Member or State accepting the same obligation, that is to say, on the sole condition of reciprocity, the jurisdiction of the Court as compulsory, *ipso facto* and without special convention.

Geneva, 30 September 1924.

(Signed) Jacinto R. DE CASTRO.

EGYPT

22 VII 57.

I, Mahmoud Fawzi, Minister for Foreign Affairs of the Republic of Egypt, declare on behalf of the Government of the Republic of Egypt, that, in accordance with Article 36 (2) of the Statute of the International Court of Justice and in pursuance and for the purposes of paragraph 9 *(b)* of the Declaration of the Government of the Republic of Egypt dated 24 April 1957, on "the Suez Canal and the arrangements for its operation"[2], the Government of the Republic of Egypt accept as compulsory *ipso facto*, on condition of reciprocity and without special agreement, the jurisdiction of the International Court of Justice in all legal disputes that may arise under the said paragraph 9 *(b)* of the above Declaration dated 24 April 1957, with effect as from that date.

18 July 1957.

(Signed) Mahmoud FAWZI.

---

[1] The instrument of ratification was deposited on 4 February 1933.

[2] United Nations, *Treaty Series*, I, No. 3821, Vol. 265.

Estonia

21 X 91.

I, Arnold Rüütel, Chairman of the Supreme Council of the Republic of Estonia, declare on behalf of the Republic of Estonia and in accordance with the Resolution of September 26, 1991 of the Supreme Council of the Republic of Estonia, that the Republic of Estonia recognizes as compulsory *ipso facto* and without special agreement, in relation to any other State accepting the same obligation, on condition of reciprocity, the jurisdiction of the International Court of Justice, in conformity with paragraph 2 of Article 36 of the Statute of the Court,

provided that this declaration shall not apply to disputes, the solution of which the parties shall entrust to other tribunals by virtue of agreements already in existence or which may be concluded in the future.

Tallinn, 10 October 1991.

(Signed) A. Rüütel,
Chairman of the Supreme Council.

Finland

[Translation from the French] 25 VI 58.

On behalf of the Finnish Government, I hereby declare that I recognize as compulsory *ipso facto* and without special agreement, in relation to any other State accepting the same obligation, that is to say, on condition of reciprocity, the jurisdiction of the International Court of Justice, in accordance with Article 36, paragraph 2, of the Statute of the Court, for a period of five years from 25 June 1958. This declaration shall be renewed by tacit agreement for further periods of the same duration, unless it is denounced not later than six months before the expiry of any such period. This declaration shall apply only to disputes arising in regard to situations or facts subsequent to 25 June 1958.

New York, 25 June 1958.

(Signed) G. A. Gripenberg,
Permanent Representative of Finland
to the United Nations.

Gambia

22 VI 66.

In accordance with Article 36, paragraph 2, of the Statute of the International Court of Justice, I declare, on behalf of the Government of the Gambia, that the Gambia recognizes as compulsory *ipso facto* and without special agreement, in relation to any other State accepting the same obligation, the jurisdiction of the International Court of Justice until such time as notice may be given to terminate the acceptance, over all disputes arising in the future concerning:

(a) the interpretation of a treaty;
(b) any question of international law;
(c) the existence of any fact which, if established, would constitute a breach of an international obligation;
(d) the nature or extent of the reparation to be made for the breach of an international obligation;

with the reservation, however, that this declaration does not apply to

(a) disputes in regard to which the parties have agreed to a settlement other than by recourse to the International Court of Justice;
(b) disputes with any country in the Commonwealth;
(c) disputes which, by international law, fall exclusively within the jurisdiction of the Gambia.

Bathurst, 14 June 1966.

(Signed) A. B. N'JIE,
Minister of State for External Affairs.

GEORGIA

20 VI 95.

I have the honour on behalf of the Republic of Georgia to declare that, in accordance with paragraph 2 of Article 36 of the Statute of the International Court of Justice, the Republic of Georgia recognizes as compulsory *ipso facto* and without special agreement, in relation to any other State accepting the same obligation, the jurisdiction of the Court in all legal disputes referred to in paragraph 2 of Article 36 of the Statute of the International Court of Justice.

Tbilisi, 16 June 1995.

(Signed) Alexander CHIKVAIDZE,
Minister of Foreign Affairs
of the Republic of Georgia.

GREECE

[Translation from the French] 10 I 94.

I declare, on behalf of the Greek Government, that I recognize as compulsory *ipso facto* and without special agreement, on condition of reciprocity, in relation to any other State accepting the same obligation, the jurisdiction of the International Court of Justice in all legal disputes referred to in Article 36, paragraph 2, of the Statute of the Court. However, the Greek Government excludes from the competence of the

Court any dispute relating to defensive military action taken by the Hellenic Republic for reasons of national defence.

This declaration shall remain in force for a period of five years. Upon the expiry of that period, it shall continue to have effect until notice of its termination is given.

Athens, 20 December 1993.

(Signed) Karolos PAPOULIAS,
Minister for Foreign Affairs.

GUINEA-BISSAU

[Translation from the French] 7 VIII 89.

In accordance with Article 36, paragraph 2, of the Statute of the International Court of Justice, the Republic of Guinea-Bissau accepts as compulsory *ipso facto* and without special agreement, in relation to any other State accepting the same obligation, the jurisdiction of the Court in all legal disputes referred to in Article 36, paragraph 2, of the Statute thereof.

This declaration will remain in force until six months following the date on which the Government of Guinea-Bissau makes known its intention of terminating it.

New York, 7 August 1989.

(Signed) Raul A. DE MELO CABRAL,
Chargé d'affaires a.i.

HAITI

[Translation from the French] 4 X 21.

On behalf of the Republic of Haiti, I recognize the jurisdiction of the Permanent Court of International Justice as compulsory.

(Signed) F. ADDOR,
Consul.

HONDURAS

[Translation from the Spanish] 6 VI 86.

The Government of the Republic of Honduras, duly authorized by the National Congress under Decree No. 75-86 of 21 May 1986 to modify the Declaration made on 20 February 1960 concerning Article 36, paragraph 2, of the Statute of the International Court of Justice, *hereby declares* that it modifies the Declaration made by it on 20 February 1960[1] as follows:

[1] *I.C.J. Yearbook 1984-1985*, pp. 78-79.

1. It recognizes as compulsory *ipso facto* and without special agreement, in relation to any other State accepting the same obligation, the jurisdiction of the International Court of Justice in all legal disputes concerning:

   (a) the interpretation of a treaty;
   (b) any question of international law;
   (c) the existence of any fact which, if established, would constitute a breach of an international obligation;
   (d) the nature or extent of the reparation to be made for the breach of an international obligation.

2. This Declaration shall not apply, however, to the following disputes to which the Republic of Honduras may be a party:

   (a) disputes in respect of which the parties have agreed or may agree to resort to other means for the pacific settlement of disputes;
   (b) disputes concerning matters subject to the domestic jurisdiction of the Republic of Honduras under international law;
   (c) disputes relating to facts or situations originating in armed conflicts or acts of a similar nature which may affect the territory of the Republic of Honduras, and in which it may find itself involved directly or indirectly;
   (d) disputes referring to:

      (i) territorial questions with regard to sovereignty over islands, shoals and keys; internal waters, bays, the territorial sea and the legal status and limits thereof;
      (ii) all rights of sovereignty or jurisdiction concerning the legal status and limits of the contiguous zone, the exclusive economic zone and the continental shelf;
      (iii) the airspace over the territories, waters and zones referred to in this subparagraph.

3. The Government of Honduras also reserves the right at any time to supplement, modify or withdraw this Declaration or the reservations contained therein by giving notice to the Secretary-General of the United Nations.

4. This Declaration replaces the Declaration made by the Government of Honduras on 20 February 1960.

National Palace, Tegucigalpa, D.C., 22 May 1986.

(Signed) José AZCONA H.,
President of the Republic.

(Signed) Carlos LÓPEZ CONTRERAS,
The Secretary of State for Foreign Affairs.

Hungary

22 X 92.

The Republic of Hungary hereby recognizes as compulsory *ipso facto* and without special agreement, on condition of reciprocity, the jurisdiction of the International Court of Justice, in accordance with Article 36, paragraph 2, of the Statute of the Court in all disputes which may arise in respect of facts or situations subsequent to this declaration, other than:

(a) disputes in regard to which the parties to the dispute have agreed or shall agree to have recourse to some other method of peaceful settlement;

(b) disputes in regard to matters which by international law fall exclusively within the domestic jurisdiction of the Republic of Hungary;

(c) disputes relating to, or connected with, facts or situations of hostilities, war, armed conflicts, individual or collective actions taken in self-defence or the discharge of any functions pursuant to any resolution or recommendation of the United Nations, and other similar or related acts, measures or situations in which the Republic of Hungary is, has been or may in the future be involved;

(d) disputes in respect of which any other party to the dispute has accepted the compulsory jurisdiction of the Court only in relation to or for the purpose of such dispute; or where the acceptance of the Court's compulsory jurisdiction on behalf of any other party to the dispute was deposited less than twelve months prior to the filing of the application bringing the dispute before the Court.

The Government of the Republic of Hungary reserves the right at any time, by means of a notification addressed to the Secretary-General of the United Nations, and with effect of six months of such notification to amend, add to or withdraw any of the foregoing reservations or any that may hereafter be added.

This declaration shall remain in force until the expiration of six months after notification has been given of its termination.

Budapest, 7 October 1992.

(Signed) Dr. GÉZA JESZENSZKY,
Minister for Foreign Affairs
of the Republic of Hungary.

India

18 IX 74.

I have the honour to declare, on behalf of the Government of the Republic of India, that they accept, in conformity with paragraph 2 of Article 36 of the Statute of the Court, until such time as notice may be given to terminate such acceptance, as compulsory *ipso facto* and without special agreement, and on the basis and condition of reciprocity, the jurisdiction of the International Court of Justice over all disputes other than:

(1) disputes in regard to which the parties to the dispute have agreed or shall agree to have recourse to some other method or methods of settlement;

(2) disputes with the government of any State which is or has been a Member of the Commonwealth of Nations;

(3) disputes in regard to matters which are essentially within the domestic jurisdiction of the Republic of India;

(4) disputes relating to or connected with facts or situations of hostilities, armed conflicts, individual or collective actions taken in self-defence, resistance to aggression, fulfilment of obligations imposed by international bodies, and other similar or related acts, measures or situations in which India is, has been or may in future be involved;

(5) disputes with regard to which any other party to a dispute has accepted the compulsory jurisdiction of the International Court of Justice exclusively for or in relation to the purposes of such dispute; or where the acceptance of the Court's compulsory jurisdiction on behalf of a party to the dispute was deposited or ratified less than 12 months prior to the filing of the application bringing the dispute before the Court;

(6) disputes where the jurisdiction of the Court is or may be founded on the basis of a treaty concluded under the auspices of the League of Nations, unless the Government of India specially agree to jurisdiction in each case;

(7) disputes concerning the interpretation or application of a multilateral treaty unless all the parties to the treaty are also parties to the case before the Court or Government of India specially agree to jurisdiction;

(8) disputes with the government of any State with which, on the date of an application to bring a dispute before the Court, the Government of India has no diplomatic relations or which has not been recognized by the Government of India;

(9) disputes with non-sovereign States or territories;

(10) disputes with India concerning or relating to:

(a) the status of its territory or the modification or delimitation of its frontiers or any other matter concerning boundaries;

(b) the territorial sea, the continental shelf and the margins, the exclusive fishery zone, the exclusive economic zone, and other zones of national maritime jurisdiction including for the regulation and control of marine pollution and the conduct of scientific research by foreign vessels;

(c) the condition and status of its islands, bays and gulfs and that of the bays and gulfs that for historical reasons belong to it;

(*d*) the airspace superjacent to its land and maritime territory; and

(*e*) the determination and delimitation of its maritime boundaries.

(11) disputes prior to the date of this declaration, including any dispute the foundations, reasons, facts, causes, origins, definitions, allegations or bases of which existed prior to this date, even if they are submitted or brought to the knowledge of the Court hereafter.

2. This declaration revokes and replaces the previous declaration made by the Government of India on 14 September 1959[1].

New Delhi, 15 September 1974.

(Signed) Swaran SINGH,
Minister for External Affairs.

JAPAN

15 IX 58.

I have the honour, by direction of the Minister for Foreign Affairs, to declare on behalf of the Government of Japan, that in conformity with paragraph 2 of Article 36 of the Statute of the International Court of Justice, Japan recognizes as compulsory *ipso facto* and without special agreement, in relation to any other State accepting the same obligation and on condition of reciprocity, the jurisdiction of the International Court of Justice, over all disputes which arise on and after the date of the present declaration with regard to situations or facts subsequent to the same date and which are not settled by other means of peaceful settlement.

This declaration does not apply to disputes which the parties thereto have agreed or shall agree to refer for final and binding decision to arbitration or judicial settlement.

This declaration shall remain in force for a period of five years and thereafter until it may be terminated by a written notice.

New York, 15 September 1958.

(Signed) Koto MATSUDAIRA,
Permanent Representative of Japan
to the United Nations.

KENYA

19 IV 65.

I have the honour to declare, on behalf of the Government of the Republic of Kenya that it accepts, in conformity with paragraph 2 of

---

[1] United Nations, *Treaty Series,* I, No. 4871, Vol. 340.

Article 36 of the Statute of the International Court of Justice until such time as notice may be given to terminate such acceptance, as compulsory *ipso facto* and without special agreement, and on the basis and condition of reciprocity, the jurisdiction over all disputes arising after 12 December 1963 with regard to situations or facts subsequent to that date, other than:

(1) disputes in regard to which the parties to the dispute have agreed or shall agree to have recourse to some other method or methods of settlement;
(2) dispute with the government of any State which, on the date of this Declaration is a Member of the Commonwealth of Nations or may so become subsequently;
(3) disputes with regard to questions which by general rules of international law fall exclusively within the jurisdiction of Kenya;
(4) disputes concerning any question relating to or arising out of belligerent or military occupation or the discharge of any functions pursuant to any recommendation or decision of an organ of the United Nations, in accordance with which the Government of the Republic of Kenya have accepted obligations.

The Government of the Republic of Kenya reserves the right at any time by means of a notification addressed to the Secretary-General of the United Nations to add to, amend, or withdraw any of the foregoing reservations. Such notifications shall be effective on the date of their receipt by the Secretary-General of the United Nations.

Nairobi, 12 April 1965.

(Signed) Joseph MURUMBI,
Minister for External Affairs.

LIBERIA

20 III 52.

On behalf of the Government of the Republic of Liberia, I, Gabriel L. Dennis, Secretary of State of Liberia, subject to ratification, declare that the Republic of Liberia recognizes as compulsory *ipso facto* and without special agreement, in relation to any other State, also a party to the Statute pursuant to Article 93 of the United Nations Charter, which accepts the same obligation (i.e., subject to reciprocity), the jurisdiction of the International Court of Justice in all legal disputes arising after ratification concerning:

(a) the interpretation of a treaty;
(b) any question of international law;
(c) the existence of any fact which, if established, would constitute a breach of an international obligation;
(d) the nature or extent of the reparation to be made for the breach of an international obligation.

This declaration does not apply:

(a) to any dispute which the Republic of Liberia considers essentially within its domestic jurisdiction;

(b) to any dispute in regard to which the parties have agreed or may agree to bring before other tribunals as a result of agreements already existing or which may be made in the future.

The present declaration has been made for a period of five years as from the date of deposit of the ratification[1] and thereafter until notice of termination is given.

Done at Monrovia this 3rd day of March 1952.

(Signed) Gabriel L. DENNIS,
Secretary of State.

LIECHTENSTEIN

[Translation from the French] 29 III 50.

The Government of the Principality of Liechtenstein, duly authorized by His Serene Highness, the Reigning Prince François Joseph II, in accordance with the Order of the Diet of the Principality of Liechtenstein dated 9 March 1950, which came into force on 10 March 1950,

declares by these presents that the Principality of Liechtenstein recognizes as compulsory *ipso facto* and without special agreement, in relation to any other State accepting the same obligation, the jurisdiction of the International Court of Justice in all legal disputes concerning:

(a) the interpretation of a treaty;

(b) any question of international law;

(c) the existence of any fact which, if established, would constitute a breach of an international obligation;

(d) the nature or extent of the reparation to be made for the breach of an international obligation.

The present declaration, which is made under Article 36 of the Statute of the International Court of Justice, shall take effect from the date on which the Principality becomes a party to the Statute[2] and shall have effect as long as the declaration has not been revoked subject to one year's notice.

Done at Vaduz, 10 March 1950.

On behalf of the Government of
the Principality of Liechtenstein,
(Signed) A. FRICK,
The Head of Government.

---

[1] The instrument of ratification, dated 30 March 1953, was deposited on 17 April 1953.

[2] Liechtenstein became a party to the Statute of the Court on 29 March 1950.

Luxembourg[1]

[Translation from the French] 15 IX 30.

The Government of the Grand-Duchy of Luxembourg recognizes as compulsory, *ipso facto* and without special agreement, in relation to any other State accepting the same obligation, that is to say on condition of reciprocity, the jurisdiction of the Court in conformity with Article 36, paragraph 2, of the Statute, in any disputes arising after the signature of the present declaration with regard to situations or facts subsequent to this signature, except in cases where the parties have agreed or shall agree to have recourse to another procedure or to another method of pacific settlement. The present declaration is made for a period of five years. Unless it is denounced six months before the expiration of that period, it shall be considered as renewed for a further period of five years and similarly thereafter.

Geneva, 15 September 1930.

(Signed) Bech.

Madagascar

[Translation from the French] 2 VII 92.

On behalf of the Government of Madagascar, I declare under Article 36, paragraph 2, of the Statute of the International Court of Justice that Madagascar accepts as compulsory *ipso facto* and without special agreement, in relation to any other State accepting the same obligation and until such time as notice may be given to terminate this acceptance, the compulsory jurisdiction of the Court in all legal disputes concerning:

- the interpretation of a treaty;
- any question of international law;
- the existence of any fact which, if established, would constitute a breach of an international obligation;
- the nature or extent of the reparation to be made for the breach of an international obligation.

The present declaration does not apply:

- to disputes in regard to which the parties have agreed to have recourse to some other method of settlement;
- disputes relating to questions which, under international law, fall exclusively within the jurisdiction of Madagascar.

The Government of Madagascar also reserves the right to add to, amend or withdraw the foregoing reservations by means of a notification

---

[1] The Government of Luxembourg had in 1921 signed the Optional Clause subject to ratification. That declaration was, however, never ratified.

addressed to the Secretary-General of the United Nations, which would take effect on the date of its receipt by the Secretary-General.

Antananarivo, 12 May 1992.

(Signed) Césaire RABENORO,
Minister for Foreign Affairs.

MALAWI

12 XII 66.

On behalf of the Government of Malawi, I declare under Article 36, paragraph 2, of the Statute of the International Court of Justice that I recognize as compulsory *ipso facto* and without special agreement, in relation to any other State accepting the same obligation, on condition of reciprocity, the jurisdiction of the International Court of Justice in all legal disputes which may arise in respect of facts or situations subsequent to this declaration concerning –

(a) the interpretation of a treaty;
(b) any question of international law;
(c) the existence of any fact which, if established, would constitute a breach of an international obligation;
(d) the nature or extent of the reparation to be made for the breach of an international obligation:

Provided that this declaration shall not apply to –

(i) disputes with regard to matters which are essentially within the domestic jurisdiction of the Republic of Malawi as determined by the Government of Malawi;
(ii) disputes in regard to which the parties of the dispute have agreed or shall agree to have recourse to some other method of peaceful settlement; or
(iii) disputes concerning any question relating to or arising out of belligerent or military occupation.

The Government of Malawi also reserves the right at any time, by means of a notification addressed to the Secretary-General of the United Nations, to add to, amend, or withdraw any of the foregoing reservations or any that may hereafter be added. Such notifications shall be effective on the date of their receipt by the Secretary-General of the United Nations.

Given under my hand in Zomba this 22nd day of November 1966.

(Signed) H. KAMUZU BANDA,
President and
Minister for External Affairs.

MALTA[1]

6 XII 66.

I have the honour to declare, on behalf of the Government of Malta, that Malta accepts as compulsory *ipso facto* and without special convention, on condition of reciprocity, the jurisdiction of the International Court of Justice, in conformity with paragraph 2 of Article 36 of the Statute of the Court, until such time as notice may be given to terminate the acceptance, over all disputes other than:

(i) disputes in regard to which the Parties to the dispute have agreed or shall agree to have recourse to some other method of peaceful settlement;

(ii) disputes with the government of any other country which is a Member of the British Commonwealth of Nations, all of which disputes shall be settled in such manner as the Parties have agreed or shall agree;

(iii) disputes with regard to questions which by international law fall exclusively within the jurisdiction of Malta;

(iv) disputes concerning any question relating to or arising out of belligerent or military occupation or the discharge of any functions pursuant to any recommendation or decision of an organ of the United Nations, in accordance with which the Government of Malta have accepted obligations;

(v) disputes arising under a multilateral treaty, unless (1) all Parties to the treaty affected by the decision are also Parties to the case before the Court, or (2) the Government of Malta specially agrees to jurisdiction;

(vi) disputes relating to any matter excluded from compulsory adjudication or arbitration under any treaty, convention or other international agreement or instrument to which Malta is a Party;

(vii) disputes in respect of which arbitral or judicial proceedings are taking, or have taken place with any State which, at the date of the commencement of the proceedings, had not itself accepted the compulsory jurisdiction of the International Court of Justice; and

(viii) disputes in respect of which any other Party to the dispute has accepted the compulsory jurisdiction of the International Court of Justice only in relation to or for the purposes of the dispute; or where the acceptance of the Court's compulsory jurisdiction on

[1] By letter of 13 May 1983 to the Secretary-General of the United Nations, the Minister for Foreign Affairs notified the withdrawal, with immediate effect, of a declaration concerning a particular category of disputes which was filed on 23 January 1981 and which is reproduced in *I.C.J. Yearbook 1981-1982*, p. 78.

behalf of any other Party to the dispute was deposited or ratified less than twelve months prior to the filing of the application bringing the dispute before the Court.

The Government of Malta also reserves the right at any time, by means of a notification addressed to the Secretary-General of the United Nations, and with effect as from the moment of such notification either to add to, amend or withdraw any of the foregoing reservations or any that may hereafter be added.

Valletta, 29 November 1966.

(Signed) G. FELICE,
Acting Minister of Commonwealth
and Foreign Affairs.

2 IX 83.

I have the honour to refer to the declaration made by the Government of Malta on 29 November 1966, and notified on 6 December 1966, concerning the compulsory jurisdiction of the International Court of Justice and to give notice that, with effect from the moment this notification is received by Your Excellency, the acceptance of the Government of Malta of the jurisdiction of the Court shall be limited to all disputes with Malta other than

(1) the disputes mentioned in paragraphs (i) to (viii) both inclusive, of the said declaration, and
(2) the following categories of disputes, that is to say:

Disputes with Malta concerning or relating to:

(a) its territory, including the territorial sea, and the status thereof,
(b) the continental shelf or any other zone of maritime jurisdiction, and the resources thereof,
(c) the determination or delimitation of any of the above,
(d) the prevention or control of pollution or contamination of the marine environment in marine areas adjacent to the coast of Malta.

The Government of Malta also reserves the right at any time, by means of a notification addressed to the Secretary-General of the United Nations, and with effect from the moment of such notification, either to add to, amend or withdraw any of the foregoing reservations or any that may hereafter be added.

(Signed) Alex SCEBERAS TRIGON,
Minister for Foreign Affairs.

MAURITIUS

23 IX 68.

I have the honour to declare, on behalf of the Government of Mauritius, that Mauritius accepts as compulsory *ipso facto* and without special convention, on condition of reciprocity, the jurisdiction of the International Court of Justice, in conformity with paragraph 2 of Article 36 of the Statute of the Court, until such time as notice may be given to terminate the acceptance, over all disputes other than:

(i) disputes in regard to which the Parties to the dispute have agreed or shall agree to have recourse to some other method of peaceful settlement;

(ii) disputes with the Government of any other country which is a Member of the British Commonwealth of Nations, all of which disputes shall be settled in such manner as the parties have agreed or shall agree;

(iii) disputes with regard to questions which by international law fall exclusively within the jurisdiction of Mauritius;

(iv) disputes concerning any question relating to or arising out of belligerent or military occupation or the discharge of any functions pursuant to any recommendation or decision of an organ of the United Nations, in accordance with which the Government of Mauritius has accepted obligations;

(v) disputes relating to any matter excluded from compulsory adjudication or arbitration under any treaty, convention or other international agreement or instrument to which Mauritius is a party;

(vi) disputes in respect of which arbitral or judicial proceedings are taking, or have taken place with any State which, at the date of the commencement of the proceedings, had not itself accepted the compulsory jurisdiction of the International Court of Justice; and

(vii) disputes in respect of which any other Party to the dispute has accepted the compulsory jurisdiction of the International Court of Justice only in relation to or for the purposes of the dispute; or where the acceptance of the Court's compulsory jurisdiction on behalf of any other Party to the dispute was deposited or ratified less than twelve months prior to the filing of the application bringing the dispute before the Court.

The Government of Mauritius also reserves the right at any time, by means of a notification addressed to the Secretary-General of the United Nations, and with effect as from the moment of such notification either to add to, amend or withdraw any of the foregoing reservations or any that may hereafter be added.

Port Louis, 4 September 1968.

(Signed) S. RAMGOOLAM,
Prime Minister and
Minister for External Affairs.

MEXICO

[Translation from the Spanish] 28 X 47.

In regard to any legal dispute that may in future arise between the United States of Mexico and any other State out of events subsequent to the date of this Declaration, the Mexican Government recognizes as compulsory *ipso facto*, and without any special agreement being required therefor, the jurisdiction of the International Court of Justice in accordance with Article 36, paragraph 2, of the Statute of the said Court, in relation to any other State accepting the same obligation, that is, on condition of strict reciprocity. This Declaration, which does not apply to disputes arising from matters that, in the opinion of the Mexican Government, are within the domestic jurisdiction of the United States of Mexico, shall be binding for a period of five years as from 1 March 1947 and after that date shall continue in force until six months after the Mexican Government gives notice of denunciation.

Mexico, D.F., 23 October 1947.

(Signed) Jaime TORRES BODET,
Secretary of State for External Relations.

NAURU

9 IX 92.

On behalf of the Government of the Republic of Nauru, I have the honour to refer to the Republic's Declaration dated 30 December 1987[1], deposited with the United Nations Secretary-General on 29 January 1988, whereby the Republic has accepted as compulsory, *ipso facto* and without special agreement, in relation to any other State accepting the same obligation, the jurisdiction of the International Court of Justice, in accordance with Article 36, paragraph 2, of the Statute of the Court, and stipulated that the acceptance of the Court's jurisdiction shall extend to all disputes to which the Republic is or may be a party, other than any dispute with respect to which there exists a dispute settlement mechanism under an agreement between the Republic of Nauru and another State.

I have the further honour to declare that the aforesaid Declaration shall stand renewed and extended on 29 January 1993 and continue to be in force for a further period of five years from that date.

In witness whereof, I set my hand and the Common Seal of the Republic of Nauru, this fourth day of the month of September one thousand nine hundred and ninety-two.

(Signed) Hammer DEROBURT,
President
and Minister for External Affairs,
Republic of Nauru.

[1] *I.C.J. Yearbook 1987-1988*, p. 84.

NETHERLANDS

[Translation from the French] 1 VIII 56.

I hereby declare that the Government of the Kingdom of the Netherlands recognizes, in accordance with Article 36, paragraph 2, of the Statute of the International Court of Justice, with effect from 6 August 1956, as compulsory *ipso facto* and without special agreement, in relation to any other State accepting the same obligation, that is on condition of reciprocity, the jurisdiction of said Court in all disputes arising or which may arise after 5 August 1921, with the exception of disputes in respect of which the parties, excluding the jurisdiction of the International Court of Justice, may have agreed to have recourse to some other method of pacific settlement.

The aforesaid obligation is accepted for a period of five years and will be renewed by tacit agreement for additional periods of five years, unless notice is given, not less than six months before the expiry of any such period, that the Government of the Kingdom of the Netherlands does not wish to renew it.

The acceptance of the jurisdiction of the Court founded on the declaration of 5 August 1946[1] is terminated with effect from 6 August 1956.

New York, 1 August 1956.

(Signed) E. L. C. SCHIFF,
Acting Permanent Representative of the
Kingdom of the Netherlands to the United Nations.

NEW ZEALAND

22 IX 77.

I have the honour, by direction of the Minister of Foreign Affairs of New Zealand, to declare on behalf of the Government of New Zealand:

(I) The acceptance by the Government of New Zealand of the compulsory jurisdiction of the International Court of Justice by virtue of the Declaration made on 1 April 1940[2] under Article 36 of the Statute of the Permanent Court of International Justice and made applicable to the International Court of Justice by paragraph 5 of Article 36 of the Statute of that Court, is hereby terminated.

(II) The Government of New Zealand accept as compulsory, *ipso facto*, and without special agreement, on condition of reciprocity, the jurisdiction of the International Court of Justice in conformity with paragraph 2 of Article 36 of the Court over all disputes other than:

[1] United Nations, *Treaty Series*, I, No. 2, Vol. 1.

[2] *I.C.J. Yearbook 1976-1977*, pp. 69 f.

(1) disputes in regard to which the parties have agreed or shall agree to have recourse to some other method of peaceful settlement;

(2) disputes in respect of which any other party to the dispute has accepted the compulsory jurisdiction of the International Court of Justice only in relation to or for the purpose of the dispute: or where the acceptance of the Court's compulsory jurisdiction on behalf of any other party to the dispute was deposited or ratified less than twelve months prior to the filing of the application bringing the dispute before the Court;

(3) disputes arising out of, or concerning, the jurisdiction or rights claimed or exercised by New Zealand in respect of the exploration, exploitation, conservation or management of the living resources in marine areas beyond and adjacent to the territorial sea of New Zealand but within 200 nautical miles from the baselines from which the breadth of the territorial sea is measured.

This Declaration shall remain in force for a period of five years from 22 September 1977 and thereafter until the expiration of six months after notice has been given of the termination of this Declaration provided that the Government of New Zealand reserves the right at any time to amend this Declaration in the light of the results of the Third United Nations Conference on the Law of the Sea in respect of the settlement of disputes.

New York, 22 September 1977.

(Signed) M. J. C. TEMPLETON,
Permanent Representative of
New Zealand to the United Nations.

NICARAGUA[1]

[Translation from the French] 24 IX 29.

On behalf of the Republic of Nicaragua I recognize as compulsory unconditionally the jurisdiction of the Permanent Court of International Justice.

Geneva, 24 September 1929.

(Signed) T. F. MEDINA.

[1] See the Court's Judgment of 26 November 1984 (*I.C.J. Reports 1984*, p. 392).

Nigeria

3 IX 65.

Whereas under Article 93 of the United Nations Charter all Member States are *ipso facto* parties to the Statute of the International Court of Justice;

And whereas the Government of the Federal Republic of Nigeria has decided to accept the compulsory jurisdiction of the International Court of Justice and it is necessary to make a declaration in terms of Article 36 (2) of the Statute of the Court;

Now therefore, I, Nuhu Bamali, Minister of State for External Affairs, hereby declare that the Government of the Federal Republic of Nigeria recognizes as compulsory *ipso facto* and without special agreement, in relation to any other State accepting the same obligation, that is to say, on the sole condition of reciprocity, the jurisdiction of the International Court of Justice in conformity with Article 36, paragraph 2, of the Statute of the Court.

Done at Lagos, this 14th day of August, one thousand nine hundred and sixty-five.

(Signed) Nuhu Bamali,
Minister of State
for External Affairs.

Norway[1]

25 VI 96.

I hereby declare on behalf of the Royal Norwegian Government that Norway recognizes as compulsory *ipso facto* and without special agreement, in relation to any other State accepting the same obligation, that is on condition of reciprocity, the jurisdiction of the International Court of Justice in conformity with Article 36, paragraph 2, of the Statute of the Court, for a period of five years as from 3 October 1976. This declaration shall thereafter be tacitly renewed for additional periods of five years, unless notice of termination is given not less than six months

---

[1] This is the text of the declaration as amended by letter of 24 June 1996 received by the Secretary-General of the United Nations on the following day. The first paragraph of that letter read as follows:

> "On behalf of the Government of Norway,
>
> I give notice that I hereby amend the acceptance by Norway of the compulsory jurisdiction of the International Court of Justice hitherto effective by virtue of the declaration made on 2 April 1976 in conformity with paragraph 2 of Article 36 of the Statute of the Court. As amended, the declaration shall read . . ."

The declaration of 1976 replaced that of 17 December 1956 (United Nations, *Treaty Series*, I, No. 3642, Vol. 256).

before the expiration of the current period; provided, however, that the limitations and exceptions relating to the settlement of disputes pursuant to the provisions of, and the Norwegian declarations applicable at any given time to, the United Nations Convention on the Law of the Sea of 10 December 1982 and the Agreement of 4 December 1995 for the Implementation of the Provisions of the United Nations Convention on the Law of the Sea of 10 December 1982 relating to the Conservation and Management of Straddling Fish Stocks and Highly Migratory Fish Stocks, shall apply to all disputes concerning the law of the sea.

New York, 24 June 1996.

(Signed) Hans Jacob Biørn LIAN,
Permanent Representative of
Norway to the United Nations.

PAKISTAN[1]

13 IX 60.

I have the honour, by direction of the President of Pakistan, to make the following declaration on behalf of the Government of Pakistan under Article 36, paragraph 2, of the Statute of the International Court of Justice:

The Government of Pakistan recognize as compulsory *ipso facto* and without special agreement in relation to any other State accepting the same obligation, the jurisdiction of the International Court of Justice in all legal disputes after 24 June 1948, arising, concerning:

(a) the interpretation of a treaty;
(b) any question of international law;
(c) the existence of any fact which, if established, would constitute a breach of an international obligation;
(d) the nature or extent of the reparation to be made for the breach of an international obligation;

Provided, that the declaration shall not apply to:

(a) disputes the solution of which the parties shall entrust to other tribunals by virtue of agreements already in existence or which may be concluded in the future; or
(b) disputes relating to questions which by international law fall exclusively within the domestic jurisdiction of Pakistan;

[1] This declaration replaced that of 23 May 1957 (United Nations, *Treaty Series*, I, No. 3875, Vol. 269) notice of the withdrawal and termination of which was given by letter of 12 September 1960 received on the following day by the Secretary-General of the United Nations.

(*c*) disputes arising under a multilateral treaty unless

(i) all parties to the treaty affected by the decision are also parties to the case before the Court, or

(ii) the Government of Pakistan specially agree to jurisdiction; and

provided further, that this Declaration shall remain in force till such time as notice may be given to terminate it.

New York, 12 September 1960.

(*Signed*) Said HASAN,
Ambassador Extraordinary and Plenipotentiary,
Permanent Representative of Pakistan to the
United Nations.

PANAMA[1]

[*Translation from the French*] 25 X 21.

On behalf of the Government of Panama, I recognize, in relation to any other Member or State which accepts the same obligation, that is to say, on the sole condition of reciprocity, the jurisdiction of the Court as compulsory, *ipso facto* and without any special convention.

Paris, 25 October 1921.

(*Signed*) R. A. AMADOR,
Chargé d'affaires.

PHILIPPINES[2]

18 I 72.

I, Carlos P. Romulo, Secretary of Foreign Affairs of the Republic of the Philippines, hereby declare, under Article 36, paragraph 2, of the Statute of the International Court of Justice, that the Republic of the Philippines recognizes as compulsory *ipso facto* and without special agreement, in relation to any other State accepting the same obligation, the jurisdiction of the International Court of Justice in all legal disputes arising hereafter concerning:

(*a*) the interpretation of a treaty;
(*b*) any question of international law;

[1] An instrument of ratification was deposited on 14 June 1929. Cf. the footnote to Colombia, p. 88, above.

[2] This declaration replaced that of 12 July 1947 (United Nations, *Treaty Series*, I, No. 101, Vol. 7).

(c) the existence of any fact which, if established, would constitute a breach of an international obligation;

(d) the nature or extent of the reparation to be made for the breach of an international obligation;

Provided, that this declaration shall not apply to any dispute –

(a) in regard to which the parties thereto have agreed or shall agree to have recourse to some other method of peaceful settlement; or

(b) which the Republic of the Philippines considers to be essentially within its domestic jurisdiction; or

(c) in respect of which the other party has accepted the compulsory jurisdiction of the International Court of Justice only in relation to or for the purposes of such dispute; or where the acceptance of the compulsory jurisdiction was deposited or ratified less than 12 months prior to the filing of the application bringing the dispute before the Court; or

(d) arising under a multilateral treaty, unless (1) all parties to the treaty are also parties to the case before the Court, or (2) the Republic of the Philippines specially agrees to jurisdiction; or

(e) arising out of or concerning jurisdiction or rights claimed or exercised by the Philippines –

(i) in respect of the natural resources, including living organisms belonging to sedentary species, of the sea-bed and subsoil of the continental shelf of the Philippines, or its analogue in an archipelago, as described in Proclamation No. 370 dated 20 March 1968 of the President of the Republic of the Philippines; or

(ii) in respect of the territory of the Republic of the Philippines, including its territorial seas and inland waters; and

Provided, further, that this declaration shall remain in force until notice is given to the Secretary-General of the United Nations of its termination.

Done at Manila this 23rd day of December 1971.

(Signed) Carlos P. ROMULO,
Secretary of Foreign Affairs.

POLAND

25 III 96.

On behalf of the Government of the Republic of Poland I hereby declare that the Republic of Poland withdraws its consent to the compulsory jurisdiction of the International Court of Justice communicated on

25 September 1990[1] in light of Article 36, paragraph 2, of the Statute of the Court. At the same time, I hereby declare that the Republic of Poland shall recognize with the effect as of 25 September 1996, in accordance with the provisions of the aforementioned article, as compulsory *ipso facto* and without special agreement, in relation to any other State accepting the same obligation and subject to the sole condition of reciprocity, the jurisdiction of the International Court of Justice in all legal disputes other than:

(a) disputes prior to 25 September 1990 or disputes arisen out of facts or situations prior to the same date,
(b) disputes with regard to the territory and State boundaries,
(c) disputes with regard to environmental protection,
(d) disputes with regard to foreign liabilities or debts,
(e) disputes with regard to any State which has made a declaration accepting the compulsory jurisdiction of the International Court of Justice less than twelve months prior to the filing of the application bringing the dispute before the Court,
(f) disputes in respect whereof the parties have agreed or shall agree to have recourse to other method of peaceful settlement,
(g) disputes relating to matters which, by international law, fall exclusively within the domestic jurisdiction of the Republic of Poland.

The Government of the Republic of Poland reserves its right to withdraw or modify the present Declaration at any time and by means of a notification addressed to the Secretary-General of the United Nations, taking effect after six months from the moment whereof.

25 March 1996.

(Signed) Dariusz Rosati,
Minister of Foreign Affairs.

Portugal

19 XII 55.

Under Article 36, paragraph 2, of the Statute of the International Court of Justice, I declare on behalf of the Portuguese Government that Portugal recognizes the jurisdiction of this Court as compulsory *ipso facto* and without special agreement, as provided for in the said paragraph 2 of Article 36 and under the following conditions:

(1) the present declaration covers disputes arising out of events both prior and subsequent to the declaration of acceptance of the "optional clause" which Portugal made on 16 December 1920 as a party to the Statute of the Permanent Court of International Justice;

[1] *I.C.J. Yearbook 1994-1995*, pp. 109-110.

(2) the present declaration enters into force at the moment it is deposited with the Secretary-General of the United Nations; it shall be valid for a period of one year, and thereafter until notice of its denunciation is given to the said Secretary-General;

(3) the Portuguese Government reserves the right to exclude from the scope of the present declaration, at any time during its validity, any given category or categories of disputes, by notifying the Secretary-General of the United Nations and with effect from the moment of such notification.

Washington, D.C., 19 December 1955.

(Signed) L. ESTEVES FERNANDES.

SENEGAL[1]

[Translation from the French] 2 XII 85.

I have the honour, on behalf of the Government of the Republic of Senegal, to declare that, in conformity with Article 36, paragraph 2, of the Statute of the International Court of Justice, it accepts on condition of reciprocity as compulsory *ipso facto* and without special convention, in relation to any other State accepting the same obligation, the jurisdiction of the Court over all legal disputes arising after the present declaration, concerning:

- the interpretation of a treaty;
- any question of international law;
- the existence of any fact which, if established, would constitute a breach of an international obligation;
- the nature or extent of the reparation to be made for the breach of international obligation.

This declaration is made on condition of reciprocity on the part of all States. However, Senegal may reject the Court's competence in respect of:

- disputes in regard to which the parties have agreed to have recourse to some other method of settlement;
- disputes with regard to questions which, under international law, fall exclusively within the jurisdiction of Senegal.

Lastly, the Government of the Republic of Senegal reserves the right at any time, by means of a notification addressed to the Secretary-General

[1] This declaration replaced that of 3 May 1985 (*I.C.J. Yearbook 1984-1985*, p. 93).

of the United Nations, to add to, amend or withdraw the foregoing reservations.

Such notification would take effect on the date of its receipt by the Secretary-General.

Dakar, 22 October 1985.

(Signed) Ibrahima FALL,
Minister of Foreign Affairs
of the Republic of Senegal.

SOMALIA

11 IV 63.

I have the honour to declare on behalf of the Government of the Somali Republic that the Somali Republic accepts as compulsory *ipso facto*, and without special agreement, on condition of reciprocity, the jurisdiction of the International Court of Justice, in conformity with paragraph 2 of Article 36 of the Statute of the Court, until such time as notice may be given to terminate the acceptance, over all legal disputes arising other than disputes in respect of which any other party to the dispute has accepted the compulsory jurisdiction of the International Court of Justice only in relation to or for the purposes of the dispute; or where the acceptance of the Court's compulsory jurisdiction on behalf of any other party to the dispute was deposited or ratified less than 12 months prior to the filing of the application bringing the dispute before the Court.

The Somali Republic also reserves the right at any time by means of a notification addressed to the Secretary-General of the United Nations, and with effect as from the moment of such notification, either to add to, amend or withdraw any of the foregoing reservations, or any that may hereafter be added.

Mogadishu, 25 March 1963.

(Signed) Abdullahi ISSA,
Minister for Foreign Affairs.

SPAIN

[Translation from the Spanish] 29 X 90.

1. On behalf of the Spanish Government, I have the honour to declare that the Kingdom of Spain accepts as compulsory *ipso facto* and without special agreement, the jurisdiction of the International Court of Justice, in conformity with Article 36, paragraph 2, of the Statute of the Court, in relation to any other State accepting the same obligation, on condition of reciprocity, in legal disputes not included among the following situations and exceptions:

(*a*) disputes in regard to which the Kingdom of Spain and the other party or parties have agreed or shall agree to have recourse to some other method of peaceful settlement of the dispute;

(*b*) disputes in regard to which the other party or parties have accepted the compulsory jurisdiction of the Court only in relation to or for the purposes of the dispute in question;

(*c*) disputes in regard to which the other party or parties have accepted the compulsory jurisdiction of the Court less than 12 months prior to the filing of the application bringing the dispute before the Court;

(*d*) disputes arising prior to the date on which this Declaration was deposited with the Secretary-General of the United Nations or relating to events or situations which occurred prior to that date, even if such events or situations may continue to occur or to have effects thereafter.

2. The Kingdom of Spain may at any time, by means of a notification addressed to the Secretary-General of the United Nations, add to, amend or withdraw, in whole or in part, the foregoing reservations or any that may hereafter be added. These amendments shall become effective on the date of their receipt by the Secretary-General of the United Nations.

3. The present Declaration, which is deposited with the Secretary-General of the United Nations in conformity with Article 36, paragraph 4, of the Statute of the International Court of Justice, shall remain in force until such time as it has been withdrawn by the Spanish Government or superseded by another declaration by the latter.

The withdrawal of the Declaration shall become effective after a period of six months has elapsed from the date of receipt by the Secretary-General of the United Nations of the relevant notification by the Spanish Government. However, in respect of States which have established a period of less than six months between notification of the withdrawal of their Declaration and its becoming effective, the withdrawal of the Spanish Declaration shall become effective after such shorter period has elapsed.

Madrid, 15 October 1990.

(Signed) Francisco FERNÁNDEZ ORDÓÑEZ,
Minister for Foreign Affairs.

SUDAN

2 I 58.

I have the honour by direction of the Ministry of Foreign Affairs to declare, on behalf of the Government of the Republic of the Sudan, that in pursuance of paragraph 2 of Article 36 of the Statute of the

International Court of Justice, the Government of the Republic of the Sudan recognize as compulsory *ipso facto* and without special agreement, on condition of reciprocity, until such time as notice may be given to terminate this declaration, the jurisdiction of the International Court of Justice in all legal disputes arising after the first day of January 1956 with regard to situations or facts subsequent to that date concerning:

(a) the interpretation of a treaty concluded or ratified by the Republic of the Sudan on or after the first day of January 1956;
(b) any question of international law;
(c) the existence of any fact, which, if established, would constitute a breach of an international obligation; or
(d) the nature or extent of the reparation to be made for the breach of an international obligation;

but excluding the following:

(i) disputes in regard to which the parties to the dispute have agreed or shall agree to have recourse to some other method of peaceful settlement;
(ii) disputes in regard to matters which are essentially within the domestic jurisdiction of the Republic of the Sudan as determined by the Government of the Republic of the Sudan;
(iii) disputes arising out of events occurring during any period in which the Republic of the Sudan is engaged in hostilities as a belligerent.

New York, 30 December 1957.

(Signed) Yacoub OSMAN,
Permanent Representative of the Sudan
to the United Nations.

SURINAME

31 VIII 87.

I have the honour by direction of the Minister of Foreign Affairs of the Republic of Suriname, to declare on behalf of the Government of Suriname:

The Government of the Republic of Suriname recognizes, in accordance with Article 36, paragraph 2, of the Statute of the International Court of Justice, with effect from the seventh September 1987, as compulsory *ipso facto* and without special agreement, in relation to any other State accepting the same obligation, that is on condition of reciprocity, the jurisdiction of the said Court in all disputes, which have arisen prior to this Declaration or may arise after this Declaration, with the exception of:

(A) disputes which have arisen or may arise with respect to or in relation with the borders of the Republic of Suriname;

(B) disputes in respect of which the parties, excluding the jurisdiction of the International Court of Justice, have agreed to settlement by means of arbitration, mediation or other methods of conciliation and accommodation.

This Declaration shall be binding for a period of five years and shall continue in force after that period until twelve months after the Government of the Republic of Suriname has given notice of its termination.

New York, 31 August 1987.

(Signed) W. H. Werner VREEDZAAM,
Chargé d'affaires of the Permanent Mission
of the Republic of Suriname
to the United Nations.

SWAZILAND

26 V 69.

I, Prince Makhosini Jameson Dlamini, Prime Minister of the Kingdom of Swaziland to whom His Majesty has delegated responsibility for the conduct of foreign affairs, have the honour to declare on behalf of the Government of the Kingdom of Swaziland, that it recognizes as compulsory *ipso facto* and without special agreement, on condition of reciprocity, the jurisdiction of the International Court of Justice, in accordance with paragraph 2 of Article 36 of the Statute of the Court.

This Declaration does not extend:

(a) to disputes in respect of which the parties have agreed or shall agree to have recourse to another means of peaceful settlement; or

(b) to disputes relating to matters which, by international law, are essentially within the domestic jurisdiction of the Kingdom of Swaziland.

The Government of the Kingdom of Swaziland also reserves the right to add to, amend or withdraw this Declaration by means of a notification addressed to the Secretary-General of the United Nations, with effect as from the moment of such notification.

Mbabane, 9 May 1969.

(Signed) Makhosini Jameson DLAMINI,
Prime Minister and Minister
for Foreign Affairs.

SWEDEN[1]

[Translation from the French] 6 IV 57.

On behalf of the Royal Swedish Government, I declare that it accepts as compulsory *ipso facto* and without special agreement, in relation to any other State accepting the same obligation, the jurisdiction of the International Court of Justice, in accordance with Article 36, paragraph 2, of the Statute of the said Court, for a period of five years as from 6 April 1957. This obligation shall be renewed by tacit agreement for further periods of the same duration unless notice of abrogation is made at least six months before the expiration of any such period. The above-mentioned obligation is accepted only in respect of disputes which may arise with regard to situations or facts subsequent to 6 April 1947.

New York, 6 April 1957.

(Signed) Claes CARBONNIER,
Permanent Representative *a.i.*
of Sweden to the United Nations.

SWITZERLAND

[Translation from the French] 28 VII 48.

The Swiss Federal Council, duly authorized for that purpose by a Federal decree which was adopted on 12 March 1948 by the Federal Assembly of the Swiss Confederation and became operative on 17 June 1948,

Hereby declares that the Swiss Confederation recognizes as compulsory *ipso facto* and without special agreement, in relation to any other State accepting the same obligation, the jurisdiction of the International Court of Justice in all legal disputes concerning:

(a) the interpretation of a treaty;
(b) any question of international law;
(c) the existence of any fact which, if established, would constitute a breach of an international obligation;
(d) the nature or extent of the reparation to be made for the breach of an international obligation.

This declaration, which is made under Article 36 of the Statute of the International Court of Justice, shall take effect from the date on which the Swiss Confederation becomes a party to that Statute[2] and

[1] This declaration replaced that of 5 April 1947, which had been made for a period of ten years (United Nations, *Treaty Series*, I, No. 16, Vol. 2).
[2] Switzerland became a party to the Statute of the Court on 28 July 1948.

shall have effect as long as it has not been abrogated subject to one year's notice.

Done at Berne, 6 July 1948.

On behalf of the Swiss Federal Council:

(Signed) CELIO,
The President of the Confederation.

(Signed) LEIMGRUBER,
The Chancellor of the Confederation.

TOGO

[Translation from the French] 25 X 1979.

The Togolese Republic,

Represented by His Excellency Mr. Akanyi-Awunyo Kodjovi, Ambassador Extraordinary and Plenipotentiary, Permanent Representative of Togo to the United Nations,

Acting pursuant to the provisions of Article 36, paragraphs 2 and 3, of the Statute of the International Court of Justice, annexed to the Charter of the United Nations,

Guided by its constant concern to ensure the peaceful and equitable settlement of all international disputes, particularly those in which it might be involved, and desiring to contribute to the strengthening of the international legal order based on the principles set forth in the Charter of the United Nations,

Declares that it recognizes as compulsory *ipso facto* and without special agreement in relation to any other State accepting the same obligation, that is, subject to reciprocity, the jurisdiction of the International Court of Justice in all disputes concerning:

(a) the interpretation of a treaty;
(b) any question of international law;
(c) the existence of any fact which, if established, would constitute a breach of an international obligation;
(d) the nature or extent of the reparation to be made for the breach of an international obligation.

The present declaration has been made for an unlimited period subject to the power of denunciation and modification attached to any obligation assumed by a sovereign State in its international relations. It will enter into force on the day on which it is received by the United Nations Secretariat.

New York, 24 October 1979.

(Signed) Akanyi-Awunyo KODJOVI.

UGANDA

3 X 63.

I hereby declare on behalf of the Government of Uganda that Uganda recognizes as compulsory *ipso facto* and without special agreement, in relation to any other State accepting the same obligation, and on condition of reciprocity, the jurisdiction of the International Court of Justice in conformity with paragraph 2 of Article 36 of the Statute of the Court.

New York, 3 October 1963.

(Signed) Apollo K. KIRONDE,
Ambassador and Permanent Representative
of Uganda to the United Nations.

UNITED KINGDOM OF GREAT BRITAIN AND NORTHERN IRELAND[1]

1 I 69.

I have the honour, by direction of Her Majesty's Principal Secretary of State for Foreign and Commonwealth Affairs, to declare on behalf of the Government of the United Kingdom of Great Britain and Northern Ireland that they accept as compulsory *ipso facto* and without special convention, on condition of reciprocity, the jurisdiction of the International Court of Justice, in conformity with paragraph 2 of Article 36 of the Statute of the Court, until such time as notice may be given to terminate the acceptance, over all disputes arising after 24 October 1945, with regard to situations or facts subsequent to the same date, other than:

(i) any dispute which the United Kingdom

(a) has agreed with the other Party or Parties thereto to settle by some other method of peaceful settlement; or

(b) has already submitted to arbitration by agreement with any State which had not at the time of submission accepted the compulsory jurisdiction of the International Court of Justice;

(ii) disputes with the government of any other country which is a Member of the Commonwealth with regard to situations or facts existing before 1 January 1969;

(iii) disputes in respect of which any other Party to the dispute has accepted the compulsory jurisdiction of the International Court of Justice only in relation to or for the purpose of the dispute; or where the acceptance of the Court's compulsory jurisdiction on behalf of any other Party to the dispute was deposited or ratified less than twelve months prior to the filing of the application bringing the dispute before the Court.

---

[1] This declaration replaced that of 27 November 1963 (United Nations, *Treaty Series*, I, No. 6995, Vol. 482), notice of the withdrawal and termination of which was given by letter of 1 January 1969, received by the Secretary-General of the United Nations on that date.

2. The Government of the United Kingdom also reserve the right at any time, by means of a notification addressed to the Secretary-General of the United Nations, and with effect as from the moment of such notification, either to add to, amend or withdraw any of the foregoing reservations, or any that may hereafter be added.

New York, 1 January 1969.

(Signed) L. C. GLASS.

URUGUAY[1]

[Translation from the French] *Prior to* 28 I 21[2].

On behalf of the Government of Uruguay, I recognize, in relation to any Member or State accepting the same obligation, that is to say, on the sole condition of reciprocity, the jurisdiction of the Court as compulsory, *ipso facto* and without special convention.

(Signed) B. FERNANDEZ Y MEDINA.

ZAIRE

[Translation from the French] 8 II 89.

. . . in accordance with Article 36, paragraph 2, of the Statute of the International Court of Justice:

The Executive Council of the Republic of Zaire recognizes as compulsory *ipso facto* and without special agreement, in relation to any other State accepting the same obligation, the jurisdiction of the Court in all legal disputes concerning:

(a) the interpretation of a treaty;
(b) any question of international law;
(c) the existence of any fact which, if established, would constitute a breach of an international obligation;
(d) the nature or extent of the reparation to be made for the breach of an international obligation.

It is understood further that this declaration will remain in force until notice of its revocation is given.

(Signed) Bagbeni Adeito NZENGEYA,
Ambassador Extraordinary and Plenipotentiary,
Permanent Representative of Zaire
to the United Nations.

---

[1] An instrument of ratification was deposited on 27 September 1921. Cf. the footnote to Colombia, p. 88, above.

[2] The date on which this declaration (undated) was first published in a League of Nations document.

III. Chronological List of Other Instruments Governing the Jurisdiction of the Court

Below is a chronological list of treaties and other instruments *notified to the Registry* following registration, classification or recording at the Secretariat of the United Nations which (in addition to certain texts referred to in Section I of the present chapter, the declarations reproduced in Section II and the special agreements whereby particular cases were submitted to the Court) contain clauses relating to the jurisdiction of the Court in contentious proceedings. Such clauses generally provide that disputes concerning the application or interpretation of the instrument may be referred to the Court for decision. For each instrument, the table mentions the date and place of signature, the title of the instrument, the relevant clause and the contracting parties, and also, as far as available, the number under which it has been registered or filed and recorded by the Secretariat and the volume in the United Nations *Treaty Series* in which it has been or will be published.

Where instruments prior to 1946 are mentioned they are instruments relating to the jurisdiction of the *Permanent Court of International Justice* which have been filed and recorded by the Secretariat of the United Nations and appear in the *Treaty Series* of the United Nations.

The fact that a treaty is or is not included in this section is without prejudice to its possible application by the Court in a particular case.

Any instrument not mentioned in previous *I.C.J. Yearbooks* is indicated by an asterisk.

1933	*Place*	*Title and Clause*	*Contracting Parties*	*Treaty Series*
12 May	Ottawa	Convention concerning the rights of nationals and commercial and shipping matters (Art. 20)	Canada/France	II:545 Vol. 253
1939				
17 Dec.	Bogotá	Treaty of non-aggression, conciliation and judicial settlement (Art. XXIV)	Colombia/ Venezuela	II:896 Vol. 1257
1940				
30 Mar.	Caracas	Treaty for the pacific settlement of disputes	Brazil/Venezuela	II:195 Vol. 51
1944				
7 Dec.	Chicago	International air services transit agreement (Art. II, Sec. 2)	Multilateral	II:252 Vol. 84
7 Dec.	Chicago	International air transport agreement (Art. IV, Sec. 3)	Multilateral	II:502 Vol. 171
1946				
17 Apr.	Luxembourg	Convention concerning the Luxembourg railways (Art. 12)	Luxembourg/ Belgium/France	I:402 Vol. 27

1946 (cont.)	Place	Title and Clause	Contracting Parties	Treaty Series
4 Nov.	Nanking	Treaty of friendship, commerce and navigation (Art. XXVIII)	China[1]/ United States	I:359 Vol. 25
11 Dec.[2]	Lake Success	International convention relating to dangerous drugs, signed at Geneva, 19 Feb. 1925, as amended (Art. 32)	Multilateral	I:186 Vol. 12
11 Dec.[2]	Lake Success	International convention for limiting the manufacture and regulating the distribution of narcotic drugs, signed at Geneva on 13 July 1931, as amended (Art. 25)	Multilateral	I:186 Vol. 12
11 Dec.[2]	Lake Success	International convention for the suppression of illicit traffic in dangerous drugs, signed at Geneva on 26 June 1936, as amended (Art. 17)	Multilateral	I:186 Vol. 12
1947				
18 Apr.	Manila	Treaty of amity (Art. 2)	China[1]/Philippines	I:175 Vol. 11
9 July	Rome	Treaty of friendship and general relations (Art. V)	Italy/Philippines	I:674 Vol. 44
17 Oct.	London	Treaty regarding recognition of Burmese independence (Art. 14)	United Kingdom/ Burma	I:904 Vol. 70
12 Nov.[2]	Lake Success	Convention (concluded at Geneva on 12 Sep. 1923) for the suppression of the circulation of and traffic in obscene publications, as amended (Art. 15)	Multilateral	I:710 Vol. 46
12 Nov.[2]	Lake Success	Convention (concluded at Geneva on 11 Oct. 1933) for the suppression of traffic in women of full age, as amended (Art. 4)	Multilateral	I:772 Vol. 53
1948				
24 Jan.	Paris	Agreement concerning monetary and financial relations (Art. 23)	France/Lebanon	I:2263 Vol. 173
2 Feb.	Rome	Treaty of friendship, commerce and navigation (Art. XXVI)	United States/Italy	I:1040 Vol. 79

[1] All entries recorded throughout this Section in respect of China refer to actions taken by the authorities representing China in the United Nations at the time of those actions, and are to be understood in the light of General Assembly resolution 2758 (XXVI) of 25 October 1971.

[2] The date and place given here are those of the signature of the amending protocol.

1948 (cont.)	Place	Title and Clause	Contracting Parties	Treaty Series
30 Apr.	Bogotá	American treaty on pacific settlement	Multilateral	I:449 Vol. 30
21 May	New Delhi	Agreement relating to air services (Art. XI)	India/Sweden	I:543 Vol. 34
23 June	Karachi	Agreement relating to air services (Art. XI)	Pakistan/India	I:423 Vol. 28
28 June	Rome	Economic co-operation agreement (Art. X)	United States/Italy	I:314 Vol. 20
28 June	Paris	Economic co-operation agreement (Art. X)	United States/ France	I:302 Vol. 19
29 June	Copenhagen	Economic co-operation agreement (Art. X)	United States/ Denmark	I:338 Vol. 22
2 July	Vienna	Economic co-operation agreement (Art. IX)	United States/ Austria	I:323 Vol. 21
2 July	The Hague	Economic co-operation agreement (Art. X)	United States/ Netherlands	I:315 Vol. 20
2 July	Athens	Economic co-operation agreement (Art. X)	United States/ Greece	I:342 Vol. 23
2 July	Brussels	Economic co-operation agreement (Art. X)	United States/ Belgium	I:309 Vol. 19
3 July	Oslo	Economic co-operation agreement (Art. X)	United States/ Norway	I:317 Vol. 20
3 July	Reykjavik	Economic co-operation agreement (Art. X)	United States/ Iceland	I:316 Vol. 20
3 July	Nanking	Economic co-operation agreement (Art. XI)	United States/ China[1]	I:273 Vols. 17 and 45
3 July	Luxembourg	Economic co-operation agreement (Art. X)	United States/ Luxembourg	I:350 Vol. 24
3 July	Stockholm	Economic co-operation agreement (Art. IX)	United States/ Sweden	I:343 Vol. 23
4 July	Ankara	Economic co-operation agreement (Art. IX)	United States/ Turkey	I:351 Vol. 24
6 July	London	Economic co-operation agreement (Art. X)	United States/ United Kingdom	I:339 Vol. 22
28 Sep.	Lisbon	Economic co-operation agreement, as amended (Art. X)	United States/ Portugal	I:442 Vol. 29
6 Oct.	Beirut	Treaty concerning consular arrangements, navigation, civil and commercial rights and establishment (Art. 33)	Greece/Lebanon	I:1179 Vol. 87
15/29 Nov.	Washington	*cf.* 1961, 23 Nov.		
9 Dec.	Paris (opened for signature)	Convention on the prevention and punishment of the crime of genocide (Art. IX)	Multilateral	I:1021 Vol. 78

[1] See note 1, p. 123.

1949	*Place*	*Title and Clause*	*Contracting Parties*	*Treaty Series*
3 Jan.	Karachi	Agreement relating to air services (Art. XI)	Pakistan/Ceylon	I:428 Vol. 28
28 Apr.	Lake Success (opened for accession)	Revised general act for the pacific settlement of international disputes	Multilateral	I:912 Vol. 71
14 June	Washington	Treaty of friendship (Art. II)	Thailand/ Philippines	I:1062 Vol. 81
4 July	Berne	Convention concerning the construction and use of the Bâle-Mulhouse airport at Blotzheim (Art. 20)	France/Switzerland	I:22048 Vol. 1323
15 July	Lake Success (opened for signature)	Agreement for facilitating the international circulation of visual and auditory materials of an educational, scientific and cultural character (Art. IX)	Multilateral	I:2631 Vol. 197
30 Aug.	Ottawa	Agreement relating to air services (Art. 9)	Canada/Belgium	I:782 Vol. 53
10 Sep.	Guatemala City	Treaty of peace, friendship and co-operation (Art. 7)	Guatemala/Italy	I:1410 Vol. 102
19 Sep.	Geneva	Convention on road traffic (Art. 33)	Multilateral	I:1671 Vol. 125
20 Sep.	Beirut	Air transport agreement (Art. IX)	Netherlands/ Lebanon	I:1474 Vol. 108
20 Oct.	New Delhi	Agreement relating to air services (Art. XI)	India/Philippines	I:934 Vol. 72
31 Oct.	Tehran	Agreement relating to air services (Art. 12)	Netherlands/Iran	I:3596 Vol. 254
1950				
12 Jan.	Canberra	Agreement relating to air services (Art. XII)	Australia/Ceylon	I:789 Vol. 53
21 Jan.	Dublin	Treaty of friendship, commerce and navigation (Art. XXIII)	United States/ Ireland	I:2792 Vol. 206
27 Jan.	Mexico City	Commercial agreement (Art. VII)	Netherlands/ Mexico	I:1661 Vol. 123
18 Feb.	Tehran	Treaty of friendship (Art. IV)	Iran/Pakistan	I:2119 Vol. 161
21 Mar.	Lake Success (opened for signature)	Convention for suppression of traffic in persons and of exploitation of prostitution of others (Art. 22)	Multilateral	I:342 Vol. 96
24 Mar.	Rome	Treaty of friendship, conciliation and judicial settlement (Arts. 18-24)	Turkey/Italy	I:1338 Vol. 96
6 Aug.	Cairo	Agreement relating to air transport services (Art. XVI)	Egypt/France	I:1710 Vol. 127
16 Aug.	Wellington	Agreement relating to air services (Art. X)	New Zealand/ Canada	I:1002 Vol. 77

1950 (cont.)	Place	Title and Clause	Contracting Parties	Treaty Series
28 Aug.	Manila	Treaty of friendship, consular services and establishment (Art. II)	Greece/Philippines	I:3097 Vol. 225
16 Sep.	Brussels	Commercial agreement (Art. 7)	Belgo-Luxembourg Economic Union/ Mexico	I:2523 Vol. 188
15 Dec.	London	Trade agreement (Art. 8)	United Kingdom/ Norway	I:1459 Vol. 106
1951				
2 Feb.	Paris	Treaty of cession of the territory of the Free Town of Chandernagore (Art. XI)	India/France	I:2744 Vol. 203
22 Feb.	Oslo	Consular convention (Art. 34)	United Kingdom/ Norway	I:4713 Vol. 326
8 May	London	Agreement for air services (Art. 10)	Belgium/ United Kingdom	I:2079 Vol. 158
24 May	New Delhi	Agreement relating to air services (Art. XI)	India/Netherlands	I:1471 Vol. 108
18 June	Tehran	Agreement relating to air services (Art. 12)	Denmark/Iran	I:3602 Vol. 255
28 July	Geneva (opened for signature)	Convention relating to the status of refugees (Art. 38)	Multilateral	I:2545 Vol. 189
3 Aug.	Athens	Treaty of friendship, commerce and navigation (Art. XXVI)	Greece/ United States	I:3080 Vol. 224
23 Aug.	Washington	Treaty of friendship, commerce and navigation (Art. XXIV)	Israel/ United States	I:2979 Vol. 219
7 Sep.	Addis Ababa	Treaty of amity and economic relations (Art. XVII)	United States/ Ethiopia	I:2785 Vol. 206
8 Sep.	San Francisco	Treaty of peace with Japan (Art. 22)	Multilateral	I:1832 Vol. 136
25 Sep.	Canberra	Agreement relating to air services (Art. VIII)	Netherlands/ Australia	I:1713 Vol. 128
1 Oct.	Copenhagen	Treaty of friendship, commerce and navigation (Art. XXIV)	United States/ Denmark	I:6056 Vol. 421
31 Dec.	Paris	Consular convention (Art. 49)	France/ United Kingdom	I:4744 Vol. 330
1952				
14 Mar.	Stockholm	Consular convention (Art. 34)	Sweden/ United Kingdom	I:2731 Vol. 202
9 May	Tel Aviv	Agreement for economic assistance (Art. VIII)	United States/Israel	I:226 Vol. 177
14 June	Cairo	Agreement relating to air services (Art. XIV)	Australia/Egypt	I:2269 Vol. 173
11 July	Manila	Treaty of friendship (Art. II)	India/Philippines	I:2741 Vol. 203

1952 (cont.)	Place	Title and Clause	Contracting Parties	Treaty Series
17 July	Karachi	Agreement relating to air services (Art. XI)	Pakistan/ Netherlands	I:1980 Vol. 150
29 Aug.	Cairo	Agreement relating to air services (Art. XI)	Ethiopia/Pakistan	I:1979 Vol. 150
6 Sep.	Geneva	Universal copyright convention (Art. XV)	Multilateral	I:2937 Vol. 216
1953				
*9 Jan.		Treaty of permanent friendship (Art. VI)	Costa Rica/Spain	
31 Mar.	New York (opened for signature)	Convention on the political rights of women (Art. IX)	Multilateral	I:2613 Vol. 193
31 Mar.	New York (opened for signature)	Convention on the international right of correction (Art. V)	Multilateral	I:6280 Vol. 435
2 Apr.	Tokyo	Treaty of friendship, commerce and navigation (Art. XXIV)	United States/Japan	I:2788 Vol. 206
17 Apr.	Athens	Consular convention (Art. 35)	Greece/ United Kingdom	I:2582 Vol. 191
27 Apr.	Bangkok	Agreement relating to air services (Art. 10)	Thailand/ Philippines	I:2274 Vol. 174
23 June	New York (opened for signature)	Protocol for limiting and regulating cultivation of poppy plant, production of, international and wholesale trade in, and use of opium (Art. 15)	Multilateral	I:6555 Vol. 456
1 July	Paris (opened for signature)	Convention for the establishment of a European Organization for Nuclear Research (Art. XI)	Multilateral	I:2701 Vol. 200
14 Sep.	Colombo	Agreement for air services (Art. 11)	Netherlands/Ceylon	I:2608 Vol. 193
24 Sep.	Helsinki	Agreement concerning a supplement to the convention of 30 January 1926 for the pacific settlement of disputes	Finland/Denmark	I:2532 Vol. 188
26 Sep.	Madrid	Economic aids agreement (Art. IX)	Spain/United States	I:2802 Vol. 207
19 Oct.	Venice	Constitution of the Intergovernmental Committee for European Migration (Art. 30)	Multilateral	I:2807 Vol. 207
7 Dec.[1]	New York	Slavery convention signed at Geneva on 25 Sep. 1926, as amended (Art. 8)	Multilateral	I:2861 Vol. 212
24 Dec.	Beirut	Agreement for air services (Art. 10)	Belgium/Lebanon	I:2972 Vol. 219

[1] The date and the place given here are those at which the amending protocol was opened for signature.

1954	*Place*	*Title and Clause*	*Contracting Parties*	*Treaty Series*
16 Feb.	Paris	Convention on conditions of residence and navigation (Art. 13)	Sweden/France	I:3147 Vol. 228
3 Mar.	Bangkok	Treaty of friendship (Art. VI)	Thailand/Indonesia	I:2893 Vol. 213
20 Mar.	Mexico City	Consular convention (Art. 36)	United Kingdom/ Mexico	I:4750 Vol. 331
17 Apr.	Beirut	Agreement relating to air services (Art. XIII)	Yugoslavia/ Lebanon	I:8713 Vol. 602
12 May	London (opened for signature)	International convention for the prevention of pollution of the sea by oil (Art. XIII)	Multilateral	I:4714 Vol. 327
1 June	Rome	Consular convention (Art. 37)	United Kingdom/ Italy	I:5798 Vol. 403
28 Sep.	New York	Convention relating to the status of stateless persons (Art. 34)	Multilateral	I:5158 Vol. 360
13 Oct.	Paris (opened for signature)	International convention on the standardization of methods of analysing and appreciating wines (Art. 6)	Multilateral	I:10416 Vol. 724
23 Oct.[1]	Paris	Treaty for collaboration in economic, social and cultural matters and for collective self-defence, signed at Brussels on 17 March 1948, as amended (Art. X)	Belgium, France, Luxembourg, Netherlands, United Kingdom, Fed. Rep. of Germany, Italy	I:304 Vols. 19 and 211
29 Oct.	Washington	Treaty of friendship, commerce and navigation (Art. XXVII)	United States/ Fed. Rep. of Germany	I:3943 Vol. 273
5 Nov.	Rangoon	Treaty of peace (Art. IX)	Burma/Japan	I:3542 Vol. 251
24 Nov.	Rio de Janeiro	Agreement concerning conciliation and judicial settlement (Arts. 16-22)	Italy/Brazil	I:4146 Vol. 284
1 Dec.[2]	Paris	Agreement concerning the International Institute of Refrigeration, replacing the convention of 21 June 1920 (Art. XXXIII)	Multilateral	I:11837 Vol. 826
14 Dec.	Quito	Air transport agreement (Art. VIII)	Netherlands/ Ecuador	I:3233 Vol. 232
1955				
31 Jan.	Manila	Agreement for air services (Art. 11)	Philippines/ United Kingdom	I:2932 Vol. 216
5 Mar.	Paris	Consular convention (Art. 44)	Sweden/France	I:6150 Vol. 427

[1] The date and the place given here are those of the signature of the protocol modifying and completing the Treaty, by which Article VIII of the Treaty became Article X.

[2] The date and place given here are those of the signature of the revised Convention.

1955 *(cont.)*	*Place*	*Title and Clause*	*Contracting Parties*	*Treaty Series*
10 Aug.	Tripoli	Treaty of friendship and good neighbourliness (Art. 8)	France/Libya	
15 Aug.	Tehran	Treaty of amity, economic relations and consular rights (Art. XXI)	United States/Iran	I:4132 Vol. 284
17 Sep.	Lugano	Convention concerning the regulation of Lake Lugano (Art. XI)	Italy/Switzerland	I:4257 Vol. 291
20 Oct.	Berne	Additional protocol to the convention concerning the constitution of "Eurofima" (Art. 14)	Multilateral	I:5425 Vol. 378
21 Oct.	Beirut	Air transport agreement (Art. 11)	Denmark/Lebanon	I:3482 Vol. 248
13 Dec.	Paris	European convention on establishment (Art. 31)	Multilateral	I:7660 Vol. 529
1956				
27 Mar.	The Hague	Treaty of friendship, commerce and navigation (Art. XXV)	Netherlands/ United States	I:4154 Vol. 285
30 Apr.	Paris	Agreement on commercial rights of non-scheduled air services in Europe (Art. 4)	Multilateral	I:4494 Vol. 310
19 May	Geneva (opened for signature)	Convention on the contract for the international carriage of goods by road (Art. 47)	Multilateral	I:5742 Vol. 399
20 June	New York (opened for signature)	Convention on the recovery abroad of maintenance (Art. 16)	Multilateral	I:3850 Vol. 268
30 July	Bonn	Consular convention (Art. 41)	United Kingdom/ Fed. Rep. of Germany	I:4748 Vol. 330
30 Aug.	Manila	Treaty of friendship (Art. 2)	Philippines/ Switzerland	I:4284 Vol. 293
7 Sep.	Geneva	Supplementary convention on the abolition of slavery, the slave trade, and institutions and practices similar to slavery (Art. 10)	Multilateral	I:3822 Vol. 266
28 Nov.	Seoul	Treaty of friendship, commerce and navigation (Art. XXIV)	United States/ Rep. of Korea	I:4367 Vol. 302
11 Dec.	Athens	Convention on judicial settlement	Greece/Sweden	I:4316 Vol. 299
1957				
20 Feb.	New York (opened for signature)	Convention on the nationality of married women (Art. 10)	Multilateral	I:4468 Vol. 309
28 Feb.	Tokyo	Treaty of commerce and navigation (Art. XVIII, para. 2)	Norway/Japan	I:4054 Vol. 280

1957 (cont.)	Place	Title and Clause	Contracting Parties	Treaty Series
24 Apr.	Cairo	Declaration on the Suez Canal and the arrangements for its operation (para. 9)	Egypt[1]	I:3821 Vol. 265
29 Apr.	Strasbourg (opened for signature)	European convention of the peaceful settlement of disputes	Multilateral	I:4646 Vol. 230
23 June	Kabul	Agreement relating to air services (Art. XI)	Pakistan/ Afghanistan	I:4717 Vol. 327
23 Nov.	The Hague	Agreement relating to refugee seamen (Art. 14)	Multilateral	I:7384 Vol. 506
1958				
20 Jan.	Djakarta	Treaty of peace (Art. 6)	Japan/Indonesia	I:4688 Vol. 324
3 Feb.	The Hague	Treaty instituting the Benelux Economic Union (Art. 50)	Belgium, Luxembourg, Netherlands	I:5471 Vol. 381
5 Mar.	Stockholm	Agreement relating to air services (Art. XI)	Norway/Pakistan	I:4769 Vol. 334
6 Mar.	Stockholm	Agreement relating to air services (Art. XI)	Sweden/Pakistan	I:5656 Vol. 393
10 Apr.	Copenhagen	Agreement relating to air services (Art. XI)	Denmark/Pakistan	I:4353 Vol. 302
14 Apr.	Tehran	Agreement concerning air transport (Art. 13)	Belgium/Iran	I:5473 Vol. 381
29 Apr.	Geneva (opened for signature)	Optional protocol of signature concerning the compulsory settlement of disputes[2]	Multilateral	I:6466 Vol. 450
7 June	Karachi	Agreement relating to air services (Art. XI)	Pakistan/Portugal	I:4645 Vol. 320
4 July	Karachi	Agreement relating to air services (Art. XI)	Belgium/Pakistan	I:5569 Vol. 387
21 July	Vienna	Agreement relating to air services (Art. XI)	Austria/Afghanistan	I:9236 Vol. 645
28 Nov.	Monrovia	Agreement for the establishment and operation of air services (Art. 9)	Liberia/Netherlands	I:5651 Vol. 393
1959				
30 Jan.	Tegucigalpa	Agreement on commerce (Art. XII)	Belgium, Luxembourg, Netherlands/ Honduras	I:9234 Vol. 645
16 July	Rome	Agreement relating to air services (Art. XI)	India/Italy	I:6714 Vol. 464
12 Nov.	Washington	Treaty of friendship and commerce (Art. XXIII)	United States/ Pakistan	I:5816 Vol. 404

[1] See Sec. II, p. 90, above.

[2] This Protocol relates to disputes concerning the Geneva Conventions on the Law of the Sea of 29 April 1958.

1959 *(cont.)*	*Place*	*Title and Clause*	*Contracting Parties*	*Treaty Series*
19 Nov.	Rome	Convention placing the International Poplar Commission within the framework of FAO (Art. XV)	Multilateral	I:5902 Vol. 410
25 Nov.	Paris	Convention of establishment (Art. XVI)	United States/ France	I:5764 Vol. 401
25 Nov.	Bonn	Treaty for the promotion and protection of investments (Art. 11)	Pakistan/ Fed. Rep. of Germany	I:6575 Vol. 457
1 Dec.	Washington	Antarctic treaty (Art. XI)	Multilateral	I:5778 Vol. 402
9 Dec.	Monrovia	Agreement relating to air services (Art. VIII)	Sweden/Liberia	I:6716 Vol. 464
1960				
13 Feb.[1]	Beirut	Agreement for air transport of 24 Jan. 1949, as amended (Art. 9)	Italy/Lebanon	I:3223 Vol. 497
9 Mar.	Conakry	Air transport agreement (Art. 9)	Netherlands/Guinea	I:5646 Vol. 392
15 Mar.	Geneva	Convention relating to the unification of certain rules concerning collisions in inland navigation (Art. 14)	Multilateral	I:8310 Vol. 572
24 Mar.	Berne	Agreement concerning air services (Art. 9)	Belgium/ Switzerland	I:5996 Vol. 416
8 Apr.	The Hague	Treaty concerning arrangements for co-operation in the Ems estuary (Art. 46)	Netherlands/ Fed. Rep. of Germany	I:7404 Vol. 509
8 Apr.	The Hague	Agreement to accept the compulsory jurisdiction of the International Court of Justice in disputes concerning the interpretation or application of the revised convention on Rhine navigation, 1868	Netherlands/ Fed. Rep. of Germany	I:7404 Vol. 509
24 June	Vienna	Consular convention (Art. 45)	United Kingdom/ Austria	I:7327 Vol. 502
19 Oct.	Amman	Agreement relating to air services (Art. 9)	Belgium/Jordan	I:6959 Vol. 479
14 Dec.	Paris	Convention against discrimination in education (Art. 8)	Multilateral	I:6193 Vol. 429
14 Dec.[2]	New Delhi	Agreement of 11 July 1949 relating to air services, as amended (Art. X)	India/Australia	I:552 Vols. 35 and 425
18 Dec.	Tokyo	Treaty of friendship and commerce (Art. XIII)	Pakistan/Japan	I:6093 Vol. 423

[1] The date given here is the date of signature of the amending protocol.

[2] The date given here is that of the exchange of notes which modified the Agreement and by which Article XI became Article X.

1961	*Place*	*Title and Clause*	*Contracting Parties*	*Treaty Series*
21 Feb.	Brussels	Treaty of friendship, establishment and navigation (Art. 19)	Belgium/ United States	I:6967 Vol. 480
8 Mar.	Brussels	Consular convention (Art. 43)	Belgium/ United Kingdom	I:7554 Vol. 523
11 Mar.	Reykjavik	Exchange of notes constituting an agreement settling the fisheries dispute (para. 4)	Iceland/ United Kingdom	I:5710 Vol. 397
30 Mar.	New York	Single convention on narcotic drugs (Art. 48)	Multilateral	I:7515 Vol. 520
3 Apr.	Saigon	Treaty of amity and economic relations (Art. XIV)	United States/ Republic of Viet Nam	I:6106 Vol. 424
18 Apr.	Vienna	Optional protocol to the Vienna convention on diplomatic relations concerning the compulsory settlement of disputes	Multilateral	I:7312 Vol. 500
30 May	Madrid	Consular convention (Art. 53)	United Kingdom/ Spain	I:8198 Vol. 562
17 June	Conakry	Air transport agreement (Art. 9)	Sweden/Guinea	I:6729 Vol. 465
19 July	Reykjavik	Exchange of notes constituting an agreement concerning the fishery zone round Iceland (para. 5)	Iceland/ Fed. Rep. of Germany	I:5877 Vol. 409
27 July	Beirut	Agreement for the establishment and operation of air services (Art. XII)	Lebanon/Liberia	I:11304 Vol. 794
24 Aug.	Amman	Agreement relating to air services (Art. 9)	Netherlands/Jordan	I:6733 Vol. 466
30 Aug.	New York	Convention on the reduction of statelessness (Art. 14)	Multilateral	I:14458 Vol. 989
31 Aug.	Monrovia	Agreement relating to air services (Art. XII)	Switzerland/Liberia	I:8160 Vol. 559
26 Oct.	Rome	International convention for the protection of performers, producers of phonograms and broadcasting organizations (Art. 30)	Multilateral	I:7247 Vol. 496
23 Nov.[1]	Rome	Constitution of the International Rice Commission, adopted at Washington 15/29 Nov. 1948, as amended (Art. XI)	Multilateral	I:1613 Vol. 418
23 Nov.[1]	Rome	Agreement for the establishment of Indo-Pacific Fisheries Council, adopted at Washington 15/29 Nov. 1948, as amended (Art. III)	Multilateral	I:1615 Vol. 418

[1] The date and the place given here are those on which the Conference of the Food and Agriculture Organization of the United Nations approved the amendments to the instrument.

1962	*Place*	*Title and Clause*	*Contracting Parties*	*Treaty Series*
23 Feb.	Luxembourg	Treaty of friendship, establishment and navigation (Art. XVII)	United States/ Luxembourg	I:6868 Vol. 474
19 Mar.	Evian	*cf.* 1962, 3 July		
21 June	Paris	Air transport agreement (Art. 9)	Norway/Guinea	I:6738 Vol. 466
27 June	Copenhagen	Consular convention (Art. 36)	United Kingdom/ Denmark	I:8197 Vol. 562
29 June	Bonn	Agreement relating to air services (Art. VIII)	Norway/Liberia	I:6739 Vol. 466
3 July[1]	Paris and Rocher-Noir	Exchange of letters and declarations adopted on 19 March 1962 at the close of the Evian talks, constituting an agreement (declaration of principles relating to the settlement of disputes)	France/Algeria	I:7395 Vol. 507
14 Nov.	London	Treaty of commerce, establishment and navigation (Art. 31)	United Kingdom/ Japan	I:6934 Vol. 478
10 Dec.	New York (opened for signature)	Convention on consent to marriage, minimum age for marriage and registration of marriages (Art. 8)	Multilateral	I:7525 Vol. 521
1963				
8 Jan.	Seoul	Consular convention (Art. 16)	United States/ Republic of Korea	I:7211 Vol. 493
24 Apr.	Vienna	Optional protocol to the Vienna convention on consular relatons concerning the compulsory settlement of disputes	Multilateral	I:8640 Vol. 596
13 Aug.	Asunción	Agreement on trade and navigation (Art. XVI)	Belgium, Luxembourg, Netherlands/ Paraguay	I:8572 Vol. 592
14 Sep.	Tokyo	Convention on offences and certain other acts committed on board aircraft (Art. 24)	Multilateral	I:10106 Vol. 704
26 Oct.	Niamey	Act regarding navigation and economic co-operation between the States of the Niger Basin (Art. 7)	Multilateral	I:8506 Vol. 587
31 Oct.	Paris (opened for signature)	Protocol on privileges and immunities of the European Space Research Organization (Art. 29)	Multilateral	I:11473 Vol. 805

[1] The date and the places given here are those of the exchange of letters.

1963 *(cont.)*	*Place*	*Title and Clause*	*Contracting Parties*	*Treaty Series*
3 Dec.[1]	Rome	Agreement for the establishment of a General Fisheries Council for the Mediterranean, drawn up at Rome on 24 Sep. 1949, as amended (Art. XIII)	Multilateral	I:1691 Vol. 490
3 Dec.	Rome	Agreement for the establishment of a Commission for Controlling the Desert Locust in the Eastern Region of Its Distribution Area in South-West Asia (Art. XVII)	Multilateral	I:7663 Vol. 529
1964				
4 Feb.	Karachi	Agreement relating to scheduled air services (Art. XII, para. B, ii)	Pakistan/Lebanon	I:8863 Vol. 614
4 May	Tokyo	Consular convention (Art. 39)	United Kingdom/ Japan	I:8179 Vol. 561
19 Sep.	Beirut	Agreement relating to air services (Art. XI)	India/Lebanon	I:11820 Vol. 825
1965				
25 Jan.	Geneva	Convention on the registration of inland navigation vessels (Art. 20)	Multilateral	I:21114
18 Mar.	Washington (opened for signature)	Convention on the settlement of investment disputes between States and nationals of other States (Art. 64)	Multilateral	I:8359 Vol. 575
21 Apr.	Belgrade	Consular convention (Art. 45)	United Kingdom/ Yugoslavia	I:8620 Vol. 595
2 July	Rome	Agreement for establishment of a commission for controlling the desert locust in the Near East (Art. XVI)	Multilateral	I:8575 Vol. 592
7 July	London	Treaty for conciliation, judicial settlement and arbitration (Art. 14)	United Kingdom/ Switzerland	I:8765 Vol. 605
1966				
8 Feb.	Lomé	Treaty of amity and economic relations (Art. XIV)	United States/ Togo	I:9677 Vol. 680
15 Feb.	Geneva	Convention on the measurement of inland navigation vessels (Art. 14)	Multilateral	I:13899 Vol. 964
7 Mar.	New York (opened for signature)	International convention on the elimination of all forms of racial discrimination (Art. 22)	Multilateral	I:9464 Vol. 660

[1] The date and the place given here are those on which the Conference of the Food and Agriculture Organization of the United Nations approved the amendments to the Agreement.

1967	*Place*	*Title and Clause*	*Contracting Parties*	*Treaty Series*
31 Jan.	New York	Protocol relating to the status of refugees (Art. IV)	Multilateral	I:8791 Vol. 606
14 Feb.	Mexico City	Treaty for the prohibition of nuclear weapons in Latin America (Art. 24)	Multilateral	I:9068 Vol. 634
14 Mar.	Manila	Trade agreement (Art. IX)	Belgium, Luxembourg, Netherlands/ Philippines	I:12382 Vol. 863
24 May	Kabul	Agreement relating to air services (Art. IX)	Denmark/ Afghanistan	I:9951 Vol. 695
1 June	London	Convention on conduct of fishing operations in the North Atlantic (Art. 13)	Multilateral	I:15849 Vol. 1051
10 July	Paris	International agreement on the procedure for the establishment of tariffs for scheduled air services (Art. 4)	Multilateral	I:9971 Vol. 696
14 July[1]	Stockholm	Convention for the protection of industrial property signed at Paris on 20 March 1883, as revised (Art. 28)	Multilateral	I:11851 Vol. 828
1968				
23 Feb.	Brussels	Protocol amending the international convention for the unification of certain rules of law relating to bills of lading, signed at Brussels on 25 August 1925 (Art. 8)	Multilateral	I:23643
8 Nov.	Vienna	Convention on road traffic (Art. 52)	Multilateral	I:15705 Vol. 1042
8 Nov.	Vienna	Convention on road signs and signals (Art. 44)	Multilateral	I:16743 Vol. 1091
1969				
13 Feb.	Geneva	Agreement establishing the European Molecular Biology Conference (Art. VIII)	Multilateral	I:10462 Vol. 727
23 May	Vienna	Convention on the law of treaties (Art. 66)	Multilateral	I:18232 Vol. 1155
25 July	Boston	International health regulations (Art. 106)	Multilateral	I:10921 Vol. 764
2 Sep.	Washington	Consular convention (Art. 46)	Belgium/ United States	I:13178 Vol. 924
8 Sep.	Mexico City	Convention on the privileges and immunities of the Agency for the Prohibition of Nuclear Weapons in Latin America (Art. 7)	Multilateral	I:16545
30 Dec.	Belgrade	Consular convention (Art. 46)	Belgium/ Yugoslavia	I:13441 Vol. 943

[1] The date and the place given here are those of the signature of the revised Convention.

1970	*Place*	*Title and Clause*	*Contracting Parties*	*Treaty Series*
23 Apr.	Brussels	International convention on travel contracts (Art. 32, para. 2)	Multilateral	I:21051
19 June	Washington	Treaty on patent co-operation (Art. 59)	Multilateral	I:18336 Vol. 1160
1 Dec.	Rome	Agreement for the establishment of a commission for controlling the desert locust in North-West Africa (Art. XVI)	Multilateral	I:11354 Vol. 797
16 Dec.	The Hague	Convention on the suppression of the unlawful seizure of aircraft (Art. 12, para. 1)	Multilateral	I:12325 Vol. 860
1971				
21 Feb.	Vienna	Convention on psychotropic substances (Art. 31)	Multilateral	I:14956 Vol. 1019
14 July	Brussels	Treaty of commerce (Art. 11)	Belgium, Luxembourg, Netherlands/ USSR	I:12656 Vol. 883
17 July	Accra	Agreement for the provision of a special loan to the Government of the Republic of Ghana to facilitate the payment of medium term commercial debts (Art. VII)	United Kingdom/ Ghana	I:11467 Vol. 805
24 July[1]	Paris	Convention for the protection of literary and artistic works signed at Berne on 9 September 1886, as revised (Art. 33)	Multilateral	I:25986
24 July	Paris	Universal copyright convention, signed at Geneva on 6 September 1952, as revised (Art. XV)	Multilateral	I:13444 Vol. 943
23 Sep.	Montreal	Convention for the suppression of unlawful acts against the safety of civil aviation (Art. 14)	Multilateral	I:14118 Vol. 974
6 Oct.	Paris	Convention on the establishment of the International Institute for the Management of Technology (Art. 7)	Multilateral	I:14566 Vol. 995
1972				
28 Apr.	Ankara	Consular convention (Art. 58)	Belgium/Turkey	I:15142 Vol. 1029
16 May	Basle	European convention on State immunity (Art. 34)	Multilateral	I:25699

[1] The date and the place given here are those of the signature of the revised Convention.

1973	*Place*	*Title and Clause*	*Contracting Parties*	*Treaty Series*
10 May	Geneva	Agreement establishing the European Molecular Biology Laboratory (Art. XII)	Multilateral	I: 13668 Vol. 954
12 June	The Hague	Protocol relating to refugee seamen (Art. II)	Multilateral	I: 13928 Vol. 965
22 June	Rome	Agreement for the establishment of a Regional Animal Production and Health Commission for Asia, the Far East and the South-West Pacific (Art. XX)	Multilateral	I: 14604 Vol. 997
5 Oct.	Munich	Convention on the grant of European patents (Art. 173)	Multilateral	I: 16208
19 Nov.	Montevideo	Treaty of the La Plata River and its maritime limits (Art. 87)	Uruguay/Argentina	I: 21424 Vol. 1295
30 Nov.	New York	International convention on the suppression and punishment of the crime of *apartheid* (Art. XII)	Multilateral	I: 14861 Vol. 1015
14 Dec.	New York	Convention on the prevention and punishment of crimes against internationally protected persons, including diplomatic agents (Art. 13)	Multilateral	I: 15410 Vol. 1035
1974				
19 Feb.	Madrid	Agreement on the delimitation of the continental shelf (Art. 3, para. 2)	Italy/Spain	
22 Mar.	Helsinki	Convention on the protection of the marine environment of the Baltic Sea area (Art. 18, para. 2)	Multilateral	I: 18338
16 May	Khartoum	Agreement relating to the joint exploitation of the natural resources of the sea-bed and subsoil of the Red Sea in the common zone (Art. XVI)	Sudan/ Saudi Arabia	I: 13605 Vol. 952
1975				
26 Feb.	Salto	Treaty concerning the status of the river Uruguay (Art. 60)	Uruguay/ Argentina	I: 21425 Vol. 1295
8 Aug.	New York	Single convention on narcotic drugs, 1961, as amended (Art. 48)	Multilateral	I: 14152 Vol. 1976
1977				
24 May	Athens	Agreement on the delimitation of the respective continental shelves of the two States (Art. IV)	Greece/Italy	I: 21048 Vol. 1275

1978	Place	Title and Clause	Contracting Parties	Treaty Series
5 July	Geneva	Protocol to the convention on the contract for the international carriage of goods by road (CMR) (Art. 8)	Multilateral	I:19487 Vol. 1208
1979				
30 Mar.	Geneva	International agreement on olive oil (Art. 14, para. 2)	Multilateral	I:19674 Vol. 1219
10 May	Manila	Treaty of amity, commerce and navigation (Art. XV, para. 2)	Japan/Philippines	I:20979 Vol. 1272
8 Apr.	Vienna	Constitution of the United Nations Industrial Development Organization (UNIDO) (Art. 22, para. 1 *(b)*)	Multilateral	I:23432 Vol. 1401
17 Dec.	New York	International convention against the taking of hostages (Art. 16, para. 1)	Multilateral	I:21931 Vol. 1316
18 Dec.	New York	Convention on the elimination of all forms of discrimination against women (Art. 29)	Multilateral	I:20378 Vol. 1249
1980				
20 May	Canberra	Convention on the conservation of Antarctic marine living resources	Multilateral	I:22301
30 Oct.	Lima	General peace treaty (Arts. 31-36 and 39)	El Salvador/ Honduras	I:21856 Vol. 1310
1981				
23 Jan.	Cotonou	Agreement concerning technical co-operation (Art. XI)	Switzerland/Benin	I:19804 Vol. 1226
1984				
10 Dec.	New York	Convention against torture and other cruel, inhuman or degrading treatment or punishment (Art. 30, para. 1)	Multilateral	I:24841
1985				
22 Mar.	Vienna	Vienna convention for the protection of the ozone layer (Art. 11)	Multilateral	I:26164
10 Dec.	New York	International convention against *apartheid* in sports (Art. 19)	Multilateral	I:25822
1986				
21 Mar.	Vienna	Vienna convention on the law of treaties between States and international organizations or between international organizations (Art. 66, para. 2)	Multilateral	
1988				
10 Mar.	Rome	Convention for the suppression of unlawful acts against the safety of maritime navigation (Art. 18, para. 1)	Multilateral	I:29004

1988 *(cont.)*	*Place*	*Title and Clause*	*Contracting Parties*	*Treaty Series*
20 Dec.	Vienna	United Nations convention against illicit traffic in narcotic drugs and psychotropic substances (Art. 32)	Multilateral	I:27627
1989				
4 Dec.	New York	International convention against the recruitment, use, financing and training of mercenaries (Art. 17, para. 1)	Multilateral	
1991				
*25 Feb.	Espoo	Convention on environmental impact assessment in a transboundary context (Art. 15, para. 2)	Multilateral	
1 Mar.	Montreal	Convention on the marking of plastic explosives for the purpose of detection (Art. XI, para. 1)	Multilateral	
1992				
17 March	Helsinki	Convention on the protection and use of transboundary watercourses and international lakes (Art. 22, para. 1)	Multilateral	
9 May	New York	United Nations framework convention on climate change	Multilateral	
5 June	Rio de Janeiro	Convention on biological diversity (Art. 27, para. 3)	Multilateral	
1993				
13 Jan.	Paris	Convention on the prohibition of the development, production, stockpiling and use of chemical weapons and on their destruction (Art. XIV, para. 2)	Multilateral	
1994				
14 June	Oslo	Protocol to the 1979 Convention on long-range transboundary air pollution on further reduction of sulphur emissions (Art. 9)	Multilateral	

CHAPTER V

FUNCTIONING AND PRACTICE OF THE COURT

In matters concerning its administration and procedure, the International Court of Justice applies Articles 21, 22 and 39-68 of its Statute and Articles 12, 19-31 and 38-109 of its Rules.

I. Seat

The seat of the Court is established at The Hague (Netherlands); this however, does not prevent the Court from sitting and exercising its functions elsewhere whenever the Court considers it desirable to do so (Statute, Art. 22, para. 1; Rules, Art. 55).

The Court occupies, in the Peace Palace at The Hague, the premises formerly occupied by the *Permanent Court of International Justice* as well as a new wing built at the expense of the Netherlands Government and inaugurated in 1978.

An agreement of 21 February 1946 between the United Nations and the Carnegie Foundation, which is responsible for the administration of the Peace Palace, determines the conditions under which the Court uses these premises. The agreement was approved by the General Assembly of the United Nations in resolution 84 (I) of 11 December 1946. It provides for the payment to the Carnegie Foundation of an annual contribution (see Chap. VIII, p. 322, below).

II. Administration

1. The Presidency and the Committees of the Court

The President shall preside at all meetings of the Court; he shall direct the work and supervise the administration of the Court (Rules, Art. 12)[1].

Decisions which have to be taken by the Court on administrative matters are prepared by a Budgetary and Administrative Committee composed of the President, the Vice-President and five judges who are elected annually (at present Judges Guillaume, Shahabuddeen, Ranjeva, Shi and Fleischhauer).

---

[1] Occasionally the President is requested by third persons to undertake tasks outside the judicial work of the Court. These activities are described at the end of this chapter (pp. 158-159, below).

In 1967 the Court established a Committee on Relations. Its present members are Judges Weeramantry, Herczegh and Vereshchetin. This committee is responsible for preparing plans and programmes with a view to the wider dissemination of information on the work of the Court and the maintenance of its relations with other United Nations organs, the specialized agencies, and international bodies and conferences concerned with the codification and progressive development of international law.

In 1970 the Court established a Library Committee (at present Judges Weeramantry, Ranjeva, Herczegh, Shi and Koroma) to review the programme of acquisitions for the library of the Court and supervise the continuous modernization of its services.

In 1979 the Court constituted the Rules Committee as a standing body. Its members are at present Judges Oda, Guillaume, Fleischhauer, Koroma, Ferrari Bravo and Higgins.

Each year, in application of Article 11 of the Staff Regulations for the Registry, which came into force in 1979, the Court elects a Judge and Alternate Judge for Staff Appeals. Judges Weeramantry and Fleischhauer, respectively, hold these offices at present.

2. *The Registry*

The Registry is the administrative organ of the Court. Its role is defined by the Statute and the Rules (in particular Rules, Arts. 22-29). The organization of the Registry is prescribed by the Court on proposals submitted by the Registrar, and Instructions for the Registry are drawn up by the Registrar and approved by the Court (Rules, Art. 28, paras. 2 and 3). The instructions drawn up in October 1946 were amended in March 1947 and September 1949 (*I.C.J. Yearbook 1946-1947*, pp. 72-87; *I.C.J. Yearbook 1949-1950*, p. 24).

(a) *The Registrar and the Deputy-Registrar*

The Court appoints its Registrar from among candidates proposed by Members of the Court; he is elected for a term of seven years and may be re-elected (Statute, Art. 21, para. 2; Rules, Art. 22). The Court also appoints a Deputy-Registrar, under the same conditions and in the same way as the Registrar (Rules, Art. 23).

The general functions of the Registrar are defined by the Rules of Court (Art. 26) and the Instructions for the Registry (Art. 1). Under the Instructions: "the Registrar is responsible for all departments of the Registry. The Staff is under his control and he alone is authorized to direct the work of the Registry, of which he is the Head." He is assisted by the Deputy-Registrar and, in the event of his absence, is replaced by the Deputy-Registrar or, failing him, an official of the Registry appointed by the President (Rules, Art. 27; Instructions for the Registry, Arts. 2 and 42).

The present Registrar is Mr. Eduardo Valencia-Ospina, of Colombian nationality, who was elected on 19 February 1987 and re-elected on 15 February 1994 for a term of 7 years, as from 19 February 1994. He was previously the Court's Deputy-Registrar (1984-1987) and before that had served as the senior legal officer of the Codification Division at the Office of Legal Affairs in the United Nations Secretariat.

On 15 February 1994 the Court elected Mr. Jean-Jacques Arnaldez to the post of Deputy-Registrar for a term of 7 years, as from 19 February 1994. Mr. Arnaldez, who is of French nationality, was previously Legal Counsel in a Paris international law firm (1977-1982) and Counsel in the International Court of Arbitration of the International Chamber of Commerce (ICC) in Paris (1982-1994).

Previous Registrars of the Court were E. Hambro (1946-1953), J. López-Oliván (1953-1960), J. Garnier-Coignet (1960-1966), S. Aquarone (1966-1980) and S. Torres Bernárdez (1980-1986). Previous Deputy-Registrars were J. Garnier-Coignet (1946-1960), S. Aquarone (1960-1966), W. Tait (1966-1976), A. Pillepich (1977-1984), E. Valencia-Ospina (1984-1987), and B. Noble (1987-1994).

(b) *Departments of the Registry*

The officials of the Registry are appointed by the Court on proposals submitted by the Registrar (Statute, Art. 21, para. 2; Rules, Art. 25). General Service category and temporary staff, however, are appointed by the Registrar (Rules, Art. 25; Staff Regulations for the Registry, Art. 5; Instructions for the Registry, Art. 4).

All officials of the Registry, whether permanent or temporary, must be proficient in English and French and those whose work involves linguistic responsibilities must have one of these languages as their first language.

The following table gives a list of officials employed by the Registry (both on a permanent basis and under fixed-term contracts) as at 31 July 1996, showing the posts they occupy with references, where appropriate, to the articles of the Instructions for the Registry in which their duties are defined.

	Date of assumption of duties	*Nationality*
Secretaries of the Court (Art. 43)		
Principal Legal Secretary		
Ph. Couvreur	13 April 1982	Belgian
First Secretaries		
Ms F. Meadows	1 January 1995	British
A. Brouillet	13 June 1988	French

Secretary		
A. Th. Witteveen In charge of information matters	15 July 1975	Dutch
Linguistic Staff		
Mrs. J. E. Bouri	1 July 1986	British
F. Mengin	5 May 1986	French
H. Sutcliffe	1 January 1995	British
Mrs. D. M. Pierfederici	1 January 1994	French
Legal Officers		
J.-P. Isselé	5 April 1988	French
F. Ouguergouz	1 February 1995	Algerian
E. Ward	1 January 1996	American
Administrative Assistants		
Miss M. D. Donnelly	1 January 1985	British
Mrs. M. G. A. van Haasbergen	1 March 1985	French
Miss V. Primas	1 January 1990	French
Mrs. C. Wainwright	1 January 1990	Australian
Establishment (Arts. 54-66)		
M. Mendella Accountant/Establishment Officer, Head of Department	1 April 1986	Canadian
Mrs. S. Claesson	1 January 1996	Swedish
C. Uriot	1 March 1981	Dutch
B. J. van Veen	1 March 1982	Dutch
T. Komnenović	1 August 1973	Yugoslav
H. Laeijendecker	1 January 1994	Dutch
Telephonists-Receptionists		
Mrs. J. Koot-Jager	1 March 1978	Dutch
Mrs. E. Keijman	1 April 1978	Dutch
Messengers		
I. J. van der Meer Co-ordinator	1 June 1980	Dutch
F. Koch	1 September 1985	Dutch
D. Driessen	1 April 1982	Dutch
Security Guards		
R. Pijl	1 January 1990	Dutch
Mrs. M. Buan	1 October 1991	Dutch

Shorthand and Typewriting Department (Art. 53)

Mrs. N. Juszezak Head of Department	1 January 1979	French
Mrs. C. Blom-Rakoto	5 September 1983	French and Malagasy
Mrs. D. Roodbol-Sourisseau	1 January 1990	French
Mrs. N. Barnes	1 January 1996	British
Mrs. M. Steenbergen	9 April 1996	Belgian
G. D'Olivo	4 February 1982	Italian and Dutch
E. van Heeswijk	16 August 1993	Dutch

Judges' Secretaries

Mrs. M. de Meyier Co-ordinator	1 January 1982	French and Dutch
Mrs. R. Snoeck	10 January 1977	French and Dutch
Miss W. Ch. Deelder	1 July 1982	Dutch
Mrs. J. E. van Hamel-Newall	1 November 1985	British
Mrs. L. Speeleveld	1 January 1986	Belgian
Miss H. H. Muyen	1 June 1987	Dutch
Mrs. M. Cleary-Cogan	1 January 1990	British
Mrs. A. Rowland-Moore	1 January 1990	British
Miss M. Sullivan	1 January 1990	British
Mrs. D. Bloemendaal	1 April 1990	British
Mrs. J. Devisme	1 January 1986	French
Miss Ch. L. Kamers	8 March 1993	Dutch
Miss H. E. Jeffares	1 October 1993	Irish
Mrs. M.-F. Teven	1 February 1995	French

Archives (Arts. 44-52)

S. R. S. Bedi Head of Department	16 September 1985	Indian
P. Ferreira	1 December 1995	Portuguese
D. van Rooy	16 April 1975	Dutch
S. Cantarella	9 April 1981	Italian
M. Sow	1 August 1985	Senegalese
J. Pronk	1 January 1981	Dutch

Printing Department (Arts. 67-69)

P. Vio Head of Department	1 June 1974	Italian
S. H. Herd	1 August 1987	British

Documents Department (Arts. 70-73)

A. C. G. M. Eyffinger Librarian, Head of Department	1 February 1988	Dutch
Mrs. R. S. B. van Megen	13 August 1973	Dutch
M. Schiethart	1 January 1981	Dutch
G. Vooijs	1 January 1981	Dutch

(c) *Staff Regulations for the Registry*

Article 28, paragraph 4, of the Rules of Court states:

> "The staff of the Registry shall be subject to Staff Regulations drawn up by the Registrar, so far as possible in conformity with the United Nations Staff Regulations and Staff Rules, and approved by the Court."

On 7 March 1979 the Court adopted new Staff Regulations for the Registry, which are reproduced in Chapter VI of the *I.C.J. Yearbook 1978-1979* (pp. 127-131). In November 1987 these Staff Regulations were amended (see *I.C.J. Yearbook 1988-1989*, pp. 163-164).

Before 1979 staff members of the Registry had been subject to Staff Regulations adopted by the President and approved by the Court in March 1947 in accordance with Article 18, paragraph 2, of the 1946 Rules of Court; these Staff Regulations had been amended in February and March 1950 and in June 1951 (see *I.C.J. Yearbook 1946-1947*, pp. 66-71; *I.C.J. Yearbook 1949-1950*, pp. 23-24; *I.C.J. Yearbook 1950-1951*, pp. 25-27).

(d) *Privileges and immunities*

In the Netherlands, in accordance with the terms of an exchange of letters, dated 26 June 1946, between the President of the Court and the Minister for Foreign Affairs of the Netherlands, the Registrar is, in a general way, accorded the same treatment as heads of diplomatic missions accredited to Her Majesty the Queen of the Netherlands, and officials of the Registry are treated as officials of comparable rank attached to diplomatic missions at The Hague (*I.C.J. Acts and Documents No. 5*, pp. 201-207).

By resolution 90 (I) of 11 December 1946 (*ibid.*, pp. 207-211) the General Assembly of the United Nations recommended that, on journeys in connection with the exercise of his functions, the Registrar should enjoy all the privileges, immunities and facilities granted to diplomatic envoys and that the officials of the Registry should, in the same circumstances, enjoy such privileges, immunities and facilities for residence and travel as may be necessary for the independent exercise of their functions.

This resolution also contains a recommendation calling upon Members of the United Nations to recognize and accept the United Nations laissez-passer issued to the Registrar and officials of the Registry by the Court. Such laissez-passer have been issued since 1950. They are similar in form to those issued by the Secretary-General of the United Nations. They are signed by the President of the Court and by the Registrar.

3. *Relations with the Public*

(a) *Correspondence*

Article 26, paragraph 1 *(a)*, of the Rules of Court states that the Registrar shall "be the regular channel for communications to and from the Court".

Consequently, correspondence should be addressed to *The Registrar, International Court of Justice, Peace Palace, 2517 KJ The Hague, Netherlands* (telegraphic address: INTERCOURT THE HAGUE; Telex: 32323; Telefax (3170) 364 99 28). It should be written in either English or French[1].

A special issue of postage stamps is used by the Netherlands postal administration for the franking of correspondence from the Court.

The Court's telephone number is (3170) 302 23 23.

(b) *Access to the Court's library and archives*

The library of the Court is separate from the library of the Peace Palace, which is situated in the same building but is administered by the Carnegie Foundation. The relations between the two libraries were the subject of an exchange of notes dated 29 and 30 July 1946 (*I.C.J. Yearbook 1946-1947*, pp. 98-99). The public has access to the Peace Palace Library, but the library of the Court is private.

The Court's library keeps the archives of the Nuremberg *International Military Tribunal*, as entrusted to the Court pursuant to a decision of that Tribunal dated 1 October 1946. These archives, which relate solely to the trial of the major war criminals tried in 1945-1946, may be consulted on written application to the Registrar.

Neither the archives of the Court itself nor those of the *Permanent Court of International Justice* are open to the public (Rules, Art. 26, para. 1 *(n)*).

(c) *Information*

Article 26, paragraph 1 *(k)* and *(m)*, of the Rules of Court provides that the Registrar shall "deal with enquiries concerning the Court and its work" and "ensure that information concerning the Court and its activities is made accessible to governments, the highest national courts of justice, professional and learned societies, legal faculties and schools

---

[1] It is not possible for the Registry to give legal advice or to enter into correspondence with private persons concerning any matter at issue between them and the authorities of their own or another country.

of law, and public information media". For the purpose of carrying out this function, the Registrar is assisted by one of the Secretaries.

The Registrar arranges as he considers necessary for the publication of information concerning the composition, jurisdiction and work of the Court, and the cases before the Court[1].

The following documentation, issued separately in English and in French, is available free of charge on application to the Registry:

Press Communiqués;

Background Notes, of which four are available:

- *II* and *II bis. Synopsis of cases referred to the International Court of Justice (1947-1969* and *1969-1976);*
- *IV. Note by the Registry indicating the Rules of Court amended on 10 May 1972;*
- *V. Note by the Registry on the Revised Rules of Court (1978);*
- *VI. Collected unofficial summaries of decisions concerning the law of the sea (1946-1986).*

Also obtainable, from the Registry or United Nations Information Centres, are:

– a popular handbook on *The International Court of Justice*, published in Arabic, Chinese, English, French, Russian, Spanish and German editions, which is in particular distributed in the framework of the United Nations Programme of Assistance in the Teaching, Study, Dissemination and Wider Appreciation of International Law;

– unofficial Arabic, Chinese, Russian and Spanish texts of the Rules of Court.

A film on the Court by the United Nations Department of Public Information is also available on application to that Department or to a United Nations Information Centre.

Groups often ask to visit the Registry and have the way the Court functions explained to them. So far as the work of the Court permits, the Registrar accedes to requests of this kind. During the period under review the Court received a great number of groups including diplomats, scholars and academics, judges and representatives of judicial authorities, lawyers and legal professionals, as well as others, amounting to some 3,500 persons in all.

Information on the assistance given members of the public and representatives of the press to help them follow the proceedings in cases before the Court will be found within the following section (pp. 152, 153, 157).

---

[1] These publications are distinct from the publications of the Court issued by the Registry: see below, Chap. VII, pp. 287-289.

III. Practice in Regard to Procedure[1]

1. General

(a) *Official languages*

The official languages of the Court are French and English (Statute, Art. 39; Rules, Arts. 51, 70 and 71).

(b) *Official communications*

In all cases submitted to the Court, communications and documents for the Court are delivered to the Registrar and he is the regular channel for communications or notifications from the Court (Rules, Art. 26, para. 1, and Art. 30; Instructions for the Registry, Arts. 3, 11 and 13).

Communications in a case which are intended for a State party thereto are sent to its agent at the Hague address it designates for the purpose (Rules, Art. 40, para. 1).

For communications with other States, the Registrar requests the foreign ministers of States entitled to appear before the Court to indicate the channel through which their governments would wish to receive such communications. The channel of communication indicated is usually the Embassy in The Hague or the Ministry of Foreign Affairs of the State in question.

For public international organizations, the Registrar addresses the communications of the Court to the Director-General or Secretary-General of the organization as the case may be.

(c) *Minutes*

The Registrar is present at all sittings and meetings of the Court and is responsible for drawing up the minutes. After being signed by the President and the Registrar, these minutes are filed in the archives

---

[1] For decisions taken by the Court involving the application of its Statute and Rules in procedural matters, see *I.C.J. Yearbook 1962-1963*, pp. 91-137; *I.C.J. Yearbook 1963-1964*, pp. 99-109; *I.C.J. Yearbook 1964-1965*, pp. 87-88; *I.C.J. Yearbook 1965-1966*, pp. 91-92; *I.C.J. Yearbook 1966-1967*, p. 87; *I.C.J. Yearbook 1967-1968*, pp. 87-92; *I.C.J. Yearbook 1968-1969*, pp. 108-112; *I.C.J. Yearbook 1969-1970*, pp. 113-115; *I.C.J. Yearbook 1970-1971*, pp. 109-113; *I.C.J. Yearbook 1971-1972*, pp. 123-125; *I.C.J. Yearbook 1972-1973*, pp. 136-143; *I.C.J. Yearbook 1973-1974*, pp. 125-129; *I.C.J. Yearbook 1974-1975*, pp. 120-123; *I.C.J. Yearbook 1975-1976*, pp. 118-123; *I.C.J. Yearbook 1976-1977*, pp. 113-114; *I.C.J. Yearbook 1977-1978*, pp. 111-119; *I.C.J. Yearbook 1978-1979*, pp. 124-131; *I.C.J. Yearbook 1979-1980*, pp. 125-129; *I.C.J. Yearbook 1980-1981*, pp. 133-137; *I.C.J. Yearbook 1981-1982*, pp. 141-147; *I.C.J. Yearbook 1982-1983*, pp. 125-126; *I.C.J. Yearbook 1983-1984*, pp. 140-141; *I.C.J. Yearbook 1984-1985*, pp. 173-184; *I.C.J. Yearbook 1985-1986*, pp. 164-172; *I.C.J. Yearbook 1986-1987*, pp. 158-163; *I.C.J. Yearbook 1987-1988*, pp. 146-151; *I.C.J. Yearbook 1988-1989*, pp. 159-164; *I.C.J. Yearbook 1989-1990*, pp. 157-162; *I.C.J. Yearbook 1990-1991*, pp. 174-182; *I.C.J. Yearbook 1991-1992*, pp. 198-204; *I.C.J. Yearbook 1992-1993*, pp. 242-248; *I.C.J. Yearbook 1993-1994*, pp. 209-216; *I.C.J. Yearbook 1994-1995*, pp. 199-206; and pp. 224-240 in Chapter VI, below.

(Statute, Art. 47; Rules, Art. 21, Art. 26, para. 1 *(f)-(i)*, and Art. 71; Instructions for the Registry, Art. 19).

(d) *General List*

The Registrar prepares and keeps up to date a General List of cases submitted to the Court (Rules, Art. 26, para. 1 *(b)*, and Art. 38, para. 5; Instructions for the Registry, Art. 6, para. 1, and Art. 46, para. 3).

Extracts from the General List are supplied by the Registry on request, in the form of *Background Notes II* and *II bis: Synopsis of cases referred to the International Court of Justice (1947-1969* and *1969-1976)*.

(For the General List of the *Permanent Court of International Justice*, see *P.C.I.J., Series E, No. 16,* pp. 92-147.)

2. *Procedure in Contentious Cases*

(a) *Institution of proceedings and appointment of agents*

As soon as proceedings are instituted (see Chap. III, pp. 70-71, above), the special agreement or the application, filed in one of the two official languages of the Court, is translated and printed in a bilingual edition by the Registry, then communicated to all concerned and to the States entitled to appear before the Court (Statute, Art. 40; Rules, Art. 38, paras. 4 and 5; Art. 39, para. 1, and Art. 42).

The Registrar arranges for the publication of a communiqué informing the general public and the press that proceedings have been instituted. Copies of the special agreement or application may be obtained on request.

The party which files a document instituting proceedings informs the Court at the same time of the name of the agent who will be its representative in the proceedings and take steps on its behalf; the other party then appoints its agent as soon as possible (Statute, Art. 42; Rules, Art. 40). A party may also appoint a co-agent, a deputy-agent or an additional agent. Agents, and counsel and advocates also, enjoy such privileges and immunities as may be required for the independent exercise of their duties (Statute, Art. 42, para. 3; *I.C.J. Acts and Documents No. 5*, pp. 205 and 209).

The President, who is required to ascertain the views of the parties on questions of procedure, summons the agents to meet him as soon as possible after their appointment and whenever necessary thereafter (Rules, Art. 31).

(b) *Written proceedings*

The written proceedings comprise the filing of pleadings within time-limits fixed in orders made by the Court or, if it is not sitting, the

President; the pleadings are in principle confined to a Memorial and a Counter-Memorial, though the Court may if it thinks fit authorize or direct that there be a Reply and a Rejoinder (Statute, Art. 43; Rules, Arts. 44-46 and 48; Instructions for the Registry, Art. 14).

The party's submissions are set out in each pleading (Rules, Art. 49).

The agent of the party filing the pleading supplies the Registry (Statute, Art. 43, paras. 3 and 4; Rules, Arts. 50-52) with the following:

- an original copy of the pleading, signed by him, to which is annexed a certified copy of any relevant document adduced in support of the contentions put forward;
- an English or French translation, certified by him to be accurate, of any part of a pleading or annexed document submitted in another language;
- a copy, certified by him, of the pleading and annexed documents, for communication to the other party;
- 125 further copies of the pleading and annexed documents;
- in the case of any document of which only parts are relevant and only necessary extracts have been annexed to the pleading, a copy of the whole document.

The format for the pleadings and annexes is 19 × 26 cm. If they are submitted in printed form, which is not compulsory, it is recommended that the Court's Typographical Rules (supplied by the Registry on request) be complied with. If the composition is entrusted to one of the printers who work for the Court, so that it is not necessary to re-compose the texts when they come to be used in the Court's series *Pleadings, Oral Arguments, Documents* (see *(e)* below), the Court will at that stage reimburse half the cost, at the normal rate, of the composition of the pleading itself and of such annexes as are to be reproduced in the *Pleadings* series (but excluding any text in a language other than English or French or entirely reproduced from another printed pleading).

The Registry usually translates, for the judges, pleadings and annexed documents, filed in one of the official languages of the Court, into the other official language (Rules, Art. 26, para. 1 *(g)*).

The Registrar arranges for the publication of communiqués giving information concerning the course of the written proceedings. Moreover, the Court may, after ascertaining the views of the parties, communicate the pleadings on request to any State entitled to appear before the Court. It may also, after ascertaining the parties' views, make the pleadings available to the general public and the press on or after the opening of the oral proceedings (Rules, Art. 53); this is generally done by depositing copies in a number of Information Centres and libraries, including the Peace Palace Library. The pagination of the pleadings and annexed documents which may thus be made accessible is provisional in character. They are not given their final pagination until they are published in the *I.C.J. Pleadings* series (see *(e)* below).

(c) *Oral proceedings*

Upon the closure of the written proceedings, a case is ready for hearing. The opening date of the oral proceedings is fixed by the Court or, if it is not sitting, the President (Rules, Art. 54). Public sittings are held at the seat of the Court, usually from 10 a.m. to 1 p.m. on weekdays. They are devoted to hearing the arguments of counsel and such evidence of witnesses or experts as the parties may call; the Court itself may also arrange for a witness to be heard, entrust any individual, body or organization with the task of giving an expert opinion or decide on an inspection *in loco*[1] (Statute, Arts. 43-46 and 48-51; Rules, Arts. 57-68; Instructions for the Registry, Art. 20).

The Court settles the order in which the parties are heard, the number of counsel who will address the Court, and the method of handling the evidence (Rules, Art. 58, para. 2). It is customary for the parties to present their arguments in the order in which their pleadings have been deposited or, in the case of proceedings instituted by special agreement, in the order laid down by the Court after consultations with the agents of the parties. Speeches and statements are normally made in one of the Court's two official languages and are (simultaneously) interpreted into the other; arrangements may be made for some other language to be used (Statute, Art. 39; Rules, Art. 70; Instructions for the Registry, Art. 17).

When the Court or a judge puts a question to the agents, counsel and advocates, the answer may be given either immediately or within a time-limit fixed by the President; if given in writing it is communicated to the other party (Rules, Art. 61, paras. 2-4, and Art. 72).

A provisional verbatim record of each public sitting is drawn up by the Registry in the official language used, and translated into the other; copies in the original official language are then communicated to the parties

---

[1] In the *Corfu Channel (United Kingdom* v. *Albania)* case, the Court heard witnesses and experts presented by each of the Parties, appointed experts by Order and prescribed an enquiry on the spot. In the *Temple of Preah Vihear (Cambodia* v. *Thailand)* case, it heard witnesses and experts presented by each of the Parties. In the *South West Africa (Ethiopia* v. *South Africa; Liberia* v. *South Africa)* cases, it heard witnesses and experts presented by one Party, but did not accede to a request concerning an inspection *in loco*. In *Continental Shelf (Tunisia/Libyan Arab Jamahiriya)*, it heard an expert presented by one Party. The Chamber constituted in the *Delimitation of the Maritime Boundary in the Gulf of Maine Area (Canada/United States of America)* case heard an expert presented by one Party and itself appointed, by Order, at the request of the Parties and in accordance with the Special Agreement concluded between them, a technical expert to assist it in its work. In the case concerning the *Continental Shelf (Libyan Arab Jamahiriya/Malta)*, the Court heard experts presented by each of the Parties. In the case concerning *Military and Paramilitary Activities in and against Nicaragua (Nicaragua* v. *United States of America)* it heard witnesses presented by one Party. The Chamber constituted in the case concerning *Elettronica Sicula S.p.A. (ELSI) (United States of America* v. *Italy)* heard witnesses presented by one of the Parties and experts presented by each of them. In the case concerning the *Land, Island and Maritime Frontier Dispute (El Salvador/Honduras: Nicaragua intervening)* the Court heard a witness presented by one of the Parties, but did not accede to a request concerning an inspection *in loco*.

and to the witnesses and experts in order that mistakes may be corrected under the supervision of the Court (Statute, Art. 47; Rules, Art. 71). A period of 24 hours is usually allowed for the submission of corrections.

In the course of the hearings each party reads out its final submissions and hands the Registrar copies of the text (Rules, Art. 60, para. 2). The filing of new documents after closure of the written proceedings is permissible only with the other party's consent or the authorization of the Court; such documents must be filed in the same number of copies as the pleadings (see *(b)* above); the Registrar transmits them to the other party with a request for observations. No reference may be made to the contents of any document which has not been duly produced, unless the document is part of a publication readily available (Statute, Art. 52; Rules, Art. 56).

The Registrar issues communiqués giving all necessary information as to the dates of the hearings (Instructions for the Registry, Art. 12). Admission cards are issued to members of the diplomatic corps and to representatives of the press and also to any person who makes application either in writing or in person at the Peace Palace on the occasion of a hearing. Photographs may be taken before the opening of hearings. Filming for cinema or television purposes is, however, subject to special authorization. There is a Press Room within the Peace Palace, and also a Post Office where a number of telephones are available for the use of journalists. As soon as the provisional, uncorrected verbatim records of each hearing have been duplicated they are made available to representatives of the press, though neither the text nor the pagination is final at that stage (see *(e)* below).

(d) *Deliberations*

After the close of the oral proceedings, the Court withdraws to deliberate in private and to prepare a judgment. The deliberations of the Court are conducted *in camera* and remain confidential. This applies to all aspects of the deliberations, including the schedule of meetings (Statute, Arts. 54-55; Rules, Arts. 19-21; Instructions for the Registry, Art. 16).

The manner in which the Court conducts its deliberations is governed by a resolution concerning the internal judicial practice of the Court, the most recent version of which was adopted on 12 April 1976 (see *I.C.J. Acts and Documents No. 5*, pp. 165-173).

(e) *Judgment*

The judgment is read out at a public sitting for which similar arrangements are made as for a hearing in open court, in particular with regard to the admission of the public and the assistance provided to representatives of the press (see *(c)* above).

The judgment is prepared in both official languages, of which one is indicated as authoritative (Statute, Art. 39; Rules, Art. 96). If it does not represent in whole or in part the unanimous opinion of the judges, any judge is entitled to attach a dissenting or separate opinion, or a declaration which records his position without stating his reasons; the judgment indicates the names of the judges constituting the majority (Statute, Arts. 56-58; Rules, Arts. 94 and 95).

Three original copies of the judgment are signed by the President and the Registrar and are then sealed; one is placed in the archives of the Court and the others are handed to the parties (Rules, Art. 95, para. 3; Instructions for the Registry, Art. 21).

Immediately after the public reading, copies of a special duplicated *tirage* are placed at the disposal of the judges and the representatives of the parties. At the same time an unofficial communiqué summarizing the decision is issued on the authority of the Registrar.

As soon as possible, the printed text of the judgment becomes available as a separate fascicle in the *I.C.J. Reports* series, which is sent to States entitled to appear before the Court and is placed on sale. Subsequently, the documentation of the case is published in one or more printed volumes of the series entitled *I.C.J. Pleadings, Oral Arguments, Documents*. It is these printed texts (see Chap. VII, pp. 309-316, below) which should be used for all purposes of quotation or citation.

(f) *Expenses and costs*

The expenses of the Court, including amounts payable to witnesses or experts appearing at the instance of the Court (Rules, Art. 68; Instructions for the Registry, Art. 18), are borne out of the United Nations budget; if a party to a case does not contribute to the United Nations budget, the Court itself fixes the amount payable by that party as a contribution towards the expenses of the Court for the case (see Chap. VIII, p. 317, below).

Each party bears its own costs, unless the Court makes an order in favour of a party for the payment of the costs (Statute, Art. 64; Rules, Art. 95, para. 1, and Art. 97).

In addition, there exists a Secretary-General's Trust Fund to Assist States in the Settlement of Disputes through the International Court of Justice, established on 1 November 1989[1]. The Fund is designed to encourage States to settle their disputes peaceably by submitting them to the Court. To be eligible for funding, a State must be entitled to appear before the Court (see Chap. III, pp. 62-69, for an explanation of which States are so entitled) and demonstrate a need for financial assistance. In addition, the dispute must be submitted to the Court by Special Agreement.

[1] Cf. United Nations doc. A/44/PV.43 (1989).

3. *Occasional Rules in Contentious Cases*

(a) *Provisional measures*

The Court has the power to indicate provisional measures (Statute, Art. 41). A request for such measures is treated as a matter of urgency, and the Court's decision is given in an order (Rules, Arts. 73-78)[1].

(b) *Joinder of proceedings*

The Court may direct that the proceedings in two or more cases be joined (Rules, Art. 47). It does this by means of an order[2].

(c) *Preliminary objections*

Preliminary objections (see Chap. III, p. 72, above) must be filed within the time-limit fixed for the filing of the Counter-Memorial (Rules, Art. 79). They suspend the proceedings on the merits and may be answered by the observations and submissions of the opposing party, to be filed within a time-limit fixed by an order. Oral proceedings on the objections ensue, the party which raised them being called upon to speak first. The Court gives its decision on the objections in a judgment; if it dismisses them, the proceedings on the merits are resumed from the point of interruption; they are likewise resumed if it declares that the objections do not possess an exclusively preliminary character[3]. The Court may also

---

[1] Such provisional measures have been requested in the following 19 cases: *Anglo-Iranian Oil Co. (United Kingdom* v. *Iran); Interhandel (Switzerland* v. *United States of America); Fisheries Jurisdiction (United Kingdom* v. *Iceland) (Federal Republic of Germany* v. *Iceland); Nuclear Tests (Australia* v. *France) (New Zealand* v. *France); Trial of Pakistani Prisoners of War (Pakistan* v. *India); Aegean Sea Continental Shelf (Greece* v. *Turkey); United States Diplomatic and Consular Staff in Tehran (United States of America* v. *Iran); Military and Paramilitary Activities in and against Nicaragua (Nicaragua* v. *United States of America); Frontier Dispute (Burkina Faso/Republic of Mali)* (case referred to a Chamber); *Border and Transborder Armed Actions (Nicaragua* v. *Honduras)* (in this case the request was withdrawn); *Arbitral Award of 31 July 1989 (Guinea-Bissau* v. *Senegal); Passage through the Great Belt (Finland* v. *Denmark)*; *Questions of Interpretation and Application of the 1971 Montreal Convention arising from the Aerial Incident at Lockerbie (Libyan Arab Jamahiriya* v. *United Kingdom) (Libyan Arab Jamahiriya* v. *United States of America); Application of the Convention on the Prevention and Punishment of the Crime of Genocide (Bosnia and Herzegovina* v. *Yugoslavia)* (in this case two requests were made by Bosnia and Herzegovina and one by Yugoslavia; *Land and Maritime Boundary between Cameroon and Nigeria (Cameroon* v. *Nigeria); Request for an Examination of the Situation in Accordance with Paragraph 63 of the Court's Judgment of 20 December 1974 in the Nuclear Tests* (New Zealand *v.* France) *Case.*

[2] Proceedings were joined in the following cases: *South West Africa (Ethiopia* v. *South Africa; Liberia* v. *South Africa); North Sea Continental Shelf (Federal Republic of Germany/Denmark; Federal Republic of Germany/Netherlands).*

[3] The Court gave its decision on the preliminary objections raised in the following 15 cases: *Corfu Channel (United Kingdom* v. *Albania); Ambatielos (Greece* v. *United Kingdom); Anglo-Iranian Oil Co. (United Kingdom* v. *Iran); Nottebohm (Liechtenstein* v. *Guatemala); Monetary Gold Removed from Rome in 1943 (Italy* v. *France, United Kingdom and United States of America); Certain Norwegian Loans (France* v. *Norway); Right of Passage over Indian*

give effect to an agreement between the parties that objections should be heard and determined within the framework of the merits[1].

(d) *Intervention, presentation of information*

A third State may request to be permitted to intervene if it considers that it has an interest of a legal nature which may be affected by the decision in the case; it is for the Court to decide upon such a request (Statute, Art. 62; Rules, Arts. 81 and 83-85)[2]. If the dispute relates to the construction of a convention to which States other than those concerned in the case are parties, these States are notified forthwith and have the right to intervene in the proceedings (Statute, Art. 63; Rules, Arts. 43, 82-84 and 86)[3].

Territory (Portugal v. *India); Interhandel (Switzerland* v. *United States of America); Aerial Incident of 27 July 1955 (Israel* v. *Bulgaria); Temple of Preah Vihear (Cambodia* v. *Thailand); South West Africa (Ethiopia* v. *South Africa; Liberia* v. *South Africa); Northern Cameroons (Cameroon* v. *United Kingdom); Barcelona Traction, Light and Power Company, Limited (New Application: 1962) (Belgium* v. *Spain); Elettronica Sicula S.p.A. (ELSI) (United States of America* v. *Italy); Certain Phosphate Lands in Nauru (Nauru* v. *Australia)*. Preliminary objections on which the Court will yet have to give a decision have also been raised in two pending cases: *Oil Platforms (Islamic Republic of Iran* v. *United States of America)* and *Land and Maritime Boundary between Cameroon and Nigeria (Cameroon* v. *Nigeria)*. In other cases the Court was not called upon to give a decision on the preliminary objections, either because they were withdrawn *(Rights of Nationals of the United States of America in Morocco (France* v. *United States of America))* or as the result of a discontinuance *(Aerial Incident of 27 July 1955 (United States of America* v. *Bulgaria); Barcelona Traction, Light and Power Company, Limited* (first application) *(Belgium* v. *Spain); Compagnie du Port, des Quais et des Entrepôts de Beyrouth and Société Radio-Orient (France* v. *Lebanon); Aerial Incident of 3 July 1988 (Islamic Republic of Iran* v. *United States of America))*. The Court also dealt with questions of jurisdiction or admissibility in the following 11 cases: *Appeal Relating to the Jurisdiction of the ICAO Council (India* v. *Pakistan); Fisheries Jurisdiction (United Kingdom* v. *Iceland) (Federal Republic of Germany* v. *Iceland); Nuclear Tests (Australia* v. *France) (New Zealand* v. *France); Aegean Sea Continental Shelf (Greece* v. *Turkey); United States Diplomatic and Consular Staff in Tehran (United States of America* v. *Iran); Military and Paramilitary Activities in and against Nicaragua (Nicaragua* v. *United States of America); Border and Transborder Armed Actions (Nicaragua* v. *Honduras); Maritime Delimitation and Territorial Questions between Qatar and Bahrain (Qatar* v. *Bahrain)*; and *East Timor (Portugal* v. *Australia)*. The Court has still to decide questions of jurisdiction and admissibility in the pending case concerning *Fisheries Jurisdiction (Spain* v. *Canada)*.

[1] This was done in the cases concerning *Elettronica Sicula S.p.A. (ELSI) (United States of America* v. *Italy)* and *East Timor (Portugal* v. *Australia)*. Preliminary objections were joined to the merits under the pre-1972 Rules of Court after agreement between the Parties in the case concerning *Certain Norwegian Loans (France* v. *Norway)* and by decision of the Court in the following two cases: *Right of Passage over Indian Territory (Portugal* v. *India); Barcelona Traction, Light and Power Company, Limited (New Application: 1962) (Belgium* v. *Spain)*.

[2] Permission to intervene was applied for in the *Nuclear Tests* cases *(Australia* v. *France) (New Zealand* v. *France)*, in the cases concerning the *Continental Shelf (Tunisia/Libyan Arab Jamahiriya)* and the *Continental Shelf (Libyan Arab Jamahiriya/Malta)*; in the case concerning the *Land, Island and Maritime Frontier Dispute (El Salvador/Honduras)* and in the *Request for an Examination of the Situation in Accordance with Paragraph 63 of the Court's Judgment of 20 December 1974 in the* Nuclear Tests (New Zealand *v.* France) *Case*. In the last case, several States filed a document entitled "Application for Permission to Intervene under Article 62/Declaration of Intervention under Article 63".

[3] A third State intervened in the *Haya de la Torre (Colombia* v. *Peru)* case and a Declaration of Intervention was submitted in the case concerning *Military and Paramilitary Activities in and against Nicaragua (Nicaragua* v. *United States of America)*. (See also footnote 2 above.)

Similarly, public international organizations may, at the request of the Court or a party or on their own initiative, furnish the Court with information relevant to cases before it; whenever the construction of their constituent instruments or of a convention adopted thereunder is in question, they are notified (Statute, Art. 34, paras. 2 and 3; Rules, Art. 69).

(e) *Default, settlement, discontinuance*

If one of the parties does not appear before the Court or fails to defend its case, the other party may call upon the Court to decide in favour of its claim (Statute, Art. 53)[1].

The Court, or the President if the Court is not sitting, may, by way of an order, officially record the conclusion of a settlement or a discontinuance (Rules, Arts. 88 and 89)[2].

(f) *Execution, interpretation or revision of judgments*

The judgments of the Court are binding, final and without appeal (Charter, Art. 94, para. 1; Statute, Arts. 59-60; Rules, Art. 94, para. 2). The parties may, however, make a request for interpretation or, in certain circumstances, for revision of a judgment (see above, Chap. III, pp. 72-73). The decision of the Court on such requests is given in the form of a judgment (Statute, Arts. 60-61; Rules, Arts. 98-100)[3,4].

---

[1] A number of judgments and orders were delivered in the absence of one of the parties: *Corfu Channel (United Kingdom* v. *Albania), Assessment of Amount of Compensation; Anglo-Iranian Oil Co. (United Kingdom* v. *Iran), Interim Protection; Nottebohm (Liechtenstein* v. *Guatemala), Preliminary Objection; Fisheries Jurisdiction (United Kingdom* v. *Iceland) (Federal Republic of Germany* v. *Iceland), Interim Protection, Jurisdiction of the Court* and *Merits; Nuclear Tests (Australia* v. *France) (New Zealand* v. *France), Interim Protection* and *Second Phase; Trial of Pakistani Prisoners of War (Pakistan* v. *India), Interim Protection; Aegean Sea Continental Shelf (Greece* v. *Turkey), Interim Protection* and *Jurisdiction of the Court; United States Diplomatic and Consular Staff in Tehran (United States of America* v. *Iran), Provisional Measures* and *Merits; Military and Paramilitary Activities in and against Nicaragua (Nicaragua* v. *United States of America), Merits; Maritime Delimitation and Territorial Questions between Qatar and Bahrain (Qatar* v. *Bahrain), Jurisdiction and Admissibility.*

[2] The following 13 cases ended in discontinuance: *Protection of French Nationals and Protected Persons in Egypt (France* v. *Egypt); Electricité de Beyrouth Company (France* v. *Lebanon); Aerial Incident of 27 July 1955 (United States of America* v. *Bulgaria) (United Kingdom* v. *Bulgaria); Barcelona Traction, Light and Power Company, Limited (Belgium* v. *Spain)* (first application); *Compagnie du Port, des Quais et des Entrepôts de Beyrouth and Société Radio-Orient (France* v. *Lebanon); Trial of Pakistani Prisoners of War (Pakistan* v. *India); Border and Transborder Armed Actions (Nicaragua* v. *Costa Rica); Border and Transborder Armed Actions (Nicaragua* v. *Honduras); Passage through the Great Belt (Finland* v. *Denmark); Certain Phosphate Lands in Nauru (Nauru* v. *Australia); Maritime Delimitation between Guinea-Bissau and Senegal (Guinea-Bissau* v. *Senegal); Aerial Incident of 3 July 1988 (Islamic Republic of Iran* v. *United States of America)*. Furthermore, the cases concerning *United States Diplomatic and Consular Staff in Tehran (United States of America* v. *Iran)* and *Military and Paramilitary Activities in and against Nicaragua (Nicaragua* v. *United States of America)* ended in discontinuance as regarded the question of reparation which the Judgment had left to be settled.

[3] The Court gave a decision on a request for interpretation of its Judgment in the *Asylum (Colombia/Peru)* case. See also pp. 72, note 2, and 73, note 1, above.

[4] The Court gave a decision on an application for revision and interpretation submitted by Tunisia in connection with its Judgment in the case concerning the *Continental Shelf (Tunisia/Libyan Arab Jamahiriya)*.

Article 94, paragraph 2, of the Charter of the United Nations states that, if any party to a case fails to perform the obligations incumbent upon it under a judgment, the other party may have recourse to the Security Council.

(g) *Special reference to the Court*

When a matter which has been the subject of proceedings before some other international body is brought before the Court, the provisions of the Statute and of the Rules apply (Rules, Art. 87)[1].

4. *Procedure in Advisory Cases*

In addition to the Rules of Court which are expressly applicable to proceedings in regard to advisory opinions, the Court is guided by the provisions which apply in contentious proceedings (Statute, Art. 68; Rules, Art. 102). It may thus be led to apply the articles of the Statute concerning judges *ad hoc* (see Chap. I, pp. 12-16, above).

The practical information given concerning the course of the procedure in contentious cases (see under 2, above) applies *mutatis mutandis* to the procedure in regard to advisory opinions, in particular as regards arrangements for the public and the representatives of the press.

(a) *Request*

Notice of a request for an advisory opinion (see Chap. III, pp. 73-74, above) is addressed to the Court by the Secretary-General of the United Nations or the chief administrative officer of the organization authorized to make the request; all documents likely to throw light upon the question are to be transmitted at the same time as the request or as soon as possible thereafter (Statute, Art. 65, para. 2; Rules, Art. 104).

Notice of the request for an advisory opinion is given to all States entitled to appear before the Court (Statute, Art. 66, para. 1).

In addition, the Court gives the States and international organizations considered likely to be able to furnish information on the question an opportunity to submit their views in writing or orally, or both (Statute, Art. 66, paras. 2-4).

(b) *Written and oral proceedings*

A request for an opinion usually gives rise to written proceedings followed by oral proceedings (Statute, Art. 66; Rules, Arts. 105 and 106).

In the case of urgency, the Court takes all necessary steps to accelerate the procedure (Rules, Art. 103)[2].

---

[1] The Court was seised of an *Appeal Relating to the Jurisdiction of the ICAO Council (India* v. *Pakistan)* in the case of that name.

[2] The Court decided to accelerate the procedure in accordance with Article 103 of the Rules in the case concerning the *Applicability of the Obligation to Arbitrate under Section 21 of the United Nations Headquarters Agreement of 26 June 1947.*

(c) *Deliberations*

The deliberations are conducted in the same manner as in contentious cases (Rules, Arts. 19-21 and 107; resolution concerning the Internal Judicial Practice of the Court, Art. 10).

(d) *Advisory opinion*

The advisory opinion is read in open Court; if it does not represent in whole or in part the unanimous opinion of the judges, any judge is entitled to attach a dissenting or separate opinion, or a declaration which records his position without stating his reasons; the advisory opinion indicates the names of the judges constituting the majority (Statute, Art. 67; Rules, Arts. 107 and 108).

One of the original copies of the advisory opinion is transmitted to the body which made the request (Rules, Art. 109).

The opinions given by the Court are purely advisory in character. The body requesting the opinion may however be committed to accepting it as binding by the terms of the instrument under which it is authorized to request advisory opinions of the Court.

IV. Occasional Functions Entrusted to the President of the International Court of Justice

1. International Instruments Providing for Appointment of Arbitrators, etc.

There are many international instruments which provide that in certain eventualities the President of the Court may be requested by the contracting parties to appoint arbitrators, umpires, members of conciliation commissions, etc. Requests of this sort have always been acceded to.

States proposing to insert such a provision in a treaty generally consult the President as to his willingness to accept such a task, and submit the draft provision to him. This frequently provides that, if the President is of the nationality of one of the parties to the dispute, the appointment should be made either by the Vice-President or by the senior Member of the Court not so disqualified.

Such a provision is found, for instance, in bilateral agreements relating to air transport, social security, reparations or guarantees, loans, technical co-operation and the protection of investments; in multilateral treaties; in conventions or agreements concerning the constitution, status or privileges and immunities of international organizations; and in agreements or contracts concluded between States and international organs.

2. Other Requests for Appointment of Arbitrators

The President of the Court is sometimes requested to appoint arbitrators under the terms of contracts concluded between a State and a corporation or between corporations. Such requests are generally acceded to.

In such cases, too, the usual practice is to consult the President in advance and to submit the draft contract to him. It is usually provided that if the President is of the same nationality as one of the parties to the contract, the appointment should be made either by the Vice-President or by the senior Member of the Court not so disqualified.

3. Other Appointments

The President has also at times been requested by States or international organizations to appoint persons to fill other offices.

Such appointments are, for instance, provided for in texts such as Article 12 of the Protocol of 23 June 1953 for limiting and regulating the cultivation of the poppy plant, the production of, international and wholesale trade in, and use of opium, or Article 4 of the Regulations for the execution of the Convention of 14 May 1954 for the protection of cultural property in the event of armed conflict or, again, Rule 109.1 *(a)* of the Staff Rules of the United Nations and Regulation 9.1.1 of the Staff Regulations of the United Nations Educational, Scientific and Cultural Organization.

CHAPTER VI

WORK OF THE COURT IN 1995-1996

During the period under review, the Court was seised of the *Request for an Examination of the Situation in Accordance with Paragraph 63 of the Court's Judgment of 20 December 1974 in the* Nuclear Tests (New Zealand *v.* France) *Case* and of the case concerning *Kasikili/Sedudu Island (Botswana/Namibia)*. Two requests for the indication of provisional measures were made: one in the above-mentioned Request made by New Zealand and one in the case concerning the *Land and Maritime Boundary between Cameroon and Nigeria (Cameroon* v. *Nigeria)*. In that case also, preliminary objections were raised by Nigeria. Two cases were discontinued: the case concerning *Maritime Delimitation between Guinea-Bissau and Senegal (Guinea-Bissau* v. *Senegal)* was discontinued by Guinea-Bissau; the case concerning the *Aerial Incident of 3 July 1988 (Islamic Republic of Iran* v. *United States of America)* by agreement of the two Parties.

The Court held 31 public sittings and a number of private meetings. It rendered an Advisory Opinion in the case concerning the *Legality of the Use by a State of Nuclear Weapons in Armed Conflict* (*I.C.J. Reports 1996*, p. 66) and another one in the case concerning the *Legality of the Threat or Use of Nuclear Weapons* (*I.C.J. Reports 1996*, p. 226). It delivered a Judgment on jurisdiction and admissibility in the case concerning *Application of the Convention on the Prevention and Punishment of the Crime of Genocide (Bosnia and Herzegovina* v. *Yugoslavia)* (*I.C.J. Reports 1996*, p. 595); and made an Order in which it dismissed the *Request for an Examination of the Situation in Accordance with Paragraph 63 of the Court's Judgment of 20 December 1974 in the* Nuclear Tests (New Zealand *v.* France) *Case* (*I.C.J. Reports 1995*, p. 288), as well as the request for provisional measures and the applications for permission to intervene made in respect of that Request. The Court further made an Order indicating provisional measures in the case concerning the *Land and Maritime Boundary between Cameroon and Nigeria (Cameroon* v. *Nigeria)* (*I.C.J. Reports 1996*, p. 13). It also made Orders recording the discontinuance and directing the removal of the case from the list in the cases concerning *Maritime Delimitation between Guinea-Bissau and Senegal (Guinea-Bissau* v. *Senegal)* (*I.C.J. Reports 1995*, p. 423) and the *Aerial Incident of 3 July 1988 (Islamic Republic of Iran* v. *United States of America)* (*I.C.J. Reports 1996*, p. 9). By another Order, in the case concerning *Fisheries Jurisdiction (Spain* v. *Canada)* (*I.C.J. Reports 1996*, p. 58), it decided not to authorize the filing of a second round of written pleadings on the question of its jurisdiction. It, finally, made Orders concerning time-limits in the cases concerning *Maritime Delimitation and Territorial Questions between Qatar and Bahrain (Qatar* v. *Bahrain)* (*I.C.J. Reports 1996*, p. 6), *Questions of Interpretation and Application of the 1971 Montreal Convention arising from the Aerial Incident at Lockerbie (Libyan Arab Jamahiriya* v. *United Kingdom)* (*I.C.J. Reports 1995*, p. 282), *Questions of Interpretation and Application of the 1971 Montreal Convention arising from the Aerial Incident at Lockerbie (Libyan Arab Jamahiriya* v. *United States of America)* (*I.C.J. Reports 1995*, p. 285) and *Kasikili/Sedudu Island (Botswana/Namibia)* (*I.C.J. Reports 1996*, p. 63).

The President of the Court made Orders concerning time-limits in the case concerning the *Land and Maritime Boundary between Cameroon and Nigeria (Cameroon* v. *Nigeria)* (*I.C.J. Reports 1996*, p. 3) and in the case concerning *Application of the Convention on the Prevention and Punishment of the Crime of Genocide (Bosnia and Herzegovina* v. *Yugoslavia)*.

I. CASES BEFORE THE COURT

A. CONTENTIOUS CASES

1. Aerial Incident of 3 July 1988 (Islamic Republic of Iran v. *United States of America)*

On 17 May 1989, the Islamic Republic of Iran filed in the Registry of the Court an Application instituting proceedings against the United States of America, citing as bases for the Court's jurisdiction provisions of the 1944 Chicago Convention on International Civil Aviation and the 1971 Montreal Convention for the Suppression of Unlawful Acts Against the Safety of Civil Aviation.

In its Application, the Islamic Republic of Iran referred to:

> "The destruction of an Iranian aircraft, Iran Air Airbus A-300B, flight 655, and the killing of its 290 passengers and crew by two surface-to-air missiles launched from the USS *Vincennes*, a guided-missile cruiser on duty with the United States Persian Gulf/Middle East Force in the Iranian airspace over the Islamic Republic's territorial waters in the Persian Gulf on 3 July 1988."

It contended that,

> "by its destruction of Iran Air flight 655 and taking 290 lives, its refusal to compensate the Islamic Republic for damages arising from the loss of the aircraft and individuals on board and its continuous interference with the Persian Gulf aviation",

the Government of the United States had violated certain provisions of the Chicago Convention on International Civil Aviation (7 December

1944), as amended, and of the Montreal Convention for the Suppression of Unlawful Acts Against the Safety of Civil Aviation (23 September 1971), and that the Council of the International Civil Aviation Organization (ICAO) had erred in its decision of 17 March 1989 concerning the incident.

In its Application the Government of the Islamic Republic of Iran requested the Court to adjudge and declare:

"*(a)* that the ICAO Council decision is erroneous in that the Government of the United States has violated the Chicago Convention, including the Preamble, Articles 1, 2, 3 *bis* and 44 *(a)* and *(h)* and Annex 15 of the Chicago Convention as well as Recommendation 2.6/1 of the Third Middle East Regional Air Navigation Meeting of ICAO;

(b) that the Government of the United States has violated Articles 1, 3 and 10 (1) of the Montreal Convention; and

(c) that the Government of the United States is responsible to pay compensation to the Islamic Republic, in the amount to be determined by the Court, as measured by the injuries suffered by the Islamic Republic and the bereaved families as a result of these violations, including additional financial losses which Iran Air and the bereaved families have suffered for the disruption of their activities."

By an Order of 13 December 1989, the Court, having taken into account the views expressed by each of the Parties, fixed 12 June 1990 as the time-limit for the filing of the Memorial of the Islamic Republic of Iran and 10 December 1990 for the filing of the Counter-Memorial of the United States of America (*I.C.J. Reports 1989*, p. 132). Judge Oda appended a declaration to the Order of the Court (*ibid.*, p. 135); Judges Schwebel and Shahabuddeen appended separate opinions (*ibid.*, pp. 136-144 and 145-160).

By an Order of 12 June 1990 (*I.C.J. Reports 1990*, p. 86), made in response to a request by the Islamic Republic of Iran and after the views of the United States of America had been ascertained, the President of the Court extended to 24 July 1990 the time-limit for the filing of the Memorial of the Islamic Republic of Iran and to 4 March 1991 the time-limit for the Counter-Memorial of the United States of America. The Memorial was filed within the prescribed time-limit.

On 4 March 1991, within the time-limit fixed for the filing of its Counter-Memorial, the United States of America filed certain preliminary objections to the jurisdiction of the Court. By virtue of the provisions of Article 79, paragraph 3, of the Rules of Court, the proceedings on the merits were suspended and a time-limit had to be fixed for the presentation by the other Party of a written statement of its observations and submissions on the preliminary objections. By an Order of 9 April 1991 (*I.C.J. Reports 1991*, p. 6), the Court, having ascertained the views of the Parties, fixed 9 December 1991 as the time-limit within which the Islamic Republic of Iran may present such observations and submissions.

The Islamic Republic of Iran chose Mr. Mohsen Aghahosseini to sit as judge *ad hoc*.

By Orders of 18 December 1991 (*I.C.J. Reports 1991*, p. 187) and 5 June 1992 (*I.C.J. Reports 1992*, p. 225), made in response to successive requests by Iran and after the views of the United States had been ascertained, the President of the Court extended the above-mentioned time-limit for the written observations and submissions of Iran on the preliminary objections to 9 June and 9 September 1992 respectively. Those observations and submissions were filed within the prescribed time-limit and were communicated to the Secretary-General of the International Civil Aviation Organization (ICAO), together with the written pleadings previously filed, pursuant to Article 34, paragraph 3, of the Statute of the Court and Article 69, paragraph 3, of the Rules of Court. The President of the Court, acting under the same provisions, fixed 9 December 1992 as the time-limit for the eventual submission of written observations by the Council of ICAO. The ICAO's observations were duly filed within that time-limit.

The public sittings to hear the oral arguments of the Parties, scheduled to open on 12 September 1994, were postponed *sine die* at the request of the Parties.

By a letter of 22 February 1996, the Agents of the two Parties jointly notified the Court that their Governments had agreed to discontinue the case because they had entered into "an agreement in full and final settlement of all disputes, differences, claims, counterclaims and matters directly or indirectly raised by or capable of arising out of, or directly or indirectly related to or connected with, this case". By an Order of the same day (*I.C.J. Reports 1996*, p. 9), the Court placed on record the discontinuance and directed that the case be removed from the list.

2. *Maritime Delimitation between Guinea-Bissau and Senegal (Guinea-Bissau* v. *Senegal)*

On 12 March 1991, the Government of the Republic of Guinea-Bissau filed in the Registry of the Court an Application instituting proceedings against the Republic of Senegal in a dispute concerning the delimitation of all the maritime territories between the two States. Guinea-Bissau cited as bases for the Court's jurisdiction the declarations made by both States under Article 36, paragraph 2, of the Statute.

In its Application, Guinea-Bissau recalled that, by an Application dated 23 August 1989, it referred to the Court a dispute concerning the existence and validity of the Arbitral Award made on 31 July 1989 by the Arbitration Tribunal formed to determine the maritime boundary between the two States.

Guinea-Bissau claimed that the objective of the request laid before the Arbitration Tribunal was the delimitation of the maritime territories appertaining respectively to one and the other State. According to Guinea-Bissau, the decision of the Arbitration Tribunal of 31 July 1989, however, did not make it possible to draw a definitive delimitation of all the maritime areas over which the Parties had rights. Moreover, whatever the outcome of the proceedings pending before the Court, a real and definitive delimitation of all the maritime territories between the two States would still not be realized.

The Government of Guinea-Bissau asked the Court to adjudge and declare:

> "What should be, on the basis of the international law of the sea and of all the relevant elements of the case, including the future decision of the Court in the case concerning the Arbitral *'award'* of 31 July 1989, the line (to be drawn on a map) delimiting all the maritime territories appertaining respectively to Guinea-Bissau and Senegal."

In its Judgment of 12 November 1991 in the case concerning the *Arbitral Award of 31 July 1989 (Guinea-Bissau* v. *Senegal)* (*I.C.J. Reports 1991*, p. 53) the Court took note of the filing of a second Application but added:

> "67. . . . It has also taken note of the declaration made by the Agent of Senegal in the present proceedings, according to which one solution
>
> 'would be to negotiate with Senegal, which has no objection to this, a boundary for the exclusive economic zone or, should it prove impossible to reach an agreement, to bring the matter before the Court'.
>
> 68. Having regard to that Application and that declaration, and at the close of a long and difficult arbitral procedure and of these proceedings before the Court, the Court considers it highly desirable that the elements of the dispute that were not settled by the Arbitral Award of 31 July 1989 be resolved as soon as possible, as both Parties desire."

After the two Governments concerned had had time to study that Judgment, the President of the Court convened a meeting with the representatives of the Parties on 28 February 1992, at which however they requested that no time-limit be fixed for the initial pleadings in the case, pending the outcome of negotiations on the question of maritime delimitation; those negotiations were to continue for six months in the first instance, after which, if they had not been successful, a further meeting would be held with the President.

No indications having been received from the Parties as to the state of their negotiations, the President convened a further meeting with the Agents on 6 October 1992. The Agents stated that some progress had been made towards an agreement, and a joint request was made by the two Parties that a further period of three months, with a possible further extension of three months, be allowed for continuation of the negotiations. The President agreed to this, and expressed satisfaction at the efforts being made by the Parties to resolve their dispute by negotiation, in the spirit of the recommendation made in the Judgment of 12 November 1991.

After several exchanges of letters regarding extended time-limits, the President again convened the Agents of the Parties on 10 March 1994. At that meeting the Agents handed the President the text of an agreement entitled "Management and Co-operation Agreement between the Government of the Republic of Guinea-Bissau and the Government of the Republic of Senegal", done at Dakar on 14 October 1993 and signed by the two Heads of State. The Agreement, which provides, *inter alia*, for the joint exploitation, by the two Parties, of a "maritime zone situated between the 268° and 220° azimuths drawn from Cape Roxo" (Art. 1), and the establishment of an "International Agency for the exploitation of the zone" (Art. 4), will enter into force, according to the terms of its Article 7,

> "upon conclusion of the agreement concerning the establishment and functioning of the International Agency and with the exchange of the instruments of ratification of both agreements by both States".

In letters dated 16 March 1994, addressed to the Presidents of both States, the President of the Court expressed his satisfaction and informed them that the case would be removed from the list, in accordance with the terms of the Rules of Court, as soon as the Parties had notified him of their decision to discontinue the proceedings.

At a meeting held by the President with the representatives of the Parties on 1 November 1995, the latter furnished him with an additional copy of the above-mentioned agreement as well as the text of a "Protocole d'accord avant trait à l'organisation et au fonctionnement de l'agence de gestion et de coopération entre la République de Sénégal et la République de Guinée-Bissau instituée par l'accord du 14 octobre 1993", done at Bissau on 12 June 1995 and signed by the two Heads of State; the representatives at the same time notified him of the decisions of their Governments to discontinue the proceedings and the President asked them to confirm that decision in writing to the Court in whatever manner they deemed most appropriate.

By a letter of 2 November 1995, the Agent of Guinea-Bissau confirmed that his Government, by virtue of the agreement reached by the two Parties on the disputed zone, had decided to discontinue the proceedings instituted by its Application dated 12 March 1991; after the Agent of Senegal, by a letter dated 6 November 1995, had confirmed that his Government "agreed to the discontinuance of proceedings", the Court, by an Order of 8 November 1995 (*I.C.J. Reports 1995*, p. 423), placed on record the discontinuance and directed that the case be removed from the list.

3. *Maritime Delimitation and Territorial Questions between Qatar and Bahrain (Qatar* v. *Bahrain)*

On 8 July 1991, the Government of the State of Qatar filed in the Registry of the Court an Application instituting proceedings against the Government of the State of Bahrain

> "in respect of certain existing disputes between them relating to sovereignty over the Hawar islands, sovereign rights over the shoals of Dibal and Qit'at Jaradah, and the delimitation of the maritime areas of the two States".

Qatar claimed that its sovereignty over the Hawar islands was well founded on the basis of customary international law and applicable local practices and customs. It had therefore continuously opposed a decision announced by the British Government in 1939, during the time of the British presence in Bahrain and Qatar (which came to an end in 1971), that the islands belonged to Bahrain. This decision was, in the view of Qatar, invalid, beyond the power of the British in relation to the two States, and not binding on Qatar.

With regard to the shoals of Dibal and Qit'at Jaradah, a further decision of the British Government in 1947 to delimit the sea-bed boundary between Bahrain and Qatar purported to recognize that Bahrain had "sovereign rights" in the areas of those shoals. In that decision the view was expressed that the shoals should not be considered to be islands having territorial waters. Qatar had claimed and continued to claim that such sovereign rights as existed over the shoals belonged to Qatar; it also considered however that these were shoals and not islands. Bahrain claimed in 1964 that Dibal and Qit'at Jaradah were islands possessing territorial waters, and belonged to Bahrain, a claim rejected by Qatar.

With regard to the delimitation of the maritime areas of the two States, in the letter informing the Rulers of Qatar and Bahrain of the 1947 decision it was stated that the British Government considered that the line divided "in accordance with equitable principles" the sea-bed between Qatar and Bahrain, and that it was a median line based generally on the configuration of the coastline of the Bahrain main island and the peninsula of Qatar. The letter further specified two exceptions. One concerned the status of the shoals; the other that of the Hawar islands.

Qatar stated that it did not oppose that part of the delimitation line which the British Government stated was based on the configuration of the coastlines of the two States and was determined in accordance with equitable principles. It had been rejecting and still rejected the claim made in 1964 by Bahrain (which had refused to accept the above-mentioned delimitation by the British Government) of a new line delimiting the sea-bed boundary of the two States. Qatar based its claims with respect to delimitation on customary international law and applicable local practices and customs.

The State of Qatar therefore requested the Court:

"I. To adjudge and declare in accordance with international law

(A) that the State of Qatar has sovereignty over the Hawar islands; and

(B) that the State of Qatar has sovereign rights over Dibal and Qit'at Jaradah shoals;

and

II. With due regard to the line dividing the sea-bed of the two States as described in the British decision of 23 December 1947, to draw in accordance with international law a single maritime boundary between the maritime areas of sea-bed, subsoil and superjacent waters appertaining respectively to the State of Qatar and the State of Bahrain."

In the Application, Qatar founded the jurisdiction of the Court upon certain agreements between the Parties stated to have been concluded in December 1987 and December 1990, the subject and scope of the commitment to jurisdiction being determined, according to Qatar, by a formula proposed by Bahrain to Qatar on 26 October 1988 and accepted by Qatar in December 1990.

By letters addressed to the Registrar of the Court on 14 July 1991 and 18 August 1991, Bahrain contested the basis of jurisdiction invoked by Qatar.

At a meeting held on 2 October 1991 to enable the President of the Court to ascertain their views, the Parties reached agreement as to the desirability of the proceedings being initially devoted to the questions of the Court's jurisdiction to entertain the dispute and the admissibility of the Application. The President accordingly made, on 11 October 1991, an Order (*I.C.J. Reports 1991*, p. 50) deciding that the written proceedings should first be addressed to those questions; in the same Order he fixed the following time-limits in accordance with a further agreement reached between the Parties at the meeting of 2 October: 10 February 1992 for the Memorial of Qatar, and 11 June 1992 for the Counter-Memorial of Bahrain. The Memorial and Counter-Memorial were filed within the prescribed time-limits.

By an Order of 26 June 1992 (*I.C.J. Reports 1992*, p. 237), the Court, having ascertained the views of the Parties, directed that a Reply by the Applicant and a Rejoinder by the Respondent be filed on the questions of jurisdiction and admissibility. It fixed 28 September 1992 as the time-limit for the Reply of Qatar and 29 December 1992 for the Rejoinder of Bahrain. Both the Reply and the Rejoinder were filed within the prescribed time-limits.

Qatar had chosen Mr. José María Ruda and Bahrain Mr. Nicolas Valticos to sit as judges *ad hoc*. Following Mr. Ruda's death, Qatar chose Mr. Santiago Torres Bernárdez to sit as judge *ad hoc*.

Oral proceedings were held from 28 February to 11 March 1994. In the course of eight public sittings, the Court heard statements on behalf of Qatar and Bahrain. The Vice-President of the Court put questions to both the Parties.

At a public sitting held on 1 July 1994, the Court delivered a Judgment (*I.C.J. Reports 1994*, p. 112) by which it found that the exchanges of letters between the King of Saudi Arabia and the Amir of Qatar dated 19 and 21 December 1987, and between the King of Saudi Arabia and the Amir of Bahrain dated 19 and 26 December 1987, and the document headed "Minutes" and signed at Doha on 25 December 1990 by the Ministers for Foreign Affairs of Bahrain, Qatar and Saudi Arabia, were international agreements creating rights and obligations for the Parties; and that, by the terms of those agreements, the Parties had undertaken to submit to the Court the whole of the dispute between them, as circumscribed by the Bahraini formula. Having noted that it had before it only an Application from Qatar setting out that State's specific claims in connection with that formula, the Court decided to afford the Parties the opportunity to submit to it the whole of the dispute. It fixed 30 November 1994 as the time-limit within which the Parties were jointly or separately to take action to that end and reserved any other matters for subsequent decision.

Judge Shahabuddeen appended a declaration to the Judgment (*I.C.J. Reports 1994*, p. 129); Vice-President Schwebel and Judge *ad hoc* Valticos appended separate opinions (*ibid.*, pp. 130-131 and 132); and Judge Oda appended a dissenting opinion (*ibid.*, pp. 133-149).

On 30 November 1994, the date fixed in the Judgment of 1 July, the Court received from the Agent of Qatar a letter transmitting an "Act to comply with paragraphs (3) and (4) of the operative paragraph 41 of the Judgment of the Court dated 1 July 1994". On the same day, the Court received a communication from the Agent of Bahrain, transmitting the text of a document entitled "Report of the State of Bahrain to the International Court of Justice on the attempt by the Parties to implement the Court's Judgment of 1st July, 1994".

In view of those communications, the Court resumed dealing with the case.

At a public sitting held on 15 February 1995, the Court delivered a Judgment on jurisdiction and admissibility (*I.C.J. Reports 1995*, p. 6) by which it found that it had jurisdiction to adjudicate upon the dispute submitted to it between the State of Qatar and the State of Bahrain and that the Application of the State of Qatar as formulated on 30 November 1994 was admissible.

Vice-President Schwebel, Judges Oda, Shahabuddeen and Koroma, and Judge *ad hoc* Valticos appended dissenting opinions to the Judgment (*I.C.J. Reports 1995*, pp. 27-39, 40-50, 51-66, 67-73 and 74-78).

Judge *ad hoc* Valticos resigned as of the end of the jurisdiction and admissibility phase of the proceedings.

By an Order of 28 April 1995 (*I.C.J. Reports 1995*, p. 83), the Court, having ascertained the views of Qatar and having given Bahrain an opportunity of stating its views, fixed 29 February 1996 as the time-limit for the filing by each of the Parties of a Memorial on the merits. On the request of Bahrain, and after the views of Qatar had been ascertained, the Court, by an Order of 1 February 1996 (*I.C.J. Reports 1996*, p. 6), extended that time-limit to 30 September 1996.

4, 5. Questions of Interpretation and Application of the 1971 Montreal Convention arising from the Aerial Incident at Lockerbie (Libyan Arab Jamahiriya v. *United Kingdom)* and *Questions of Interpretation and Application of the 1971 Montreal Convention arising from the Aerial Incident at Lockerbie (Libyan Arab Jamahiriya* v. *United States of America)*

On 3 March 1992 the Government of the Socialist People's Libyan Arab Jamahiriya filed in the Registry of the Court two separate Applications instituting proceedings against the Government of the United Kingdom of Great Britain and Northern Ireland and against the United States of America in respect of a dispute over the interpretation and application of the Montreal Convention of 23 September 1971, a dispute arising from acts resulting in the aerial incident that occurred over Lockerbie, Scotland, on 21 December 1988.

In the Applications, Libya referred to the charging and indictment of two Libyan nationals by the Lord Advocate of Scotland and by a Grand Jury of the United States, respectively, with having caused a bomb to be placed aboard Pan Am flight 103. The bomb subsequently exploded, causing the aeroplane to crash, and all persons aboard were killed.

Libya pointed out that the acts alleged constituted an offence within the meaning of Article 1 of the Montreal Convention, which it claimed to be the only appropriate convention in force between the Parties, and claimed that it had fully complied with its own obligations under that instrument, Article 5 of which required a State to establish its own jurisdiction over alleged offenders present in its territory in the event of their non-extradition; there was no extradition treaty between Libya and the respective other Parties, and Libya was obliged under Article 7 of the Convention to submit the case to its competent authorities for the purpose of prosecution.

Libya contended that the United Kingdom and the United States were in breach of the Montreal Convention through rejection of its efforts to resolve the matter within the framework of international law, including the Convention itself, in that they were placing pressure upon Libya to surrender the two Libyan nationals for trial.

According to the Applications, it had not been possible to settle by negotiation the disputes that had thus arisen, neither had the Parties been able to agree upon the organization of an arbitration to hear the matter. The Libyan Arab Jamahiriya therefore submitted the disputes to the Court on the basis of Article 14, paragraph 1, of the Montreal Convention.

Libya requested the Court to adjudge and declare as follows:

(a) that Libya has fully complied with all of its obligations under the Montreal Convention;
(b) that the United Kingdom and the United States respectively have breached, and are continuing to breach, their legal obligations to Libya under Articles 5 (2), 5 (3), 7, 8 (2) and 11 of the Montreal Convention; and
(c) that the United Kingdom and the United States respectively are under a legal obligation immediately to cease and desist from such breaches and from the use of any and all force or threats against Libya, including the threat of force against Libya, and from all violations of the sovereignty, territorial integrity, and the political independence of Libya.

Later the same day, Libya made two separate requests to the Court to indicate forthwith the following provisional measures:

(a) to enjoin the United Kingdom and the United States respectively from taking any action against Libya calculated to coerce or compel Libya to surrender the accused individuals to any jurisdiction outside of Libya; and
(b) to ensure that no steps are taken that would prejudice in any way the rights of Libya with respect to the legal proceedings that are the subject of Libya's Applications.

In those requests Libya also requested the President, pending the meeting of the Court, to exercise the power conferred on him by Article 74, paragraph 4, of the Rules of Court, to call upon the Parties to act in such a way as to enable any Order the Court might make on Libya's request for provisional measures to have its appropriate effects.

By a letter of 6 March 1992, the Legal Adviser of the United States Department of State, referring to the specific request made by Libya under Article 74, paragraph 4, of the Rules of Court, in its request for the indication of provisional measures, stated *inter alia* that

> "taking into account both the absence of any concrete showing of urgency relating to the request and developments in the ongoing action by the Security Council and the Secretary-General in this matter . . . the action requested by Libya . . . is unnecessary and could be misconstrued".

Libya chose Mr. Ahmed S. El-Kosheri to sit as judge *ad hoc*.

At the opening of the hearings on the request for the indication of provisional measures, on 26 March 1992, the Vice-President of the Court, exercising the functions of the presidency in the case, referred to the request made by Libya under Article 74, paragraph 4, of the Rules of Court and stated that, after the most careful consideration of all the circumstances then known to him, he had come to the conclusion that it would not be appropriate for him to exercise the discretionary power conferred on the President by that provision. At five public sittings held on 26, 27 and 28 March 1992, both Parties in each of the two cases presented oral arguments on the request for the indication of provisional measures. A Member of the Court put questions to both Agents in each of the two cases and the Judge *ad hoc* put a question to the Agent of Libya.

At a public sitting held on 14 April 1992, the Court read the two Orders on the requests for indication of provisional measures filed by Libya (*I.C.J. Reports 1992*, pp. 3 and 114), in which it found that the circumstances of the cases were not such as to require the exercise of its power to indicate such measures.

Acting President Oda (*ibid.*, pp. 17-19 and 129-131) and Judge Ni (*ibid.*, pp. 20-23 and 132-135) each appended a declaration to the Orders of the Court; Judges Evensen, Tarassov, Guillaume and Aguilar-Mawdsley appended a joint declaration (*ibid.*, pp. 24-25 and 136-137). Judges Lachs (*ibid.*, pp. 26-27 and 138-139) and Shahabuddeen (*ibid.*, pp. 28-32 and 140-142) appended separate opinions; and Judges Bedjaoui (*ibid.*, pp. 33-49 and 143-159), Weeramantry (*ibid.*, pp. 50-71 and 160-181), Ranjeva (*ibid.*, pp. 72-77 and 182), Ajibola (*ibid.*, pp. 78-93 and 183-198) and Judge *ad hoc* El-Kosheri (*ibid.*, pp. 94-112 and 199-217) appended dissenting opinions to the Orders.

By Orders of 19 June 1992 (*ibid.*, pp. 231 and 234), the Court, taking into account that the length of time-limits had been agreed by the Parties at a meeting held on 5 June 1992 with the Vice-President of the Court, exercising the function of the presidency in the two cases, fixed 20 December 1993 as the time-limit for the filing of the Memorial of Libya and 20 June 1995 for the filing of the Counter-Memorials of the United Kingdom and the United States of America. The Memorial was filed within the prescribed time-limit.

On 16 and 20 June 1995 respectively the United Kingdom and the United States of America filed preliminary objections to the jurisdiction of the Court to entertain the Applications of the Libyan Arab Jamahiriya.

By virtue of Article 79, paragraph 3, of the Rules of Court, the proceedings on the merits are suspended when preliminary objections are filed; proceedings have then to be organized for the consideration of those preliminary objections in accordance with the provisions of that Article.

After a meeting had been held, on 9 September 1995, between the President of the Court and the Agents of the Parties to ascertain the latters' views, the Court, by Orders of 22 September 1995 (*I.C.J. Reports 1995*, pp. 282 and 285), fixed, in each case, 22 December 1995 as the time-limit within which the Libyan Arab Jamahiriya might present a written statement of its observations and submissions on the preliminary objections raised by the United Kingdom and the United States of America respectively. Libya filed such statements within the prescribed time-limits.

6. *Oil Platforms (Islamic Republic of Iran* v. *United States of America)*

On 2 November 1992 the Islamic Republic of Iran filed in the Registry of the Court an Application instituting proceedings against the United States of America with respect to the destruction of Iranian oil platforms.

The Islamic Republic founded the jurisdiction of the Court for the purposes of these proceedings on Article XXI (2) of the Treaty of Amity, Economic Relations and Consular Rights between the United States of America and Iran, signed at Tehran on 15 August 1955.

In its Application Iran alleged that the destruction caused by several warships of the United States Navy, on 19 October 1987 and 18 April 1988, to three offshore oil production complexes, owned and operated for commercial purposes by the National Iranian Oil Company, constituted a fundamental breach of various provisions of the Treaty of Amity and of international law. In this connection Iran referred in particular to Articles I and X(1) of the Treaty which provide respectively: "There shall be firm and enduring peace and sincere friendship between the United States of America and Iran", and "Between the territories of the two High Contracting Parties there shall be freedom of commerce and navigation".

The Islamic Republic accordingly requested the Court to adjudge and declare as follows:

"*(a)* that the Court has jurisdiction under the Treaty of Amity to entertain the dispute and to rule upon the claims submitted by the Islamic Republic;

(b) that in attacking and destroying the oil platforms referred to in the Application on 19 October 1987 and 18 April 1988, the United States breached its obligations to the Islamic Republic, *inter alia*, under Article I and X (1) of the Treaty of Amity and international law;

(c) that in adopting a patently hostile and threatening attitude towards the Islamic Republic that culminated in the attack and destruction of the Iranian oil platforms, the United States breached the object and purpose of the Treaty of Amity, including Articles I and X(1), and international law;

(d) that the United States is under an obligation to make reparations to the Islamic Republic for the violation of its international legal obligations in an amount to be determined by the Court at a subsequent stage of the proceedings. The Islamic Republic reserves the right to introduce and present to the Court in due course a precise evaluation of the reparations owed by the United States; and

(e) any other remedy the Court may deem appropriate."

By an Order of 4 December 1992 (*I.C.J. Reports 1992*, p. 763), the President of the Court, taking into account an agreement of the Parties, fixed 31 May 1993 as the time-limit for the filing of the Memorial of Iran and 30 November 1993 for the filing of the Counter-Memorial of the United States.

By an Order of 3 June 1993 (*I.C.J. Reports 1993*, p. 35), the President of the Court, upon the request of Iran and after the United States had indicated that it had no objection, extended those time-limits to 8 June and 16 December 1993, respectively. The Memorial was filed within the prescribed time-limit.

The Islamic Republic of Iran chose Mr. François Rigaux to sit as judge *ad hoc*.

On 16 December 1993, within the extended time-limit for filing the Counter-Memorial, the United States of America filed certain preliminary objections to the Court's jurisdiction. In accordance with the terms of Article 79, paragraph 3, of the Rules of Court, the proceedings on the merits were suspended; by an Order of 18 January 1994 (*I.C.J. Reports 1994*, p. 3), the Court fixed 1 July 1994 as the time-limit within which Iran could present a written statement of its observations and submissions on the objections. That written statement was filed within the prescribed time-limit.

The public sittings to hear the oral arguments of the Parties on the preliminary objections filed by the United States of America will open on 16 September 1996.

7. Application of the Convention on the Prevention and Punishment of the Crime of Genocide (Bosnia and Herzegovina v. *Yugoslavia)*

On 20 March 1993, the Republic of Bosnia and Herzegovina filed in the Registry of the Court an Application instituting proceedings against Yugoslavia "for violating the Genocide Convention".

The Application referred to several provisions of the Convention on the Prevention and Punishment of the Crime of Genocide of 9 December 1948, as well as of the Charter of the United Nations, which Bosnia and Herzegovina alleged were violated by Yugoslavia. It also referred in this respect to the four Geneva Conventions of 1949 and their Additional Protocol I of 1977, to the Hague Regulations on Land Warfare of 1907, and to the Universal Declaration of Human Rights.

The Application referred to Article IX of the Genocide Convention as the basis for the jurisdiction of the Court.

In the Application, Bosnia and Herzegovina requested the Court to adjudge and declare:

"*(a)* that Yugoslavia (Serbia and Montenegro) has breached, and is continuing to breach, its legal obligations toward the People and State of Bosnia and Herzegovina under Articles I, II *(a)*, II *(b)*, II *(c)*, II *(d)*, III *(a)*, III *(b)*, III *(c)*, III *(d)*, III *(e)*, IV and V of the Genocide Convention;

(b) that Yugoslavia (Serbia and Montenegro) has violated and is continuing to violate its legal obligations toward the People and State of Bosnia and Herzegovina under the four Geneva Conventions of 1949, their Additional Protocol I of 1977, the customary international laws of war including the Hague Regulations on Land Warfare of 1907, and other fundamental principles of international humanitarian law;

(c) that Yugoslavia (Serbia and Montenegro) has violated and

continues to violate Articles 1, 2, 3, 4, 5, 6, 7, 8, 9, 10, 11, 12, 13, 15, 16, 17, 18, 19, 20, 21, 22, 23, 25, 26 and 28 of the Universal Declaration of Human Rights with respect to the citizens of Bosnia and Herzegovina;

(d) that Yugoslavia (Serbia and Montenegro), in breach of its obligations under general and customary international law, has killed, murdered, wounded, raped, robbed, tortured, kidnapped, illegally detained, and exterminated the citizens of Bosnia and Herzegovina, and is continuing to do so;

(e) that in its treatment of the citizens of Bosnia and Herzegovina, Yugoslavia (Serbia and Montenegro) has violated, and is continuing to violate, its solemn obligations under Articles 1 (3), 55 and 56 of the United Nations Charter;

(f) that Yugoslavia (Serbia and Montenegro) has used and is continuing to use force and the threat of force against Bosnia and Herzegovina in violation of Articles 2 (1), 2 (2), 2 (3), 2 (4), and 33 (1), of the United Nations Charter;

(g) that Yugoslavia (Serbia and Montenegro), in breach of its obligations under general and customary international law, has used and is using force and the threat of force against Bosnia and Herzegovina;

(h) that Yugoslavia (Serbia and Montenegro), in breach of its obligations under general and customary international law, has violated and is violating the sovereignty of Bosnia and Herzegovina by:

- armed attacks against Bosnia and Herzegovina by air and land;
- aerial trespass into Bosnian airspace;
- efforts by direct and indirect means to coerce and intimidate the Government of Bosnia and Herzegovina;

(i) that Yugoslavia (Serbia and Montenegro), in breach of its obligations under general and customary international law, has intervened and is intervening in the internal affairs of Bosnia and Herzegovina;

(j) that Yugoslavia (Serbia and Montenegro), in recruiting, training, arming, equipping, financing, supplying and otherwise encouraging, supporting, aiding, and directing military and paramilitary actions in and against Bosnia and Herzegovina by means of its agents and surrogates, has violated and is violating its express charter and treaty obligations to Bosnia and Herzegovina and, in particular, its charter and treaty obligations under Article 2 (4) of the United Nations Charter, as well as its obligations under general and customary international law;

(k) that under the circumstances set forth above, Bosnia and Herzegovina has the sovereign right to defend Itself and its People under United Nations Charter Article 51 and customary

international law, including by means of immediately obtaining military weapons, equipment, supplies and troops from other States;

(l) that under the circumstances set forth above, Bosnia and Herzegovina has the sovereign right under United Nations Charter Article 51 and customary international law to request the immediate assistance of any State to come to its defence, including by military means (weapons, equipment, supplies, troops, etc.);

(m) that Security Council resolution 713 (1991), imposing a weapons embargo upon the former Yugoslavia, must be construed in a manner that shall not impair the inherent right of individual or collective self-defence of Bosnia and Herzegovina under the terms of United Nations Charter Article 51 and the rules of customary international law;

(n) that all subsequent Security Council resolutions that refer to or reaffirm resolution 713 (1991) must be construed in a manner that shall not impair the inherent right of individual or collective self-defence of Bosnia and Herzegovina under the terms of United Nations Charter Article 51 and the rules of customary international law;

(o) that Security Council resolution 713 (1991) and all subsequent Security Council resolutions referring thereto or reaffirming thereof must not be construed to impose an arms embargo upon Bosnia and Herzegovina, as required by Articles 24 (1) and 51 of the United Nations Charter and in accordance with the customary doctrine of *ultra vires*;

(p) that pursuant to the right of collective self-defence recognized by United Nations Charter Article 51, all other State parties to the Charter have the right to come to the immediate defence of Bosnia and Herzegovina – at its request – including by means of immediately providing It with weapons, military equipment and supplies, and armed forces (soldiers, sailors, airpeople, etc.);

(q) that Yugoslavia (Serbia and Montenegro) and its agents and surrogates are under an obligation to cease and desist immediately from its breaches of the foregoing legal obligations, and is under a particular duty to cease and desist immediately:

- from its systematic practice of so-called 'ethnic cleansing' of the citizens and sovereign territory of Bosnia and Herzegovina;
- from the murder, summary execution, torture, rape, kidnapping, mayhem, wounding, physical and mental abuse, and detention of the citizens of Bosnia and Herzegovina;
- from the wanton devastation of villages, towns, districts, cities, and religious institutions in Bosnia and Herzegovina;

- from the bombardment of civilian population centres in Bosnia and Herzegovina, and especially its capital, Sarajevo;
- from continuing the siege of any civilian population centres in Bosnia and Herzegovina, and especially its capital, Sarajevo;
- from the starvation of the civilian population in Bosnia and Herzegovina;
- from the interruption of, interference with, or harassment of humanitarian relief supplies to the citizens of Bosnia and Herzegovina by the international community;
- from all use of force – whether direct or indirect, overt or covert – against Bosnia and Herzegovina, and from all threats of force against Bosnia and Herzegovina;
- from all violations of the sovereignty, territorial integrity or political independence of Bosnia and Herzegovina, including all intervention, direct or indirect, in the internal affairs of Bosnia and Herzegovina;
- from all support of any kind – including the provision of training, arms, ammunition, finances, supplies, assistance, direction or any other form of support – to any nation, group, organization, movement or individual engaged or planning to engage in military or paramilitary actions in or against Bosnia and Herzegovina.

(r) that Yugoslavia (Serbia and Montenegro) has an obligation to pay Bosnia and Herzegovina, in its own right and as *parens patriae* for its citizens, reparations for damages to persons and property as well as to the Bosnian economy and environment caused by the foregoing violations of international law in a sum to be determined by the Court. Bosnia and Herzegovina reserves the right to introduce to the Court a precise evaluation of the damages caused by Yugoslavia (Serbia and Montenegro)."

On the same day, the Government of Bosnia and Herzegovina, stating that:

> "The overriding objective of this Request is to prevent further loss of human life in Bosnia and Herzegovina",

and that:

> "The very lives, well-being, health, safety, physical, mental and bodily integrity, homes, property and personal possessions of hundreds of thousands of people in Bosnia and Herzegovina are right now at stake, hanging in the balance, awaiting the order of this Court",

filed a request for the indication of provisional measures under Article 41 of the Statute of the Court.

The provisional measures requested were as follows:

> "1. That Yugoslavia (Serbia and Montenegro), together with its agents and surrogates in Bosnia and elsewhere, must immediately cease and desist from all acts of genocide and genocidal acts against the People and State of Bosnia and Herzegovina, including but not limited to murder; summary executions; torture; rape; mayhem; so-called 'ethnic cleansing'; the wanton devastation of villages, towns, districts and cities; the siege of villages, towns, districts and cities; the starvation of the civilian population; the interruption of, interference with, or harassment of humanitarian relief supplies to the civilian population by the international community; the bombardment of civilian population centres; and the detention of civilians in concentration camps or otherwise.
>
> 2. That Yugoslavia (Serbia and Montenegro) must immediately cease and desist from providing, directly or indirectly, any type of support – including training, weapons, arms, ammunition, supplies, assistance, finances, direction or any other form of support – to any nation, group, organization, movement, militia or individual engaged in or planning to engage in military or paramilitary activities in or against the People, State and Government of Bosnia and Herzegovina.
>
> 3. That Yugoslavia (Serbia and Montenegro) itself must immediately cease and desist from any and all types of military or paramilitary activities by its own officials, agents, surrogates, or forces in or against the People, State and Government of Bosnia and Herzegovina, and from any other use or threat of force in its relations with Bosnia and Herzegovina.
>
> 4. That under the current circumstances, the Government of Bosnia and Herzegovina has the right to seek and receive support from other States in order to defend Itself and its People, including by means of immediately obtaining military weapons, equipment and supplies.
>
> 5. That under the current circumstances, the Government of Bosnia and Herzegovina has the right to request the immediate assistance of any State to come to its defence, including by means of immediately providing weapons, military equipment and supplies, and armed forces (soldiers, sailors, airpeople, etc.).
>
> 6. That under the current circumstances, any State has the right to come to the immediate defence of Bosnia and Herzegovina – at its request – including by means of immediately providing weapons, military equipment and supplies, and armed forces (soldiers, sailors, and airpeople, etc.)."

Hearings on the request for the indication of provisional measures were held on 1 and 2 April 1993. At two public sittings the Court heard the oral observations of each of the Parties. A Member of the Court put a question to both Agents.

At a public sitting held on 8 April 1993, the President of the Court read out the Order on the request for provisional measures made by Bosnia and Herzegovina (*I.C.J. Reports 1993*, p. 3) by which the Court indicated, pending its final decision in the proceedings instituted on 20 March 1993 by the Republic of Bosnia and Herzegovina against the Federal Republic of Yugoslavia, the following provisional measures:

(a) The Government of the Federal Republic of Yugoslavia should immediately, in pursuance of its undertaking in the Convention on the Prevention and Punishment of the Crime of Genocide of 9 December 1948, take all measures within its power to prevent commission of the crime of genocide; and the Government of the Federal Republic of Yugoslavia should in particular ensure that any military, paramilitary or irregular armed units which may be directed or supported by it, as well as any organizations and persons which may be subject to its control, direction or influence, do not commit any acts of genocide, of conspiracy to commit genocide, of direct and public incitement to commit genocide, or of complicity in genocide, whether directed against the Muslim population of Bosnia and Herzegovina or against any other national, ethnical, racial or religious group.

(b) The Government of the Federal Republic of Yugoslavia and the Government of the Republic of Bosnia and Herzegovina should not take any action and should ensure that no action is taken which may aggravate or extend the existing dispute over the prevention or punishment of the crime of genocide, or render it more difficult of solution.

Judge Tarassov appended a declaration to the Order (*ibid.*, pp. 26-27).

By an Order of 16 April 1993 (*I.C.J. Reports 1993*, p. 29), the President of the Court, taking into account an agreement of the Parties, fixed 15 October 1993 as the time-limit for the filing of the Memorial of Bosnia and Herzegovina and 15 April 1994 for the filing of the Counter-Memorial of Yugoslavia.

Bosnia and Herzegovina chose Mr. Elihu Lauterpacht and Yugoslavia Mr. Milenko Kreća to sit as judges *ad hoc*.

On 27 July 1993 the Republic of Bosnia and Herzegovina filed a second request for the indication of provisional measures, stating that:

> "This extraordinary step is being taken because the Respondent has violated each and every one of the three measures of protection on behalf of Bosnia and Herzegovina that were indicated by this Court on 8 April 1993, to the grave detriment of both the People and State of Bosnia and Herzegovina. In addition to continuing its campaign of genocide against the Bosnian People – whether Muslim, Christian, Jew, Croat or Serb – the Respondent is now planning, preparing, conspiring to, proposing, and negotiating the partition, dismemberment, annexation and incorporation of the sovereign State

of Bosnia and Herzegovina – a Member of the United Nations Organization – by means of genocide."

The provisional measures then requested were as follows:

> "1. That Yugoslavia (Serbia and Montenegro) must immediately cease and desist from providing, directly or indirectly, any type of support – including training, weapons, arms, ammunition, supplies, assistance, finances, direction or any other form of support – to any nation, group, organization, movement, military, militia or paramilitary force, irregular armed unit, or individual in Bosnia and Herzegovina for any reason or purpose whatsoever.
>
> 2. That Yugoslavia (Serbia and Montenegro) and all of its public officials – including and especially the President of Serbia, Mr. Slobodan Milosevic – must immediately cease and desist from any and all efforts, plans, plots, schemes, proposals or negotiations to partition, dismember, annex or incorporate the sovereign territory of Bosnia and Herzegovina.
>
> 3. That the annexation or incorporation of any sovereign territory of the Republic of Bosnia and Herzegovina by Yugoslavia (Serbia and Montenegro) by any means or for any reason shall be deemed illegal, null, and void *ab initio*.
>
> 4. That the Government of Bosnia and Herzegovina must have the means 'to prevent' the commission of acts of genocide against its own People as required by Article I of the Genocide Convention.
>
> 5. That all Contracting Parties to the Genocide Convention are obliged by Article I thereof 'to prevent' the commission of acts of genocide against the People and State of Bosnia and Herzegovina.
>
> 6. That the Government of Bosnia and Herzegovina must have the means to defend the People and State of Bosnia and Herzegovina from acts of genocide and partition and dismemberment by means of genocide.
>
> 7. That all Contracting Parties to the Genocide Convention have the obligation thereunder 'to prevent' acts of genocide, and partition and dismemberment by means of genocide, against the People and State of Bosnia and Herzegovina.
>
> 8. That in order to fulfil its obligations under the Genocide Convention under the current circumstances, the Government of Bosnia and Herzegovina must have the ability to obtain military weapons, equipment, and supplies from other Contracting Parties.
>
> 9. That in order to fulfil their obligations under the Genocide Convention under the current circumstances, all Contracting Parties thereto must have the ability to provide military weapons, equipment, supplies and armed forces (soldiers, sailors, airpeople) to the Government of Bosnia and Herzegovina at its request.
>
> 10. That United Nations Peacekeeping Forces in Bosnia and Herzegovina (i.e., UNPROFOR) must do all in their power to ensure

> the flow of humanitarian relief supplies to the Bosnian People through the Bosnian city of Tuzla."

On 5 August 1993 the President of the Court addressed a message to both Parties, referring to Article 74, paragraph 4, of the Rules of Court, which enables him, pending the meeting of the Court,

> "to call upon the parties to act in such a way as will enable any order the Court may make on the request for provisional measures to have its appropriate effects",

and stating:

> "I do now call upon the Parties so to act, and I stress that the provisional measures already indicated in the Order which the Court made after hearing the Parties, on 8 April 1993, still apply.
>
> Accordingly I call upon the Parties to take renewed note of the Court's Order and to take all and any measures that may be within their power to prevent any commission, continuance, or encouragement of the heinous international crime of genocide."

On 10 August 1993 Yugoslavia filed a request, dated 9 August 1993, for the indication of provisional measures, whereby it requested the Court to indicate the following provisional measure:

> "The Government of the so-called Republic of Bosnia and Herzegovina should immediately, in pursuance of its obligation under the Convention on the Prevention and Punishment of the Crime of Genocide of 9 December 1948, take all measures within its power to prevent commission of the crime of genocide against the Serb ethnic group."

The hearings concerning the further requests for the indication of provisional measures were held on 25 and 26 August 1993. In the course of two public sittings the Court heard statements from each of the Parties. Judges put questions to both Parties.

At a public sitting held on 13 September 1993, the President of the Court read out the Order concerning the further requests for the indication of provisional measures (*I.C.J. Reports 1993*, p. 325), by which the Court reaffirmed the provisional measures indicated in its order of 8 April 1993, which measures, the Court stated, should be immediately and effectively implemented.

Judge Oda appended a declaration to the Order (*I.C.J. Reports 1993*, pp. 351-352); Judges Shahabuddeen, Weeramantry and Ajibola and Judge *ad hoc* Lauterpacht appended separate opinions (*ibid.*, pp. 353-369, 370-389, 390-406 and 407-448); and Judge Tarassov and Judge *ad hoc* Kreća appended dissenting opinions (*ibid.*, pp. 449-452 and 453-465).

By an Order of 7 October 1993 (*I.C.J. Reports 1993*, p. 470), the Vice-President of the Court, at the request of Bosnia and Herzegovina and after Yugoslavia had expressed its opinion, extended to 15 April 1994 the time-limit for the filing of the Memorial of Bosnia and Herzegovina, and to 15 April 1995 the time-limit for the filing of the Counter-Memorial of Yugoslavia. The Memorial was filed within the prescribed time-limit.

By an Order of 21 March 1995 (*I.C.J. Reports 1995*, p. 80), the President of the Court, upon a request of the Agent of Yugoslavia and after the views of Bosnia and Herzegovina had been ascertained, extended to 30 June 1995 the time-limit for the filing of the Counter-Memorial of Yugoslavia.

On 26 June 1995, within the extended time-limit for the filing of its Counter-Memorial, Yugoslavia filed certain preliminary objections. The objections related, firstly, to the admissibility of the Application and, secondly, to the jurisdiction of the Court to deal with the case.

By virtue of Article 79, paragraph 3, of the Rules of Court, the proceedings on the merits are suspended when preliminary objections are filed; proceedings have then to be organized for the consideration of those preliminary objections in accordance with the provision of that Article.

By an Order of 14 July 1995 (*I.C.J. Reports 1995*, p. 279), the President of the Court, taking into account the views expressed by the Parties, fixed 14 November 1995 as the time-limit within which the Republic of Bosnia and Herzegovina might present a written statement of its observations and submissions on the preliminary objections raised by the Federal Republic of Yugoslavia. Bosnia and Herzegovina filed such a statement within the prescribed time-limit.

Public sittings to hear the oral arguments of the Parties on the preliminary objection raised by Yugoslavia were held between 29 April and 3 May 1996.

At a public sitting held on 11 July 1996, the Court delivered its Judgment on the preliminary objections, a summary of which is given below, followed by the text of the operative paragraph:

Institution of proceedings and history of the case (paras. 1-15)

The Court began by recalling that on 20 March 1993, the Republic of Bosnia and Herzegovina (hereinafter called "Bosnia and Herzegovina") had instituted proceedings against the Federal Republic of Yugoslavia (hereinafter called "Yugoslavia") in respect of a dispute concerning alleged violations of the Convention on the Prevention and Punishment of the Crime of Genocide (hereinafter called "the Genocide Convention"), adopted by the General Assembly of the United Nations on 9 December 1948, as well as various matters which Bosnia and Herzegovina claimed were connected therewith. The Application had invoked Article IX of the Genocide Convention as the basis of the jurisdiction of the Court.

On 20 March 1993, immediately after the filing of its Application,

Bosnia and Herzegovina had submitted a request for the indication of provisional measures under Article 41 of the Statute. On 31 March 1993, the Agent of Bosnia and Herzegovina had filed in the Registry, invoking it as an additional basis of the jurisdiction of the Court in the case, the text of a letter dated 8 June 1992, addressed to the President of the Arbitration Commission of the International Conference for Peace in Yugoslavia by the Presidents of the Republics of Montenegro and Serbia. On 1 April 1993, Yugoslavia had submitted written observations on Bosnia and Herzegovina's request for provisional measures, in which, in turn, it had recommended the Court to order the application of provisional measures to Bosnia and Herzegovina. By an Order dated 8 April 1993, the Court, after hearing the Parties, had indicated certain provisional measures with a view to the protection of rights under the Genocide Convention.

On 27 July 1993, Bosnia and Herzegovina had submitted a new request for the indication of provisional measures; and, by a series of subsequent communications, had stated that it was amending or supplementing that request, as well as, in some cases, the Application, including the basis of jurisdiction relied on therein. By letters of 6 August and 10 August 1993, the Agent of Bosnia and Herzegovina had indicated that his Government was relying, as additional bases of the jurisdiction of the Court in the case, on, respectively, the Treaty between the Allied and Associated Powers and the Kingdom of the Serbs, Croats and Slovenes on the Protection of Minorities, signed at Saint-Germain-en-Laye on 10 September 1919, and on customary and conventional international laws of war and international humanitarian law. On 10 August 1993, Yugoslavia had also submitted a request for the indication of provisional measures; and, on 10 August and 23 August 1993, it had filed written observations on Bosnia and Herzegovina's new request, as amended or supplemented. By an Order dated 13 September 1993, the Court, after hearing the Parties, had reaffirmed the measures indicated in its Order of 8 April 1993 and declared that those measures should be immediately and effectively implemented.

Within the extended time-limit of 30 June 1995 for the filing of the Counter-Memorial, Yugoslavia had raised preliminary objections concerning, respectively, the admissibility of the Application and the jurisdiction of the Court to entertain the case. (In view of its length, the text of the preliminary objections is not reproduced in this summary.)

By a letter dated 2 February 1996, the Agent of Yugoslavia had submitted to the Court, "as a document relevant to the case", the text of the General Framework Agreement for Peace in Bosnia and Herzegovina and the annexes thereto (collectively "the peace agreement"), initialled in Dayton, Ohio, on 21 November 1995 and signed in Paris on 14 December 1995 (hereinafter called the "Dayton-Paris Agreement").

Public hearings on the preliminary objections raised by Yugoslavia had been held between 29 April and 3 May 1996.

Jurisdiction ratione personae (paras. 16-26)

Recalling that Bosnia and Herzegovina had principally relied, as a basis for the jurisdiction of the Court in this case, on Article IX of the Genocide Convention, the Court initially considered the preliminary objections raised by Yugoslavia on this point. It took note of the withdrawal by Yugoslavia of its fourth preliminary objection, which therefore need no longer be dealt with. In its third objection, Yugoslavia, on various grounds, had disputed the contention that the Convention bound the two Parties or that it had entered into force between them; and in its fifth objection, Yugoslavia had objected, for various reasons, to the argument that the dispute submitted by Bosnia and Herzegovina fell within the provisions of Article IX of the Convention.

The proceedings instituted before the Court were between two States whose territories were located within the former Socialist Federal Republic of Yugoslavia. At the time of the proclamation of the Federal Republic of Yugoslavia, on 27 April 1992, a formal declaration had been adopted on its behalf which expressed the intention of Yugoslavia to remain bound by the international treaties to which the former Yugoslavia was party. The Court observed, furthermore, that it had not been contested that Yugoslavia was party to the Genocide Convention. Thus, Yugoslavia was bound by the provisions of the Convention on the date of the filing of the Application in the instant case, namely, on 20 March 1993.

For its part, on 29 December 1992, Bosnia and Herzegovina had transmitted to the Secretary-General of the United Nations, as depositary of the Genocide Convention, a Notice of Succession. Yugoslavia had contested the validity and legal effect of that Notice, as, in its view, Bosnia and Herzegovina was not qualified to become a party to the Convention.

The Court noted that Bosnia and Herzegovina had become a Member of the United Nations following the decisions adopted on 22 May 1992 by the Security Council and the General Assembly, bodies competent under the Charter. Article XI of the Genocide Convention opened it to "any Member of the United Nations"; from the time of its admission to the Organization, Bosnia and Herzegovina had thus been able to become a party to the Convention. It was of the view that the circumstances of Bosnia and Herzegovina's accession to independence, which Yugoslavia referred to in its third preliminary objection, were of little consequence.

It was clear from the foregoing, that Bosnia and Herzegovina was able to become a party to the Convention through the mechanism of State succession. The Parties to the dispute differed, however, as to the legal consequences to be drawn from the occurrence of a State succession in the present case.

The Court did not consider it necessary, in order to decide on its jurisdiction in this case, to make a determination on the legal issues concerning State succession in respect to treaties which had been raised by the Parties. Whether Bosnia and Herzegovina had automatically become a party to the Genocide Convention on the date of its accession to independence on 6 March 1992, or whether it had become a party as a result – retroactive or not – of its Notice of Succession of 29 December 1992, at all events it had been a party to it on the date of the filing of its Application on 20 March 1993.

Yugoslavia had submitted that, even supposing that Bosnia and Herzegovina had been bound by the Convention in March 1993, it could not, at that time, have entered into force between the Parties, because the two States did not recognize one another and the conditions necessary to found the consensual basis of the Court's jurisdiction were therefore lacking. The Court observed, however, that this situation no longer obtained since the signature, and the entry into force on 14 December 1995, of the Dayton-Paris Agreement, Article X of which stipulated that the Parties "recognize each other as sovereign independent States within their international borders". It took note moreover that, even if it were to be assumed that the Genocide Convention did not enter into force between the Parties until the signature of the Dayton-Paris Agreement, all the conditions were currently fulfilled to found the jurisdiction of the Court *ratione personae*. It added that, indeed, the jurisdiction of the Court had normally to be assessed on the date of the filing of the act instituting proceedings, but that the Court, like its predecessor, the Permanent Court of International Justice, had always had recourse to the principle according to which it ought not to penalize a defect in a procedural act which the applicant could easily remedy.

In the light of the foregoing, the Court considered that it must reject Yugoslavia's third preliminary objection.

Jurisdiction ratione materiae (paras. 27-33)

In order to determine whether it had jurisdiction to entertain the case on the basis of Article IX of the Genocide Convention, it remained for the Court to verify whether there was a dispute between the Parties that fell within the scope of that provision. Article IX of the Convention is worded as follows:

> "Disputes between the Contracting Parties relating to the interpretation, application or fulfilment of the present Convention, including those relating to the responsibility of a State for genocide or for any of the other acts enumerated in Article III, shall be submitted to the International Court of Justice at the request of any of the parties to the dispute."

It is jurisdiction *ratione materiae*, as so defined, to which Yugoslavia's fifth objection related.

The Court noted that there persisted between the Parties before it,

> "a situation in which the two sides hold clearly opposite views concerning the question of the performance or non-performance of

> certain treaty obligations" (*Interpretation of Peace Treaties with Bulgaria, Hungary and Romania, First Phase, Advisory Opinion, I.C.J. Reports 1950*, p. 74)

and that, by reason of the rejection by Yugoslavia of the complaints formulated against it by Bosnia and Herzegovina, there was a legal dispute.

To found its jurisdiction, the Court had, however, still to ensure that the dispute in question did indeed fall within the provisions of Article IX of the Genocide Convention.

Yugoslavia disputed this. It contested the existence in this case of an "international dispute" within the meaning of the Convention, basing itself on two propositions: first, that the conflict occurring in certain parts of the Applicant's territory was of a domestic nature, Yugoslavia was not party to it and did not exercise jurisdiction over that territory at the time in question; and, second, that State responsibility, as referred to in the requests of Bosnia and Herzegovina, was excluded from the scope of application of Article IX.

With regard to Yugoslavia's first proposition, the Court considered that, irrespective of the nature of the conflict forming the background to the acts referred to in Articles II and III of the Convention, the obligations of prevention and punishment which were incumbent upon the States parties to the Convention remained identical. It further noted that it could not, at that stage in the proceedings, settle the question whether Yugoslavia took part – directly or indirectly – in the conflict at issue, which clearly belonged to the merits. Lastly, as to the territorial problems linked to the application of the Convention, the Court was of the view that it followed from the object and purpose of the Convention that the rights and obligations enshrined by the Convention were rights and obligations *erga omnes*. The Court noted that the obligation each State thus had to prevent and to punish the crime of genocide was not territorially limited by the Convention.

Concerning the second proposition advanced by Yugoslavia, regarding the type of State responsibility envisaged in Article IX of the Convention, the Court observed that the reference in Article IX to "the responsibility of a State for genocide or for any of the other acts enumerated in Article III", did not exclude any form of State responsibility. Nor was the responsibility of a State for acts of its organs excluded by Article IV of the Convention, which contemplated the commission of an act of genocide by "rulers" or "public officials". In the light of the foregoing, the Court considered that it had to reject the fifth preliminary objection of Yugoslavia.

Jurisdiction ratione temporis (para. 34)

In this regard, the Court confined itself to the observation that the Genocide Convention – and in particular Article IX – did not contain any clause the object or effect of which was to limit in such manner the scope of its jurisdiction *ratione temporis*, and observed that neither had the Parties themselves made any reservation to that end, either to the Convention or on the occasion of the signature of the Dayton-Paris Agreement. The Court thus found that it had jurisdiction in that case to give effect to the Genocide Convention with regard to the relevant facts which had occurred since the beginning of the conflict which took place in Bosnia and Herzegovina. As a result, the Court considered that it had to reject Yugoslavia's sixth and seventh preliminary objections.

Additional basis of jurisdiction invoked by Bosnia and Herzegovina (paras. 35-41)

The Court found further that it was unable to uphold as a basis for its jurisdiction in the instant case a letter dated 8 June 1992 addressed to the President of the Arbitration Commission of the International Conference for Peace in Yugoslavia by Mr. Momir Bulatović, President of the Republic of Montenegro, and Mr. Slobodan Milosević, President of the Republic of Serbia; the Treaty between the Allied and Associated Powers (the United States of America, the British Empire, France, Italy and Japan) and the Kingdom of the Serbs, Croats and Slovenes, that was signed at Saint-Germain-en-Laye on 10 September 1919 and entered into force on 16 July 1920; or any other of the additional bases of jurisdiction invoked by Bosnia and Herzegovina. Nor did the Court find that Yugoslavia had given in this case a "voluntary and indisputable" consent which would have conferred upon the Court a jurisdiction exceeding that which it had already acknowledged to have been conferred upon it by Article IX of the Genocide Convention. Its only jurisdiction to entertain the case was on the basis of Article IX of the Genocide Convention.

Admissibility of the Application (paras. 42-45)

According to the first preliminary objection of Yugoslavia, the Application was said to be inadmissible on the ground that it referred to events that had taken place within the framework of a civil war, and there was consequently no international dispute upon which the Court could make a finding.

That objection was very close to the fifth objection which the Court had already considered. In responding to the latter objection, the Court had in fact also answered it. Having noted that there did indeed exist between the Parties a dispute falling within the provisions of Article IX of the Genocide Convention – that is to say an international dispute –, the Court could not find that the Application was inadmissible on the sole ground that, in order to decide the dispute, it would have been impelled to take account of events that might have occurred in a context of civil war. It followed that the first objection of Yugoslavia had to be rejected.

According to the second objection of Yugoslavia, the Application was inadmissible because, as Mr. Alija Izetbegović had not been serving as President of the Republic – but only as President of the Presidency – at the time at which he had granted the authorization to initiate proceedings, that authorization had been granted in violation of certain rules of domestic law of fundamental significance. Yugoslavia had likewise contended that Mr. Izetbegović was not even acting legally at that time as President of the Presidency.

The Court observed that, according to international law, there was no doubt that every Head of State was presumed to be able to act on behalf of the State in its international relations and that at the time of the filing of the Application, Mr. Izetbegović had been recognized, in particular by the United Nations, as the Head of State of Bosnia and Herzegovina. It therefore also rejected the second preliminary objection of Yugoslavia.

The Court emphasized, finally, that it did not consider that Yugoslavia had, in presenting its objections, abused its rights to do so under Article 36, paragraph 6, of the Statute of the Court and Article 79 of the Rules of Court, and concluded that having established its jurisdiction under Article IX of the Genocide Convention, and having concluded that the Application was admissible, the Court might now proceed to consider the merits of the case on that basis.

Operative paragraph (para. 47)

"For these reasons,

THE COURT,

(1) Having taken note of the withdrawal of the fourth preliminary objection raised by the Federal Republic of Yugoslavia,

Rejects

(a) by fourteen votes to one,

the first, second and third preliminary objections;

IN FAVOUR: *President* Bedjaoui; *Vice-President* Schwebel; *Judges* Oda, Guillaume, Shahabuddeen, Weeramantry, Ranjeva, Herczegh, Shi, Koroma, Vereshchetin, Ferrari Bravo, Parra-Aranguren; *Judge* ad hoc Lauterpacht;

AGAINST: *Judge* ad hoc Kreća;

(b) by eleven votes to four,

the fifth preliminary objection;

IN FAVOUR: *President* Bedjaoui; *Vice-President* Schwebel; *Judges* Guillaume, Shahabuddeen, Weeramantry, Ranjeva, Herczegh, Koroma, Ferrari Bravo, Parra-Aranguren; *Judge* ad hoc Lauterpacht;

AGAINST: *Judges* Oda, Shi, Vereshchetin; *Judge* ad hoc Kreća;

(c) by fourteen votes to one,

the sixth and seventh preliminary objections;

IN FAVOUR: *President* Bedjaoui; *Vice-President* Schwebel; *Judges* Oda, Guillaume, Shahabuddeen, Weeramantry, Ranjeva, Herczegh, Shi, Koroma, Vereshchetin, Ferrari Bravo, Parra-Aranguren; *Judge* ad hoc Lauterpacht;

AGAINST: *Judge* ad hoc Kreća;

(2) *(a)* by thirteen votes to two,

Finds that, on the basis of Article IX of the Convention on the Prevention and Punishment of the Crime of Genocide, it has jurisdiction to adjudicate upon the dispute;

IN FAVOUR: *President* Bedjaoui; *Vice-President* Schwebel; *Judges* Guillaume, Shahabuddeen, Weeramantry, Ranjeva, Herczegh, Shi, Koroma, Vereshchetin, Ferrari Bravo, Parra-Aranguren; *Judge* ad hoc Lauterpacht;

AGAINST: *Judge* Oda; *Judge* ad hoc Kreća;

(b) by fourteen votes to one,

Dismisses the additional bases of jurisdiction invoked by the Republic of Bosnia and Herzegovina;

IN FAVOUR: *President* Bedjaoui; *Vice-President* Schwebel; *Judges* Oda, Guillaume, Shahabuddeen, Weeramantry, Ranjeva, Herczegh, Shi, Koroma, Vereshchetin, Ferrari Bravo, Parra-Aranguren; *Judge* ad hoc Kreća;

AGAINST: *Judge* ad hoc Lauterpacht;

(3) by thirteen votes to two,

Finds that the Application filed by the Republic of Bosnia and Herzegovina on 20 March 1993 is admissible.

IN FAVOUR: *President* Bedjaoui; *Vice-President* Schwebel; *Judges* Guillaume, Shahabuddeen, Weeramantry, Ranjeva, Herczegh, Shi, Koroma, Vereshchetin, Ferrari Bravo, Parra-Aranguren; *Judge* ad hoc Lauterpacht;

AGAINST: *Judge* Oda; *Judge* ad hoc Kreća."

*

Judge Oda appended a declaration to the Judgment of the Court; Judges Shi and Vereshchetin appended a joint declaration; Judge *ad hoc* Lauterpacht also appended a declaration; Judges Shahabuddeen, Weeramantry and Parra-Aranguren appended separate opinions; Judge *ad hoc* Kreća appended a dissenting opinion.

*

By an Order of 23 July 1996, the President of the Court, taking into account the views expressed by the Parties, fixed 23 July 1997 as the time-limit for the filing of the Counter-Memorial of Yugoslavia.

8. Gabčíkovo-Nagymaros Project (Hungary/Slovakia)

On 23 October 1992 the Ambassador of the Republic of Hungary to the Netherlands filed in the Registry of the Court an Application instituting proceedings against the Czech and Slovak Federal Republic in a dispute concerning the projected diversion of the Danube. In that document the Hungarian Government, before detailing its case, invited the Czech and Slovak Federal Republic to accept the jurisdiction of the Court.

A copy of the Application was transmitted to the Government of the Czech and Slovak Federal Republic in accordance with Article 38, paragraph 5, of the Rules of Court, which reads as follows:

> "When the Applicant State proposes to found the jurisdiction of the Court upon a consent thereto yet to be given or manifested by the State against which such application is made, the application shall be transmitted to that State. It shall not however be entered in the General List, nor any action be taken in the proceedings, unless and until the State against which such application is made consents to the Court's jurisdiction for the purposes of the case."

Following negotiations under the aegis of the European Communities between Hungary and the Czech and Slovak Federal Republic, which dissolved into two separate States on 1 January 1993, the Governments of the Republic of Hungary and of the Slovak Republic notified jointly, on 2 July 1993, to the Registrar of the Court a Special Agreement, signed at Brussels on 7 April 1993, for the submission to the Court of certain issues arising out of differences which had existed between the Republic of Hungary and the Czech and Slovak Federal Republic, regarding the implementation and the termination of the Budapest Treaty of 16 September 1977 on the Construction and Operation of the Gabčíkovo-Nagymaros Barrage System and on the construction and operation of the "provisional solution". The Special Agreement records that the Slovak Republic is in this respect the sole successor State of the Czech and Slovak Federal Republic.

In Article 2 of the Special Agreement:

> "(1) The Court is requested to decide on the basis of the Treaty and rules and principles of general international law, as well as such other treaties as the Court may find applicable,
>
> *(a)* whether the Republic of Hungary was entitled to suspend and subsequently abandon, in 1989, the works on the Nagymaros Project and on the part of the Gabčíkovo Project for which the Treaty attributed responsibility to the Republic of Hungary;

(*b*) whether the Czech and Slovak Federal Republic was entitled to proceed, in November 1991, to the 'provisional solution' and to put into operation from October 1992 this system, described in the Report of the Working Group of Independent Experts of the Commission of the European Communities, the Republic of Hungary and the Czech and Slovak Federal Republic dated 23 November 1992 (damming up of the Danube at river kilometre 1851.7 on Czechoslovak territory and resulting consequences on water and navigation course);

(*c*) what are the legal effects of the notification, on 19 May 1992, of the termination of the Treaty by the Republic of Hungary.

(2) The Court is also requested to determine the legal consequences, including the rights and obligations for the Parties, arising from its Judgment on the questions in paragraph 1 of this Article."

By an Order of 14 July 1993 (*I.C.J. Reports 1993*, p. 319) the Court decided that, as provided in Article 3, paragraph 2, of the Special Agreement and Article 46, paragraph 1, of the Rules of Court, each Party should file a Memorial and a Counter-Memorial, within the same time-limit, and fixed 2 May 1994 and 5 December 1994 as the time-limits for the filing of the Memorial and Counter-Memorial, respectively. The Memorials and Counter-Memorials were filed within the prescribed time-limits.

Slovakia chose Mr. Krzysztof J. Skubiszewski to sit as judge *ad hoc*.

By an Order of 20 December 1994 (*I.C.J. Reports 1994*, p. 151), the President of the Court, taking into account the views of the Parties, fixed 20 June 1995 as the time-limit for the filing of a Reply by each of the Parties. Those Replies were filed within the prescribed time-limit.

9. Land and Maritime Boundary between Cameroon and Nigeria (Cameroon v. *Nigeria)*

On 29 March 1994 the Republic of Cameroon filed in the Registry of the Court an Application instituting proceedings against the Federal Republic of Nigeria in a dispute concerning the question of sovereignty over the peninsula of Bakassi, and requesting the Court to determine the course of the maritime frontier between the two States in so far as that frontier had not already been established in 1975.

As a basis for the jurisdiction of the Court, the Application refers to the declarations made by Cameroon and Nigeria under Article 36, paragraph 2, of the Statute of the Court, by which they accept that jurisdiction as compulsory.

In the Application Cameroon refers to "an aggression by the Federal Republic of Nigeria, whose troops are occupying several Cameroonian localities on the Bakassi Peninsula", resulting "in great prejudice to the Republic of Cameroon", and requests the Court to adjudge and declare:

"*(a)* that sovereignty over the Peninsula of Bakassi is Cameroonian, by virtue of international law, and that that Peninsula is an integral part of the territory of Cameroon;

(b) that the Federal Republic of Nigeria has violated and is violating the fundamental principle of respect for frontiers inherited from colonization *(uti possidetis juris)*;

(c) that by using force against the Republic of Cameroon, the Federal Republic of Nigeria has violated and is violating its obligations under international treaty law and customary law;

(d) that the Federal Republic of Nigeria, by militarily occupying the Cameroonian Peninsula of Bakassi, has violated and is violating the obligations incumbent upon it by virtue of treaty law and customary law;

(e) that in view of these breaches of legal obligation, mentioned above, the Federal Republic of Nigeria has the express duty of putting an end to its military presence in Cameroonian territory, and effecting an immediate and unconditional withdrawal of its troops from the Cameroonian Peninsula of Bakassi;

(e′) that the internationally unlawful acts referred to under *(a)*, *(b)*, *(c)*, *(d)*, and *(e)* above involve the responsibility of the Federal Republic of Nigeria;

(e″) that, consequently, and on account of the material and non-material damage inflicted upon the Republic of Cameroon, reparation in an amount to be determined by the Court is due from the Federal Republic of Nigeria to the Republic of Cameroon, which reserves the introduction before the Court of [proceedings for] a precise assessment of the damage caused by the Federal Republic of Nigeria;

(f) in order to prevent any dispute arising between the two States concerning their maritime boundary, the Republic of Cameroon requests the Court to proceed to prolong the course of its maritime boundary with the Federal Republic of Nigeria up to the limit of the maritime zones which international law places under their respective jurisdictions."

On 6 June 1994 Cameroon filed in the Registry of the Court an Additional Application "for the purpose of extending the subject of the dispute" to a further dispute described as relating essentially "to the question of sovereignty over a part of the territory of Cameroon in the area of Lake Chad", while also asking the Court to specify definitively the frontier between Cameroon and Nigeria from Lake Chad to the sea. Cameroon requested the Court to adjudge and declare:

"*(a)* that sovereignty over the disputed parcel in the area of Lake Chad is Cameroonian, by virtue of international law, and that that parcel is an integral part of the territory of Cameroon;

(b) that the Federal Republic of Nigeria has violated and is violating the fundamental principle of respect for frontiers inherited from colonization *(uti possidetis juris)*, and its recent legal commitments concerning the demarcation of frontiers in Lake Chad;

(c) that the Federal Republic of Nigeria, by occupying, with the support of its security forces, parcels of Cameroonian territory in the area of Lake Chad, has violated and is violating its obligations under treaty law and customary law;

(d) that in view of these legal obligations, mentioned above, the Federal Republic of Nigeria has the express duty of effecting an immediate and unconditional withdrawal of its troops from Cameroonian territory in the area of Lake Chad;

(e) that the internationally unlawful acts referred to under *(a)*, *(b)*, and *(d)* above involve the responsibility of the Federal Republic of Nigeria;

(e') that consequently, and on account of the material and non-material damage inflicted upon the Republic of Cameroon, reparation in an amount to be determined by the Court is due from the Federal Republic of Nigeria to the Republic of Cameroon, which reserves the introduction before the Court of [proceedings for] a precise assessment of the damage caused by the Federal Republic of Nigeria;

(f) that in view of the repeated incursions of Nigerian groups and armed forces into Cameroonian territory, all along the frontier between the two countries, the consequent grave and repeated incidents, and the vacillating and contradictory attitude of the Federal Republic of Nigeria in regard to the legal instruments defining the frontier between the two countries and the exact course of that frontier, the Republic of Cameroon respectfully asks the Court to specify definitively the frontier between Cameroon and the Federal Republic of Nigeria from Lake Chad to the sea."

Cameroon further requested the Court to join the two Applications "and to examine the whole in a single case".

At a meeting between the President of the Court and the representatives of the Parties held on 14 June 1994, the Agent of Nigeria indicated that his Government had no objection to the Additional Application being treated as an amendment to the initial Application, so that the Court could deal with the whole as one case.

Cameroon chose Mr. Kéba Mbaye and Nigeria Prince Bola A. Ajibola to sit as judges *ad hoc*.

By an Order of 16 June 1994 (*I.C.J. Reports 1994*, p. 105), the Court, seeing no objection to the suggested procedure, fixed 16 March 1995 as the time-limit for filing the Memorial of Cameroon, and 18 December 1995 as the time-limit for filing the Counter-Memorial of Nigeria. The Memorial was filed within the prescribed time-limit.

On 13 December 1995, within the time-limit for the filing of its Counter-Memorial, Nigeria filed certain preliminary objections to the jurisdiction of the Court and to the admissibility of the claims of Cameroon.

By virtue of Article 79, paragraph 3, of the Rules of Court, the proceedings on the merits are suspended when preliminary objections are filed; proceedings have then to be organized for the consideration of those preliminary objections in accordance with the provisions of that Article.

By an Order of 10 January 1996 (*I.C.J. Reports 1996*, p. 3), the President of the Court, taking into account the views expressed by the Parties at a meeting between the President and the Agents of the Parties held on 10 January 1996, fixed 15 May 1996 as the time-limit within which Cameroon might present a written statement of its observations and submissions on the preliminary objections raised by Nigeria. Cameroon filed such a statement within the prescribed time-limit.

On 12 February 1996, the Registry of the International Court of Justice received from Cameroon a request for the indication of provisional measures, with reference to "serious armed incidents" which had taken place between Cameroonian and Nigerian forces in the Bakassi Peninsula beginning on 3 February 1996.

In its request Cameroon referred to the submissions made in its Application of 29 May 1994, supplemented by an Additional Application of 6 June of that year, as also summed up in its Memorial of 16 March 1995, and requested the Court to indicate the following provisional measures:

> "(1) the armed forces of the Parties shall withdraw to the position they were occupying before the Nigerian armed attack of 3 February 1996;
>
> (2) the Parties shall abstain from all military activity along the entire boundary until the judgment of the Court has taken place;
>
> (3) the Parties shall abstain from any act or action which might hamper the gathering of evidence in the present case".

Public sittings to hear the oral observations of the Parties on the request for the indication of provisional measures were held between 5 and 8 March 1996.

At a public sitting, held on 15 March 1996, the President of the Court read the Order on the request for provisional measures made by Cameroon (*I.C.J. Reports 1996*, p. 13), a summary of which is given below followed by the text of the operative paragraph.

In its Order the Court first recited the history of the proceedings as set out here above.

The Court then began by considering that the two Parties had each made a declaration recognizing the compulsory jurisdiction of the Court in accordance with Article 36, paragraph 2, of the Statute neither of which included any reservation and that those declarations constituted a prima facie basis upon which the Court's jurisdiction in the present case might be founded. The Court further considered that the consolidated Application of Cameroon did not appear prima facie to be inadmissible in the light of the preliminary objections raised by Nigeria.

The Court went on to observe that the power conferred upon it by Articles 41 of the Statute of the Court and 73 of the Rules of Court to indicate provisional measures had as its object to preserve the respective rights of the Parties, pending a decision of the Court, and presupposed that irreparable prejudice should not be caused to rights which were the subject of dispute in judicial proceedings; that it followed that the Court should be concerned to preserve by such measures the rights which might subsequently be adjudged by the Court to belong either to the Applicant or to the Respondent; and that such measures were only justified if there was urgency.

The Court found that the mediation conducted by the President of the Republic of Togo and the ensuing communiqué announcing the cessation of all hostilities published on 17 February 1996 did not deprive the Court of the rights and duties pertaining to it in the case brought before it. It was clear from the submissions of both Parties to the Court that there were military incidents and that they caused suffering, occasioned fatalities – of both military and civilian personnel – while causing others to be wounded or unaccounted for, as well as causing major material damage. The rights at issue in the proceedings were sovereign rights which the Parties claimed over territory, and these rights also concerned persons; and armed actions had regrettably occurred on territory which was the subject of proceedings before the Court.

Independently of the requests for the indication of provisional measures submitted by the Parties to preserve specific rights, the Court possessed by virtue of Article 41 of the Statute the power to indicate provisional measures with a view to preventing the aggravation or extension of the dispute whenever it considered that circumstances so required.

The Court found that the events that had given rise to the request, and more especially the killing of persons, had caused irreparable damage to the rights that the Parties might have over the Peninsula; that persons in the disputed area and, as a consequence, the rights of the Parties within that area were exposed to serious risk of further irreparable damage; and that armed actions within the territory in dispute could jeopardize the existence of evidence relevant to the present case. From the elements of information available to it, the Court took the view that there was a risk that events likely to aggravate or extend the dispute might occur again, thus rendering any settlement of that dispute more difficult.

The Court here observed that, in the context of the proceedings concerning the indication of provisional measures, it could not make definitive findings of fact or of imputability, and that the right of each Party to dispute the facts alleged against it, to challenge the attribution to it of responsibility for those facts, and to submit arguments, if appropriate, in respect of the merits, should remain unaffected by the Court's decision.

The Court then drew attention to the fact that the decision given in the current proceedings in no way prejudged the question of the jurisdiction of the Court to deal with the merits of the case, or any questions relating to the admissibility of the Application, or relating to the merits themselves and left unaffected the right of the Governments of Cameroon and Nigeria to submit arguments in respect of those questions.

After mentioning letters of the President of the Security Council, dated 29 February 1996, which called upon the two Parties "to respect the cease-fire they agreed to on 17 February in Kara, Togo", "to refrain from further violence", and "to take necessary steps to return their forces to the positions they occupied before the dispute was referred to the International Court [of Justice]"; and also the proposal of the Secretary-General of the United Nations to despatch a fact-finding mission into the Bakassi Peninsula, the Court indicated the provisional measures cited below.

Operative paragraph (para. 49)

"For these reasons,

THE COURT,

Indicates, pending a decision in the proceedings instituted as aforesaid, the following provisional measures:

(1) Unanimously,

Both Parties should ensure that no action of any kind, and particularly no action by their armed forces, is taken which might prejudice the rights of the other in respect of whatever judgment the Court may render in the case, or which might aggravate or extend the dispute before it;

(2) By sixteen votes to one,

Both Parties should observe the agreement reached between the Ministers for Foreign Affairs in Kara, Togo, on 17 February 1996, for the cessation of all hostilities in the Bakassi Peninsula;

IN FAVOUR: *President* Bedjaoui; *Vice-President* Schwebel; *Judges* Oda, Guillaume, Shahabuddeen, Weeramantry, Ranjeva, Herczegh, Shi, Fleischhauer, Koroma, Vereshchetin, Ferrari Bravo, Higgins, Parra-Aranguren; *Judge* ad hoc Mbaye;

AGAINST: *Judge* ad hoc Ajibola.

(3) By twelve votes to five,

Both Parties should ensure that the presence of any armed forces in the Bakassi Peninsula does not extend beyond the positions in which they were situated prior to 3 February 1996;

IN FAVOUR: *President* Bedjaoui; *Vice-President* Schwebel; *Judges* Oda, Guillaume, Ranjeva, Herczegh, Fleischhauer, Koroma, Ferrari Bravo, Higgins, Parra-Aranguren; *Judge* ad hoc Mbaye;

AGAINST: *Judges* Shahabuddeen, Weeramantry, Shi, Vereshchetin; *Judge* ad hoc Ajibola.

(4) By sixteen votes to one,

Both Parties should take all necessary steps to conserve evidence relevant to the present case within the disputed area;

IN FAVOUR: *President* Bedjaoui; *Vice-President* Schwebel; *Judges* Oda, Guillaume, Shahabuddeen, Weeramantry, Ranjeva, Herczegh, Shi, Fleischhauer, Koroma, Vereshchetin, Ferrari Bravo, Higgins, Parra-Aranguren; *Judge* ad hoc Mbaye;

AGAINST: *Judge* ad hoc Ajibola;

(5) By sixteen votes to one,

Both Parties should lend every assistance to the fact-finding mission which the Secretary-General of the United Nations has proposed to send to the Bakassi Peninsula.

IN FAVOUR: *President* Bedjaoui; *Vice-President* Schwebel; *Judges* Oda, Guillaume, Shahabuddeen, Weeramantry, Ranjeva, Herczegh, Shi, Fleischhauer, Koroma, Vereshchetin, Ferrari Bravo, Higgins, Parra-Aranguren; *Judge* ad hoc Mbaye;

AGAINST: *Judge* ad hoc Ajibola."

*

Judges Oda, Shahabuddeen, Ranjeva and Koroma appended declarations to the Order of the Court (*I.C.J. Reports 1996*, pp. 26-27, 28, 29 and 30); Judges Weeramantry, Shi and Vereshchetin appended a joint declaration (*ibid.*, p. 31); Judge *ad hoc* Mbaye appended a declaration (*ibid.*, pp. 32-34). Judge *ad hoc* Ajibola appended a separate opinion (*ibid.*, pp. 35-56).

10. Fisheries Jurisdiction (Spain v. *Canada)*

On 28 March 1995 the Kingdom of Spain filed in the Registry of the Court an Application instituting proceedings against Canada with respect to a dispute relating to the Canadian Coastal Fisheries Protection Act, as amended on 12 May 1994, and to the implementing regulations of that Act, as well as to certain measures taken on the basis of that legislation, more particularly the boarding on the high seas, on 9 March 1995, of a fishing boat, the *Estai*, sailing under the Spanish flag.

The Application indicated, *inter alia*, that by the amended Act "an attempt was made to impose on all persons on board foreign ships a broad prohibition on fishing in the NAFO [Northwest Atlantic Fisheries Organization] Regulatory Area – that is, on the high seas, outside Canada's exclusive economic zone"; that the Act "expressly permits (Art. 8) the use of force against foreign fishing boats in the zones that Article 2.1 unambiguously terms the 'high seas' "; that the rules of application of 25 May 1994 provided, in particular, for "the use of force by fishery protection officers against the foreign fishing boats covered by those regulations . . . which infringe their mandates in the zone of the high seas within the scope of those regulations"; and that the implementing regulations of 3 March 1995 "expressly permit [. . .] such conduct as regards Spanish and Portuguese ships on the high seas".

The Application alleged the violation of various principles and norms of international law and stated that there was a dispute between the Kingdom of Spain and Canada which, going beyond the framework of fishing, seriously affected the very principle of the freedom of the high seas and, moreover, implied a very serious infringement of the sovereign rights of Spain.

As a basis of the Court's jurisdiction, the Applicant referred to the declarations of Spain and of Canada made in accordance with Article 36, paragraph 2, of the Statute of the Court.

In that regard, the Application specified that:

> "The exclusion of the jurisdiction of the Court in relation to disputes which may arise from management and conservation measures taken by Canada with respect to vessels fishing in the NAFO Regulatory Area and the enforcement of such measures (Declaration of Canada, para. 2 *(d)*, introduced as recently as 10 May 1994, two days prior to the amendment of the Coastal Fisheries Protection Act), does not even partially affect the present dispute. Indeed, the Application of the Kingdom of Spain does not refer exactly to the disputes concerning those measures, but rather to their origin, to the Canadian legislation which constitutes their frame of reference. The Application of Spain directly attacks the title asserted to justify the Canadian measures and their actions to enforce them, a piece of legislation which, going a great deal further than the mere management and conservation of fishery resources, is in itself an internationally wrongful act of Canada, as it is contrary to the fundamental principles and norms of international law; a piece of legislation which for that reason does not fall exclusively within the jurisdiction of Canada either, according to its own Declaration (para. 2 *(c)* thereof). Moreover, only as from 3 March 1995 has an attempt been made to extend that legislation, in a discriminatory manner, to ships flying the flags of Spain and Portugal, which has led to the serious offences against international law set forth above."

While expressly reserving the right to modify and extend the terms of the Application, as well as the grounds invoked, and the right to request the appropriate provisional measures, the Kingdom of Spain requested:

> "(A) that the Court declare that the legislation of Canada, in so far as it claims to exercise a jurisdiction over ships flying a foreign flag on the high seas, outside the exclusive economic zone of Canada, is not opposable to the Kingdom of Spain;
>
> (B) that the Court adjudge and declare that Canada is bound to refrain from any repetition of the acts complained of, and to offer to the Kingdom of Spain the reparation that is due, in

the form of an indemnity the amount of which must cover all the damages and injuries occasioned; and

(C) that, consequently, the Court declare also that the boarding on the high seas, on 9 March 1995, of the ship *Estai* flying the flag of Spain, and the measures of coercion and the exercise of jurisdiction over that ship and over its captain constitute a concrete violation of the aforementioned principles and norms of international law."

By a letter dated 21 April 1995, the Ambassador of Canada to the Netherlands informed the Court that, in the view of his Government, the Court manifestly lacked jurisdiction to deal with the Application filed by Spain by reason of paragraph 2 *(d)* of the Declaration, dated 10 May 1994, whereby Canada accepted the compulsory jurisdiction of the Court.

Taking into account an agreement concerning the procedure reached between the Parties at a meeting with the President of the Court, held on 27 April 1995, the President, by an Order of 2 May 1995 (*I.C.J. Reports 1995*, p. 87), decided that the written proceedings should first be addressed to the question of the jurisdiction of the Court to entertain the dispute and fixed 29 September 1995 as the time-limit for the filing of the Memorial of the Kingdom of Spain and 29 February 1996 for the filing of the Counter-Memorial of Canada. The Memorial and Counter-Memorial were filed within the prescribed time-limits.

Spain chose Mr. Santiago Torres-Bernárdez and Canada the Honourable Marc Lalonde to sit as judges *ad hoc*.

The Spanish Government subsequently expressed its wish to be authorized to file a Reply; the Canadian Government opposed this. By an Order of 8 May 1996 (*I.C.J. Reports 1996*, p. 58), the Court, considering that it was "sufficiently informed, at this stage, of the contentions of fact and law on which the Parties rely with respect to its jurisdiction in the case and whereas the presentation by them of other written pleadings on that question therefore does not appear necessary", decided by fifteen votes to two, not to authorize the filing of a Reply by the Applicant and a Rejoinder by the Respondent on the question of jurisdiction.

Judge Vereshchetin and Judge *ad hoc* Torres-Bernárdez voted against; the latter appended a dissenting opinion to the Order (*I.C.J. Reports 1996*, p. 61).

The written proceedings on the question of the jurisdiction of the Court to entertain the dispute were thus concluded.

11. Request for an Examination of the Situation in Accordance with Paragraph 63 of the Court's Judgment of 20 December 1974 in the Nuclear Tests (New Zealand *v.* France) *Case*

On 21 August 1995, New Zealand submitted to the Court a Request for an Examination of the Situation "arising out of a proposed action announced by France which will, if carried out, affect the basis of the

Judgment rendered by the Court on 20 December 1974 in the *Nuclear Tests (New Zealand* v. *France)* case". The Request referred to a media statement of 13 June 1995 by President Chirac "which said that France would conduct a final series of eight nuclear weapons tests in the South Pacific starting in September 1995". New Zealand stated that the request was made "under the right granted to New Zealand in paragraph 63 of the Judgment of 20 December 1974".

Paragraph 63 reads as follows:

> "Once the Court has found that a State has entered into a commitment concerning its future conduct it is not the Court's function to contemplate that it will not comply with it. However, the Court observes that if the basis of this Judgment were to be affected, the Applicant could request an examination of the situation in accordance with the provisions of the Statute; the denunciation by France, by letter dated 2 January 1974, of the General Act for the Pacific Settlement of International Disputes, which is relied on as a basis of jurisdiction in the present case, cannot constitute by itself an obstacle to the presentation of such a request."

New Zealand asserted that the rights for which it sought protection "all fall within the scope of the rights invoked by New Zealand in paragraph 28 of the 1973 Application" in the above-mentioned case, but that at the present time New Zealand sought

> "recognition only of those rights that would be adversely affected by entry into the marine environment of radioactive material in consequence of the further tests to be carried out at Mururoa or Fangataufa Atolls, and of its entitlement to the protection and benefit of a properly conducted Environmental Impact Assessment".

New Zealand asked the Court to adjudge and declare:

> "(i) that the conduct of the proposed nuclear tests will constitute a violation of the rights under international law of New Zealand, as well as of other States;
>
> further or in the alternative;
>
> (ii) that it is unlawful for France to conduct such nuclear tests before it has undertaken an Environmental Impact Assessment according to accepted international standards. Unless such an assessment establishes that the tests will not give rise, directly or indirectly, to radioactive contamination of the marine environment the rights under international law of New Zealand, as well as the rights of other States, will be violated."

On the same day, New Zealand, referring to the Court's Order of 22 June 1973 indicating interim measures of protection and to the Court's Judgment of 20 December 1974 in the above-mentioned case, requested the Court, in accordance with Article 33, paragraph 1, of the General

Act for the Pacific Settlement of Disputes, 1928, and Article 41 of the Statute of the Court, to indicate the following further provisional measures:

"(1) that France refrain from conducting any further nuclear tests at Mururoa and Fangataufa Atolls;
(2) that France undertake an environmental impact assessment of the proposed nuclear tests according to accepted international standards and that, unless the assessment establishes that the tests will not give rise to radioactive contamination of the marine environment, France refrain from conducting the tests;
(3) that France and New Zealand ensure that no action of any kind is taken which might aggravate or extend the dispute submitted to the Court or prejudice the rights of the other Party in respect of the carrying out of whatever decisions the Court may give in this case".

New Zealand chose Sir Geoffrey Palmer to sit as judge *ad hoc*.

Applications for permission to intervene were submitted by Australia, Samoa, Solomon Islands, the Marshall Islands and the Federated States of Micronesia, while the last four States also made declarations on intervention.

At the invitation of the President of the Court, informal *aides-mémoire* regarding the legal nature of the New Zealand Requests and of their effects were presented by New Zealand and France. Public sittings to hear the oral arguments of the two States on the following question, "Do the Requests submitted to the Court by the Government of New Zealand on 21 August 1995 fall within the provisions of paragraph 63 of the Judgment of the Court of 20 December 1974 in the case concerning *Nuclear Tests (New Zealand* v. *France)*", were held on 11 and 12 September 1995.

At a public sitting held on 22 September 1995, the President of the Court read the Order (*I.C.J. Reports 1995*, p. 288), a summary of which is given below, followed by the text of the operative paragraph:

In its Order the Court first recalled the history of the proceedings as set out here above. It observed that New Zealand's "Request for an Examination of the Situation" submitted under paragraph 63 of the 1974 Judgment, even if it was disputed *in limine* whether it fulfilled the conditions set in that paragraph, should nonetheless be the object of entry in the General List of the Court for the sole purpose of enabling the latter to determine whether those conditions were fulfilled; and that it had accordingly instructed the Registrar.

The Court began its reasoning by citing paragraph 63 of the Judgment of 20 December 1974, which provides:

> "Once the Court has found that a State has entered into a commitment concerning its future conduct it is not the Court's function to contemplate that it will not comply with it. However, the Court

> observes that if the basis of this Judgment were to be affected, the Applicant could request an examination of the situation in accordance with the provisions of the Statute; the denunciation by France, by letter dated 2 January 1974, of the General Act for the Pacific Settlement of International Disputes, which is relied on as a basis of jurisdiction in the present case, cannot constitute by itself an obstacle to the presentation of such a request."

It then indicated that the following question had to be answered *in limine*: "Do the Requests submitted to the Court by the Government of New Zealand on 21 August 1995 fall within the provisions of paragraph 63 of the Judgment of the Court of 20 December 1974 in the case concerning *Nuclear Tests (New Zealand* v. *France)*?"; and that the present proceedings had consequently been limited to that question. The question had two elements; one concerned the courses of procedure envisaged by the Court in paragraph 63 of its 1974 Judgment, when it stated that "the Applicant could request an examination of the situation *in accordance with the provisions of the Statute*"; the other concerned the question whether the "basis" of that Judgment had been "affected" within the meaning of paragraph 63 thereof.

As to the first element of the question before it, the Court recalled that New Zealand expressed the following view:

> "paragraph 63 is a mechanism enabling the continuation or the resumption of the proceedings of 1973 and 1974. They were not fully determined. The Court foresaw that the course of future events might in justice require that New Zealand should have that opportunity to continue its case, the progress of which was stopped in 1974. And to this end in paragraph 63 the Court authorized these derivative proceedings. . . . the presentation of a Request for such an examination is to be part of the same case and not of a new one."

New Zealand added that paragraph 63 could only refer to the procedure applicable to the examination of the situation once the Request was admitted; it furthermore explicitly stated that it was not seeking an interpretation of the 1974 Judgment under Article 60 of the Statute, nor a revision of that Judgment under Article 61.

France, for its part, stated as follows:

> "As the Court itself has expressly stated, the possible steps to which it alludes are subject to compliance with the 'provisions of the Statute'. . . . The French Government incidentally further observes that, even had the Court not so specified, the principle would nevertheless apply: any activity of the Court is governed by the Statute, which circumscribes the powers of the Court and prescribes the conduct that States must observe without it being possible for them to depart therefrom, even by agreement . . .; as a result and *a fortiori*, a State cannot act unilaterally before the Court in the absence of any basis in the Statute.

> Now New Zealand does not invoke any provision of the Statute and could not invoke any that would be capable of justifying its procedure in law. It is not a request for interpretation or revision . . ., nor a new Application, whose entry in the General List would, for that matter, be quite out of the question . . ."

The Court observed that in expressly laying down, in paragraph 63 of its Judgment of 20 December 1974, that, in the circumstances set out therein, "the Applicant could request an examination of the situation *in accordance with the provisions of the Statute*", the Court could not have intended to limit the Applicant's access to legal procedures such as the filing of a new application (Statute, Art. 40, para. 1), a request for interpretation (Statute, Art. 60) or a request for revision (Statute, Art. 61), which would have been open to it in any event; by inserting the above-mentioned words in paragraph 63 of its Judgment, the Court did not exclude a special procedure, in the event that the circumstances defined in that paragraph were to arise, in other words, circumstances which "affected" the "basis" of the Judgment. The Court went on to point out that such a procedure appeared to be indissociably linked, under that paragraph, to the existence of those circumstances; and that if the circumstances in question did not arise, that special procedure was not available.

The Court then considered that it should determine the second element of the question raised, namely whether the basis of its Judgment of 20 December 1974 had been affected by the facts to which New Zealand referred and whether the Court might consequently proceed to examine the situation as contemplated by paragraph 63 of that Judgment; to that end, it first had to define the basis of that Judgment by an analysis of its text. The Court observed that, in 1974, it took as the point of departure of its reasoning the Application filed by New Zealand in 1973; that in its Judgment of 20 December 1974 it affirmed that

> "In the circumstances of the present case, as already mentioned, the Court must ascertain the true subject of the dispute, the object and purpose of the claim . . . In doing so it must take into account not only the submission, but the Application as a whole, the arguments of the Applicant before the Court, and other documents referred to . . ." (*I.C.J. Reports 1974*, p. 467, para. 31.)

Referring, among other things, to a statement made by the Prime Minister of New Zealand, the Court found that

> "for purposes of the Application, the New Zealand claim is to be interpreted as applying only to atmospheric tests, not to any other form of testing, and as applying only to atmospheric tests so conducted as to give rise to radio-active fall-out on New Zealand territory" (*I.C.J. Reports 1974*, p. 466, para. 29).

In making, in 1974, this finding and the one in the *Nuclear Tests (Australia* v. *France)* case (for the Court, the two cases appeared identical as to their subject-matter which concerned exclusively atmospheric tests), the Court had addressed the question whether New Zealand, when filing its 1973 Application might have had broader objectives than the cessation of atmospheric nuclear tests – the "primary concern" of the Government of New Zealand, as it now put it. The Court concluded that it could not now reopen this question since its current task was limited to an analysis of the Judgment of 1974.

The Court recalled that moreover it had taken note, at that time, of the communiqué issued by the Office of the President of the French Republic on 8 June 1974, stating that

> "in view of the stage reached in carrying out the French nuclear defence programme France will be in a position to pass on to the stage of underground explosions as soon as the series of tests planned for this summer is completed" (*I.C.J. Reports 1974*, p. 469, para. 35);

and to other official declarations of the French authorities on the same subject, made publicly outside the Court and *erga omnes*, and expressing the French Government's intention to put an end to its atmospheric tests; that, comparing the undertaking entered into by France with the claim asserted by New Zealand, it had found that it faced "a situation in which the objective of the Applicant [had] in effect been accomplished" (*I.C.J. Reports 1974*, p. 475, para. 55) and accordingly had indicated that "the object of the claim having clearly disappeared, there is nothing on which to give judgment" (*I.C.J. Reports 1974*, p. 477, para. 62). The Court concluded that the basis of the 1974 Judgment was consequently France's undertaking not to conduct any further atmospheric nuclear tests; that it was only, therefore, in the event of a resumption of nuclear tests in the atmosphere that that basis of the Judgment would have been affected; and that that hypothesis had not materialized.

The Court observed further that in analysing its Judgment of 1974, it reached the conclusion that that Judgment dealt exclusively with atmospheric nuclear tests; that consequently, it was not possible for the Court now to take into consideration questions relating to underground nuclear tests; and that the Court could not, therefore, take account of the arguments derived by New Zealand, on the one hand from the conditions in which France had conducted underground nuclear tests since 1974, and on the other from the development of international law in recent decades – and particularly the conclusion, on 25 November 1986, of the Noumea Convention – any more than of the arguments derived by France from the conduct of the New Zealand Government since 1974. It finally observed that its Order was without prejudice to the obligations of States to respect and protect the natural environment, obligations to which both New Zealand and France had in the present instance reaffirmed their commitment.

The Court therefore found that the basis of the 1974 Judgment had not been affected; that New Zealand's Request did not therefore fall within the provisions of paragraph 63 of that Judgment; and that that Request had consequently to be dismissed. It also pointed out that following its Order, the Court had instructed the Registrar to remove that Request from the General List as of 22 September 1995.

Finally the Court indicated that it likewise had to dismiss New Zealand's "Further Request for the Indication of Provisional Measures" as well as the applications for permission to intervene submitted by Australia, Samoa, Solomon Islands, the Marshall Islands and the Federated States of Micronesia and the declarations of intervention made by the last four States – all of which were proceedings incidental to New Zealand's main request.

Operative paragraph (para. 68)

"Accordingly,

THE COURT,

(1) By twelve votes to three,

Finds that the 'Request for an Examination of the Situation' in accordance with paragraph 63 of the Judgment of the Court of 20 December 1974 in the *Nuclear Tests (New Zealand* v. *France)* case, submitted by New Zealand on 21 August 1995, does not fall within the provisions of the said paragraph 63 and must consequently be dismissed;

IN FAVOUR: *President* Bedjaoui; *Vice-President* Schwebel; *Judges* Oda, Guillaume, Shahabuddeen, Ranjeva, Herczegh, Shi, Fleischhauer, Vereshchetin, Ferrari Bravo, Higgins;

AGAINST: *Judges* Weeramantry, Koroma; *Judge* ad hoc Sir Geoffrey Palmer;

(2) By twelve votes to three,

Finds that the 'Further Request for the Indication of Provisional Measures' submitted by New Zealand on the same date must be dismissed;

IN FAVOUR: *President* Bedjaoui; *Vice-President* Schwebel; *Judges* Oda, Guillaume, Shahabuddeen, Ranjeva, Herczegh, Shi, Fleischhauer, Vereshchetin, Ferrari Bravo, Higgins;

AGAINST: *Judges* Weeramantry, Koroma; *Judge* ad hoc Sir Geoffrey Palmer;

(3) By twelve votes to three,

Finds that the 'Application for Permission to Intervene' submitted by Australia on 23 August 1995, and the 'Applications for Permission to Intervene' and 'Declarations of Intervention' submitted by Samoa and Solomon Islands on 24 August 1995, and by the Marshall Islands and the Federated States of Micronesia on 25 August 1995, must likewise be dismissed.

IN FAVOUR: *President* Bedjaoui; *Vice-President* Schwebel; *Judges* Oda, Guillaume, Shahabuddeen, Ranjeva, Herczegh, Shi, Fleischhauer, Vereshchetin, Ferrari Bravo, Higgins;

AGAINST: *Judges* Weeramantry, Koroma; *Judge* ad hoc Sir Geoffrey Palmer."

*

Vice-President Schwebel and Judges Oda and Ranjeva appended declarations to the Order of the Court (*I.C.J. Reports 1995*, pp. 309, 310 and 311). Judge Shahabuddeen appended a separate opinion (*ibid.*, pp. 312-316); and Judges Weeramantry, Koroma and Judge *ad hoc* Sir Geoffrey Palmer appended dissenting opinions (*ibid.*, pp. 317-362, 363-380, 381-421).

12. Kasikili/Sedudu Island (Botswana/Namibia)

On 29 May 1996 the Government of the Republic of Botswana and the Government of the Republic of Namibia notified jointly to the Registrar of the Court a Special Agreement between the two States signed at Gaborone on 15 February 1996 and which came into force on 15 May 1996, for the submission to the Court of the dispute existing between them concerning the boundary around Kasikili/Sedudu Island and the legal status of that island.

The Special Agreement refers to a Treaty between Great Britain and Germany respecting the spheres of influence of the two countries, signed on 1 July 1890, and to the appointment, on 24 May 1992, of a Joint Team of Technical Experts "to determine the boundary between Namibia and Botswana around Kasikili/Sedudu Island" on the basis of that Treaty and of the applicable principles of international law. Unable to reach a conclusion on the question the Joint Team of Technical Experts recommended "recourse to the peaceful settlement of the dispute on the basis of the applicable rules and principles of international law". At the Summit Meeting held in Harare, Zimbabwe, on 15 February 1995, President Masire of Botswana and President Nujoma of Namibia agreed "to submit the dispute to the International Court of Justice for a final and binding determination".

Under the terms of the Special Agreement, the Parties ask the Court to

> "determine, on the basis of the Anglo-Germany Treaty of 1 July 1890 and the rules and principles of international law, the boundary between Namibia and Botswana around Kasikili/Sedudu Island and the legal status of the island".

By an Order of 24 June 1996 (*I.C.J. Reports 1996*, p. 63), the Court fixed 28 February and 28 November 1997 respectively as the time-limits for the filing by each of the Parties of a Memorial and a Counter-Memorial.

B. REQUESTS FOR ADVISORY OPINION

Legality of the Use by a State of Nuclear Weapons in Armed Conflict

On 14 May 1993 the World Health Assembly of the World Health Organization adopted resolution WHA46.40 by which the Assembly requested the International Court of Justice to give an advisory opinion on the following question:

> "In view of the health and environmental effects, would the use of nuclear weapons by a State in war or other armed conflict be a breach of its obligations under international law including the WHO Constitution?"

The letter of the Director-General of the World Health Organization (WHO) transmitting to the Court the request for an advisory opinion, together with certified true copies of the English and French texts of the aforesaid resolution, dated 27 August 1993, was received in the Registry on 3 September 1993.

By an Order of 13 September 1993 (*I.C.J. Reports 1993*, p. 467), the Court fixed 10 June 1994 as the time-limit within which written statements might be submitted to the Court by the World Health Organization and by those of its member States which were entitled to appear before the Court, in accordance with Article 66, paragraph 2, of the Statute of the Court.

By an Order of 20 June 1994 (*I.C.J. Reports 1994*, p. 109), the President of the Court, following requests from several of the aforesaid States, extended that time-limit to 20 September 1994.

By the same Order, the President fixed 20 June 1995 as the time-limit within which States and organizations having presented written statements might submit written comments on the other written statements (Art. 66, para. 4, of the Statute of the Court).

Written statements were filed by Australia, Azerbaijan, Colombia, Costa Rica, the Democratic People's Republic of Korea, Finland, France, Germany, India, Ireland, the Islamic Republic of Iran, Italy, Japan, Kazakhstan, Lithuania, Malaysia, Mexico, Moldova, Nauru, the Netherlands, New Zealand, Norway, Papua New Guinea, the Philippines, the Russian Federation, Rwanda, Samoa, Saudi Arabia, the Solomon Islands, Sri Lanka, Sweden, Uganda, Ukraine, the United Kingdom of Great Britain and Northern Ireland and the United States of America.

Written comments were filed by France, India, Malaysia, Nauru, the Russian Federation, the Solomon Islands, the United Kingdom of Great Britain and Northern Ireland and the United States of America. The written proceedings in this case were thus concluded.

Public sittings to hear oral statements or comments on the request for advisory opinion made by the World Health Organization were held between 30 October 1995 and 15 November 1995. These oral proceedings also covered the request for an advisory opinion submitted by the

General Assembly of the United Nations on the question of the *Legality of the Threat or Use of Nuclear Weapons*. During the hearings statements were made by the WHO, Australia, Egypt, France, Germany, Indonesia, Mexico, Iran, Italy, Japan, Malaysia, New Zealand, Philippines, Russian Federation, Samoa, Marshall Islands, Solomon Islands, Costa Rica, United Kingdom of Great Britain and Northern Ireland, United States of America and Zimbabwe.

At a public sitting held on 8 July 1996, the Court delivered its Advisory Opinion (*I.C.J. Reports 1996*, p. 66), a summary of which is given below, followed by the text of the final paragraph.

Submission of the request and subsequent procedure (paras. 1-9)

The Court began by recalling that by a letter dated 27 August 1993, filed in the Registry on 3 September 1993, the Director-General of the World Health Organization (hereinafter called "the WHO") had officially communicated to the Registrar a decision taken by the World Health Assembly to submit a question to the Court for advisory opinion. The question set forth in resolution WHA46.40 adopted by the Assembly on 14 May 1993, read as follows:

> "In view of the health and environmental effects, would the use of nuclear weapons by a State in war or other armed conflict be a breach of its obligations under international law including the WHO Constitution?"

The Court then recapitulated the various stages of the proceedings.

Jurisdiction of the Court (paras. 10-31)

The Court began by observing that, in view of Article 65, paragraph 1, of its Statute and of Article 96, paragraph 2, of the Charter, three conditions had to be satisfied in order to found the jurisdiction of the Court when a request for an advisory opinion was submitted to it by a specialized agency: the agency requesting the opinion had to be duly authorized, under the Charter, to request opinions from the Court; the opinion requested had to be on a legal question; and that question had to be one arising within the scope of the activities of the requesting agency.

Authorization of WHO to request advisory opinions (paras. 11 and 12)

Where the WHO was concerned, the above-mentioned texts were reflected in Article 76 of that Organization's Constitution, and in paragraph 2 of Article X of the Agreement of 10 July 1948 between the United Nations and the WHO which the Court found to have left no doubt that the WHO had been duly authorized, in accordance with Article 96, paragraph 2, of the Charter, to request advisory opinions of the Court.

"Legal question" (paras. 13-17)

The Court observed that it had already had occasion to indicate that questions

> "framed in terms of law and rais[ing] problems of international law . . . are by their very nature susceptible of a reply based on law . . . [and] appear . . . to be questions of a legal character" (*Western Sahara, Advisory Opinion, I.C.J. Reports 1975*, p. 18, para. 15).

It found that the question put to the Court by the World Health Assembly did in fact constitute a legal question, as in order to rule on the question submitted to it, the Court needed to identify the obligations of States under the rules of law invoked, and assess whether the behaviour in question conforms to those obligations, thus giving an answer to the question posed based on law.

The fact that this question also had political aspects, as, in the nature of things, was the case with so many questions which arose in international life, did not suffice to deprive it of its character as a "legal question" and to "deprive the Court of a competence expressly conferred on it by its Statute". Nor were the political nature of the motives which might be said to have inspired the request, or the political implications that the opinion given might have had, of relevance in the establishment of the Court's jurisdiction to give such an opinion.

Question arising "within the scope of the activities" of WHO (paras. 18-31)

The Court observed that in order to delineate the field of activity or the area of competence of an international organization, one needed to refer to the relevant rules of the organization and, in the first place, to its constitution. From a formal standpoint, the constituent instruments of international organizations were multilateral treaties, to which the well-established rules of treaty interpretation applied. But they were also treaties of a particular type; their object was to create new subjects of law endowed with a certain autonomy, to which the parties entrusted the task of realizing common goals. Such treaties could raise specific problems of interpretation owing, *inter alia*, to their character which was conventional and at the same time institutional; the very nature of the organization created, the objectives which had been assigned to it by its founders, the imperatives associated with the effective performance of its functions, as well as its own practice, were all elements which might deserve special attention when the time came to interpret these constituent treaties.

According to the customary rule of interpretation as expressed in Article 31 of the 1969 Vienna Convention on the Law of Treaties, the terms of a treaty had to be interpreted "in their context and in the light of its object and purpose" and there were to be

> "taken into account, together with the context:
>
> . . . .

(b) any subsequent practice in the application of the treaty which establishes the agreement of the parties regarding its interpretation".

The Court had had occasion to apply this rule of interpretation several times and would also apply it in the instant case.

Interpretation of the WHO Constitution (paras. 20-26)

The Court pointed out that the functions attributed to the WHO were listed in 22 subparagraphs (subparagraphs *(a)* to *(v)*) in Article 2 of its Constitution. None of these subparagraphs expressly referred to the legality of any activity hazardous to health; and none of the functions of the WHO was dependent upon the legality of the situations upon which it was bound to act. Moreover, it was stated in the introductory sentence of Article 2 that the Organization discharged its functions "in order to achieve its objective". The objective of the Organization was defined in Article 1 as being "the attainment by all peoples of the highest possible level of health".

Also referring to the Preamble to the Constitution, the Court concluded that, interpreted in accordance with their ordinary meaning, in their context and in the light of the object and purpose of the WHO Constitution, as well as of the practice followed by the Organization, the provisions of its Article 2 might be read as authorizing the Organization to deal with the effects on health of the use of nuclear weapons, or of any other hazardous activity, and to take preventive measures aimed at protecting the health of populations in the event of such weapons being used or such activities engaged in.

It went on to observe that the question put to the Court in the instant case related, however, *not to the effects* of the use of nuclear weapons on health, but to the *legality* of the use of such weapons *in view of their health and environmental effects*. And the Court pointed out that whatever those effects might be, the competence of the WHO to deal with them was not dependent on the legality of the acts that caused them. Accordingly, it did not seem to the Court that the provisions of Article 2 of the WHO Constitution, interpreted in accordance with the criteria referred to above, could be understood as conferring upon the Organization a competence to address the legality of the use of nuclear weapons, and thus in turn a competence to ask the Court about that matter.

In the view of the Court, none of the functions referred to in the resolution by which the Court had been seised of this request for an opinion had a sufficient connection with the question before it for that question to be capable of being considered as arising "within the scope of [the] activities" of the WHO. The causes of the deterioration of human health were numerous and varied; and the legal or illegal character of these causes was essentially immaterial to the measures which the WHO had in any case to take in an attempt to remedy their effects. In particular, the legality or illegality of the use of nuclear weapons in no way determined the specific measures, regarding health or otherwise (studies, plans, procedures, etc.), which might be necessary in order to seek to prevent or cure some of their effects. The reference in the question put to the Court to the health and environmental effects, which according to the WHO the use of a nuclear weapon would always occasion, did not make the question one that fell within the WHO's functions.

The Court went on to point out that international organizations were subjects of international law which did not, unlike States, possess a general competence. International organizations were governed by the "principle of speciality", that is to say, they were invested by the States which created them with powers, the limits of which were a function of the common interests whose promotion those States entrusted to them.

The powers conferred on international organizations were normally the subject of an express statement in their constituent instruments. Nevertheless, the necessities of international life might point to the need for organizations, in order to achieve their objectives, to possess subsidiary powers which were not expressly provided for in the basic instruments which governed their activities. It was generally accepted that international organizations could exercise such powers, known as "implied" powers.

The Court was of the opinion, however, that to ascribe to the WHO the competence to address the legality of the use of nuclear weapons – even in view of their health and environmental effects – would be tantamount to disregarding the principle of speciality; for such competence could not be deemed a necessary implication of the Constitution of the Organization in the light of the purposes assigned to it by its member States.

The WHO was, moreover, an international organization of a particular kind. As indicated in the Preamble and confirmed by Article 69 of its Constitution, "the Organization shall be brought into relation with the United Nations as one of the specialized agencies referred to in Article 57 of the Charter of the United Nations". As its Articles 57, 58 and 63 demonstrated, the Charter had laid the basis of a "system" designed to organize international co-operation in a coherent fashion by bringing the United Nations, invested with powers of general scope, into relationship with various autonomous and complementary organizations, invested with sectorial powers.

If, according to the rules on which that system was based, the WHO had, by virtue of Article 57 of the Charter, "wide international responsibilities", those responsibilities were necessarily restricted to the sphere of "public health" and could not encroach on the responsibilities of other parts of the United Nations system. And there was no doubt that questions concerning the use of force, the regulation of armaments and disarmament were within the competence of the United Nations and lay outside that of the specialized agencies.

For all those reasons, the Court considered that the question raised in the request for an advisory opinion submitted to it by the WHO did not arise "within the scope of [the] activities" of that Organization as defined by its Constitution.

WHO's practice (para. 27)

A consideration of the practice of the WHO bore out these conclusions. None of the reports and resolutions referred to in the Preamble to World Health Assembly resolution WHA46.40, nor resolution WHA46.40 itself, could be taken to express, or to amount on its own to a practice establishing an agreement between the members of the Organization to interpret its Constitution as empowering it to address the question of the legality of the use of nuclear weapons, nor could, in the view of the Court, such a practice be inferred from isolated passages of certain resolutions of the World Health Assembly cited during the current proceedings.

The Court further considered that the insertion of the words "including the WHO Constitution" in the question put to the Court did not change the fact that the WHO was not empowered to seek an opinion on the interpretation of its Constitution in relation to matters outside the scope of its functions.

Other arguments (paras. 29 and 30)

The Court finally considered that other arguments put forward in the proceedings to found the jurisdiction of the Court – concerning the way in which World Health Assembly resolution WHA46.40 had been adopted and concerning the reference to that resolution in General Assembly resolution 49/75 K – did not affect the conclusions reached by the Court concerning the competence of the WHO to request an opinion on the question raised.

Having arrived at the view that the request for an advisory opinion submitted by the WHO did not relate to a question arising "within the scope of [the] activities" of that Organization in accordance with Article 96, paragraph 2, of the Charter, the Court found that an essential condition of founding its jurisdiction in the present case was absent and that it could not, accordingly, give the opinion requested.

Final paragraph (para. 32)

"For these reasons,

THE COURT,

By eleven votes to three,

Finds that it is not able to give the advisory opinion which was requested of it under World Health Assembly resolution WHA46.40 dated 14 May 1993.

IN FAVOUR: *President* Bedjaoui; *Vice-President* Schwebel; *Judges* Oda, Guillaume, Ranjeva, Herczegh, Shi, Fleischhauer, Vereshchetin, Ferrari Bravo, Higgins.

AGAINST: *Judges* Shahabuddeen, Weeramantry, Koroma."

*

Judges Ranjeva and Ferrari Bravo appended declarations to the Advisory Opinion (*I.C.J. Reports 1996*, pp. 86 and 87); Judge Oda appended a separate opinion (*ibid.*, pp. 88-96); Judges Shahabuddeen, Weeramantry and Koroma appended dissenting opinions (*ibid.*, pp. 97-100, 101-171 and 172-224).

2. *Legality of the Threat or Use of Nuclear Weapons*

On 15 December 1994, the General Assembly of the United Nations adopted resolution 49/75 K, entitled "Request for an Advisory Opinion from the International Court of Justice on the Legality of the Threat or Use of Nuclear Weapons", by which, pursuant to Article 96, paragraph 1, of the Charter of the United Nations, it requested the Court

> "urgently to render its advisory opinion on the following question: 'Is the threat or use of nuclear weapons in any circumstance permitted under international law?' "

The request was transmitted to the Court by the Secretary-General of the United Nations in a letter dated 19 December 1994, received in the Registry by facsimile on 20 December 1994 and filed in the original on 6 January 1995.

By an Order of 1 February 1995 (*I.C.J. Reports 1995*, p. 3), the Court decided that States entitled to appear before the Court and the United Nations might furnish information on the question submitted to the Court and fixed 20 June 1995 as the time-limit within which written statements might be submitted (Art. 66, para. 2, of the Statute of the Court) and 20 September 1995 as the time-limit within which States and organizations having presented written statements might present written comments on the other written statements (Art. 66, para. 4, of the Statute).

Written statements were filed by Bosnia and Herzegovina, Burundi, the Democratic People's Republic of Korea, Ecuador, Egypt, Finland, France, Germany, India, Ireland, the Islamic Republic of Iran, Italy, Japan, Lesotho, Malaysia, the Marshall Islands, Mexico, Nauru, the Netherlands, New Zealand, Qatar, the Russian Federation, Samoa, San Marino, the Solomon Islands, Sweden, the United Kingdom of Great Britain and Northern Ireland and the United States of America.

Written comments were filed by Egypt, Nauru and Solomon Islands. Nauru subsequently withdrew its comments.

Public sittings to hear oral statements or comments on the request for advisory opinion submitted by the General Assembly were held between 30 October and 15 November 1995. These oral proceedings also covered the request for advisory opinion submitted by the World Health Organization on the question of the *Legality of the Use by a State of Nuclear Weapons in Armed Conflict*. During the hearings statements were made by Australia, Costa Rica, Egypt, France, Germany, Indonesia, Mexico, Iran, Italy, Japan, Malaysia, New Zealand, Philippines, Qatar, Russian Federation, San Marino, Samoa, Marshall Islands, Solomon Islands, United Kingdom of Great Britain and Northern Ireland, United States of America and Zimbabwe.

At a public sitting held on 8 July 1996, the Court delivered its Advisory Opinion (*I.C.J. Reports 1996*, p. 226), a summary of which is given below, followed by the text of the final paragraph.

Submission of the request and subsequent procedure (paras. 1-9)

The Court began by recalling that by a letter dated 19 December 1994, filed in the Registry on 6 January 1995, the Secretary-General of the United Nations officially communicated to the Registrar the decision taken by the General Assembly to submit a question to the Court for an advisory opinion. The final paragraph of resolution 49/75 K, adopted by the General Assembly on 15 December 1994, which set forth the question, provides that the General Assembly

> "*Decides*, pursuant to Article 96, paragraph 1, of the Charter of the United Nations, to request the International Court of Justice urgently to render its advisory opinion on the following question: 'Is the threat or use of nuclear weapons in any circumstance permitted under international law?'"

The Court then recapitulated the various stages of the proceedings.

Jurisdiction of the Court (paras. 10-18)

The Court first considered whether it had the jurisdiction to give a reply to the request of the General Assembly for an Advisory Opinion and whether, should the answer be in the affirmative, there was any reason it should decline to exercise any such jurisdiction.

The Court observed that it draws its competence in respect of advisory opinions from Article 65, paragraph 1, of its Statute, while Article 96, paragraph 1, of the Charter provides that:

> "The General Assembly or the Security Council may request the International Court of Justice to give an advisory opinion on any legal question."

Some States which opposed the giving of an opinion by the Court argued that the General Assembly and Security Council might ask for an advisory opinion on any legal question only within the scope of their activities. In the view of the Court, it mattered little whether this interpretation of Article 96, paragraph 1, was or was not correct; in the present case, the General Assembly had competence in any event to seise the Court. Referring to Articles 10, 11 and 13 of the Charter, the Court found that, indeed, the question put to the Court had a relevance to many aspects of the activities and concerns of the General Assembly including those relating to the threat or use of force in international relations, the disarmament process, and the progressive development of international law.

"Legal Question" (para. 13)

The Court observed that it had already had occasion to indicate that questions

> "framed in terms of law and rais[ing] problems of international law . . . are by their very nature susceptible of a reply based on law . . . [and] appear . . . to be questions of a legal character" (*Western Sahara, Advisory Opinion, I.C.J. Reports 1975*, p. 18, para. 15).

It found that the question put to the Court by the General Assembly was indeed a legal one, since the Court was asked to rule on the compatibility of the threat or use of nuclear weapons with the relevant principles and rules of international law. To do this, the Court had to identify the existing principles and rules, interpret them and apply them to the threat or use of nuclear weapons, thus offering a reply to the question posed based on law.

The fact that this question also had political aspects, as, in the nature of things, was the case with so many questions which arose in international life, did not suffice to deprive it of its character as a "legal question" and to "deprive the Court of a competence expressly conferred on it by its Statute". Nor were the political nature of the motives which might be said to have inspired the request or the political implications that the opinion given might have of relevance in the establishment of the Court's jurisdiction to give such an opinion.

Discretion of the Court to give an advisory opinion (paras. 14-19)

Article 65, paragraph 1, of the Statute provides: "The Court *may* give an advisory opinion . . ." (Emphasis added.) This was more than an enabling provision. As the Court had repeatedly emphasized, the Statute left a discretion as to whether or not the Court would give an advisory opinion that had been requested of it, once it had established its competence to do so. In this context, the Court had previously noted as follows:

> "The Court's Opinion is given not to the States, but to the organ which is entitled to request it; the reply of the Court, itself an 'organ of the United Nations', represents its participation in the activities of the Organization, and, in principle, should not be refused." (*Interpretation of Peace Treaties with Bulgaria, Hungary and Romania, First Phase, Advisory Opinion, I.C.J. Reports 1950*, p. 71.)

In the history of the present Court there had been no refusal, based on the discretionary power of the Court, to act upon a request for advisory opinion; in the case concerning the *Legality of the Use by a State of Nuclear Weapons in Armed Conflict* the refusal to give the World

Health Organization the advisory opinion requested by it had been justified by the Court's lack of jurisdiction in that case.

Several reasons were adduced in the proceedings in order to persuade the Court that in the exercise of its discretionary power it should decline to render the opinion requested by the General Assembly. Some States, in contending that the question put to the Court was vague and abstract, appeared to mean by this that there existed no specific dispute on the subject-matter of the question. In order to respond to this argument, it was necessary to distinguish between requirements governing contentious procedure and those applicable to advisory opinions. The purpose of the advisory function was not to settle – at least directly – disputes between States, but to offer legal advice to the organs and institutions requesting the opinion. The fact that the question put to the Court did not relate to a specific dispute should consequently not lead the Court to decline to give the opinion requested. Other arguments concerned the fear that the abstract nature of the question might lead the Court to make hypothetical or speculative declarations outside the scope of its judicial function; the fact that the General Assembly had not explained to the Court for what precise purposes it sought the advisory opinion; that a reply from the Court in this case might adversely affect disarmament negotiations and would, therefore, be contrary to the interest of the United Nations; and that in answering the question posed, the Court would be going beyond its judicial role and would be taking upon itself a law-making capacity.

The Court did not accept those arguments and concluded that it had the authority to deliver an opinion on the question posed by the General Assembly, and that there existed no "compelling reasons" which would lead the Court to exercise its discretion not to do so. It pointed out, however, that it was an entirely different question whether, under the constraints placed upon it as a judicial organ, it would be able to give a complete answer to the question asked of it. But that was a different matter from a refusal to answer at all.

Formulation of the question posed (paras. 20 and 22)

The Court found it unnecessary to pronounce on the possible divergences between the English and French texts of the question put. Its real objective was clear: to determine the legality or illegality of the threat or use of nuclear weapons. And the argument concerning the legal conclusions to be drawn from the use of the word "permitted", and the questions of burden of proof to which it was said to give rise, were found by the Court to be without particular significance for the disposition of the issues before it.

The applicable law (paras. 23-34)

The Court observed that, in seeking to answer the question put to it by the General Assembly, it had to decide, after consideration of the great corpus of international law norms available to it, what might be the relevant applicable law.

The Court considered that the question whether a particular loss of life, through the use of a certain weapon in warfare, was to be considered an arbitrary deprivation of life contrary to Article 6 of the International Covenant on Civil and Political Rights, as argued by some of the proponents of the illegality of the use of nuclear weapons, could only be decided by reference to the law applicable in armed conflict and not deduced from the terms of the Covenant itself. The Court also pointed out that the prohibition of genocide would be pertinent in this case if the recourse to nuclear weapons did indeed entail the element of intent, towards a group as such, required by Article II of the Convention on the Prevention and Punishment of the Crime of Genocide. In the view of the Court, it would only be possible to arrive at such a conclusion after having taken due account of the circumstances specific to each case. And the Court further found that while the existing international law relating to the protection and safeguarding of the environment did not specifically prohibit the use of nuclear weapons, it indicated important environmental factors that are properly to be taken into account in the context of the implementation of the principles and rules of the law applicable in armed conflict.

In the light of the foregoing the Court concluded that the most directly relevant applicable law governing the question of which it was seised was that relating to the use of force enshrined in the United Nations Charter and the law applicable in armed conflict which regulates the conduct of hostilities, together with any specific treaties on nuclear weapons that the Court might determine to be relevant.

Unique characteristics of nuclear weapons (paras. 35 and 36)

The Court noted that in order correctly to apply to the case before it the Charter law on the use of force and the law applicable in armed conflict, in particular humanitarian law, it was imperative for it to take account of the unique characteristics of nuclear weapons, and in particular their destructive capacity, their capacity to cause untold human suffering, and their ability to cause damage to generations to come.

Provisions of the Charter relating to the threat or use of force (paras. 37-50)

The Court then addressed the question of the legality or illegality of recourse to nuclear weapons in the light of the provisions of the Charter relating to the threat or use of force.

In Article 2, paragraph 4, of the Charter the use of force against the territorial integrity or political independence of another State or in any other manner inconsistent with the purposes of the United Nations was prohibited.

This prohibition of the use of force was to be considered in the light of other relevant provisions of the Charter. In Article 51, the Charter recognized the inherent right of individual or collective self-defence in case of an armed attack. A further lawful use of force was envisaged in Article 42, whereby the Security Council might take military enforcement measures in conformity with Chapter VII of the Charter.

These provisions did not refer to specific weapons. They applied to any use of force, regardless of the weapons employed. The Charter neither expressly prohibited, nor permitted, the use of any specific weapon, including nuclear weapons.

The entitlement to resort to self-defence under Article 51 was subject to the conditions of necessity and proportionality. As the Court had stated in the case concerning *Military and Paramilitary Activities in and against Nicaragua (Nicaragua* v. *United States of America) (I.C.J. Reports 1986*, p. 94, para. 176): "there is a specific rule whereby self-defence would warrant only measures which are proportional to the armed attack and necessary to respond to it, a rule well established in customary international law".

The proportionality principle might thus not in itself exclude the use of nuclear weapons in self-defence in all circumstances. But at the same time, a use of force that was proportionate under the law of self-defence should, in order to be lawful, also meet the requirements of the law applicable in armed conflict which comprised in particular the principles and rules of humanitarian law. And the Court noted that the very nature of all nuclear weapons and the profound risks associated therewith were further considerations to be borne in mind by States believing they could exercise a nuclear response in self-defence in accordance with the requirements of proportionality.

In order to lessen or eliminate the risk of unlawful attack, States sometimes signalled that they possessed certain weapons to use in self-defence against any State violating their territorial integrity or political independence. Whether a signalled intention to use force if certain events occurred was or was not a "threat" within Article 2, paragraph 4, of the Charter depended upon various factors. The notions of "threat" and "use" of force under Article 2, paragraph 4, of the Charter stood together in the sense that if the use of force itself in a given case was illegal – for whatever reason – the threat to use such force would likewise be illegal. In short, if it was to be lawful, the declared readiness of a State to use force had to be a use of force that was in conformity with the Charter. For the rest, no State – whether or not it defended the policy of deterrence – had suggested to the Court that it would be lawful to threaten to use force if the use of force contemplated would be illegal.

Rules on the lawfulness or unlawfulness of nuclear weapons as such (paras. 49-73)

Having dealt with the Charter provisions relating to the threat or use of force, the Court turned to the law applicable in situations of armed conflict. It first addressed the question whether there were specific rules in international law regulating the legality or illegality of recourse to nuclear weapons *per se*; it then examined the question put to it in the light of the law applicable in armed conflict proper, i.e. the principles and rules of humanitarian law applicable in armed conflict, and the law of neutrality.

The Court noted by way of introduction that international customary and treaty law did not contain any specific prescription authorizing the threat or use of nuclear weapons or any other weapon in general or in certain circumstances, in particular those of the exercise of legitimate self-defence. Nor, however, was there any principle or rule of international law which would make the legality of the threat or use of nuclear weapons or of any other weapons dependent on a specific authorization. State practice showed that the illegality of the use of certain weapons as such did not result from an absence of authorization but, on the contrary, was formulated in terms of prohibition.

It did not seem to the Court that the use of nuclear weapons could be regarded as specifically prohibited on the basis of certain provisions of the Second Hague Declaration of 1899, the Regulations annexed to the Hague Convention IV of 1907 or the 1925 Geneva Protocol. The pattern had been for weapons of mass destruction to be declared illegal by specific instruments. But the Court did not find any specific prohibition of recourse to nuclear weapons in treaties expressly prohibiting the use of certain weapons of mass destruction; and observed that, although, in the last two decades, a great many negotiations had been conducted regarding nuclear weapons, they had not resulted in a treaty of general prohibition of the same kind as for bacteriological and chemical weapons.

The Court noted that the treaties dealing exclusively with acquisition, manufacture, possession, deployment and testing of nuclear weapons, without specifically addressing their threat or use, certainly pointed to an increasing concern in the international community with these weapons; it concluded from this that these treaties could therefore be seen as foreshadowing a future general prohibition of the use of such weapons, but that they did not constitute such a prohibition by themselves. As to the treaties of Tlatelolco and Rarotonga and their Protocols, and also the declarations made in connection with the indefinite extension of the Treaty on the Non-Proliferation of Nuclear Weapons, it emerged from these instruments that:

(a) a number of States had undertaken not to use nuclear weapons in specific zones (Latin America; the South Pacific) or against certain other States (non-nuclear-weapon States which are parties to the Treaty on the Non-Proliferation of Nuclear Weapons);

(b) nevertheless, even within this framework, the nuclear-weapon States had reserved the right to use nuclear weapons in certain circumstances; and

(c) these reservations had met with no objection from the parties to the Tlatelolco or Rarotonga Treaties or from the Security Council.

The Court then turned to an examination of customary international law to determine whether a prohibition of the threat or use of nuclear weapons as such flowed from that source of law.

It noted that the members of the international community were profoundly divided on the matter of whether non-recourse to nuclear weapons over the past 50 years constituted the expression of an *opinio juris*. Under these circumstances the Court did not consider itself able to find that there was such an *opinio juris*. It pointed out that the adoption each year by the General Assembly, by a large majority, of resolutions recalling the content of resolution 1653 (XVI), and requesting the Member States to conclude a convention prohibiting the use of nuclear weapons in any circumstance, revealed the desire of a very large section of the international community to take, by a specific and express prohibition of the use of nuclear weapons, a significant step forward along the road to complete nuclear disarmament. The emergence, as *lex lata*, of a customary rule specifically prohibiting the use of nuclear weapons as such was hampered by the continuing tensions between the nascent *opinio juris* on the one hand, and the still strong adherence to the doctrine of deterrence (in which the right to use those weapons in the exercise of the right to self-defence against an armed attack threatening the vital security interests of the State was reserved) on the other.

International humanitarian law (paras. 74-87)

Not having found a conventional rule of general scope, nor a customary rule specifically proscribing the threat or use of nuclear weapons *per se*, the Court then dealt with the question whether recourse to nuclear weapons should be considered as illegal in the light of the principles and rules of international humanitarian law applicable in armed conflict and of the law of neutrality.

After sketching the historical development of the body of rules which originally were called "laws and customs of war" and later came to be termed "international humanitarian law", the Court observed that the cardinal principles contained in the texts constituting the fabric of humanitarian law were the following. The first was aimed at the protection of the civilian population and civilian objects and established the distinction between combatants and non-combatants; States should never make civilians the object of attack and should consequently never use weapons that were incapable of distinguishing between civilian and military targets. According to the second principle, it was prohibited to cause unnecessary suffering to combatants: it was accordingly prohibited to use weapons causing them such harm or uselessly aggravating their suffering. In application of that second principle, States did not have unlimited freedom of choice of means in the weapons they used.

The Court also referred to the Martens Clause, which was first included in the Hague Convention II with Respect to the Laws and Customs of War on Land of 1899 and which has proved to be an effective means of addressing the rapid evolution of military technology. A modern version of that clause was to be found in Article 1, paragraph 2, of Additional Protocol I of 1977, which reads as follows:

> "In cases not covered by this Protocol or by other international agreements, civilians and combatants remain under the protection and authority of the principles of international law derived from established custom, from the principles of humanity and from the dictates of public conscience."

The extensive codification of humanitarian law and the extent of the accession to the resultant treaties, as well as the fact that the denunciation clauses that existed in the codification instruments have never been used, had provided the international community with a corpus of treaty rules the great majority of which had already become customary and which reflected the most universally recognized humanitarian principles. These rules indicated the normal conduct and behaviour expected of States.

Turning to the applicability of the principles and rules of humanitarian law to a possible threat or use of nuclear weapons, the Court noted that nuclear weapons were invented after most of the principles and rules of humanitarian law applicable in armed conflict had already come into existence; the Conferences of 1949 and 1974-1977 had left these weapons aside, and there was a qualitative as well as quantitative difference between nuclear weapons and all conventional arms. However, in the Court's view, it could not be concluded from this that the established principles and rules of humanitarian law applicable in armed conflict did not apply to nuclear weapons. Such a conclusion would have been incompatible with the intrinsically humanitarian character of the legal principles in question which permeated the entire law of armed conflict and applied to all forms of warfare and to all kinds of weapons, those of the past, those of the present and those of the future. In this respect it seemed significant that the thesis that the rules of humanitarian law did not apply to the new weaponry, because of the newness of the latter, had not been advocated in the course of the proceedings.

The principle of neutrality (paras. 88 and 89)

The Court found that as in the case of the principles of humanitarian law applicable in armed conflict, international law left no doubt that the principle of neutrality, whatever its content, which was of a fundamental character similar to that of the humanitarian principles and rules, was applicable (subject to the relevant provisions of the United Nations Charter), to all international armed conflict, whatever type of weapons might be used.

Conclusions to be drawn from the applicability of international humanitarian law and the principle of neutrality (paras. 90-97)

The Court observed that, although the applicability of the principles and rules of humanitarian law and of the principle of neutrality to nuclear weapons was hardly disputed, the conclusions to be drawn from this applicability were, on the other hand, controversial.

According to one point of view, the fact that recourse to nuclear weapons was subject to and regulated by the law of armed conflict did not necessarily mean that such recourse was as such prohibited. Another view held that recourse to nuclear weapons, in view of the necessarily indiscriminate consequences of their use, could never be compatible with the principles and rules of humanitarian law and was therefore prohibited. A similar view had been expressed with respect to the effects of the principle of neutrality. Like the principles and rules of humanitarian law, that principle had therefore been considered by some to rule out the use of a weapon the effects of which simply could not be contained within the territories of the contending States.

The Court observed that, in view of the unique characteristics of nuclear weapons, to which the Court had referred earlier, the use of such weapons in fact seemed scarcely reconcilable with respect for the requirements of the law applicable in armed conflict. It considered nevertheless, that it did not have sufficient elements to enable it to conclude with certainty that the use of nuclear weapons would necessarily be at variance with the principles and rules of law applicable in armed conflict in any circumstance. Furthermore, the Court could not lose sight of the fundamental right of every State to survival, and thus its right to resort to self-defence, in accordance with Article 51 of the Charter, when its survival was at stake. Nor could it ignore the practice referred to as "policy of deterrence", to which an appreciable section of the international community adhered for many years.

Accordingly, in view of the present state of international law viewed as a whole, as examined by the Court, and of the elements of fact at its disposal, the Court was led to observe that it could not reach a definitive conclusion as to the legality or illegality of the use of nuclear weapons by a State in an extreme circumstance of self-defence, in which its very survival would be at stake.

Obligation to negotiate nuclear disarmament (paras. 98-103)

Given the eminently difficult issues that arose in applying the law on the use of force and above all the law applicable in armed conflict to nuclear weapons, the Court considered that it needed to examine one further aspect of the question before it, seen in a broader context.

In the long run, international law, and with it the stability of the international order which it was intended to govern, were bound to suffer from the continuing difference of views with regard to the legal status of weapons as deadly as nuclear weapons. It was consequently important to put an end to this state of affairs: the long-promised complete nuclear disarmament appeared to be the most appropriate means of achieving that result.

In those circumstances, the Court appreciated the full importance of the recognition by Article VI of the Treaty on the Non-Proliferation of Nuclear Weapons of an obligation to negotiate in good faith a nuclear disarmament. The legal import of that obligation went beyond that of a mere obligation of conduct; the obligation involved here was an obligation to achieve a precise result – nuclear disarmament in all its aspects – by adopting a particular course of conduct, namely, the pursuit of negotiations on the matter in good faith. This two-fold obligation to pursue and to conclude negotiations formally concerned the 182 States parties to the Treaty on the Non-Proliferation of Nuclear Weapons, or, in other words, the vast majority of the international community. Indeed, any realistic search for general and complete disarmament, especially nuclear disarmament, necessitated the co-operation of all States.

The Court finally emphasized that its reply to the question put to it by the General Assembly rested on the totality of the legal grounds set forth by the Court above (paras. 20-103), each of which was to be read in the light of the others. Some of these grounds were not such as to form the object of formal conclusions in the final paragraph of the Opinion; they nevertheless retained, in the view of the Court, all their importance.

Final paragraph (para. 105)

"For these reasons,

THE COURT,

(1) By thirteen votes to one,

Decides to comply with the request for an advisory opinion;

IN FAVOUR: *President* Bedjaoui; *Vice-President* Schwebel; *Judges* Guillaume, Shahabuddeen, Weeramantry, Ranjeva, Herczegh, Shi, Fleischhauer, Koroma, Vereshchetin, Ferrari Bravo, Higgins;

AGAINST: *Judge* Oda.

(2) *Replies* in the following manner to the question put by the General Assembly:

A. Unanimously,

There is in neither customary nor conventional international law any specific authorization of the threat or use of nuclear weapons;

B. By eleven votes to three,

There is in neither customary nor conventional international law any comprehensive and universal prohibition of the threat or use of nuclear weapons as such;

IN FAVOUR: *President* Bedjaoui; *Vice-President* Schwebel; *Judges* Oda, Guillaume, Ranjeva, Herczegh, Shi, Fleischhauer, Vereshchetin, Ferrari Bravo, Higgins;

AGAINST: *Judges* Shahabuddeen, Weeramantry, Koroma.

C. Unanimously,

A threat or use of force by means of nuclear weapons that is contrary to Article 2, paragraph 4, of the United Nations Charter and that fails to meet all the requirements of Article 51, is unlawful;

D. Unanimously,

A threat or use of nuclear weapons should also be compatible with the requirements of the international law applicable in armed conflict, particularly those of the principles and rules of international humanitarian law, as well as with specific obligations under treaties and other undertakings which expressly deal with nuclear weapons;

E. By seven votes to seven, by the President's casting vote,

It follows from the above-mentioned requirements that the threat or use of nuclear weapons would generally be contrary to the rules of international law applicable in armed conflict, and in particular the principles and rules of humanitarian law;

However, in view of the current state of international law, and of the elements of fact at its disposal, the Court cannot conclude definitively whether the threat or use of nuclear weapons would be lawful or unlawful in an extreme circumstance of self-defence, in which the very survival of a State would be at stake;

IN FAVOUR: *President* Bedjaoui; *Judges* Ranjeva, Herczegh, Shi, Fleischhauer, Vereshchetin, Ferrari Bravo;

AGAINST: *Vice-President* Schwebel; *Judges* Oda, Guillaume, Shahabuddeen, Weeramantry, Koroma, Higgins.

F. Unanimously,

There exists an obligation to pursue in good faith and bring to a conclusion negotiations leading to nuclear disarmament in all its aspects under strict and effective international control."

*

President Bedjaoui, Judges Herczegh, Shi, Vereshchetin and Ferrari Bravo appended declarations to the Advisory Opinion of the Court (*I.C.J. Reports 1996,* pp. 268-274, 275-276, 277-278, 279-281 and 282-286); Judges Guillaume, Ranjeva and Fleischhauer appended separate opinions (*ibid.*, pp. 287-293, 294-304 and 305-310); Vice-President Schwebel, Judges Oda, Shahabuddeen, Weeramantry, Koroma and Higgins appended dissenting opinions (*ibid.*, pp. 311-329, 330-374, 375-428, 429-555, 556-582 and 583-593).

II. Application of the Statute and Rules of Court

1. Organization of the Court

(a) *Death in office of a judge and election of a new judge*
(Statute, Arts. 14 and 15; Rules, Arts. 2 and 3)

During the period under review, one of the Members of the Court died in office. An election was held by the General Assembly and the Security Council to fill the resulting vacancy (see Chap. I, p. 9, above).

(b) *Installation of a new judge*
(Statute, Art. 20; Rules, Art. 4)

The newly elected judge referred to under *(a)* above made his solemn declaration at a public sitting of the Court, on 5 March 1996.

(c) *The Presidency*
(Statute, Art. 48; Rules, Arts. 31, 44, 48 and 79)

The President made an Order fixing the time-limit for the deposit of the Counter-Memorial in the case concerning *Application of the Convention on the Prevention and Punishment of the Crime of Genocide (Bosnia and Herzegovina* v. *Yugoslavia)* (see above, p. 189).

In the case concerning the *Land and Maritime Boundary between Cameroon and Nigeria (Cameroon* v. *Nigeria)* the President fixed the time-limit for the deposit of Cameroon's written statement of its observations and submissions on the preliminary objections raised by Nigeria (see above, p. 193).

(d) *Non-participation of a judge in a case*
(Statute, Arts. 17, para. 2, 23, para. 3, and 24, para. 1; Rules, Art. 20, para. 2)

Two Members of the Court informed the President that they felt they could not participate in the case concerning the *Application of the Convention on the Prevention and Punishment of the Crime of Genocide (Bosnia and Herzegovina* v. *Yugoslavia)*, having previously dealt, in their respective capacities as Legal Counsel of the United Nations and Member of the United Nations Human Rights Committee, with certain matters likely to be material to the present case. One of those Members also excused herself from the cases concerning *Questions of Interpretation and Application of the 1971 Montreal Convention arising from the Aerial Incident at Lockerbie (Libyan Arab Jamahiriya* v. *United Kingdom)* and *Questions of Interpretation and Application of the 1971 Montreal Convention arising from the Aerial Incident at Lockerbie (Libyan Arab Jamahiriya* v. *United States of America)*, and from the case concerning the *Gabčíkovo-Nagymaros Project (Hungary/Slovakia)*, having been counsel for one of the Parties in those cases.

Due to illness, one of the Members of the Court was not able to participate in the hearings, the deliberation and final vote with regard to the *Request for an Examination of the Situation in Accordance with Paragraph 63 of the Court's Judgment of 20 December 1974 in the* Nuclear Tests (New Zealand *v.* France) *Case.*

The newly elected judge referred to under *(a)* and *(b)* above did not participate in the deliberation and final vote in the advisory cases concerning the *Legality of the Use by a State of Nuclear Weapons in Armed Conflict* and concerning the *Legality of the Threat or Use of Nuclear Weapons.*

(e) *Judges* ad hoc

(Statute, Arts. 20 and 31; Rules, Arts. 4 and 8)

At the opening of the hearings on the request for the indication of provisional measures made by Cameroon in the case concerning the *Land and Maritime Boundary between Cameroon and Nigeria (Cameroon* v. *Nigeria)*, the two judges *ad hoc* chosen by the Parties (see above, p. 16) made the solemn declaration required by the Statute and Rules of Court.

Spain and Canada, in the case concerning *Fisheries Jurisdiction (Spain* v. *Canada)*, also exercised the power to choose judges *ad hoc* (see above, p. 198).

The *Request for an Examination of the Situation in Accordance with Paragraph 63 of the Court's Judgment of 20 December 1974 in the Nuclear Tests* (New Zealand *v.* France) *Case* was accompanied by a letter which informed the Court of the resignation of the judge *ad hoc* chosen by New Zealand in 1973 and the choice of a new judge *ad hoc* to replace him (see above, p. 200). The new judge *ad hoc* made the solemn declaration at the opening of the hearings, on 11 September 1995.

(f) *Chamber of Summary Procedure*

(Statute, Art. 29)

The Court composed the Chamber of Summary Procedure, consisting of five judges and two alternate judges (see Chap. I, p. 17, above).

2. *Jurisdiction of the Court*

(a) *Jurisdiction in contentious cases*

(Statute, Art. 36)

(i) *General*

In the case concerning the *Application of the Convention on the Prevention and Punishment of the Crime of Genocide (Bosnia and Herzegovina* v. *Yugoslavia),* the Court noted that, with regard to the question of its jurisdiction *ratione personae*, Yugoslavia, in the oral proceedings, submitted that, even supposing that Bosnia and Herzegovina had been bound by the Convention in March 1993, it could not, at that time, have entered into force between the Parties, because the two States did not recognize one another and the conditions necessary to found the consensual basis of the Court's jurisdiction were therefore lacking.

The Court observed, however, that that situation no longer obtained since the signature, and the entry into force on 14 December 1995, of the Dayton-Paris Agreement, Article X of which stipulated that:

> "The Federal Republic of Yugoslavia and the Republic of Bosnia and Herzegovina recognize each other as sovereign independent States within their international borders. Further aspects of their mutual recognition will be subject to subsequent discussions."

The Court made the following observations in this connection:

> "26. For the purposes of determining its jurisdiction in this case, the Court has no need to settle the question of what the effects of a situation of non-recognition may be on the contractual ties between parties to a multilateral treaty. It need only note that, even if it were to be assumed that the Genocide Convention did not enter into force between the Parties until the signature of the Dayton-Paris Agreement, all the conditions are now fulfilled to found the jurisdiction of the Court *ratione personae*.
>
> It is the case that the jurisdiction of the Court must normally be assessed on the date of the filing of the act instituting proceedings. However, the Court, like its predecessor, the Permanent Court of International Justice, has always had recourse to the principle according to which it should not penalize a defect in a procedural act which the applicant could easily remedy. Hence, in the case concerning the *Mavrommatis Palestine Concessions*, the Permanent Court said:
>
> > 'Even if the grounds on which the institution of proceedings was based were defective for the reason stated, this would not be an adequate reason for the dismissal of the applicant's suit. The Court, whose jurisdiction is international, is not bound to attach to matters of form the same degree of importance which they might possess in municipal law. Even, therefore, if the application were premature because the Treaty of Lausanne had not yet been ratified, this circumstance would now be covered by the subsequent deposit of the necessary ratifications.' (*P.C.I.J., Series A, No. 2*, p. 34.)
>
> The same principle lies at the root of the following *dictum* of the Permanent Court of International Justice in the case concerning *Certain German Interests in Polish upper Silesia:*
>
> > 'Even if, under Article 23, the existence of a definite dispute were necessary, this condition could at any time be fulfilled by means of unilateral action on the part of the applicant Party. And

the Court cannot allow itself to be hampered by a mere defect of form, the removal of which depends solely on the Party concerned.' (*P.C.I.J., Series A, No. 6*, p. 14.)

The present Court applied this principle in the case concerning the *Northern Cameroons* (*I.C.J. Reports 1963,* p. 28), as well as *Military and Paramilitary Activities in and against Nicaragua (Nicaragua* v. *United States of America)* when it stated: 'It would make no sense to require Nicaragua now to institute fresh proceedings based on the Treaty, which it would be fully entitled to do.' (*I.C.J. Reports 1984*, pp. 428-429, para. 83.)

In the present case, even if it were established that the Parties, each of which was bound by the Convention when the Application was filed, had only been bound as between themselves with effect from 14 December 1995, the Court could not set aside its jurisdiction on this basis, inasmuch as Bosnia and Herzegovina might at any time file a new application, identical to the present one, which would be unassailable in this respect."

According to one of the arguments advanced by Bosnia and Herzegovina in the course of the above proceedings, Yugoslavia, by calling itself, on 1 April 1993, for the indication of provisional measures some of which were aimed at the preservation of rights not covered by the Genocide Convention, had, in accordance with the doctrine of *forum prorogatum (stricto sensu)*, given its consent to the exercise by the Court, in the present case, of a wider jurisdiction than that provided for in Article IX of the Convention. Given the nature of both the provisional measures subsequently requested by Yugoslavia on 9 August 1993 – which were aimed exclusively at the preservation of rights conferred by the Genocide Convention – and the unequivocal declarations whereby Yugoslavia consistently contended during the subsequent proceedings that the Court lacked jurisdiction – whether on the basis of the Genocide Convention or on any other basis – the Court found that it should confirm the provisional conclusion that it reached on that subject in its Order of 13 September 1993 (*I.C.J. Reports 1993*, pp. 341-342, para. 34). The Court did not find that the Respondent had given in this case a "voluntary and indisputable" consent (see *Corfu Channel, Preliminary Objection, Judgment, 1948, I.C.J. Reports 1947-1948*, p. 27) which would confer upon it a jurisdiction exceeding that which it had already acknowledged to have been conferred upon it by Article IX of the Genocide convention.

*

In its Order on the request for the indication of provisional measures made by Cameroon in the case concerning *Land and Maritime Boundary between Cameroon and Nigeria (Cameroon* v. *Nigeria)*, the Court, at the outset, took note of the fact that the two Parties had each made a declaration recognizing the compulsory jurisdiction of the Court, in accordance with Article 36, paragraph 2, of the Statute, deposited with the Secretary-General of the United Nations, that neither of the two declarations included any reservation, and that Nigeria had made it clear in its declaration that it was made on the sole condition of reciprocity. It further noted that Nigeria had raised preliminary objections to the jurisdiction of the Court in the present case, and had claimed *inter alia* that there was no substantive reciprocity in the recognition of the jurisdiction of the Court by the Parties; and that in the course of the proceedings its Agent had expressed the opinion that the Court did not have even "prima facie jurisdiction over the substantive issues".

The Court's considerations regarding the question of its jurisdiction were as follows:

> "30. Whereas on a request for the indication of provisional measures the Court need not, before deciding whether or not to indicate them, finally satisfy itself that it has jurisdiction on the merits of the case, yet it may not indicate them unless the provisions invoked by the Applicant appear, prima facie, to afford a basis on which the jurisdiction of the Court might be founded;
>
> 31. Whereas the Court, which has taken note of the opinion expressed by the Agent of Nigeria with respect to its prima facie jurisdiction, is of the view that the preliminary objections raised by that State are not such as to exclude that jurisdiction; whereas the Court, in fact, considers that the declarations made by the Parties in accordance with Article 36, paragraph 2, of the Statute constitute a prima facia basis upon which its jurisdiction in the present case might be founded." (*I.C.J. Reports 1996*, p. 13).

*

In the Order which the Court made on 22 September 1995 concerning the *Request for an Examination of the Situation in Accordance with Paragraph 63 of the Court's Judgment of 20 December 1974 in the Nuclear Tests* (New Zealand *v.* France) *Case*, it dismissed the "Request for an Examination of the Situation" submitted by New Zealand. That State had based its Request on paragraph 63 of the Judgment of 20 December 1974, which provides:

> "Once the Court has found that a State has entered into a commitment concerning its future conduct it is not the Court's function to contemplate that it will not comply with it. However, the Court observes that if the basis of this Judgment were to be affected, the Applicant could request an examination of the situation in accordance with the provisions of the Statute; the denunciation by France, by letter dated 2 January 1974, of the General Act for the Pacific Settlement of International Disputes, which is relied on as a basis of jurisdiction in the present case, cannot constitute by itself

an obstacle to the presentation of such a request." (*I.C.J. Reports 1974*, p. 477.)

In paragraph 65 of its Order, the Court actually considered that

> "the basis of the Judgment delivered on 20 December 1974 in the *Nuclear Tests (New Zealand* v. *France)* case has not been affected; whereas the 'Request for an Examination of the Situation' submitted by New Zealand on 21 August 1995 does not therefore fall within the provisions of paragraph 63 of that Judgment; and whereas that Request must consequently be dismissed" (*I.C.J. Reports 1995*, p. 306).

(ii) *Preliminary objections*
(Rules, Art. 79)

In the case concerning the *Land and Maritime Boundary between Cameroon and Nigeria (Cameroon* v. *Nigeria)* Nigeria, within the time-limit for the filing of its Counter-Memorial, filed certain preliminary objections. The objections related to the jurisdiction of the Court and to the admissibility of the claims of Cameroon. In accordance with Article 79, paragraph 3, of the Rules of Court, the proceedings on the merits were suspended and after having ascertained the views of the Parties in accordance with Article 31 of the Rules of Court, the President of the Court fixed the time-limit within which Cameroon might present the written statement of its observations and submissions on the objections. That written statement was filed within the time-limit fixed (see above, p. 193).

(b) *Advisory jurisdiction*
(Statute, Art. 65)

In its Advisory Opinion in the case concerning the *Legality of the Use by a State of Nuclear Weapons in Armed Conflict*, the Court observed that, in view of Article 65, paragraph 1, of its Statute and of Article 96, paragraph 2, of the Charter, three conditions had to be satisfied in order to found the jurisdiction of the Court when a request for an advisory opinion was submitted to it by a specialized agency: the agency requesting the opinion had to be duly authorized, under the Charter, to request opinions from the Court; the opinion requested had to be on a legal question; and this question had to be one arising within the scope of the activities of the requesting agency.

Where the World Health Organization (WHO) was concerned, the above-mentioned texts were reflected in Article 76 of that organization's Constitution, and in paragraph 2 of Article X of the Agreement of 10 July 1948 between the United Nations and the WHO which the Court found left no doubt that the WHO had been duly authorized, in accordance with Article 96, paragraph 2, of the Charter, to request advisory opinions of the Court.

It further found that the question put to the Court by the World Health Assembly did in fact constitute a legal question, as in order to rule on the question submitted to it, the Court had to identify the obligations of States under the rules of law invoked, and assess whether the behaviour in question conformed to those obligations, thus giving an answer to the question posed based on law.

After examining the WHO Constitution the Court concluded, however, that the question raised in the request for an advisory opinion submitted to it by the WHO did not arise "within the scope of [the] activities" of that organization as defined by its constitution, a conclusion which was borne out by a consideration of the practice of the WHO.

*

In the case concerning the *Legality of the Threat or Use of Nuclear Weapons* the Court first considered whether it had the jurisdiction to give a reply to the request of the General Assembly for an advisory opinion and whether, should the answer be in the affirmative, there was any reason it should decline to exercise any such jurisdiction.

The Court observed that it drew its competence in respect of advisory opinions from Article 65, paragraph 1, of the Statute, while Article 96, paragraph 1, of the Charter provided that: "The General Assembly or the Security Council may request the International Court of Justice to give an advisory opinion on any legal question."

Some States which opposed the giving of an opinion by the Court argued that the General Assembly and Security Council might ask for an advisory opinion on any legal question only within the scope of their activities. In the view of the Court, it mattered little whether this interpretation of Article 96, paragraph 1, was or was not correct; in the actual case, the General Assembly had competence in any event to seise the Court. Referring to Articles 10, 11 and 13 of the Charter, the Court found that, indeed, the question put to the Court had a relevance to many aspects of the activities and concerns of the General Assembly including those relating to the threat or use of force in international relations, the disarmament process, and the progressive development of international law.

The Court further found that the question put to it by the General Assembly was indeed a legal one, since the Court was asked to rule on the compatibility of the threat or use of nuclear weapons with relevant principles and rules of international law. To do this, the Court had to identify the existing principles and rules, interpret them and apply them to the threat or use of nuclear weapons, thus offering a reply to the question posed based on law.

The Court also considered the question of its discretion to give an advisory opinion. It referred to Article 65, paragraph 1, of the Statute which provides: "The Court *may* give an advisory opinion . . ." (Emphasis added.) This was more than an enabling provision. As the Court had repeatedly emphasized, the Statute leaves a discretion as to whether or not it will give an advisory opinion that has been requested of it, once it has established its competence to do so. In this context, the Court had previously noted as follows:

> "The Court's Opinion is given not to the State, but to the organ which is entitled to request it; the reply of the Court, itself an 'organ of the United Nations', represents its participation in the activities of the Organization, and, in principle, should not be refused." *Interpretation of Peace Treaties with Bulgaria, Hungary and Romania, First Phase, Advisory Opinion, I.C.J. Reports 1950*, p. 71.)

In the history of the present Court there had been no refusal, based on the discretionary power of the Court, to act upon a request for advisory opinion; in the case concerning the *Legality of the Use by a State of Nuclear Weapons in Armed Conflict* the refusal to give the World Health Organization the advisory opinion requested by it was justified by the Court's lack of jurisdiction in that case.

The Court observed that several reasons were adduced in these proceedings in order to persuade the Court that in the exercise of its discretionary power it should decline to render the opinion requested by the General Assembly. Some States, in contending that the question put to the Court was vague and abstract, appeared to mean by this that there existed no specific dispute on the subject-matter of the question. In order to respond to this argument, it was necessary to distinguish between requirements governing contentious procedure and those applicable to advisory opinions. The purpose of the advisory function was not to settle – at least directly – disputes between States, but to offer legal advice to the organs and institutions requesting the opinion. The fact that the question put to the Court did not relate to a specific dispute should consequently not lead the Court to decline to give the opinion requested. Other arguments concerned the fear that the abstract nature of the question might lead the Court to make hypothetical or speculative declarations outside the scope of its judicial function; the fact that the General Assembly had not explained to the Court for what precise purposes it sought the advisory opinion; that a reply from the Court in this case might adversely affect disarmament negotiations and would, therefore, be contrary to the interest of the United Nations; and that in answering the question posed, the Court would be going beyond its judicial role and would be taking upon itself a law-making capacity.

The Court did not accept those arguments and concluded that it had the authority to deliver an opinion on the question posed by the General Assembly, and that there existed no "compelling reasons" which would lead the Court to exercise its discretion not to do so. It pointed out, however, that it was an entirely different question whether, under the constraints placed upon it as a judicial organ, it would be able to give a complete answer to the question asked of it. But that was a different matter from a refusal to answer at all.

3. *Contentious Procedure*

(a) *Institution of proceedings*

(Statute, Art. 40; Rules, Arts. 26, para. 1 *(b)*, 39 and 42)

In the case concerning the *Kasikili/Sedudu Island (Botswana/Namibia)*, proceedings were instituted by the joint notification of a Special Agreement. The Registrar proceeded with the requisite communications, in accordance with the Statute and Rules of Court.

By its *Request for an Examination of the Situation in Accordance with Paragraph 63 of the Court's Judgment of 20 December 1974 in the Nuclear Tests* (New Zealand *v.* France) *Case*, New Zealand allegedly sought a resumption of the proceedings instituted in 1973. The Court decided that

> "such a request, even if it is disputed *in limine* whether it fulfils the conditions set in that paragraph, must nonetheless be the object of entry in the General List of the Court for the sole purpose of enabling the latter to determine whether those conditions are fulfilled;"

and consequently instructed the Registrar, pursuant to Article 26, paragraph 1 *(b)*, of its Rules, to enter that Request in the General List.

(b) *Fixing of time-limits*

(Statute, Art. 48; Rules, Arts. 31, 44, 46 and 79)

In the case concerning *Maritime Delimitation and Territorial Questions between Qatar and Bahrain (Qatar* v. *Bahrain)*, the Court extended the time-limit for the filing by each of the Parties of a Memorial on the merits (see above, p. 169). The Court fixed a time-limit for the deposit by Libya of a written statement of its observations and submissions on the preliminary objection raised by the United Kingdom and the United States in the cases concerning *Questions of Interpretation and Application of the 1971 Montreal Convention arising from the Aerial Incident at Lockerbie (Libyan Arab Jamahiriya* v. *United Kingdom)* and *Questions of Interpretation and Application of the 1971 Montreal Convention arising from the Aerial Incident at Lockerbie (Libyan Arab Jamahiriya* v. *United States of America)*, respectively (see above, p. 171). It also fixed time-limits for the filing by each of the Parties of a Memorial and a Counter-Memorial in the case concerning *Kasikili/Sedudu Island (Botswana/Namibia)* (see above, p. 205). (For the fixing of time-limits by the President of the Court, see above, p. 224, under paragraph 1 *(c)*.)

(c) *Filing of pleadings*

Libya, in the cases concerning *Questions of Interpretation and Application of the 1971 Montreal Convention arising from the Aerial*

Incident at Lockerbie (Libyan Arab Jamahiriya v. *United Kingdom)* and *Questions of Interpretation and Application of the 1971 Montreal Convention arising from the Aerial Incident at Lockerbie (Libyan Arab Jamahiriya* v. *United States of America)*, Bosnia and Herzegovina, in the case concerning the *Application of the Convention on the Prevention and Punishment of the Crime of Genocide (Bosnia and Herzegovina* v. *Yugoslavia)*, and Cameroon, in the case concerning the *Land and Maritime Boundary between Cameroon and Nigeria (Cameroon* v. *Nigeria)*, filed the written statement of their observations and submissions on the preliminary objections raised by the respective respondent Parties within the time-limits fixed (see above, pp. 173, 181 and 193).

In the case concerning *Fisheries Jurisdiction (Spain* v. *Canada)*, Spain filed its Memorial and Canada its Counter-Memorial on the question of the jurisdiction of the Court to entertain the dispute within the time-limits fixed. After Spain had subsequently requested authorization to file a Reply and Canada had opposed this, the Court, by an Order, observing that it was "sufficiently informed, at this stage, of the contentions of fact and law on which the Parties rely with respect to its jurisdiction in the case", decided "not to authorize the filing of a Reply by the Applicant and a Rejoinder by the Respondent on the question of the jurisdiction of the Court to entertain the dispute" (see above, p. 198).

In the proceedings on the *Request for an Examination of the Situation in Accordance with Paragraph 63 of the Court's Judgment of 20 December 1974 in the Nuclear Tests* (New Zealand *v.* France) *Case*, informal aides-mémoire on the legal nature of the New Zealand Requests and of their effects were presented by New Zealand and France, at the invitation of the President of the Court.

(d) *Public international organization whose constituent instrument is in question*

(Statute, Art. 34, para. 3; Rules, Art. 69, para. 3)

In the cases concerning *Questions of Interpretation and Application of the 1971 Montreal Convention arising from the Aerial Incident at Lockerbie (Libyan Arab Jamahiriya* v. *United Kingdom)* and *Questions of Interpretation and Application of the 1971 Montreal Convention arising from the Aerial Incident at Lockerbie (Libyan Arab Jamahiriya* v. *United States of America)*, the Registrar, upon the instructions of the Court, communicated copies of the written proceedings to the ICAO. In his covering letter to the Secretary-General of ICAO the Registrar referred to an earlier letter by which he had informed ICAO that the interpretation of the Convention for the Suppression of Unlawful Acts Against the Safety of Civil Aviation, concluded in Montreal on 23 September 1971, was in issue in the two above-mentioned cases, and had informed it that he would await instruction from the Court with regard to the communication of the written proceedings in accordance with Article 34, paragraph 3, of the Statute. The Registrar, in his above-mentioned covering letter further referred to Article 69, paragraph 3, of the Rules of Court which provides *inter alia*:

> "The Court, or the President if the Court is not sitting, may, as from the date on which the Registrar has communicated copies of the written proceedings and after consulting the chief administrative officer of the public international organization concerned, fix a time-limit within which the organization may submit to the Court its observations in writing"

stating that, taking into account the fact that the proceedings on the merits were suspended in the two cases, the "observations in writing" to which this provision referred should only address the question of jurisdiction and admissibility. The Secretary-General of ICAO replied that the Organization had "no observation to make for the time being", requesting, however, to be kept informed of the development of the two cases, in order to determine whether it would be appropriate to submit observations at a later stage.

(e) *Accessibility of pleadings to the public*

(Rules, Art. 53, para. 2)

In the case concerning the *Application of the Convention on the Prevention and Punishment of the Crime of Genocide (Bosnia and Herzegovina* v. *Yugoslavia) (Preliminary Objections)*, the Court, after ascertaining the views of the Parties, decided to make the pleadings and documents annexed thereto accessible to the public on the opening of the oral proceedings.

With regard to the *Request for an Examination of the Situation in Accordance with Paragraph 63 of the Court's Judgment of 20 December 1974 in the Nuclear Tests* (New Zealand *v.* France) *Case*, the Court, with the agreement of the Governments of New Zealand and France, decided that the request submitted by New Zealand on 21 August 1995, the letter from the French Ambassador of 28 August 1995 and the aides-mémoire deposited by the two States would be made available to the public.

(f) *Oral proceedings*

(Statute, Arts. 43, para. 5, 45 and 46; Rules, Arts. 54 and 58)

The hearings on the *Request for an Examination of the Situation in Accordance with Paragraph 63 of the Court's Judgment of 20 December 1974 in the Nuclear Tests* (New Zealand *v.* France) *Case* (see above, p. 200) as well as those in the case concerning the *Application of the Convention on the Prevention and Punishment of the Crime of Genocide (Bosnia and Herzegovina* v. *Yugoslavia) (Preliminary Objections)* (see above, p. 181), consisted of two rounds of oral arguments in which, in each case, both States participated.

The Court also held two rounds of hearings on the request for the indication of provisional measures made by Cameroon in the case concerning the *Land and Maritime Boundary between Cameroon and Nigeria (Cameroon* v. *Nigeria)* (see above, p. 193).

(g) *Questions by judges*

(Statute, Art. 45; Rules, Arts. 61 and 72)

During the first round of hearings on the *Request for an Examination of the Situation in Accordance with Paragraph 63 of the Court's Judgment of 20 December 1974 in the Nuclear Tests* (New Zealand *v.* France) *Case*, questions were put to either or both of the States by the Vice-President, by three other judges and by the judge *ad hoc*. The replies were given in writing, within the prescribed time-limits.

The replies to the questions addressed by the Vice-President to the two Parties and by two other judges to Nigeria during the first round of the hearings on the request for the indication of provisional measures made by Cameroon in the case concerning the *Land and Maritime Boundary between Cameroon and Nigeria (Cameroon* v. *Nigeria)* were given orally during the second round of those hearings.

(h) *Final submissions*

(Rules, Art. 60, para. 2)

In the second round of oral arguments in the case concerning the *Application of the Convention on the Prevention and Punishment of the Crime of Genocide (Bosnia and Herzegovina* v. *Yugoslavia) (Preliminary Objections)*, the Agents of both Parties read the final submissions of their Governments, which they also submitted in writing.

(i) *Provisional measures*

(Statute, Arts. 41 and 48; Rules, Arts. 73, 74 and 75)

In the case concerning the *Land and Maritime Boundary between Cameroon and Nigeria (Cameroon* v. *Nigeria)*, the applicant State filed a request for the indication of provisional measures on 12 February 1996. In the course of the hearings, which were held on 5, 6 and 8 March 1996, one of the questions put by a Member of the Court to the respondent State was as follows:

> "In his letter to the Registrar of the Court of 16 February 1996, H.E. the Minister of Justice and Attorney-General of Nigeria stated:
>
> > 'The Nigerian Government hereby invites the International Court of Justice to note these protests and call the Government of Cameroon to order . . . Finally, the Government of Cameroon should be warned to desist from further harassment of Nigerian citizens in the Bakassi Peninsula until the final determination of the case pending at the International Court of Justice.'
>
> In expressing itself in this way, does the Government of Nigeria intend to present to the Court a counter-claim for provisional measures?"

In its oral reply to that question the respondent State indicated that its communication of 16 February 1996 did not constitute a counter-claim for the indication of provisional measures. In an Order of 15 March 1996 the Court indicated provisional measures (see above, p. 193).

In addition to its *Request for an Examination of the Situation in Accordance with Paragraph 63 of the Court's Judgment of 20 December 1974 in the Nuclear Tests* (New Zealand *v.* France) *Case*, New Zealand filed a "Further Request for the Indication of Provisional Measures", at the end of which it "separately request[ed] the President of the Court to exercise his powers under the Rules pending the exercise by the Court of its powers". In accompanying letters from New Zealand's Minister of Foreign Affairs and from its Ambassador, the urgency of the situation was referred to and the President was also asked to exercise the powers provided for under Article 66, paragraph 3, of the 1972 Rules of Court, "in force at the time of the institution of the proceedings in 1973". At the opening of the hearings which were devoted to the question "Do the Requests submitted to the Court by the Government of New Zealand on 21 August 1995 fall within the provisions of paragraph 63 of the Judgment of the Court of 20 December 1974 in the case concerning *Nuclear Tests (New Zealand* v. *France)*?", the President of the Court, referring to a subsequent letter from the Prime Minister of New Zealand reiterating those requests, stated

> "that he had been fully aware of the import of those Requests, to which he had given his full attention, but that the powers conferred upon him by the above-mentioned provision of the 1972 Rules of Court, as well as by Article 74, paragraph 4, of the Rules now in force, expressly applied to incidental proceedings for the indication of provisional measures, and that it would therefore have been difficult for him to accede to those Requests without necessarily prejudging the issues submitted to the Court".

In its Order of 22 September 1995, the Court, dismissing New Zealand's "Request for an Examination of the Situation", likewise dismissed its "Further Request for the Indication of Provisional Measures".

(j) *Intervention*

(Statute, Arts. 62 and 63)

With respect to the *Request for an Examination of the Situation in Accordance with Paragraph 63 of the Court's Judgment of 20 December 1974 in the Nuclear Tests* (New Zealand *v.* France) *Case* the Australian Government filed an "Application for Permission to Intervene under the Terms of Article 62 of the Statute Submitted by the Government of Australia". A day later the Governments of Samoa and Solomon Islands each filed a document, similar in content, entitled "Application for Permission to Intervene under Article 62/Declaration of Intervention under Article 63". Again a day later similar documents bearing the same titles were filed by the Governments of the Marshall Islands and of the

Federated States of Micronesia. These five documents referred both to the "Request for and Examination of the Situation" and to the "Further Request for the Indication of Provisional Measures" submitted by New Zealand.

In its Order of 22 September 1995, the Court, dismissing New Zealand's "Request for an Examination of the Situation", likewise dismissed the "Application for Permission to Intervene" submitted by Australia, and the "Application for Permission to Intervene" and "Declarations of Intervention" submitted by Samoa, Solomon Islands, the Marshall Islands and the Federated States of Micronesia – "all of which are proceedings incidental to the 'Request for an Examination of the Situation' submitted by New Zealand" (*I.C.J. Reports 1995*, p. 306, para. 67).

(k) *Discontinuance*

(Statute, Art. 48; Rules, Arts. 88 and 89)

In the case concerning the *Aerial Incident of 3 July 1988 (Islamic Republic of Iran* v. *United States of America)*, the two Parties jointly notified the Court that they had agreed to discontinue the case because they had entered into "an agreement in full and final settlement . . ."; the Court made an Order recording the discontinuance and directing the removal of the case from the list.

In the case concerning the *Maritime Delimitation between Guinea-Bissau and Senegal*, the Agent of the Applicant confirmed, as had been indicated at a previous meeting of the President of the Court with the two Parties, that his Government, by virtue of the agreement reached by the two Parties on the disputed zone, had decided to discontinue the proceedings. After the other Party had confirmed that it agreed to the discontinuance, the Court made an Order recording the discontinuance and directing the removal of the case from the list.

(l) *Separate and dissenting opinions and declarations*

(Statute, Art. 57; Rules, Art. 95, para. 2)

In the case concerning *Application of the Convention on the Prevention and Punishment of the Crime of Genocide (Bosnia and Herzegovina* v. *Yugoslavia) (Preliminary Objections)* one of the judges and one judge *ad hoc* appended a declaration to the judgment of the Court; two judges appended a joint declaration. Three judges appended separate opinions and one judge *ad hoc* appended a dissenting opinion (see above, p. 188).

To the Order on the request for the indication of provisional measures in the case concerning the *Land and Maritime Boundary between Cameroon and Nigeria (Cameroon* v. *Nigeria)*, four judges and one judge *ad hoc* appended a declaration; three judges appended a joint declaration. One judge *ad hoc* appended a separate opinion (see above, p. 196).

The judge *ad hoc* in the case concerning *Fisheries Jurisdiction (Spain*

v. *Canada)* appended a dissenting opinion to the Court's Order of 8 May 1996 (see above, p. 198).

Declarations were appended to the Court's Order concerning the *Request for an Examination of the Situation in Accordance with Paragraph 63 of the Court's Judgment of 20 December 1974 in the Nuclear Tests* (New Zealand *v.* France) *Case* by the Vice-President and two other judges. One judge appended a separate opinion to the Order; two judges and the judge *ad hoc* appended dissenting opinions (see above, p. 205).

(m) *Reading of the decision of the Court*

(i) *Judgment*

(Statute, Art. 58; Rules, Art. 95)

The Judgment of the Court in the case concerning the *Application of the Convention on the Prevention and Punishment of the Crime of Genocide (Bosnia and Herzegovina* v. *Yugoslavia) (Preliminary Objections)* was read at a public sitting; in view of the length of the text, the President omitted or summarized certain passages.

(ii) *Orders*

The Order on the request for the indication of provisional measures in the case concerning the *Land and Maritime Boundary between Cameroon and Nigeria (Cameroon* v. *Nigeria)* and the Order concerning the *Request for an Examination of the Situation in Accordance with Paragraph 63 of the Court's Judgment of 20 December 1974 in the Nuclear Tests* (New Zealand *v.* France) *Case* were also read by the President of the Court at a public sitting.

4. Advisory Proceedings

(a) *Submission of written comments*

(Statute, Art. 66, para. 4; Rules, Art. 105)

In the case concerning the *Legality of the Threat or Use of Nuclear Weapons*, three States submitted written comments, which were communicated by the Registrar to all States having taken part in the written proceedings. One of the three States subsequently requested the Court's permission to withdraw its written comment. The Court granted the request and the Deputy-Registrar notified the States to which the document had been communicated, specifying that the document consequently did not form part of the record before the Court.

(b) *Accessibility of documentation to the public*

(Rules, Art. 106)

In the cases concerning the *Legality of the Use by a State of Nuclear Weapons in Armed Conflict* and the *Legality of the Threat or Use of Nuclear Weapons*, the Court decided to make the written statements and comments submitted to it accessible to the public, with effect from the opening of the oral proceedings.

(c) *Oral proceedings*

(Statute, Art. 66; Rules, Art. 105, para. 2 *(b)*)

In the case concerning the *Legality of the Use by a State of Nuclear Weapons in Armed Conflict* and the *Legality of the Threat or Use of Nuclear Weapons* oral proceedings were held, which covered both requests for advisory opinion. In the case concerning the *Legality of the Use by a State of Nuclear Weapons in Armed Conflict*, oral statements were made by the World Health Organization and by 20 States. Twenty-two States made oral statements in the case concerning the *Legality of the Threat or Use of Nuclear Weapons.*

(d) *Questions put by judges*

(Statute, Art. 68; Rules, Arts. 61 and 102)

During the oral proceedings in the cases concerning the *Legality of the Use by a State of Nuclear Weapons in Armed Conflict* and the *Legality of the Threat or Use of Nuclear Weapons*, questions were put by Members of the Court to particular participants in the oral proceedings, which replied in writing, as requested, within the prescribed time-limits; the Court having decided that the other participants could also reply to those questions on the same terms, several of them did so. Other questions put by Members of the Court were addressed, more generally, to any participant in the oral proceedings; several of them replied in writing, as requested, within the prescribed time-limits.

(e) *Voting*

(Statute, Arts. 55, para. 2, and 68)

In the case concerning the *Legality of the Threat or Use of Nuclear Weapons*, the votes of the Members of the Court on subparagraph 2 E of the final paragraph of the Advisory Opinion were equally divided; in accordance with the provisions of the Statute the President had a casting vote.

(f) *Separate and dissenting opinions and declarations*

(Rules, Art. 107, para. 3)

In the case concerning the *Legality of the Use by a State of Nuclear Weapons in Armed Conflict*, two judges appended declarations to the Advisory Opinion, one judge a separate opinion and three judges dissenting opinions.

In the case concerning the *Legality of the Threat or Use of Nuclear Weapons*, the President and four other judges appended declarations to the Advisory Opinion, three judges appended separate opinions and the Vice-President and five other judges appended dissenting opinions.

(g) *Public reading of the Advisory Opinions*
(Statute, Art. 69; Rules, Art. 107)

The Advisory Opinions in the cases concerning the *Legality of the Use by a State of Nuclear Weapons in Armed Conflict* and the *Legality of the Threat or Use of Nuclear Weapons* were read at a public sitting; in view of the length of the text, the President omitted or summarized certain passages.

III. Fiftieth Anniversary of the Court

In April 1996 the Court celebrated its fiftieth anniversary. On 18 April, the anniversary of its inaugural sitting in 1946, a ceremonial sitting was held in the presence of Her Majesty Queen Beatrix of the Netherlands. Addresses were given by H.E. Professor Diogo Freitas do Amaral, President of the General Assembly, by H.E. Mr. Hans van Mierlo, Minister for Foreign Affairs of the Netherlands and by the President of the Court, H.E. Judge Mohammed Bedjaoui. (The text of those addresses is reproduced below.) The Prime Minister and the Minister of Justice of the Netherlands also attended the sitting, as well as former Members of the Court and Judges *ad hoc*, the diplomatic corps, special emissaries of States (including a great many legal advisers), representatives of United Nations organs, many authorities of the host country and representatives of the Press. Prior to the sitting a two-day colloquium had been organized in co-operation with UNITAR on the theme: "Increasing the Effectiveness of the International Court of Justice". During the whole of the week of the ceremonial sitting combined sessions of the Telders Moot Court Competition/Concours Rousseau (for students) were held.

*

"ADDRESS BY H.E. PROFESSOR DIOGO FREITAS DO AMARAL, PRESIDENT OF THE UNITED NATIONS GENERAL ASSEMBLY

Your Majesty,

Distinguished President and Members of the International Court of Justice,

Mr. Prime Minister, Mr. Minister for Foreign Affairs,

Your Excellencies, Ladies and Gentlemen,

I feel deeply privileged and honoured to participate today in the celebrations of the fiftieth anniversary of the International Court of Justice, one of the principal organs of the United Nations.

At the outset, I should like to address the illustrious Members of this Court and its President, Mr. Mohammed Bedjaoui, to express my admiration and my satisfaction at the great prestige the

International Court of Justice deservedly enjoys. I praise you all for your untiring efforts and complete dedication in performing the duties of your lofty posts.

In my capacity as President of the General Assembly of the United Nations, I have repeatedly stressed, since the very first day of my mandate, that the United Nations, more than any other organization, has contributed to establishing (and has attempted to guarantee in practice) the primacy of international law. Indeed, it was not without meaning that the founding fathers of our Organization set out in the preamble of the Charter that the peoples of the United Nations resolved to establish conditions under which justice and respect for the obligations arising from treaties and other sources of international law can be maintained.

The goal of establishing and maintaining the primacy of international law is crucial. Without the rule of law Humanity cannot achieve the peace, freedom and security which will permit it to continue to develop a civilized society.

When speaking of the contribution of the United Nations to the recognition of the primacy of international law, I cannot but hail the outstanding action and lofty prestige achieved throughout the past 50 years by the International Court of Justice, to which I wish to pay my very sincere tribute.

By coming here and joining you in celebrating the fiftieth anniversary of the International Court of Justice, I am seeking to give public testimony of the importance attributed to this Court by the General Assembly of the United Nations.

Institutions, like individuals, have a character of their own. In this sense, allow me to say that the merit of this prestigious international institution resides fundamentally in the main features of its character. I refer to:

- its *authority and integrity*, namely in the manner it has been interpreting and executing the principles governing its mission;
- its *impartiality and total independence* as guaranteed by the intellectual honesty of its member judges and other personnel;
- its *judicial realism* as displayed when assisting the parties in achieving a political settlement, a solution often seen as preferable to a judicial decision.

Such characteristics or principles of action have shaped the contribution the International Court of Justice has given to the advancement of the rule of law and to the promotion of justice among nations, for which the Court deserves every praise.

It is commonly accepted that the end of the Cold War era has brought with it new challenges to the world and consequently to the United Nations.

But a changing world demands change: a change in international institutions and in the political attitudes of its members. Indeed, reform of the United Nations is now accepted by all as necessary and indispensable.

In this context, the General Assembly has established over the last few years five Working Groups specifically entrusted with the mission of reforming the United Nation system.

Although the process of reform has been focused mainly on sensitive issues such as the acute financial crisis of the Organization and the enlargement of the Security Council, one has to point out, indeed to underline, that the International Court of Justice, as the principal judicial organ of the United Nations, is unequivocally an important, inseparable and indispensable part of the system.

Allow me, therefore, to say that, although the International Court of Justice has been, for the past few years, much more active and has seen its jurisdiction expanding both in terms of the number of declarations made and of compromissory clauses included in treaties, I also have no doubts that the adjustment of this prestigious judicial organ to a changing United Nations and a changing world is indispensable and inevitable.

I believe that it is an absolute obligation of any member of an organization to abide faithfully by the rules of law applicable to it. If disagreements arise concerning the application of these rules, the principle of separation of powers requires that those disagreements should be settled impartially by a court of law. The Charter of the United Nations provides for such a judicial body: the International Court of Justice.

As I remarked in my inaugural statement as President of the General Assembly:

> 'it is therefore utterly desirable for all countries which are Members of the United Nations to accept within a relatively short time the jurisdiction of the Court at The Hague. That it should still be possible to refuse the Court's jurisdiction strikes me as an anachronism left over from the days of unlimited State sovereignty, which is inconsistent with the prevailing principle of the primacy of international law.'

Although the breakdown of State sovereignty remains a matter of intense controversy, we have been witnessing a change in the defining parameters of the concept of sovereignty and it is undeniable, today, that the old doctrine of absolute and exclusive sovereignty no longer stands.

I believe that submission to international jurisdiction and international law by all States must be left out of the defining parameters of modern States' sovereignty.

When urging the Member States of the United Nations either to accept the Court's binding jurisdiction if they have not done so or to withdraw or attenuate the crippling reservations accompanying their acceptance, I do not find myself alone. I am merely adding my voice to that of several others, including many Member States, who have, in the past, sought the same goal.

I am also adding my voice to that of the President of the International Court of Justice, Your Excellency Mr. Mohammed Bedjaoui; to the Secretary-General who, in his Agenda for Peace, invited all States to accept such jurisdiction without reservations before the end of the United Nations Decade of International Law; and to the voice of former President Mikhail Gorbachev who in 1987 proposed the acceptance of the compulsory jurisdiction of the International Court of Justice, calling upon the five permanent members of the Security Council to set the example.

Nevertheless, despite all the discussions on the role of the Court held by the General Assembly, the reality is that the International Court of Justice still remains what it was at its inception. Moreover, regretfully, the appeal for compulsory jurisdiction of the Court made by Mr. Gorbachev found no response in as much as of the five permanent members of the Security Council, only the United Kingdom is currently accepting in general terms the compulsory jurisdiction of the Court.

We, however, will continue to appeal to those who can lead and to the willingness of all that can contribute to achieve a system of more effective enforcement of international law. We will continue to strive for the need of international courts with binding jurisdiction to determine when international laws are violated and to better serve as a forum for the peaceful settlement of conflicts.

Finally, I would like to briefly call attention to some proposals, which have been put forward in several fora, and which seek to reform and further extend the jurisdiction of the Court.

If it is not expected, for the time being, that all Member States will be willing or prepared to accept in general terms the jurisdiction of the Court, it would be pragmatic to concentrate our efforts on defining certain categories of cases in which all States might be persuaded to accept the unconditional and compulsory jurisdiction of the Court. Among those categories one could certainly consider cases involving human rights issues, genocide and diplomatic protection, for example.

Beyond these possible mandatory categories, Article 36, paragraph 2, of the Statute of the Court could be amended in order to accommodate the possibility of States voluntarily accepting the unconditional jurisdiction of further categories of cases. Such flexibility could also harbour the idea put forward by the Netherlands at the time of General Assembly resolution 3232 (XXIX) of 5 November 1974 suggesting that parties to a dispute could agree to submit certain legal questions to the Court, the political aspects of which would be settled separately.

It can be noted, in the second place, that the composition of the Court has not changed sufficiently to respond to the evolving world situation, and that, therefore, its membership should be enlarged to better reflect the actual reality of the international community.

It has also been frequently pointed out that the State is today no longer the sole actor in international relations. As international organizations have taken over several prerogatives traditionally within the scope of State sovereignty, it would be important to consider extending the jurisdiction of the Court to such organizations.

Likewise, within the Court's advisory procedure, serious consideration should be given to extending such a procedure to other organs of the United Nations and entities of the United Nations system not currently envisaged in the Charter.

In my capacity as President of the General Assembly, I cannot fail, here, in this august body, to reveal my intention of proposing that the question of the reform of the International Court of Justice be considered as a main item in the future programme of work of the High Level Working Group on the Strengthening of the United Nations System.

Mr. President,

No one seems to question that this century, despite the lethal wars and all the atrocities committed, is a century of progress for international law.

Far from the traditional concept of international law as a set of rules of peace and war, international law, nowadays, is also focused on co-operation, development, and in the protection of individuals.

This, however, is not sufficient. It is not sufficient to have fair and progressive rules of international law. Indeed, for the primacy of international law to prevail it is also necessary, it is indispensable, to have international courts seeking the just interpretation and application of those rules.

I, for my part, am sure, I have full confidence that this prestigious Court will continue to strive to discharge such a noble mission in the most illustrious manner."

*

"ADDRESS BY H.E. MR. HANS VAN MIERLO,
MINISTER FOR FOREIGN AFFAIRS OF THE NETHERLANDS

Your Majesty,

Honourable President and Members of the International Court of Justice,

Your Excellencies, Ladies and Gentlemen,

On behalf of the Netherlands Government, may I too welcome you here today, as one of my predecessors welcomed your predecessors exactly 50 years ago. I should like, if I may, to delve a little further into the past to recall the events that explain why you are here today in The Hague.

This month, too, it is 97 years since Her Majesty Queen Wilhelmina, the grandmother of Her Majesty Queen Beatrix, invited Governments from all over the world to attend the First Hague Peace Conference in 1899 in her Palace of Huis ten Bosch, in The Hague. The Conference, as we are all aware, ended with the adoption of a treaty, which, *inter alia*, stipulated that a Permanent Court of Arbitration was to be established in The Hague. This magnificent building, the Peace Palace, was subsequently constructed for it thanks to the vision of Andrew Carnegie. And I may say, not without pride, that it is widely recognized that the reputation this city subsequently acquired in the field of international law prompted the Secretary-General of the League of Nations to propose that The Hague also be the seat of the Permanent Court of International Justice, the predecessor of the International Court of Justice.

It will therefore come as no surprise to you that the Netherlands, not only as a Member of the United Nations and a party to the Statute of the Court, but also as the host State, takes a particularly keen interest in the Court's destiny.

Support for the successful functioning of the Court is an essential element in the long-standing Dutch policy of promoting, where possible, the peaceful settlement of international disputes through adjudication or arbitration. This policy is reflected both in the uninterrupted acceptance by the Netherlands of the compulsory jurisdiction of the Court by virtue of a unilateral declaration, and in its acceptance of the Court's jurisdiction in numerous international agreements.

I need hardly point out to you that the International Court of Justice and the Permanent Court of Arbitration are not the only international judicial bodies established in The Hague. This city has, over the years, also been the seat of such other important international judicial institutions as the Iran-United States Claims Tribunal and the International Criminal Tribunal for the Former Yugoslavia. The latter Tribunal has, moreover, certain organs in common with the International Criminal Tribunal for Rwanda. The Netherlands Government sincerely hopes that these *ad hoc* International Criminal Courts will shortly be followed by a Permanent International Criminal Court, and indeed negotiations on the statute for that Court *in statu nascendi* are currently taking place within the framework of the Sixth Committee of the United Nations General Assembly in New York.

However, the International Court of Justice unquestionably has pride of place among the international judicial institutions in The Hague and elsewhere in the world, by virtue of its being the principal judicial organ of the United Nations, the worldwide participation in its Statute, its permanent nature, the wide range of international legal questions it is entitled to adjudicate or advise on, and the composition of its bench, on which the main forms of civilization and the principal legal systems of the world are represented. It is popularly known, quite rightly, as the 'World Court'.

Your Majesty,

Your Excellencies, Ladies and Gentlemen,

There is some cause for concern about the position of the Court and the international law of which it is the guardian, as a result of what a former President of the Court has called 'the contemporary phenomenon of the proliferation of international tribunals'. Of course, international arbitral tribunals were in existence long before the Court and its predecessor and they continue to operate alongside it.

To the extent that such tribunals are established on an *ad hoc* basis by a small number of States and are charged with settling a specific dispute or group of disputes, resort to international arbitration is, of course, justified. This is the case, in particular, if highly specialized knowledge is required, or if a large number of similar claims have to be examined which would impose too heavy a burden on the Court, or in cases where it is deemed appropriate that claimants other than States should be able to initiate proceedings or, as in the case of international criminal courts, should become the subject of international criminal prosecution.

However, in the view of the Netherlands the establishment of new permanent tribunals should not be encouraged if they are intended to be generally accessible to States and to be invested with jurisdiction over inter-State disputes in matters which have been in the past and could again be successfully dealt with by the International Court of Justice itself. In this connection I would also like to mention that the Court has now made it possible for States to submit their disputes not to the full Court but to a chamber established by it in consultation with the parties to the dispute.

The co-existence of various international judicial institutions increases the danger of diversity in the interpretation, application or even development of international law. In this regard it should be noted that domestic courts, too, are increasingly being called upon to apply, directly or indirectly, rules and principles of international law.

In today's world there is no mechanism to ensure that international law is ultimately interpreted and applied in a uniform way. Although the International Court of Justice is generally considered the most authoritative international judicial institution, other international judicial institutions or domestic courts involved in the interpretation and application of international law are not subordinate to the Court. While it may not be possible as things stand, and perhaps not even desirable, to achieve such a situation of subordination, it would nonetheless seem advisable to develop a mechanism which would promote the uniform interpretation and application of international law. One approach could be to entitle other international judicial institutions or even national courts of Member States of the United Nations, if certain conditions have been met, to submit to the Court through the General Assembly requests for an advisory opinion on questions of international law with which they are confronted.

The fiftieth anniversary of the Court prompts a natural inclination not only to celebrate the Court, but also to evaluate its achievements and effectiveness. The past, present and future of the Court have just been discussed in a colloquium sponsored jointly by the Court itself and the United Nations Institute for Training and Research. Senior legal advisers from Member States of the United Nations, professors and other scholars of international law who have studied the Court, and current and former judges of the Court were asked to participate. I look forward with great interest to the conclusions of this colloquium, which focused, *inter alia*, on how to improve the effectiveness of the Court. The considerable increase in the case load in recent years is compelling the Court to manage its work more effectively. The Court is facing the danger of a backlog. On this subject some recent studies seem to suggest a reduction in the length of the Court's decisions and in the number of separate opinions produced by the judges, and an overall more efficient handling of the cases in the written and oral phases. The Netherlands supports efforts to improve the functioning of the Court.

As is well known, under Article 34 of the Statute only States are entitled to initiate contentious proceedings before the Court. Although historic reasons may account for this provision, doubts may be expressed as to whether it is appropriate to the present day. It should not be necessary for international organizations to resort to arbitration in order to settle their disputes in a legally binding manner or to compel them to request, where possible, advisory opinions from the Court which they agree to accept as legally binding.

I would like to conclude by congratulating the Court warmly, on behalf of the Netherlands, on its fiftieth anniversary and on all that it has achieved since its foundation. The increasing number of cases and questions submitted to the Court in recent years are convincing evidence of a renewed confidence in the Court's ability to act as the principal judicial organ of the United Nations and, indeed, of the community of States as a whole.

The Netherlands, as the host State of the Court, has continuously supported the Court in the past in material and other ways and hopes to be in a position to do so in the future.

Thank you."

*

"ADDRESS BY H.E. JUDGE MOHAMMED BEDJAOUI,
PRESIDENT OF THE INTERNATIONAL COURT OF JUSTICE

The International Court of Justice in Its Heyday

Your Majesty, Excellencies, Ladies and Gentlemen,

Fifty years, half-a-century, this is the mature age attained by the International Court of Justice today, 18 April 1996. Indeed, it was in this very setting, on 18 April 1946, that the inaugural sitting of the Court was held, in the discreet beauty of this Great Hall of Justice. It was under the benevolent eye of this goddess of peace, admirably restored by the talent of Albert Besnard in his fresco *Peace through Justice*, that a major new page in international judicial settlement was turned, in the still soft light of a lovely sunny spring day filtered, like this morning, through the lead lattices of the thousand-and-one panes in the four magnificent stained glass windows by Douglas Strachan.

It was in these surroundings, within these very walls in fact, which I like to think still resound with the voice of the first of my predecessors, the Salvadorian President, José Gustavo Guerrero, who had the privilege of opening and closing the inaugural sitting of the International Court of Justice, principal judicial organ of the United Nations.

On this jubilee day, the privilege which falls to me in my capacity as President of this Court is just as exceptional and no less awesome. My first duty, and also the most pleasant one, is to add my voice to this respectful tribute addressed by the Court to Your Majesty, who has generously agreed to honour this commemorative sitting with her august presence. The Court deeply appreciates this kind gesture. It interprets Your Majesty's presence as a new and eloquent testimony to the interest which the Royal Family has traditionally shown in our Court and in the reign of international peace and justice. This fidelity to such ideals is rooted in the distant past.

As early as 1922, when Their Majesties Queen Wilhelmina and Queen Emma the Queen Mother honoured with their presence the inaugural ceremony of the Permanent Court of International Justice.

In 1946 too, on the installation of the present Court, Their Royal Highnesses Princess Juliana and Prince Bernhard were so kind as to mark by their presence the rebirth of international judicial settlement, which the tragic interlude of the Second World War had condemned to a slumber lasting almost seven years. Like the phoenix, international justice was then reborn from its own ashes.

Your Majesty, your people and Government, in words as in action, have staunchly upheld the ideals of peace and justice. The support given by the Netherlands for several centuries to all the efforts to achieve peace in international society scarcely needs to be mentioned.

Your people, as I was saying Your Majesty, are imbued with a dogged faith in the reign of peace and justice. 'Action has no need of hope nor perseverance of success.' This enlightened motto of William I of Orange-Nassau, which perfectly sums up the character traits and particular genius of your people, comes naturally to mind.

These estimable qualities of your people have been illustrated by Jan Wagenaar throughout his major 20-volume work *Vaderlandsche Historie (History of the Fatherland)*, a huge bestseller despite its proportions. More recently, these qualities have been encapsulated in a national creed, described in the following terms by the historian Louis de Jong, in his vast 31-volume work *Het Koninkrijk der Nederlanden in de Tweede Wereldoorlog:*

> 'Our basic concepts were [and remain] that a people cannot invade and dominate another people . . . that the democratic freedoms are worth defending, that any discrimination against or persecution of persons is to be condemned and that deportation and genocide are to be condemned *a fortiori*.' (Part XI, p. 1109.)

A glance at the genesis of international judicial settlement shows perfectly the unflagging interest always displayed by the Dutch nation in the supreme values of peace and justice. It was in this spirit that it played host to the celebrated Hague Conferences of 1899 and 1907, which marked the first attempts to institutionalize international justice.

Convened at the initiative of Tsar Nicolas II of Russia, the Hague Conference of 1899 took place in the delightful setting of the Royal Family's summer residence, which Queen Wilhelmina, then only 18 years of age, generously placed at the disposal of this Conference. Among other things the Conference adopted the Convention for the Pacific Settlement of International Disputes, which envisaged the creation of a Permanent Court of Arbitration. Then the second Peace Conference of 1907 established the International Prize Court. A third Peace Conference was to be held in The Hague in 1915, but the outbreak of the First World War prevented it from being convened. Yet the idea nevertheless continued to develop.

So it was here, in The Hague, in 1899, beneath the panels of the 'House in the Woods' *(Huis ten Bosch)*, that the first stirrings of international judicial organization were heard.

When 21 years later, in February 1920, the Council of the League of Nations decided to set up an advisory committee of jurists entrusted with the task of preparing a draft for the establishment of a Permanent Court of International Justice, the Netherlands provided one of their most talented servants: Mr. Bernard Cornelius Johannes Loder. This brilliant jurist, who was also an independent spirit, was appointed to serve beside Messrs. Adatci (Japan),

Altamira (Spain), Bevilaqua (Brazil), Descamps (Belgium), Hagerup (Norway), de La Pradelle (France), Phillimore (Great Britain), Ricci Busatti (Italy) and Root (United States of America) in order to find a solution, together with these other great jurists, to the bulk of the difficulties which had defeated so many statesmen and jurists at the 1907 Peace Conference.

Elected Judge and, shortly thereafter, first President of the Permanent Court of International Justice, Dr. Loder placed his knowledge and clear-sightedness at the service of judicial settlement until 1930. His memory and his work at the Court were nevertheless perpetuated in the person of another enormously cultured Dutch jurist, Professor Willem Jan Marie van Eysinga. A keen specialist on Hugo Grotius, a reputed expert on river law, ardent defender of freedom of navigation, Judge van Eysinga was also to leave his mark in the annals of the Court in The Hague by dint of the role entrusted to him during the dark days, when the Court temporarily transferred its headquarters to the shores of Lake Geneva. The reversals of history were in fact to make of Judge van Eysinga, then officiating as Vice-President, the 'guardian' of the premises of the Court, he whose breath was symbolically to keep the flame of international justice burning in this city of his birth.

It therefore comes as no surprise that the Permanent International Court should have continued to make the Netherlands its natural setting, a choice which has now earned for The Hague the much-coveted title of capital of international justice; indeed, four judicial bodies, and by no means unimportant ones, have their headquarters here, these being the Permanent Court of Arbitration, our own Court, the Iran-United States Claims Tribunal and the International Criminal Tribunal for the Former Yugoslavia. Besides these courts in the strict sense another important institution should also be mentioned, namely, the Conference on Private International Law which, by virtue of its powers in the field of conflicts of law and jurisdiction, is not without contributing to the establishment of – at long last – harmonious relations between the peoples of the world.

The Court therefore has more than ever reason to be proud that it is still today the guest of the Dutch nation, the native land of Grotius, Bynckershoek, Asser, Verzijl, Röling, Loder and van Eysinga, but also of Erasmus, Spinoza, Huygens, Vondel, Rembrandt, Van Gogh and Vermeer – Vermeer, this poet of light and colour, of whom the score of paintings currently exhibited at the Mauritshuis is delighting hundreds of thousands of visitors from all corners of the world. Favoured land of international law and international justice, the Netherlands is thus also the cradle of several generations of women and men who have left their mark on civilization with a universal dimension.

A kingdom of creativity, the Netherlands has, in turn, inspired many minds throughout the world, stimulated the imagination of

Verlaine and Baudelaire, that same Baudelaire who did not hesitate to depict this beautiful land of Northern Europe as

> 'a veritable earthly paradise, where everything is beautiful, sumptuous, quiet, authentic; where luxury is glad to reflect itself in orderliness; where life is full and sweet to breathe; from which disorder, turmoil and the unexpected are banned; where happiness is married to silence...'

And he added:

> 'Yes, it is in that atmosphere that it would be good to be alive, yonder, where the slower hours contain more thoughts, where the clocks chime happiness with a deeper and more meaningful solemnity.'

It is with this evocation that I once more turn to Your Majesty, in order to reiterate to you the expression of the Court's deep respect and gratitude for your great and constant solicitude towards it; this is a tribute which the Court also wishes to pay, through Your Person, to the Dutch people as a whole, a people superbly described by Her Majesty The Queen Regent, Queen Emma de Waldeck Pyrmont, when, in her proclamation of 1898 on the occasion of the majority of Her Royal Highness, Princess Wilhelmina, who, in turn, was to become Queen of the Netherlands, she referred to it as: 'A great people in all things in which a small country can be great.'

May I make so bold as to rectify these historic words by saying that the Netherlands is by no means today what is termed a 'small country'?

Your Majesty, Excellencies, Ladies and Gentlemen,

There is another pleasant duty which I am particularly keen to perform; on behalf of the Court and on my own behalf, it is also a great pleasure for me to extend a warm welcome to H.E. Professor Diogo Freitas do Amaral, President of the United Nations General Assembly, who represents the Parliament of the Peoples of the World, which has just celebrated its fiftieth anniversary. Mr. President, the Court thanks you for kindly agreeing to traverse oceans in order to accept its invitation, thereby testifying to the closeness of the ties which unite our two institutions, both of them principal organs of the United Nations, notwithstanding their geographical remoteness; your encouraging words on the Court are all the more appreciated by it inasmuch as you are, as it were, the incarnation of *'these peoples of the United Nations'* on behalf of whom international justice is pronounced.

On behalf of the Court and on my own behalf, it is also a very real pleasure for me to welcome in our midst H.E. Mr. Wim Kok, H.E. Mr. Hans van Mierlo, H.E. Mrs. Winnie Sorgdrager, respectively Prime Minister, Minister for Foreign Affairs and Minister for

Justice of the Netherlands. Ministers, the Court is greatly honoured by this fresh mark of esteem shown to it through your persons by the Government of the Netherlands. Mr. Minister for Foreign Affairs, the Court greatly appreciates the generous words which you were kind enough to address to it and which confirm, if there was any need, the excellent relations which the Court has always had with the host country here represented at the highest level.

I am also greatly pleased to see that a number of other personalities have honoured the Court by their presence today. Accordingly, I welcome the members of the Diplomatic Corps appointed to the Netherlands and all the representatives of the international organizations with headquarters in the Netherlands.

Lastly, I cordially welcome all the other people whose presence here is a clear sign of their unfailing interest and support with respect to the Court; I am thinking, among others, of its occasional interlocutors, the agents and counsel; I am also thinking of the staff of the Registry of the Court, to whose dedication I wish to pay a particular tribute here.

Your Majesty, Excellencies, Ladies and Gentlemen,

As a rule, the celebration of a fiftieth anniversary is an occasion for reflection on the ground covered and on the ground which still lies ahead, an occasion for a retrospective glance at the past and a prospective glance at the future. However, the past of the International Court of Justice cannot be evaluated solely in the light of the last 50 years. For the present Court is but the continuation of an international justice born at the dawn of this century in the delicious coolness of this charming tree-lined city of The Hague.

In his speech inaugurating the Permanent Court of International Justice on 15 February 1922, President Bernard Cornelis Loder compared that Court to a precious plant, which would put down deep roots into the fertile soil of Holland and whose gardener would be the whole world. He had nourished the hope that this plant *'might develop and become a tree with a solid trunk, with strong wide-spreading branches and with thick foliage, in the shade of which the peoples might find rest'*. There is no doubt that his wish has been fulfilled beyond all expectation. A miraculous plant if ever there was one, international justice has flourished against all the odds, notwithstanding the shadow of the vigorous principle of State sovereignty, that sovereignty which, all things considered, judicial settlement has learned to live with and which, in itself, remains the guarantee of a balanced international society.

However, the past 50 years were to have their share of stormy weather. Scarcely had the deafening thunder of the Second World War died away than international society was trapped in the ice of East-West dissension, only to be assailed later by the burning sirocco of decolonization.

However, in no way did these upheavals thwart the principal judicial organ of the United Nations from flourishing. In almost 50 years of judicial activity, the International Court of Justice has been seised of 73 contentious cases and 23 requests for advisory opinion; it has delivered 60 judgments and 21 advisory opinions.

With a pride which, however, does not exclude humility, we therefore practise a profession unique in the world. We pass judgment on major questions linked to the sacrosanct sovereignty of States. Yesterday this was a mad dream of men in advance of their time. Today it is a reality. But a reality still unsatisfactory in certain respects, such as the scope of the personal or material jurisdiction of the Court. International justice has taken time, has taken its time, to become effective. But the breakthrough was definitive and the progress made irreversible. With each case judged, we experience the renewed wonder of this progress.

Though now 50 years old, the International Court of Justice would nevertheless still appear to be in the springtime of its life, if the great solicitude of which it is the object on the part of the States both in contentious and advisory proceedings is anything to go by. No less than eight contentious cases are currently pending before the Court and it is still seised of two important requests for advisory opinion. Ultimately, the present vitality of the Court is no more than an expression of the confidence which it inspires in the States and this confidence is not measured solely by the number of cases of which it is seised, but also, and above all, by the nature of those cases. In reality, the Court is not seised of cases of minor importance, quite the contrary.

In more general terms, the Court can take pride in having not only conferred its letters patent on a judicial settlement which had long been marginalized, but also, through the respect it inspires, for having to some extent *'secularized'* international justice, for having made it become part of its time, as evinced by the pre-eminent role which the States induce it to play by involving it in the process of getting to grips with the major preoccupations of the contemporary world, foremost among which are the questions of security and the environment.

On the threshold of the twenty-first century, the Court more than ever wishes to see itself as sensitive to the great anxieties which prey on the conscience of mankind. This *'secularization'* of international justice could not be more salutary, for the judge is always, ultimately, the interpreter of a state of civilization. Like all men, he journeys through the world by *'situating'* himself in his environment. Thus, the international judge remains attentive to all the commonly accepted values, which international public opinion usually echoes in our Court.

The opening up of the Court to the world and to its aspirations is nothing new. At the same time, the Court has succeeded in proving that it practises neither a justice of castes nor of rich States. Witness the case concerning *South West Africa*, which occupied the centre of the international stage and strongly mobilized public opinion in the sixties and seventies. Now in its heyday, the Court is more than ever in the limelight, as witness the attention devoted to it by civil society, proof of this being the avalanche of petitions addressed to the Court by individuals or legal entities relating to certain cases pending.

But it must be clearly stated: the fact that international justice is more than ever a house of glass in no way means that the Court is influenced by international public opinion in making its decisions. For the judges have no need at all of the approval of public opinion, only of their own consciences.

Let me emphasize, in this respect, that the justice rendered by men relating to *other men* is always a difficult matter and poses quasi-metaphysical problems for the conscience. *'Judges of the Earth, You are Gods!'* I interpret this exclamation of the French Chancellor d'Aguessau more as an overwhelming responsibility than as an expression of admiration. But what else can be said of the justice rendered by men regarding *States*, which is just as difficult, just as agonizing, bearing in mind the interests at stake, which are always substantial? The Members of the Court are acutely aware of this to the point of obsession. The protracted deliberations procedure, the numerous stages in the production of a judgment, provide ample evidence of this by the infinite but necessary meanders through which its drafts must pass before receiving the *imprimatur* of a publicly delivered judgment.

However, in this jubilee year, the Court in The Hague is at a crossroads as it were; other challenges are looming on the horizon and its ability to respond to them to a large extent determines its very existence as a universal Court. If it is to remain effective, the Court must adapt to the new international realities.

Your Majesty, Excellencies, Ladies and Gentlemen,

Fifty years ago to the day, referring to the work of the Permanent Court of International Justice, President Guerrero said that:

> 'This work will be carried on by us in the spirit which animated our predecessors. We shall preserve its continuity and devote ourselves to maintaining its prestige and authority. The activities of the Court, which we hope will continually increase in volume, will be dependent on the readiness of governments to refer to the international jurisdiction disputes capable of judicial settlement and on the readiness of the Security Council and General Assembly to seek from it advisory opinions. If the Court therefore is to be kept constantly employed, they must be faithful to the principle

of the pacific settlement of disputes, while it will depend on the conscience of the judges to ensure that the decisions to be rendered are in accordance with the principles of justice.'

This promise made on 18 April 1946 by one of my most illustrious predecessors has been kept and will continue to be so by all those who have succeeded one another or will succeed one another on the Bench of this Court and its message of hope will be heard by the States and the organs to which it was addressed. Today, 50 years later, on behalf of the Court and on my own behalf, I venture to express the wish that those chief players in international life, the States, will remain faithful to the principle of the judicial settlement of their disputes; I also endorse the promise that the work of the International Court of Justice will be carried out with all the authority of its experience and its now mature years."

IV. Fiftieth Anniversary of the United Nations

On 21 October 1995, an open day to mark the fiftieth anniversary of the United Nations was organized at the seat of the Court, in co-operation with the Netherlands National Committee for the 50th Anniversary of the United Nations. The twelve hundred visitors were addressed in the morning on the work of the International Court of Justice, the Permanent Court of Arbitration and the Carnegie Foundation. In the afternoon a panel discussion was held on the future of the United Nations, presided over by the Chairman of the First Chamber of the Dutch States General. Visitors were further able to visit information stands of Unesco, UNICEF, FAO and UNHCR, an exhibition of photographs put together by the Roosevelt Study Centre, Middelburg, and entitled "Fifty Years of the United Nations: A Dream of One World", a youth postage stamp exhibition (UNOPHILEX 95) with, in particular, a "Senior Citizens Collection", a series of slides on the United Nations in postage stamps, as well as the specially developed multi-media Exhibit for the Fiftieth Anniversary.

V. Visit of a Head of State

On 4 March 1996 the President of the Republic of Costa Rica, His Excellency Mr. José Maria Figueres Olsen, was received by the Court at a formal sitting in the Great Hall of Justice of the Peace Palace. At the sitting, which was attended by the diplomatic corps authorities from the host country and representatives of the Press, the President of the Court made a welcoming speech, to which the President of Costa Rica responded.

VI. Report and Representation of the Court at the General Assembly

On the occasion of the fiftieth session of the General Assembly, the Court submitted a report on its activities covering the period from 1 August 1994 to 31 July 1995 (A/50/4). This report was divided into seven parts, relating to the composition, jurisdiction and judicial work of the Court, the role of the Court, visits, administrative questions, and the Court's publications and documents. The General Assembly took note of the report at its 30th plenary meeting held on 12 October 1995.

On that occasion the President, who, with the Registrar, represented the Court at the forty-ninth session of the General Assembly, addressed that body on the role and functioning of the Court. The text of that address is reproduced in the Appendix to this Chapter (see below, pp. 262-270). Those Members of the Court who were present in New York also attended part of the fiftieth session of the General Assembly.

A report dealing with the period 1 August 1995 to 31 July 1996 will be submitted on the occasion of the fifty-first session of the General Assembly (A/51/4).

VII. Applications from Private Persons

Private persons frequently apply to the Court for the purpose of obtaining a decision on matters at issue between them and the authorities of their own or of another country. Between 1 August 1995 and 31 July 1996 the Court received approximately 1,200 requests of this kind. The writers were informed that, according to Article 34 of the Statute, "only States may be parties in cases before the Court".

APPENDIX

1. Action Pursuant to Decisions of the Court

The present section contains the information received in the Registry concerning action taken pursuant to decisions of the Court. The Registry, which does not take the initiative of seeking such information, publishes it without comment as and when it is received and can accept no responsibility in connection with it.

Cases concerning the *Corfu Channel (United Kingdom* v. *Albania)* and *Monetary Gold Removed from Rome in 1943 (Italy* v. *France, United Kingdom and United States)*

A copy of the Memorandum of Understanding between the Government of Albania and of the United Kingdom, which is reproduced below, was received in the Registry in 1992 and has been erroneously omitted from the Appendix to Chapter VI of *I.C.J. Yearbook 1992-1993*.

"MEMORANDUM OF UNDERSTANDING

The Governments of Albania and of the United Kingdom,

Having already re-established diplomatic relations;

Desiring now to settle the outstanding issues between them;

have reached an understanding on the following points:

(1) The Government of the United Kingdom will approve the delivery to Albania of some 1574 kgms of gold previously identified for allocation to Albania from the gold pool maintained by the Tripartite Commission for the Restitution of Monetary Gold.

(2) Closely linked to the delivery of the gold to the Government of Albania, the Government of Albania will pay to the Government of the United Kingdom the sum of US$2 million.

(3) Once the Government of Albania have paid the said sum, the Government of the United Kingdom will regard as fully and finally settled the financial claims put forward by the Government of the United Kingdom.

(4) Both Governments understood that the delivery of the gold to Albania will require the consent not only of the Government of the United Kingdom but also of the Governments of France and the United States of America.

The foregoing records the understandings of the Governments of Albania and of the United Kingdom on the matters specified therein.

Done at Rome on 8 May 1992.

For the Government of Albania:	For the Government of the United Kingdom:
(Signed) ILLEGIBLE	*(Signed)* Michael TAIT."

2. THE ROLE AND FUNCTIONING OF THE COURT

"PRESENT DIFFICULTIES OF THE COURT[1]

In recent years, the Court has been busier than ever before, as recounted more fully elsewhere in the present Report. Its calendar in the year under review has been crowded and demanding. On 21 August 1995, New Zealand, in response to France's resumption of nuclear testing, filed a *Request for an Examination of the Situation in Accordance with Paragraph 63 of the Court's Judgment of 20 December 1974 in the* Nuclear Tests (New Zealand *v.* France) *Case.* The

[1] This text is a reproduction of Chapter IV of the Court's Report to the General Assembly for 1 August 1995 to 31 July 1996 (*Official Records of the General Assembly, Fifty-first Session, Supplement No. 4* (A/51/4)).

Court, after hearings on whether the Request submitted by New Zealand fell within paragraph 63 of the 1974 Judgment, found, in an Order of 22 September 1995, that it did not. It then held three weeks of hearings in October and November conjointly on two requests for advisory opinions, one filed by the World Health Assembly on the *Legality of the Use by a State of Nuclear Weapons in Armed Conflict*, the other filed by the General Assembly on the *Legality of the Threat or Use of Nuclear Weapons*. An unprecedented number of States submitted written statements and written comments on these statements and took part in the hearings on what may be the most important questions ever put to the Court in advisory proceedings. The Opinions, which required consideration of problems of exceptional difficulty, were rendered on 8 July 1996. In the midst of that consideration, the Court was required to deal with a request for the indication of provisional measures in the case concerning the *Land and Maritime Boundary between Cameroon and Nigeria (Cameroon* v. *Nigeria)*; an Order indicating provisional measures was issued on 15 March 1996. The Court also held hearings between 29 April and 3 May on issues of jurisdiction and admissibility raised by Yugoslavia in the case concerning *Application of the Convention on the Prevention and Punishment of the Crime of Genocide (Bosnia and Herzegovina* v. *Yugoslavia)*; it handed down a Judgment on 11 July 1996.

It will thus be seen that the Court has been deliberating on three cases simultaneously, in contrast with its traditional practice of taking one case, or one phase of a case, at a time. The Court has accordingly been placed under exceptional strain in a period in which the staff and resources of its Registry have been subjected to severe cuts. At a time of substantial recourse to the Court by States and international organizations, staff and budgetary reductions required of it inevitably are beginning to curtail its established levels of judicial service. Yet the Court, unlike other bodies, cannot eliminate programmes; it is bound by its Statute to deal with the cases and advisory opinions brought before it.

The financial crisis of the Organization in fact is seriously prejudicing the work of the Court. The Court is informing the Secretary-General and the Advisory Committee on Administrative and Budgetary Questions of the dimensions and details of the financial difficulties with which the Court is beset. However, the situation is grave enough to be brought to the attention of the General Assembly in the present Annual Report.

In 1995, the Court submitted to the General Assembly through the Secretary-General tightly drawn budgetary proposals, fashioned to respond to the high level of recourse to the Court by States and international organizations. The Court's limited budgetary proposals were reduced by the General Assembly when it approved, by its resolution 50/215 A of 23 December 1995, the programme budget of the Organization for the biennium 1996-1997, which among other cuts eliminated four of the total of 61 positions which the Registrar had had during the previous biennium. An additional reduction of 4.1 per cent in that already reduced budget was imposed pursuant to part IV of General Assembly resolution 50/216 of the same date. In addition, three of the total of 54 permanent posts in the Registry which became vacant in 1996 have been frozen pursuant to United Nations directives. The result is that, in a period of months, the Court's small staff has sustained an effective reduction of 11.5 per cent, and professional staff has been cut by 16.7 per cent.

The impact of these budgetary restrictions and staff reductions is particularly preoccupying for conference services, in particular translation services, which can no longer be supplied as required. The shortfall in translation services – a problem not easily appreciated or even perceived by the outside world – jeopardizes the functioning of the Court in accordance with its Statute, which provides that its official languages shall be French and English (it may be observed that the fact that the Court operates in two rather than six official languages results in great savings as compared with other United Nations organs). There are perceived – and real – problems of delay by the Court in discharging its duties, but such delay will ineluctably increase if the Court continues to be deprived of sufficient staff and funds to meet its translation requirements.

The reality is that the funding of the Court falls considerably short of what is required for it to fulfil its functions. Current budget allocations take insufficient account of the extraordinary and sustained increase of recent years in the number of cases on the Court's General List and in the increase in the volume of pleadings filed by parties to those cases.

The costs to the Court of ensuring that a case is fairly and impartially heard may not be sufficiently appreciated. Among the many burdens are the translating and publication not only of the pleadings themselves but also of their annexes. The current budget of the Court as revised and reduced by the General Assembly and by the Secretary-General acting in pursuance of its decisions affords the Court neither the staff nor the financial resources properly to carry out these tasks. Yet it has always been recognized that the Court cannot render justice without performing those tasks and that it falls to the United Nations to provide it with the requisite means.

States submitting documentary annexes to support their written arguments are entitled to expect that they will be fully understood by all Members of the Court and that the Judges will be able to study them in their working language, whether French or English. The problem of under-funding of the Court is graphically illustrated by the *Gabčíkovo-Nagymaros Project (Hungary/Slovakia)* case. This case, concerning a dam project on the Danube, is of critical importance to the Parties. It is also likely to contribute significantly to the clarification and development of international treaty and environmental law. Some 3,351 pages of documentary annexes have been submitted to the Court. There is simply not the staff or funds to do the work of translating all of the pages not already available in both languages. Using the traditional means of freelance translation of written pleadings submitted by parties before the Court, the confidential nature of which require them to be translated within the premises of the Court, the estimated costs are of the order of $530,000. That sum exceeds the balance available to the Court for translation for the 1996-1997 biennium. This situation will doubtless occasion serious difficulties, not only for adjudication of the *Gabčíkovo-Nagymaros Project (Hungary/Slovakia)* case but also for other pending cases, not to speak of other such cases as may be brought to the Court.

Mindful of its obligations under its Statute, the Court nevertheless has ordered, in so far as its resources permit, the translation of the documentation in preparation for the hearings to be held in early 1997 in the case concerning the *Gabčíkovo-Nagymaros Project (Hungary/Slovakia)*.

Restoration of the cuts in the Court's budget and staff is urgently required if the Court is to regain the traditional pace of its proceedings, not to speak of accelerating them. The budget of the Court even before these cuts was a smaller percentage of the budget of the United Nations in 1995 than it was 50 years earlier in 1946. If the total budget of the Court – some $10,000,000 a year – is compared not only with that of the other principal organs of the United Nations, but with lesser organs (including that of a subsidiary organ of the Security Council, the International Tribunal for the Former Yugoslavia), the modesty of its resources is clear. If the Court is to operate more expeditiously, there are steps that could be taken to enhance its productivity, which will require increased funding. For example, Judges of the Court unlike the Members of that International Tribunal or the Court of the European Communities or some national courts have no clerks and no research assistance. The case-law of the Court has not been computerized in the Court and the Court has no access to such beginnings as have been made in this regard outside of the Court, nor does it have access to the vast and readily retrievable body of information that is available via computer in much of the world. Introduction of clerks and computerization would materially expedite the work of the Court.

A great restraint on the size of the Registry – lack of physical space – is about to be overcome. With the completion of the extension and renovation of its facilities in the Peace Palace by the end of 1996, the Court, for the first time in its history, will have adequate space, not only for Judges and Judges *ad hoc* (of which there are currently 11) but for an expanded Registry. Apart from other constraints, before 1997 the Court would have lacked the office space in which clerks could work. In its next budget request, the Court will seek funds for the appointment of an initial contingent of clerks, to be internationally recruited and appointed by the Court for two-year terms, who as a pool will collectively assist the Judges. It will also submit a request for funds to computerize both its case-law and current caseload, and other data, and to afford it access to the world of computerized information.

The Court is gratified that, in recent years, States have increasingly submitted international legal disputes to the Court for resolution, a development long sought by the General Assembly which promises to be sustained. At the same time, the Court is conscious of the fact that its List is long and that its possibilities of expeditiously disposing of the cases brought to it hobbled by the inadequacy of its material resources. Although it is to be kept in mind that some of the lengthiest cases, for example, the *South West Africa* cases and the *Barcelona Traction* case, were before the Court in the 1960s, it may still be said that over the last years the length of time elapsing between the filing of an application and the rendering of a judgment has been growing. Parties to a case are generally accorded the time they request for preparation of pleadings, in the course of which they may seek extensions. But the problem of particular concern is that, when written pleadings are complete – pleadings which may require the Members of the Court to study many thousands of pages – and when the case is ready for hearing, the disposition of prior cases on the List may lead to considerable delay in the holding of hearings. This recent but serious development has occasioned criticism within and outside the Court.

The procedures for the Court's deliberations are described in its *Resolution concerning the Internal Judicial Practice of the Court* of 12 April 1976. Those procedures were subjected to searching evaluation at the Colloquium convened by the Court with the assistance of the United Nations Institute for Training and Research (UNITAR) in celebration of the fiftieth anniversary of the Court in April 1996. The theme chosen by the Court for its Colloquium evidenced its appreciation of the position: 'Increasing the Effectiveness of the International Court of Justice'. The Colloquium was attended by the Legal Advisers of the Foreign Ministries of some 45 States, by leading counsel in the Court and by scholars, as well as all Judges of the Court and the Registrar and his colleagues.

The Court's internal procedures, devised when the Court had few cases on its List, currently are the subject of reconsideration by the Court's Rules Committee. While on the one hand they ensure a scrupulous consideration of the plenitude of issues raised by a case by every Member of the Court and enable every Member to influence the content and drafting of the Court's decisions – great advantages in a court of universal composition and mission – on the other hand they take a great deal of time. The Rules Committee is reconsidering their utility in the light of these competing considerations.

In 1996, the Court has taken steps to avoid gaps in its work occasioned by the settlement of cases, by forward planning of oral hearings. Hearings are scheduled in *Oil Platforms (Islamic Republic of Iran* v. *United States of America)* for September 1996, and in the case concerning the *Gabčíkovo-Nagymaros Project (Hungary/Slovakia)* for February 1997. It is to be hoped that, with the practice of forward planning in place, States parties will be in a position in future to accelerate their appearance in Court at the Court's request when an earlier scheduled set of hearings is cancelled by reason of settlement of the prior case.

In its Report of 12 December 1995 (A/50/7/Add.11), the Advisory Committee on Administrative and Budgetary Questions has raised questions about the practice of the Court in permitting its Members to engage in occasional activities outside of the Court that may be remunerated: acting as arbitrators in inter-State and private international arbitrations, serving in administrative tribunals or quasi-judicial organs of specialized agencies, lecturing, writing. That occasional practice goes back to the origins of the Permanent Court of International Justice. Not only is it in conformity with the Statute of the Court; the repeated endorsement by the international organs and by the States that have appointed Members of the Court as arbitrators shows their awareness of the contribution that the Members of the Court may, by this function, make to the development of international law, and of the benefits deriving therefrom for all institutions concerned. The practice, which involves a very limited number of Judges for very limited periods, has no adverse effect on the pace of the work of the Court or the total precedence given to that work by its Members. The Court has recently considered the questions respecting that practice which the Advisory Committee has raised, and has adopted new guidelines governing the matter."

*

At the 30th meeting of the fiftieth session of the General Assembly, held on 12 October 1995 (see above, p. 255), the President of the Court, Judge Mohammed Bedjaoui, gave the following address:

"THE INTERNATIONAL COURT OF JUSTICE: WHAT WILL ITS FUTURE BE?

[Translation by the Registry]

Mr. President, Mr. Secretary-General, Your Excellencies, Ladies and Gentlemen,

Portugal, which is so well endowed with intelligent citizens, was not – I am sure – long in doubt as to the choice of a politician to be put forward for election by the nations of the world to the office of President of the General Assembly. Looking behind the image of the Prime Minister, or Minister, or the Head of a democratic party – which posts you have occupied or still occupy – it chose in the first place, I am sure, the academic, the intellectual, the man of culture that you likewise personify.

In other words, the international community is honoured to be able to welcome you, as you take the chair of the highest Assembly of the world, in your capacity of a man of political action – of course – but likewise as a thinker and a humanist who has, throughout his life, made generous choices in the service of justice and progress. I would also say how delighted the International Court of Justice was to learn that an eminent professor of public law had been chosen to preside over this Assembly.

Moreover, how can the Court have failed to rejoice in your election when – in an unprecedented gesture – you made a point, from your very first statement as President on 19 September last, of ranging the work of the United Nations under the banner of the primacy of international law and paying tribute to the Court as one of the principal organs of the United Nations, dedicated to the promotion of respect for that international law that you do not cease from teaching and inculcating to the rising generations?

How can the Court fail to express its gratitude, through me as intermediary, when you have launched an exalted appeal to all States to accept the jurisdiction of our Court?

You are presiding over the Assembly of peoples of the United Nations at an exceptional period in the life of the Organization, as it celebrates its admirable fiftieth anniversary. I am sure that you will conduct this celebration with all the wisdom and the mastery that we expect of you. My warmest good wishes go with you for the complete success of this exalted task which you are so well fitted to undertake.

Giving the floor to the President of the International Court of Justice when the Court's Report is being considered has become a tradition which the General Assembly has accepted with a good grace for some years now. This gesture seems to me to be highly symbolic. In this year in which we are celebrating the fiftieth anniversary of the United Nations, I would like to lay particular stress upon the extremely privileged nature of this regular contact, an exemplary expression of the close collaboration which should unite the principal organs of the United Nations as they strive to attain the purposes of the Organization, but also providing a striking testimony to the interest that the General Assembly – and through it the whole international community – takes in the activities of the Court. I am accordingly delighted to be able to thank the General Assembly for having once again been so good as to devote a few minutes of its precious time to listening to the President of the International Court of Justice.

The celebration of the fiftieth anniversary of the United Nations – and the fiftieth anniversary of the International Court of Justice in a few months time – provides me with an opportunity to share with the Assembly, and with each of the States here represented at the highest level, some thoughts on the current role and the future of the principal judicial organ that I have the honour to represent.

When confronted by the large number of conflicts in the world of today which fall outside the jurisdiction of the International Court of Justice, the general public is frequently led to wonder *what exactly an international court is supposed to do.*

To wonder about the role and future of permanent international justice is to try to find a proper answer to that kind of question. It is to wonder how the 'scales of justice' can operate and extend their influence when not backed up by a powerful 'sword' – if I may transpose into the international sphere the familiar thought-patterns of the municipal order which has accustomed us to a trilogy – dear to Montesquieu – of legislative, executive and judicial powers. One is once more led to wonder whether, given the requirements of the municipal 'model', one can really conceive, for the international order, of a judicial power in an international community whose real existence is a matter of some doubt in certain quarters and in which there is, moreover, neither an authentic legislature nor any real power of enforcement.

One could carry on asking questions of this kind until one reached the point of paradox, such are the difficulties involved in resolving the mystery surrounding the future of international justice. Indeed the International Court of Justice, as principal judicial organ of the United Nations, is no more than one part of a whole, a mere cog – albeit an important cog – in a complex mechanism conceived in accordance with a set of precise specifications. One might properly be led to think that the future of that organ naturally depends upon the future of the United Nations. This is an obviously sensible line of argument but nonetheless implies a simplification which has to be moderated in the light of the point I would now like to make. It would seem that the current situation of the International Court of Justice is characterized by a certain singularity – I would even say a certain paradox. This relates to the good fortune currently attending the Court, at the very same time as the mother Organization as a whole is coming up against considerable difficulties on a variety of fronts.

The world legislative power exists only in outline. It is represented by your exalted Assembly, fortified by its composition representing all the peoples of the United Nations, but which can only legislate by means of resolutions which are not, as a general rule, legally binding. As for the Security Council, which is constitutionally freed from any such limitation, it may doubtless be compared to a quasi-world executive power but, as it has scarcely recovered from the paralysis to which it was long condemned by the cold war, it is currently experiencing new difficulties in maintaining and consolidating international peace and security. However, it is in this context of the laborious building of the proclaimed new world order that States, and even national public opinions, are turning to the Court – a singular but encouraging trend.

Now that we are engaged in a stock-taking exercise, the Court's stock actually seems to be in better shape than some others. It would seem that the judicial function may – on an international level as well – lay claim to a necessary measure of autonomy and independence. When the founding fathers of the 1945 Charter forged close structural links between the Court and the United Nations, they obviously intended that the Court should be fully integrated into the new system for the peaceful settlement of disputes that had just been devised, but did not in any way wish to deprive the Court of the autonomy indispensable to the sound administration of justice. In that regard, they refrained from making any fundamental changes to the situation brought into being by their predecessors at the League of Nations with respect to the former Permanent Court.

It would however be unforgivably imprudent – if not totally disproportionate – to claim to be able to predict a separate future for the United Nations and for the Court, as their mutual and indissociable fate remains sealed by the Charter, that Magna Carta of mankind.

For the time being, and more cautiously, my aim is to look briefly at the Court's current good fortune and to explore the reasons for it. I shall then consider the improvements that could well be made to a judicial institution that will soon be 50 years old, to enable it to meet the new and numerous challenges with which it is confronted.

The International Court of Justice has been thriving for the past few years. Never has it been so much in demand, never has it been so active. There seems to be every indication that that tendency will only grow stronger in the years to come.

Indeed, certain profound changes that have come about in the international community and, more particularly, the end of a world divided into two camps as a result of the cold war, are still too recent to have been able to have their full positive effect upon international judicial settlement. This new period was ushered in by a momentous event, the collapse of the Berlin Wall – on one memorable day in November 1989. However it does seem that on all sides, other walls, erected in the minds of the world's leaders and which previously constituted so many additional impediments to the work of the Court, are now beginning to fall – to such an extent that the States parties to the dozen or so contentious cases now on the Court's General List are located on every continent.

The International Court of Justice is currently displaying an unprecedented vitality. In line with the unusual number of cases of which it is seised, the Court has seen its jurisdiction steadily expand, in terms of both the number of declarations made and the compromissory clauses included in treaties – or in terms of the withdrawal of reservations to such clauses. Moreover, the Court's current vitality is not merely to be measured by the yardstick of the confidence currently placed in it by States, but must also be assessed in accordance with the way in which States comply with its decisions.

But what is the source of the Court's new vitality?

References have been made in turn, and with a greater or lesser degree of relevance, to the decisions reached by the Court in certain cases, the end of communism, the greater trust placed in the Court by Third World countries, and a more generalized psychological rallying to the applicable international law.

I must stress that the Court's success has not derived from the *'transactional justice'* or *'compromise justice'* which has sometimes been ascribed to it. It is of course true to say that, in certain cases, the seisin of the Court has been no more than a means of pressure exercised by one party upon another in a bid to lead it to a political settlement, seen as preferable to a judicial decision. Under such circumstances, the Court, fully aware of its responsibilities as an integral part of the system of peaceful settlement of international disputes established under the Charter, has displayed judicial realism and has considered itself obligated to assist in bringing the parties closer together, while not at any time departing from its primordial task of applying the law.

However that in no way signifies that the Court hands down 'judgments of Solomon'. Far from it. It goes without saying that it has never attempted to do any favours to anybody, nor has it ever compromised the integrity of its judicial function or the principles governing its mission. Its strength – and doubtless its success – will have been that it knows how to do justice in all legal rectitude, in all intellectual honesty and in a spirit of total independence without, for all that, shutting itself away in an ivory tower or failing to take account of the facts of life.

The vitality of the Court can be explained. The International Court of Justice ultimately has the strengths of its weaknesses or, if you prefer, the virtue of its principal vice. The international judicial function still bears the image of the international society whose disputes it is called upon to settle: *it operates on a consensual basis.* The success of the Court may well be due precisely to the fact that its office seems ultimately to be fairly well adapted to the concerns and the system of values predominating in the States to which it is open. Has not *consensualism* become, more than ever, a value in which to take refuge in a society of States that is still resistant to the advances of supranationalism?

Of course States may undertake in advance to accept the compulsory jurisdiction of the Court, thus giving it what may be described as a free hand, just as they give a free hand to the Security Council when they accede to the Charter. However, such a comparison immediately requires one to relativize, in so far as the abandonment of sovereignty conceded in each case is not done under identical conditions, or with identical consequences. There can be said to be a far greater exercise of free will in a State's decision to accept the jurisdiction of the Court than in a decision to submit to the decisions of the Security Council.

Another partial reason for the present good fortune of the Court might be found in a wider context, namely, that of the general evolution in international relations. It would appear to be a truth of experience that legal settlement is more widely supported, and even more sought after, when the international atmosphere is less tense. The counterpart proof is provided by the fact that it was during the periods of extreme international tension in the cold war that the Court was bereft of cases and could not perform its function. Moreover, is it not true to say that the 'tension', without any clearly defined object, generally prevented the emergence of specific legal disputes, which are the only ones appropriate for submission to the Court?

However, this argument must be treated with caution, for it is no secret that the disappearance of the bipolar international order has not resulted in the creation of a peaceful world, since the world of freedom which has succeeded it is also more fragmented and uncertain.

Be that as it may, if it is to guarantee its future, the Court needs new means to enable it to meet the new challenges with which it will be confronted in the coming years.

Before briefly outlining some of these means, let me make two introductory observations, which seem to me as self-evident as they are fundamental and also to govern the future direction of the Court.

The first of these is that, although permanent international jurisdiction made forward strides with the Charter, this progress was not as decisive in this field as it was, for example, in the political one. With the major changes which occurred on the world stage after the Second World War and the outlawing of the use of force, the overall profile of the political organs of the United Nations, as well as the links and relations between these organs, have been fundamentally reshaped and streamlined. On the other hand, the judicial organ, the International Court of Justice, has, barring a few details, remained virtually a replica or a continuation of the Permanent Court of International Justice. From the League of Nations to the United Nations, the political organs would appear to have 'matured' more than the judicial organ, which, 73 years after its birth, remains essentially the same.

My second introductory observation concerns the new functions and powers which have been granted to the United Nations and to many other international organizations since 1945. It cannot be claimed today, in 1995, that the World Organization plays the same role, is vested with the same mission and has the same legal status as its predecessor in the 1920s. Still more, at a time when the international organizations have more legal means at their disposal – which, admittedly, they do not always use – in order to become *full players* in international relations, the State, traditionally the exclusive subject of these international relations, is undergoing internal and external changes which affect this traditional role of solo player.

It is clear that these new situations create new needs and that the future of the International Court of Justice will be measured by its ability to win a status which is not simply a replica of the status of the former Permanent Court of International Justice. There can be no doubt that adjustments are necessary.

These adjustments must first of all be made to the contentious function of the Court.

The Court's jurisdiction *ratione personae* has remained frozen as it were since 1922. The Court is open only to States. Today, when inter-governmental organizations have grown up, it is important to given them access to contentious procedure.

States, subjects traditionally described as 'primary' or 'necessary' components of the international legal order, are, in reality, no longer the only players in international relations, or the only interlocutors where peacekeeping is concerned. International life shows us every single day that, at this level, greater account must be taken of other entities, notably, the international organizations. Access to the Court's contentious procedure, currently reserved for States alone, may therefore now seem too narrow. Among the remedies found for these shortcomings has been the incorporation, into certain treaties, of *ad hoc* clauses laying down that, in the event of a dispute between the international organization and the States specified therein, that organization will request the Court for an advisory opinion, which the two parties agree will have a 'decisive' or 'binding' effect. The technique referred to as that of '*compulsory* advisory *opinions*' – whose very name underlines its singularity – is, however, no more than a stopgap, which cannot be a substitute for full access by organizations with international legal personality to the contentious procedure of the Court.

Where the Court's jurisdiction *ratione materiae* in the context of contentious procedure is concerned, it would not seem, on the other hand, that there are any measures to be taken with a view to increasing accession to the optional clause of compulsory jurisdiction. To date, 59 States have acceded to the clause; this number, compared with the total number of Member States of the Organization (187 States) represents a ratio which has not appreciably altered since 1945.

I fear that this ratio cannot be significantly improved, failing a spectacular *momentum* in international relations. When President Mikhail Gorbachev called upon the five permanent member States of the Security Council to set an example by submitting their disputes to the International Court, this aroused great interest which, regrettably, quickly waned. The Five held a number of meetings at legal adviser level with a view to drawing up a list of subjects which the Court would be likely to entertain in the event of a dispute. But no agreement was reached.

It is the natural and inevitable consequence of the conception of international relations which nowadays always prevails. States remain attached to the political and diplomatic liberty available to them for settling their disputes in line with their own interests and prevailing circumstances. All they want is to see all existing procedures relating to the peaceful settlement of disputes open. And this, after all, is what counts.

Moreover, since every case has its political aspects and its legal aspects, it is difficult *a priori* to draw a distinction, in general and definitive terms, between cases which it would be desirable to submit to the Court and those which it would be appropriate to settle by other means. It is the States which must choose. This is why it seems so rash to try and predict which categories of cases could be submitted to the Court in future.

The desire for the International Court of Justice to be better known by all so that it can be better utilized and play a greater role in the day-to-day life of chancelleries and international organizations has often been expressed. With a view to this, some of them have suggested that it should be seised of small cases, whose rapid settlement would enable it to become part of the mechanics of international relations in the everyday life of peoples. This is an interesting idea but in fact an unrealistic one; States and international organizations cannot contemplate mobilizing the heavy and complex procedural apparatus of the International Court of Justice for small cases, nor exposing themselves to expenses which would seem substantial for such modest issues.

Other jurists have contended, on the contrary, that it would rather tend to be cases of medium importance which would, by nature, be suitable for submission to the Court, such as, for example, the existence, the scope or the limits of the rights of jurisdiction of States, in particular where land frontiers or maritime delimitations are concerned.

In reality these two approaches, however ingenious they may be, are not part of the political will of States, which remains the only objective determining factor of the Court's activity. Today, the Court is not seised of minor issues, nor is it seised only of disputes of medium importance. On the contrary, it is seised of a series of vital issues ranging from the application of the Convention on the

Prevention and Punishment of the Crime of Genocide to the lawfulness of the use of nuclear weapons, a question with which this Assembly is very familiar.

As regards the *advisory jurisdiction* of the Court, it seems that thought should also be given to widening its field of application *ratione personae*. The Secretariat, represented by the Secretary-General, is to date the only principal organ of the United Nations not authorized to request an advisory opinion of the Court on any legal question related to its activity in the service of the Organization.

A widening of the group of international organizations authorized to request opinions might also usefully be considered, admitting certain organizations which do not fall within the present definition of the Charter, but whose access to the advisory procedure would be desirable for various reasons. Authorizing access to this procedure might also be extended to include inter-governmental organizations with a more or less universal status, such as the World Trade Organization or the Organization for the Prohibition of Chemical Weapons, and regional governmental organizations.

Lastly, the question of the participation of non-governmental organizations in the Court's advisory procedure should be given serious study. NGOs are today important bodies representing world public opinion. Many of them enjoy permanent *consultative status* with principal organs of the United Nations. They may now have access to the Security Council or the General Assembly.

In conclusion, the future of the International Court of Justice depends on many factors which, to a broad extent, elude the control of the Court itself. These include:

(1) the emergence of certain categories of so-called internal conflict, but with clear international repercussions, which international law does not yet cover except in a very fragmentary fashion;
(2) internal and external changes in States, which affect their traditional role as key players in international relations;
(3) the emergence of international inter-governmental organizations on the world stage, including with respect to judicial settlement;
(4) the growing place of non-governmental organizations voicing the wishes of an international public opinion more concerned with and motivated by world affairs; and
(5) *last but not least*, recognition of the essential role the Court must play in sanctioning a form of international law governing a world and a society of law.

Thank you."

*

On 16 October 1995 President Bedjaoui further gave the following address to the Sixth Committee of the General Assembly:

“THE CHANGING FORTUNES OF THE JURISDICTION OF THE INTERNATIONAL COURT OF JUSTICE

[Translation by the Registry]

Your Excellencies, Ladies and Gentlemen,

Neither the Court’s need for independence nor its remoteness from the banks of the East River should mean that it is confined in isolation, which is why I see this moment in time as one that is truly propitious for relations between the Court and the international legal community you represent. I would like to take this opportunity to share with you some thoughts on what I would like to call the ‘changing fortunes’ of the jurisdiction of the International Court of Justice.

1. History shows us that Justice has only made progress when there has been a consolidation of the social order which it is required to pacify, and what applies to national judicial systems applies equally to the international judicial system. The sacrosanct principle of national sovereignty has, however, long been brandished by States like a scarecrow, to ward off any attempt to structure international society along the lines of national societies in which the task of the *judge* is to hear and determine cases on the basis of a *corpus juris* enacted by a *legislator* and where he may count upon the intervention of the *police* to ensure that his decisions are enforced.

2. As is known, the system devised 50 years ago in San Francisco did not usher in any real revolution in this regard as it is based, at the very most, upon a schema comprising an international executive function, a deliberative function and a judicial function devolving respectively upon the Security Council, the General Assembly and the International Court of Justice. As a general rule, neither the General Assembly nor the Security Council – without prejudice to the powers conferred upon the Council by Article 25 as well as under Chapter VII of the Charter – was invested with the capacity to create rules legally binding upon the Member States. Article 94 of the Charter of the United Nations provides, for its part, that the Security Council may take appropriate measures to ensure compliance with the decisions of the Court, but the implementation of that mechanism is governed by criteria of expediency which only the Council is able to assess. The lack of any real international *legislature* and *police force* accordingly rules out any conclusion that there is an international judicial power in the true sense of the term. The lack of any capacity to control the acts of the decision-making and deliberative organs, as well as the optional character of the binding jurisdiction of the International Court of Justice are the most visible consequences of this state of affairs.

3. Whereas in any social order, the *Law*, the *Sword* and the *Scales of Justice* are normally in such a relationship of interdependence that the dysfunction of one necessarily has an effect upon the functioning

of the others, the observer of the international scene will have no difficulty in perceiving that the viability and vitality of the international judicial function are not necessarily to be assessed by the same yardstick as those of the legislative and executive functions carried out respectively by the General Assembly and Security Council.

4. Indeed, for the time being, the International Court of Justice seems to be singularly blessed in its efforts to bring peace to international life. Formerly in a class apart, relegated to the sidelines of the maintenance of international peace and security, the Court is nowadays in the forefront of the action, and has become a protagonist playing a full part in the realization of this primordial purpose of the United Nations.

5. As I speak to you now, no less than ten contentious cases, involving countries on four continents, are pending before the Court, and it has been seised of two requests for advisory opinions. Moreover, in spite of what some scholars have been wont to advocate or predict, the Court is not currently seised of minor matters, neither is it seised merely of disputes of only moderate importance. It is seised of considerable and even crucial issues such as, for example, the question of nuclear weapons, through the medium of two requests for advisory opinions on the legality of the use of nuclear weapons submitted by the World Health Organization and the United Nations General Assembly. It is also seised of other questions of no lesser importance, such as the case brought by Bosnia and Herzegovina which relied upon the Convention on the Prevention and Punishment of the Crime of Genocide.

6. Both by their quantity and their quality, the cases pending before the Court undoubtedly bear witness to the current good health of a judicial institution which has been somewhat neglected in the past. That period of recession 'bottomed out' in 1971 as, between 21 June and 30 August of that year, the Court was purely and simply at a standstill, since no more cases were currently pending before it.

7. Is the Court currently enjoying a mere remission in its problems or has it really been cured of its former ills? For the time being, it is difficult to make any definite predictions as to its future health. In the same way it is difficult to isolate with any precision the factor or factors responsible for its currently healthy condition. It is more appropriate to speak of a set of circumstances which cannot easily be subjected to scientific observation and which have, for that reason, been overlooked in the efforts at systematization hitherto made in writings on the Court.

8. I would now like to try to consider, with you, this phenomenon of the alternating fortunes of the Court's jurisdiction in the light of an explanatory outline based on the facts and events of international life. The jurisdiction of the International Court of Justice would seem to be at the mercy of the reversals and sudden turns of history, and it is essentially in factors completely extraneous to the Court that one

must, in my view, seek for the origins of both its past vicissitudes and the expected – or at least hoped-for – fulfilment of its jurisdiction.

I. The Reverses of History or the Era of Changing Fortunes in Judicial Settlement

9. Of all the criticisms that are levelled at the International Court of Justice there is one which seems to be a recurrent theme, i.e., that in quantitive terms, the record of the present Court's activities would appear to be much less impressive than that of its predecessor.

10. Let us allow the figures to speak for themselves. It is true that, in 18 years of judicial activity, the Permanent Court of International Justice was seised of 66 cases and handed down 32 Judgments and 27 Advisory Opinions. It is equally true that, from 1946 to 1964 – or during a similar period of activity – the International Court of Justice, for its part, only dealt with 49 cases – both contentious and advisory – and that it handed down no more than 28 Judgments and 13 Advisory Opinions. For your information, I would add that up to the present, or in other words in 50 years of judicial activity, the Court has been seised of 74 contentious cases and 23 requests for advisory opinions, and that it has handed down 60 Judgments and 21 Advisory Opinions.

11. I will keep to the figures and carry on with my comparisons, as there has also been a great deal of speculation about the perceptibly larger number of States that made declarations of acceptance of the compulsory jurisdiction of the Permanent Court under the optional clause of Article 36, paragraph 2, of its Statute. In 1925, more than half the States parties to the Statute of the Permanent Court had made a declaration under the optional clause[1]. In 1934, that proportion attained its maximum with a record figure of 85 per cent of the States parties to the Statute[2]. It had gone down slightly in 1939 just before the outbreak of the Second World War (80 per cent)[3]. It is true that, in the context of the International Court of Justice, the optional clause has been much less successful. In 1947, 25 out of the 55 States parties to the Statute had accepted the compulsory jurisdiction of the present-day Court, i.e., a proportion of 45 per cent. That proportion has declined steadily since that time. It fell to 33 per cent in 1967[4], to 30 per cent in 1977[5], and lastly to 28 per cent in 1987[6]. It has now risen again to almost 32 per cent[7].

---

[1] Twenty States out of thirty-five.

[2] Forty-two out of forty-nine.

[3] Forty Declarations out of fifty States parties to the Statute.

[4] Forty-two Declarations for one hundred and twenty-five States parties to the Statute.

[5] Forty-five Declarations for one hundred and fifty States parties to the Statute.

[6] Forty-six Declarations for one hundred and sixty-two States parties to the Statute.

[7] Fifty-nine Declarations for one hundred and eighty-seven States parties to the Statute.

12. In this regard, I would like to engage in a brief aside and to point out that the greater or lesser degree of acceptance of the compulsory jurisdiction of the Court is far from being the only criterion for the evaluation of the extent to which States are prepared to have their disputes settled by it. I will call to witness the fact that the actual volume of cases before the Court is a great deal larger than it was 30 years ago whereas, in the past 30 years, the proportion of acceptances of its compulsory jurisdiction has stabilized at about 30 per cent. The withdrawal by the United States, in 1985, of its acceptance under the optional clause, followed two years later by the filing, by that same State, of an application instituting proceedings against Italy in the *ELSI* case, attests – if such testimony is needed – that the existence and the number of those declarations is a poor indicator of the extent to which States are well disposed towards the Court.

13. I would add that one also needs to relativize the significance of the number of declarations under the optional clause, firstly on account of the more or less extensive reservations that frequently accompany them (we all remember the so called 'automatic' reservation) and, secondly, on account of the frequent raising of preliminary objections by States that have made a declaration, when they find themselves in the position of respondents. This kind of comment applies *mutatis mutandis* to the compromissory clauses inserted into more than 270 bilateral and multilateral conventions. For that reason the considerable reduction, in relative terms, of the number of such clauses as from the mid-1970s, is not very significant either.

14. We have now finished with the figures, presented with no attempt at embellishment. I am afraid that I felt obliged to inflict this little exercise upon you and I hope you will not judge me too severely. It seemed to me that I needed to quote all those figures because some people have not hesitated to highlight the tendencies revealed by them in an attempt to show that there has been a progressive deterioration, a regression of the role and importance of international justice for the peaceful settlement of disputes since the adoption of the Charter. There can be no doubt that, in terms of raw data, the record of the activities of the present-day Court – particularly in advisory cases – is less impressive than was that of its predecessor. However, one should only compare like with like and, when making any comparison, take account of the different contexts in which the two Courts were required to operate.

15. Before laying stress upon the specificity of the international context of the inter-war period, one must begin by mentioning an important factor which helps to explain the greater extent to which the Permanent Court of International Justice was indeed favoured by States. One needs to stress that the peace treaties concluded at the end of the First World War entrusted the Permanent Court with some specific responsibilities and thus promoted its activity to a

large extent. By way of comparison, half the contentious cases and more than half the requests for advisory opinion that were dealt with by the Permanent Court can be linked to the territorial transfers effected under the peace treaties of 1919-1920. The comprehensive settlement of the questions arising from the Second World War was, on the other hand, entrusted to organs specially created for the occasion, and accordingly only provided material for two advisory opinions handed down in one single case by the present Court[1].

16. Moving on to the factors linked to the international context, one must not leave out of account the relatively greater enthusiasm for the peaceful settlement of disputes and, in particular, for judicial settlement at the time of the Permanent Court. This enthusiasm is clearly illustrated by the adoption of the General Act for the Pacific Settlement of International Disputes by the League of Nations on 26 September 1928. The General Act of 1928 was adopted in the wake of another related treaty of major significance, namely the Briand-Kellogg Pact of 26 August 1928 providing for the renunciation of the recourse to war for the settlement of international disputes. I would also like to draw your attention to a legal peculiarity which really points to the extent of the interest and faith manifested by States at that time in the matter of the peaceful settlement of international disputes. By the terms of its Article 45, the General Act could only actually be denounced at regular intervals, that is to say only every five years, and that denunciation was without prejudice to such settlement procedures as might already have been initiated by the State withdrawing from that treaty.

17. At another level, one must not lose sight of the fact that the society of States at the time of the Permanent Court was culturally and politically more homogeneous than the international society resulting from the Second World War, an international society that was almost immediately caught up in the icy climate of East-West dissension and was subsequently riven by the passionate and convulsive movements of decolonization and the difficult North-South dialogue. What was more, the face of international society of the post-war period was profoundly affected by the fact of the two-fold and then three-fold increase in the number of States with a diversity of political and legal systems which could aptly be compared to a palette showing all the colours of the rainbow. There is no point in laying stress at this stage upon the disputes about, and the development of, international law that accompanied those successive accelerations of history; suffice it to say that the present Court was, without any doubt, severely handicapped by the crisis of confidence which, at that time, affected the international law that it was bound to apply in accordance with Article 38 of its Statute.

---

[1] *Interpretation of Peace Treaties with Bulgaria, Hungary and Romania, First Phase, I.C.J. Reports 1950*, p. 65, *Second Phase, I.C.J. Reports 1950*, p. 221.

18. The defiant attitude of the newly independent countries with respect to international law, in whose formulation they did not participate, has been accompanied by suspicion directed at the Court itself. Indeed, the Judgment delivered on 18 July 1966 in the *South West Africa* case shook the confidence in the Court of a large section of the international community, which then saw in it a rigid instrument in the service of a conservative brand of international law. This also led to a hardening of the position of the Third World countries regarding the legal settlement of disputes; the Vienna Convention on the Law of Treaties of 23 May 1969 thus refers to the Court only in relation to *jus cogens* and, for its part, the important Declaration on the seven Principles of International Law concerning Friendly Relations among States, adopted by consensus on 24 October 1970, after seven years of negotiation, makes no direct reference to the Court. It is true that, at that time, the USSR and the Socialist countries in general, manifested no interest in an international jurisdiction.

19. I should like to make another important observation. Over two-thirds of the cases brought before the Permanent Court, in other words, 50 out of 66, were brought during the first decade of that Court's activity, a period which coincides with the leanest years of the League of Nations. Between 1925 and 1928, four years marked, among other things, by the thaw in Franco-German relations (Treaty of Locarno of 1925)[1], no less than 19 new cases were introduced. This fact strongly suggests that legal settlement has more appeal and receives greater support during periods with little international tension. Proof in counterpart is provided by the fact that no case was submitted to the Permanent Court in 1929, a year of major economic crisis, and that only 8 cases were submitted to it during the four years (1936-1939) preceding the Second World War. It was also during the periods of great international tension during the cold war that the present Court was bereft of cases and its role reduced to a minimum. As Charles de Visscher so admirably put it, *'So long as the individual distribution of power among sovereign States endures, peace will serve justice better than justice will serve peace.'* Indeed, a climate of tension, uncertainty and suspicion does not predispose States to abandon to a third party the solution of the conflicts between them and other States.

20. Certain profound changes in the international community,

[1] Treaty concluded on 16 October 1925 between Belgium, France, Germany and Italy, and in which Germany recognized the integrity of the French frontiers, the definitive return of Alsace-Lorraine to France, as well as the provisions relating to the demilitarized area of the Rhine; this Treaty incontestably marked an important turning point in the history of Europe, in that it ushered in the process of the integration of Germany into Western Europe beside France, Great Britain, Italy, Czechoslovakia and Poland; it thus formally abolished the demarcation line between victorious and vanquished countries.

and in particular, the end of the cold war, are still too recent for all their positive effects on international judicial settlement already to have been felt. Nevertheless, it would appear that, even before the fall of the Berlin Wall on that famous autumn day in 1989, a number of other walls of prejudice against the Court, which had grown up in the minds of world leaders, had started to crumble.

II. The Reversals of History or the Chronicle of a Fulfilment Heralded if Not Hoped for

21. The appeal launched by the General Assembly on 14 November 1947[1] and intended to encourage the Member States, the Organs of the United Nations and the specialized agencies to make greater use of the services of the International Court of Justice, was to be heard only a great many years later. It was to require a fresh appeal by the General Assembly on 12 November 1974[2], as well as a combination of various factors and events.

22. From 1970 onwards, the Court has, for example, succeeded in gaining or regaining some of the confidence of the Third World countries by seizing – if not forging – opportunities to wash itself clean of the sin with which it had been stained since its Judgment of 1966 on *South West Africa.* Indeed, you will recall the famous *obiter dictum* on obligations *erga omnes* which it introduced into its Judgment of 5 February 1970 in the *Barcelona Traction* case; the allusion in that Judgment to the *'obligations of a State towards the international community as a whole'*, and the reference made in it to protection from racial discrimination in particular, in the reasons relating to the diplomatic protection of limited companies, probably find their justification in its desire to distance itself from its Judgment of 1966. The Advisory Opinion on Namibia of 21 June 1971, as well as that on the *Western Sahara* of 16 October 1975, in which the Court recognized in the right of peoples to self-determination the character of a principle of international law, both, it seems, evince the same concern. The pledges thus given to countries then representing over half the international community, to which must be added the new equilibrium in the composition of the Court, which has become more representative of the diversity of that community, helped to set in motion the movement of those countries towards The Hague. This movement will not fail to be encouraged by the Judgment delivered a dozen years later, on 27 June 1986, in the case of the *Military and Paramilitary Activities* between Nicaragua and the United States of America. In fact, it was towards the end of the

---

[1] General Assembly resolution 171 (II), 'Need for greater use by the United Nations and its organs of the International Court of Justice'.

[2] General Assembly resolution 3232 (XXIX), 'Review of the role of the International Court of Justice'.

1980s and the beginning of the 1990s that there was to be a second surge in the number of cases brought before the Court.

23. Meanwhile, the Court had not remained idle. Far from fretting in its Palace as it awaited hypothetical cases, the Court had undertaken a revision of its Rules and of the Resolution relating to its internal judicial practice. In the framework of the limitations imposed upon it by its Statute, it thus made a number of improvements to its procedure, whose value litigant States do not fail to appreciate today; it has also appreciably facilitated the recourse by States to the institution of *ad hoc* chambers for entertaining a specific case. The chamber is composed of a limited number of judges elected by the Court in a secret ballot after its President has obtained the consent of the parties on this number and is informed of their views concerning the composition of the chamber. This facility is therefore not without a certain appeal to States, which can thus, in a way, influence the composition by which the judgment will be formed. This facility was used for the first time in 1982 in the *Gulf of Maine* case, and has subsequently been used on three other occasions, in 1985, in the case of the *Frontier Dispute*, in 1987, in the *ELSI* case, and the same year, in the *Land, Island and Maritime Frontier Dispute*.

24. Consequently, it can be seen that some of the efforts made by the Court in a move towards States, have already borne fruit and I am convinced that they will continue to do so in future. Regrettably, such efforts have escaped the attention of numerous observers of international judicial life. And yet, as one enlightened thinker has put it so well: *'There is no such thing as useless effort; Sisyphus was developing his muscles!'* (Roger Caillois, *Circonstancielles*, 1946.)

25. The fact that States are now better disposed to the Court is also mirrored by the new attitude of the States of the former Communist bloc. Indeed, Mikhail Gorbachev's famous appeal of 16 September 1987 will come to mind, calling as it did for the widest possible recognition of the compulsory jurisdiction of the Court, in particular by member States of the Security Council, and for more frequent recourse to the advisory function of the Court by the General Assembly and the Security Council.

26. This appeal has not only been followed by the withdrawal by almost all the countries of the former Communist bloc of the reservations made by them against the provisions relating to the Court's jurisdiction which form part of numerous multilateral treaties, but also by the acceptance of the compulsory jurisdiction of the Court by some of these States, such as Poland, Estonia, Bulgaria, Hungary and Georgia. Furthermore, four of these former Communist bloc countries (Bosnia, Hungary, Serbia and Slovakia) are now parties to cases before the Court. So it is now possible, I believe, to speak of a true globalization of the jurisdiction of this institution.

27. The revival in the Court's activity during recent years thus

seems to herald the start of a new phase in the life of the Court; States which are members of the international community would seem now to have vested the Court with a not inconsiderable part of *'the primary responsibility for the maintenance of international peace and security'* formally conferred by the Charter upon the Security Council.

28. It has to be acknowledged that, on many occasions, the decisions of the Court (on the merits as in incidental proceedings), and even merely the seisin of the Court, have made a decisive contribution not only to the settlement of disputes of very different kinds, but also, directly, to maintaining or restoring peace between the parties. By way of illustration, I would point out that the happy conclusion provided by the Court to the Libya/Chad territorial dispute conferred its letters patent of nobility upon a legal settlement which put an end to a conflict which had defeated all other means for the peaceful settlement of disputes hitherto employed.

29. However, the Court's contribution to the maintenance of peace and international security is measured not only against the yardstick of the confidence placed in it by States in submitting their disputes to it, but also through the action taken by the parties to the disputes concerned following the decisions of the Court.

30. Hence, in the case just mentioned, the withdrawal of the Libyan administration and troops from the Aouzou Strip was completed on 30 May 1994, in other words, less than four months after the delivery of the Judgment on 3 February 1994. On the whole, the decisions of the Court have always been complied with by the parties, even though they have not always shown the exceptional diligence displayed by the Governments of Chad and Libya.

31. Furthermore, in those admittedly rare cases in which a party has rejected a decision of the Court, its decision nevertheless ultimately had a not inconsiderable effect on the successful resolution, outside the Court, of the dispute in question.

32. Twenty years ago, Judge Manfred Lachs noted that none of the decisions of the Court before 1976 had been such as to vitally influence the cause of war and peace. Noting that States were not yet prepared to submit these vital issues to international judicial settlement, he proposed that the Court should deal with the problems of day-to-day international life. He suggested that it should play a greater role in the everyday life of the national chancelleries and the learned assemblies of international organizations, and that, in order to do so, it should be seised of small cases, whose rapid settlement would have enabled it to become part of the mechanics of international relations. Though interesting at first sight, this idea of making the Court into a simple court of first instance seems to me unrealistic. Clearly, nothing would prevent the Court from taking advantage of the opportunity provided by these 'small cases' – which have still to be defined – in

order to deal with matters of principle and state its opinion on them. But I doubt whether States and international organizations are inclined to mobilize the heavy and complex procedural apparatus of the Court for 'small cases', or to expose themselves to the heavy costs of counsel and lawyers for such insignificant matters.

33. Another eminent jurist, the late Professor Michel Virally, expressed the view that it would tend rather to be cases of 'average importance' which would, by nature, be suitable for submission to the Court; in particular, he was referring to cases relating to the existence, extent or limits of the rights of jurisdiction of States, in particular cases relating to the delimitation of land frontiers or maritime spaces.

34. To confine the Court either to the role of a simple court of first instance or to that of a major regional court seems to me to betray an excessively narrow conception of the potential role of a principal legal organ of the United Nations. Moreover, the two theories which I have just referred to now seem to be contradicted by reality. In truth, these two approaches, however ingenious they may be, are not part of the political will of States, which is the only objectively identifiable source of the Court's activity. It has to be acknowledged that an increasing number of politically important cases, which elude diplomatic settlement, are submitted to the Court.

35. I should therefore like to issue a caveat against any attempt to rigidly systematize the potential role of the Court. In my view, it is difficult to make forecasts in this matter, since the factors which lead States to turn to the Court for the settlement of their disputes are, as a rule, very subjective and bound up with considerations of national or international politics. The nature of the dispute is not decisive in itself. A State will decide whether or not to bring a dispute before the Court on the basis of the prevailing circumstances. A dispute of the same kind will be submitted to the Court by some States and not by others. For one territorial dispute of major political importance submitted to the Court, how many others of the same kind and the same importance are not and probably never will be submitted to it?

36. Having considered the past and present situation regarding the jurisdiction of the Court, I should like, by way of conclusion, to tell you my feelings regarding the future of this jurisdiction. The President of the International Court of Justice is not the Delphic oracle; consequently, you must not expect any great revelations from me on this topic. The fund of trust on which the Court now counts and the days of plenty its jurisdiction is enjoying naturally seem to me to be a good omen, but I shall nevertheless refrain from falling prey to boundless optimism. In this year of the fiftieth anniversary of the United Nations, and on the eve of the anniversary of the Court, I shall confine myself to three remarks which are also wishes:

(1) Some observers have seen in the recent flowering of the mechanisms for the judicial settlement of disputes[1], combined with the relative narrowness of the Court's jurisdiction *ratione personae* and *ratione materiae*, a more or less short-term risk of the possible marginalization of the role of the International Court of Justice. On the contrary, I believe that, far from prejudicing the future activity of the Court in The Hague, this proliferation of judicial or quasi-judicial bodies may help to relieve the Court of certain particular categories of disputes, thus enabling it to focus on disputes of major political importance. I consider that it is not unrealistic or unreasonable to cherish such hopes for a principal organ of the United Nations which is also its principal judicial organ.

(2) It is clear that the Court is currently under-used in the advisory field, not only in view of the present number of international bodies and organizations empowered to seise the Court, but also in view of the importance and the complexity of the functions which these organizations perform. Moreover, it is too often forgotten that the opinions of the Court have not inconsiderable 'pacifying' effects, directly, in the context of conflicts, or indirectly outside such contexts, even if only through their substantial contribution to the smooth functioning of world organizations, as well as to the development of law and legal science. The advisory procedure thus appears, at the minimum, to be an instrument of 'preventive diplomacy', a particularly suitable means for the Court to defuse tension and ward off conflicts by determination or law. Considering the great opportunities provided by the advisory function in this respect, I cannot stress too much the necessity for more frequent recourse to this jurisdiction of the Court.

(3) Contrary to what is often asserted, there are no political cases without a legal element, 'a point of law', however small it may be, on which the Court can pronounce. The reluctance of States to entrust to the Court the settlement of certain disputes sometimes originates in the fear of a loss of control over the resolution of the disputes concerned. States should more often consider entrusting a particular point of their dispute to legal settlement, in order to facilitate the resolution of the overall dispute between them. It is States which, by their choice, ensure the greater or lesser fortune of the Court and of its jurisdiction. It only remains to hope that the psychological barriers to the international settlement of disputes continue to fall; the States which you represent here will perhaps be sensitive to this appeal at a

[1] Such as, for example, the International Tribunal for the Law of the Sea (1982), the Central American Court of Justice (1991), the OAU's Machinery for the Prevention, Management and Settlement of Conflicts (1993), the Court of Conciliation and Arbitration of the Organization for Security and Co-operation in Europe, the International Criminal Tribunal for the Former Yugoslavia, the International Criminal Tribunal for Rwanda and the African Court on Human and People's Rights (the creation of which is currently under discussion in the OAU).

time when preparations are being made to celebrate the International Court of Justice's fiftieth anniversary, which, as people are fond of saying, is the age of maturity and wisdom.

Thank you."

*

On 19 October 1995 President Bedjaoui gave the following address to the Asian-African Legal Consultative Committee meeting in New York:

"AFRICA AND ASIA RESPOND TO THE INTERNATIONAL COURT OF JUSTICE

[Translation by the Registry]

Mr. President, Mr. Secretary-General, Ladies and Gentlemen,

I always feel truly privileged to be able to address your Committee, whose well-known achievements in the service of the primacy of law and justice, in particular in relations between the developed and developing worlds, are worthy of the highest praise. I am accordingly most grateful to you for having afforded me the opportunity of taking the floor before you this year as well.

As you all know, the International Court of Justice will be celebrating 50 years of existence in April 1996. The event is of great importance, as no other international court has ever reached such a great age. That anniversary, which will be very much in the public eye, has already provided an opportunity for stocktaking. My intention today is obviously not to present you with a retrospective summary of the Court's 50 years of activity. Any attempt to evaluate that activity with the requisite objectivity would of course mean that one would have to proceed, *inter alia*, to a detailed study of all the elements that have conditioned it over the years for a period of half a century, without overlooking the different contexts in which that activity has taken place. Moreover, it is a truism to say that the environment in which the Court has had to operate as principal judicial organ of the United Nations since 1946 has undergone some very profound transformations.

My intention today is a great deal more modest. I would simply like to share with you some thoughts on the part taken by the continents of Africa and Asia in the activity of the Court since it was set up in 1946. May I begin by reminding you, in that regard, that one of the reasons why the San Francisco Conference decided to constitute a new Court – even though its Statute was to be established on the basis of the Statute of the former Court, which had proved its worth – was that the Permanent Court of International Justice was perceived by the majority as partaking of an earlier order, in which the States of Europe played a dominant role in the political and legal affairs of the international community, and it was thought that the creation of a new Court would make it easier for the non-European States to assume their responsibilities.

The Court is a 'World Court' in several respects – in particular because it is potentially open to all the States of the world without exception, and on a completely equal footing. In accordance with Article 93, paragraph 1, of the Charter of the United Nations, all Member States are *ipso facto* parties to the Statute of the Court. Non-Members may, however, in accordance with paragraph 2 of that same provision, become parties to the Statute on conditions to be determined in each case by the General Assembly upon the recommendation of the Security Council. Moreover, access to the Court is likewise open to States which are not parties to its Statute under conditions which were fixed, in accordance with Article 35 of that Statute, by a Security Council resolution dated 15 October 1946.

Immediately after the Second World War, when the United Nations was set up, it was composed of 50 Member States (usually referred to as the 'Founder Members'). Fifty States had, then, an automatic right of access to the Court, and among them there were eight States belonging exclusively to the Asian continent, and just four States from the African continent (South Africa, Egypt, Ethiopia and Liberia).

The total number of Member States of the United Nations has now increased to 185, of which almost half belong to the continents of Africa and Asia. It can accordingly be said that those two continents together cover almost half of the Court's potential 'clientele'. Africa and Asia now seem to carry an unprecedented weight in terms of the Court's jurisdiction *ratione personae*, and if they make use of the Court, those two continents are for that reason in a position to exercise a fairly considerable influence upon its jurisprudence and, what is more, upon the development of international law – thanks to their own specific legal concepts – and by so doing to contribute to the process whereby that law is given a more authentically universal character.

The Court, which is open to all the States of the world community under conditions of perfect equality, must likewise be attentive to the concerns and arguments of each one of them, whatever their geographical, cultural and legal predispositions. Moreover, as a 'World Court', it must be able to deal with any kind of problem, in whatever setting, according to criteria reflecting, at one and the same time, the diversity of the world and its adhesion to common values. This absolute requirement is enshrined in a key provision of the Statute of the Court, Article 9, which is worded as follows:

> 'At every election, the electors shall bear in mind not only that the persons to be elected should individually possess the qualifications required, but also that in the body as a whole *the representation of the main forms of civilization and of the principal legal systems of the world should be assured.*' (Emphasis added.)

While we are dealing with this aspect, some quantitative comparisons need to be made. In its original composition of 6 April 1946, the Court, out of a total of 15 judges, included only two judges originating from African or Asian countries (i.e., an Egyptian and a Chinese). The two continents together were thus represented on the bench of the Court in a ratio of less than 14 per cent. Nowadays, the Court includes on its bench three African and three Asian judges, which means that the two continents together account for over 40 per cent of the total number of Members of the Court. The African judges, like their Asian colleagues, have moreover come from geographical and cultural areas that are sufficiently varied to ensure that there is as equitable as possible a representation of the diversities characterizing each continent. This means that Africa and Asia may be assured that their own legal concepts are sufficiently familiar to the Court.

I cannot content myself with pointing to the unexpected advent, in recent decades, of a climate that is relatively propitious for the two continents, whether in terms of the extent of the Court's jurisdiction *ratione personae* or in terms of its composition. We still need to consider whether the States of Africa and Asia have taken advantage of this new situation and to what extent the Court effectively features among their concerns.

I will begin by pointing out, with respect to the extent of the Court's jurisdiction *ratione materiae* that, out of the 25 declarations of acceptance of the Court's jurisdiction that were in force in 1947, only five emanated from African or Asian States (one from an African State, i.e., South Africa, and four from Asian States, i.e., China, India, Iran and Siam). Today there are 22 such declarations (including 17 made by African States) out of a total number of 59 – or, in other words, the ratio has increased from 20 per cent to somewhat over 35 per cent of all the declarations made. That progress, which appears particularly striking with respect to the States of Africa, must nonetheless be somewhat relativized in the light of the reservations appended to those declarations, which are sometimes fairly numerous and of quite considerable scope.

With regard to the *'implementation'* of the jurisdiction of the Court or, in other words, its effective seisin, it should be noted that, of the 74 contentious cases referred to it since 1947, 26 have involved States belonging to the continents of Africa or Asia. The ratio of these cases to the total number of contentious cases submitted to the Court is almost 50 per cent, if one sets aside those which were almost immediately struck off the list as the Court manifestly lacked jurisdiction to deal with them. I would add that, if one considers only the cases dealt with by the Court over the past 15 years, the ratio of those in which an African or Asian State has been a party is almost 60 per cent. It is moreover interesting to note that, of the 26 cases just referred to, almost half have been between States belonging to the same continent and that some two-thirds of them have been brought by unilateral application. I would also stress that, of the 23 requests for advisory opinions submitted to the Court since 1947, eight have been concerned with situations which had developed in Africa (seven opinions) or in Asia (one opinion).

In more qualitative terms, it is important to note that the *contentious cases* referred to the Court which have involved States of Africa or Asia, far from being 'small' or 'medium-sized' cases, have proved, for the most part, to be of major significance with respect to the rules of law they involved, and also, incidentally, to the political interests of the parties. Allow me, if you will, briefly to recall, merely by way of example, the substantial contribution to the jurisprudential *corpus* of the Court – and hence to the development of general international law – that has been made by the decisions handed down by the Court in the following cases:

- *Right of Passage over Indian Territory, Temple of Preah Vihear, Frontier Dispute* and *Territorial Dispute*, where territorial rights are concerned;
- *Continental Shelf (Tunisia/Libyan Arab Jamahiriya)* and *Continental Shelf (Libyan Arab Jamahiriya/Malta)*, where the law of maritime delimitations is concerned;
- *Northern Cameroons* and *Application for Revision and Interpretation of the Judgment of 24 February 1982 in the Case concerning the* Continental Shelf (Tunisia/Libyan Arab Jamahiriya), where the Court's exercise of its statutory functions is concerned; and
- *Appeal Relating to the Jurisdiction of the ICAO Council* and *Arbitral Award of 31 July 1989*, with regard to the circumstances in which the Court has to rule upon decisions made by other jurisdictional bodies.

The same could be said, *mutatis mutandis*, of the cases still pending before the Court. Major questions relating to the law of land and/or maritime delimitations are raised in cases such as those concerning the *Maritime Delimitation between Guinea-Bissau and Senegal*, the *Maritime Delimitation and Territorial Questions between Qatar and Bahrain* and the *Land and Maritime Boundary between Cameroon and Nigeria*; and major questions concerning the Law of Treaties and the organization of the respective jurisdictions of the principal organs of the United Nations have been raised in the cases relating to *Questions of Interpretation and Application of the 1971 Montreal Convention arising from the Aerial Incident at Lockerbie*. Furthermore, all these cases are politically important for the States concerned.

Where the Court's *advisory function* is concerned, I cannot, of course, omit to mention the eminent contribution that the Court has made to the law of decolonization – and in particular, to the determination of the imperatives of the principle of self-determination – in the advisory opinions it handed down with regard, respectively, to the *Legal Consequences for States of the Continued Presence of South Africa in Namibia (South West Africa) notwithstanding Security Council Resolution 276 (1970)* and the *Western Sahara*. It scarcely needs to be said that, in the first of these opinions, the Court did not hesitate to categorize as a flagrant violation of the purposes and principles of the Charter of the United Nations the former Mandatory's decision:

> 'To establish . . . and to enforce, distinctions, exclusions, restrictions and limitations exclusively based on grounds of race, colour, descent or national or ethnic origin which constitute a denial of fundamental human rights.'

Lastly, before completing this brief survey, I should like to stress that, while the African and Asian States have, as I have shown, given valuable support to the Court's action by participating in cases both numerous and substantial, their contribution to its work to promote justice and peace has been further enhanced by the often exemplary welcome given to the Court's decisions. By way of illustration, I would merely refer to the unprecedented respect shown by two young African States – Burkina Faso and the Republic of Mali – for an Order indicating provisional measures made in a particularly difficult context of recourse to force. Incidentally, I already had occasion last year to pay tribute, before this Committee, to the rapidity with which the Court's Judgment in the case concerning the *Territorial Dispute (Libyan Arab Jamahiriya/Chad)* had been complied with, despite the acute political sensibilities which prevailed at the time.

Mr. President, Mr. Secretary-General, Ladies and Gentlemen,

The few points I have just made should assuredly not lead us into the error of a self-satisfaction or triumphalism that are as facile as they are unprofitable. However, now that I am addressing this Committee in the period leading up to the Court's fiftieth anniversary, I do of course feel bound to highlight all the encouraging signs which directly contradict the peremptory assertions, so frequently encountered, that the developing world – and in particular, the newly independent States – were and still are inclined to feel somewhat suspicious of the International Court of Justice.

I thank you."

CHAPTER VII

PUBLICATIONS OF THE COURT

The publications of the International Court of Justice are published by the Registry (Rules of Court, Art. 26, para. 1 *(i)*, and Art. 71, para. 6; Instructions for the Registry, Arts. 23, 43, 67-69 and 72).

Information about the publications of the present Court and those of its forerunner, the *Permanent Court of International Justice*, is given below[1].

I. General

1. Series Published by the International Court of Justice

The publications of the Court are at present classified in series as shown hereunder. Their size is 15.6 × 24 cm when they are published in paper covers and 16 × 24.5 cm when published in hard covers.

(a) *Reports of Judgments, Advisory Opinions and Orders*

This series contains the Reports of the decisions of the Court in both the English and the French texts. Each decision is published as soon as given, in an unbound fascicle which is sold separately[2]. To allow for binding, a continuous system of pagination is adopted for all the fascicles of any one year.

In January of each year, an analytical index is published of the previous year's decisions; this also may be purchased separately. A binder is available for those who obtain the separate fascicles and the index at the time of their publication. The collected decisions, with index, for each year may also be obtained ready bound together in one volume.

Forty-five bound volumes have so far been published, the first being the *I.C.J. Reports* for the years 1947 and 1948, which are collected in a single volume. (The *I.C.J. Reports 1965*, *1967*, *1968*, *1977*, *1979* and *1983* are not indexed.)

Official citation of the series: *I.C.J. Reports*, with an indication of the year. For a separate fascicle the short title of the case and the nature of the decision should be given, e.g.: *Nottebohm, Preliminary Objection, Judgment, I.C.J. Reports 1953*, p. 111; or *Nottebohm, Order of 15 January 1954, I.C.J. Reports 1954*, p. 7. (See Sec. II, pp. 295-304, below.)

---

[1] The documents prepared and distributed by the Registry for information purposes are dealt with in Chapter V, above: see p. 147.

[2] See Chap. V, p. 153, above.

(b) *Pleadings, Oral Arguments, Documents*

Volumes in this series are published after the termination of each case and contain the documentation relating to the case in the original language, that is, in English or in French.

This comprises the document instituting proceedings[1], the written pleadings and their annexes[2], the verbatim record of the oral proceedings[3], any documents submitted to the Court after the closure of the written proceedings, and the correspondence. The Court however decided in 1967 that the annexes to the pleadings would no longer be printed in cases which had been removed from the General List either because the application instituting proceedings disclosed that the other side had not accepted the jurisdiction of the Court or because there had been a settlement or a discontinuance of the case.

Depending upon the length of the documents to be printed, one or more volumes are issued for each case. Thus far 128 volumes have been published. The volumes which appeared up to 31 December 1964 are sold in hard covers whereas subsequent volumes are in paper covers.

Abbreviated reference: *I.C.J. Pleadings*, with the short title of the case, e.g.: *I.C.J. Pleadings, Nottebohm*, Vol. I. (See Sec. III, pp. 304-316, below.)

(c) *Acts and Documents concerning the Organization of the Court*

Five volumes have appeared in this bilingual (English/French) series.

No. 1 is now out of print.

No. 2 contained, in paper covers, the text of the Rules of Court as amended in 1972.

No. 3 contained the texts of the Charter of the United Nations, the Statute and Rules of Court and the Resolution concerning the Internal Judicial Practice of the Court, together with certain documents relating to the Court's privileges and immunities. It was published in 1977, in paper covers.

No. 4 contained the same documents as *No. 3* but with the text of the 1978 revised Rules of Court replacing that of the 1972 amended Rules; it further included certain resolutions concerning States entitled to appear before the Court. It was published in July 1978, in paper covers.

No. 5 contains the same documents as *No. 4*, with some corrections and an additional resolution concerning a State entitled to appear before the Court. It was published in July 1990, the stock of *No. 4* having been exhausted, and is available in paper covers.

Abbreviated reference: *I.C.J. Acts and Documents*, with an indication of the number of the volume.

---

[1] See Chap. V, pp. 149 and 157, above.

[2] *Ibid.*, pp. 149-150, above.

[3] *Ibid.*, pp. 151-152, above.

(d) *Yearbook*

In the second half of each year there appears a *Yearbook* in which an account is given of the work of the Court during the period from 1 August of the preceding year to 31 July of the current year. There is also a French edition of this publication, the *Annuaire*.

The present *Yearbook* is the fiftieth in the series, which started with *I.C.J. Yearbook 1946-1947*. Like the 31 preceding issues, it is sold in paper covers whereas the first 18 volumes were sold in hard covers.

Abbreviated reference: *I.C.J. Yearbook*, with an indication of the year covered by the volume, e.g.: *I.C.J. Yearbook 1954-1955*.

(e) *Bibliography of the International Court of Justice*

Early each year the Registry issues a *Bibliography* listing such works and documents relating to the Court as have come to its attention during the previous year.

Bibliographies Nos. 1-18 formed Chapter IX in the appropriate *Yearbook* or *Annuaire* up to the 1963-1964 editions. Beginning with No. 19, later *Bibliographies* were issued as separate fascicles with introduction and index in both English and French, but arranged so as to facilitate the binding of several numbers together. The latest *I.C.J. Bibliography* published is No. 48 (year 1994).

Abbreviated reference: *I.C.J. Bibliography*, with the serial number of the volume, followed, if desired, by the entry number of the work cited. E.g.: *I.C.J. Bibliography No. 7:* 2528 for the *Bibliographies* prior to No. 35, and *I.C.J. Bibliography No. 35:* 81: 150 as from 1981.

2. Dissemination of the Publications of the International Court of Justice

The publications of the Court are distributed free on request and as required to the governments or public services of all States entitled to appear before the Court.

They may be consulted in major law libraries, including many university libraries, certain depository libraries for United Nations publications, and libraries aided by the United Nations programme of assistance in the teaching, study, dissemination and wider appreciation of international law.

They are sold by the Sales Sections of the United Nations Secretariat: Distribution and Sales Section, Office of the United Nations, 1211 Geneva 10, Switzerland, or the Sales Section, United Nations, New York, NY 10017, USA, and may also be obtained from any bookseller selling United Nations publications. *Orders and requests for information should be sent to these addresses and not to the Registry.*

A *Catalogue* is issued in English and French. It lists the sales number of each publication and its price in US dollars. It is brought up to date each year, by means either of an addendum or of a new edition. A free copy of the *Catalogue* may be obtained by applying to one of the Sales Sections of the United Nations or to the Registry.

3. *Publications of the Permanent Court of International Justice*

Between 1922 and 1946 the *Permanent Court of International Justice* published the following series:

Series A (Nos. 1-24): *Collection of Judgments* (up to and including 1930)
Series B (Nos. 1-18): *Collection of Advisory Opinions* (up to and including 1930)
Series A/B (Nos. 40-80): *Judgments, Orders and Advisory Opinions* (beginning in 1931)
Series C (Nos. 1-19): *Acts and Documents relating to Judgments and Advisory Opinions given by the Court* (up to and including 1930)
Series C (Nos. 52-88): *Pleadings, Oral Statements and Documents* (beginning in 1931)
Series D (Nos. 1-6): *Acts and Documents concerning the Organization of the Court*
Series E (Nos. 1-16): *Annual Reports*
Series F (Nos. 1-4): *General Indexes*

They may be consulted in certain university and other libraries with a substantial legal section.

They can also be obtained from Kraus Reprint Company, Kraus Organization Limited, Route 100, Millwood, NY 10546, USA, to whom all orders and requests for information should be addressed.

II. Official Citation of Judgments, Advisory Opinions and Orders

In order to standardize the mode of citation of the decisions of the International Court of Justice and the *Permanent Court of International Justice*, the Court decided to use the titles below, which are listed in chronological order. Orders solely fixing or extending time-limits are omitted.

1. Permanent Court of International Justice

1922

Designation of the Workers' Delegate for the Netherlands at the Third Session of the International Labour Conference, Advisory Opinion, 1922, P.C.I.J., Series B, No. 1.

Competence of the ILO in Regard to International Regulation of the Conditions of Labour of Persons Employed in Agriculture, Advisory Opinion, 1922, P.C.I.J., Series B, No. 2.

Competence of the ILO to Examine Proposals for the Organization and Development of the Methods of Agricultural Production, Advisory Opinion, 1922, P.C.I.J., Series B, No. 3.

1923

Nationality Decrees Issued in Tunis and Morocco, Advisory Opinion, 1923, P.C.I.J., Series B, No. 4.

Status of Eastern Carelia, Advisory Opinion, 1923, P.C.I.J., Series B, No. 5.

S.S. "Wimbledon", Judgments, 1923, P.C.I.J., Series A, No. 1.

German Settlers in Poland, Advisory Opinion, 1923, P.C.I.J., Series B, No. 6.

Acquisition of Polish Nationality, Advisory Opinion, 1923, P.C.I.J., Series B, No. 7.

Jaworzina, Advisory Opinion, 1923, P.C.I.J., Series B, No. 8.

1924

Mavrommatis Palestine Concessions, Judgment No. 2, 1924, P.C.I.J., Series A, No. 2.

Monastery of Saint-Naoum, Advisory Opinion, 1924, P.C.I.J., Series B, No. 9.

Treaty of Neuilly, Article 179, Annex, Paragraph 4 (Interpretation), Judgment No. 3, 1924, P.C.I.J., Series A, No. 3.

1925

Exchange of Greek and Turkish Populations, Advisory Opinion, 1925, P.C.I.J., Series B, No. 10.

Interpretation of Judgment No. 3, Judgment No. 4, 1925, P.C.I.J., Series A, No. 4.

Mavrommatis Jerusalem Concessions, Judgment No. 5, 1925, P.C.I.J., Series A, No. 5.

Polish Postal Service in Danzig, Advisory Opinion, 1925, P.C.I.J., Series B, No. 11.

Certain German Interests in Polish Upper Silesia, Jurisdiction, Judgment No. 6, 1925, P.C.I.J., Series A, No. 6.

Interpretation of Article 3, Paragraph 2, of the Treaty of Lausanne, Advisory Opinion, 1925, P.C.I.J., Series B, No. 12.

1926

Certain German Interests in Polish Upper Silesia, Merits, Judgment No. 7, 1926, P.C.I.J., Series A, No. 7.

Competence of the ILO to Regulate Incidentally the Personal Work of the Employer, Advisory Opinion, 1926, P.C.I.J., Series B, No. 13.

1927

Denunciation of the Treaty of 2 November 1865 between China and Belgium, Orders of 8 January, 15 February and 18 June 1927, P.C.I.J., Series A, No. 8.

Factory at Chorzów, Jurisdiction, Judgment No. 8, 1927, P.C.I.J., Series A, No. 9.

"Lotus", Judgment No. 9, 1927, P.C.I.J., Series A, No. 10.

Readaptation of the Mavrommatis Jerusalem Concessions, Judgment No. 10, 1927, P.C.I.J., Series A, No. 11.

Factory at Chorzów, Order of 21 November 1927, P.C.I.J., Series A, No. 12.

Jurisdiction of the European Commission of the Danube, Advisory Opinion, 1927, P.C.I.J., Series B, No. 14.

Interpretation of Judgments Nos. 7 and 8 (Factory at Chorzów), Judgment No. 11, 1927, P.C.I.J., Series A, No. 13.

1928

Denunciation of the Treaty of 2 November 1865 between China and Belgium, Order of 21 February 1928, P.C.I.J., Series A, No. 14.

Jurisdiction of the Courts of Danzig, Advisory Opinion, 1928, P.C.I.J., Series B, No. 15.

Rights of Minorities in Upper Silesia (Minority Schools), Judgment No. 12, 1928, P.C.I.J., Series A, No. 15.

Denunciation of the Treaty of 2 November 1865 between China and Belgium, Order of 13 August 1928, P.C.I.J., Series A, No. 16.

Interpretation of the Greco-Turkish Agreement of 1 December 1926 (Final Protocol, Article IV), Advisory Opinion, 1928, P.C.I.J., Series B, No. 16.

Factory at Chorzów, Merits, Judgment No. 13, 1928, P.C.I.J., Series A, No. 17.

1929

Denunciation of the Treaty of 2 November 1865 between China and Belgium, Order of 25 May 1929, P.C.I.J., Series A, No. 18.

Factory at Chorzów, Order of 25 May 1929, P.C.I.J., Series A, No. 19.

Serbian Loans, Judgment No. 14, 1929, P.C.I.J., Series A, No. 20.

Brazilian Loans, Judgment No. 15, 1929, P.C.I.J., Series A, No. 21.

Free Zones of Upper Savoy and the District of Gex, Order of 19 August 1929, P.C.I.J., Series A, No. 22.

Territorial Jurisdiction of the International Commission of the River Oder, Judgment No. 16, 1929, P.C.I.J., Series A, No. 23.

1930

Greco-Bulgarian "Communities", Advisory Opinion, 1930, P.C.I.J., Series B, No. 17.

Free City of Danzig and ILO, Advisory Opinion, 1930, P.C.I.J., Series B, No. 18.

Free Zones of Upper Savoy and the District of Gex, Order of 6 December 1930, P.C.I.J., Series A, No. 24.

1931

Access to German Minority Schools in Upper Silesia, Advisory Opinion, 1931, P.C.I.J., Series A/B, No. 40, p. 4.

Customs Régime between Germany and Austria, Advisory Opinion, 1931, P.C.I.J., Series A/B, No. 41, p. 37.

Railway Traffic between Lithuania and Poland, Advisory Opinion, 1931, P.C.I.J., Series A/B, No. 42, p. 108.

Access to, or Anchorage in, the Port of Danzig, of Polish War Vessels, Advisory Opinion, 1931, P.C.I.J., Series A/B, No. 43, p. 128.

1932

Treatment of Polish Nationals and Other Persons of Polish Origin or Speech in the Danzig Territory, Advisory Opinion, 1932, P.C.I.J., Series A/B, No. 44, p. 4.

Interpretation of the Greco-Bulgarian Agreement of 9 December 1927, Advisory Opinion, 1932, P.C.I.J., Series A/B, No. 45, p. 68.

Free Zones of Upper Savoy and the District of Gex, Judgment, 1932, P.C.I.J., Series A/B, No. 46, p. 96.

Interpretation of the Statute of the Memel Territory, Preliminary Objection, Judgment, 1932, P.C.I.J., Series A/B, No. 47, p. 243.

Legal Status of the South-Eastern Territory of Greenland, Orders of 2 and 3 August 1932, P.C.I.J., Series A/B, No. 48, p. 268.

Interpretation of the Statute of the Memel Territory, Merits, Judgment, 1932, P.C.I.J., Series A/B, No. 49, p. 294.

Interpretation of the Convention of 1919 concerning Employment of Women during the Night, Advisory Opinion, 1932, P.C.I.J., Series A/B, No. 50, p. 365.

1933

Delimitation of the Territorial Waters between the Island of Castellorizo and the Coasts of Anatolia, Order of 26 January 1933, P.C.I.J., Series A/B, No. 51, p. 4.

Prince von Pless Administration, Order of 4 February 1933, P.C.I.J., Series A/B, No. 52, p. 11.

Legal Status of Eastern Greenland, Judgment, 1933, P.C.I.J., Series A/B, No. 53, p. 22.

Prince von Pless Administration, Order of 11 May 1933, P.C.I.J., Series A/B, No. 54, p. 150.

Legal Status of the South-Eastern Territory of Greenland, Order of 11 May 1933, P.C.I.J., Series A/B, No. 55, p. 157.

Appeals from Certain Judgments of the Hungaro/Czechoslovak Mixed Arbitral Tribunal, Order of 12 May 1933, P.C.I.J., Series A/B, No. 56, p. 162.

Prince von Pless Administration, Order of 4 July 1933, P.C.I.J., Series A/B, No. 57, p. 167.

Polish Agrarian Reform and German Minority, Order of 29 July 1933, P.C.I.J., Series A/B, No. 58, p. 175.

Prince von Pless Administration, Order of 2 December 1933, P.C.I.J., Series A/B, No. 59, p. 194.

Polish Agrarian Reform and German Minority, Order of 2 December 1933, P.C.I.J., Series A/B, No. 60, p. 201.

Appeal from a Judgment of the Hungaro/Czechoslovak Mixed Arbitral Tribunal (The Peter Pázmány University), Judgment, 1933, P.C.I.J., Series A/B, No. 61, p. 208.

1934

Lighthouses case between France and Greece, Judgment, 1934, P.C.I.J., Series A/B, No. 62, p. 4.

Oscar Chinn, Judgment, 1934, P.C.I.J., Series A/B, No. 63, p. 65.

1935

Minority Schools in Albania, Advisory Opinion, 1935, P.C.I.J., Series A/B, No. 64, p. 4.

Consistency of Certain Danzig Legislative Decrees with the Constitution of the Free City, Advisory Opinion, 1935, P.C.I.J., Series A/B, No. 65, p. 41.

1936

Pajzs, Csáky, Esterházy, Order of 23 May 1936, P.C.I.J., Series A/B, No. 66, p. 4.

Losinger, Order of 27 June 1936, P.C.I.J., Series A/B, No. 67, p. 15.

Pajzs, Csáky, Esterházy, Judgment, 1936, P.C.I.J., Series A/B, No. 68, p. 30.

Losinger, Order of 14 December 1936, P.C.I.J., Series A/B, No. 69, p. 99.

1937

Diversion of Water from the Meuse, Judgment, 1937, P.C.I.J., Series A/B, No. 70, p. 4.

Lighthouses in Crete and Samos, Judgment, 1937, P.C.I.J., Series A/B, No. 71, p. 94.

Borchgrave, Judgment, 1937, P.C.I.J., Series A/B, No. 72, p. 158.

1938

Borchgrave, Order of 30 April 1938, P.C.I.J., Series A/B, No. 73, p. 4.

Phosphates in Morocco, Judgment, 1938, P.C.I.J., Series A/B, No. 74, p. 10.

Panevezys-Saldutiskis Railway, Order of 30 June 1938, P.C.I.J., Series A/B, No. 75, p. 53.

1939

Panevezys-Saldutiskis Railway, Judgment, 1939, P.C.I.J., Series A/B, No. 76, p. 4.

Electricity Company of Sofia and Bulgaria, Judgment, 1939, P.C.I.J., Series A/B, No. 77, p. 64.

Société Commerciale de Belgique, Judgment, 1939, P.C.I.J., Series A/B, No. 78, p. 160.

Electricity Company of Sofia and Bulgaria, Order of 5 December 1939, P.C.I.J., Series A/B, No. 79, p. 194.

1940

Electricity Company of Sofia and Bulgaria, Order of 26 February 1940, P.C.I.J., Series A/B, No. 80, p. 4.

2. International Court of Justice

1948

Corfu Channel, Preliminary Objection, Judgment, 1948, I.C.J. Reports 1947-1948, p. 15.

Corfu Channel, Order of 26 March 1948, I.C.J. Reports 1947-1948, p. 53.

Conditions of Admission of a State to Membership in the United Nations (Article 4 of Charter), Advisory Opinion, 1948, I.C.J. Reports 1947-1948, p. 57.

Corfu Channel, Order of 17 December 1948, I.C.J. Reports 1947-1948, p. 124.

1949

Corfu Channel, Merits, Judgment, I.C.J. Reports 1949, p. 4.

Reparation for Injuries Suffered in the Service of the United Nations, Advisory Opinion, I.C.J. Reports 1949, p. 174.

Corfu Channel, Order of 19 November 1949, I.C.J. Reports 1949, p. 237.

Corfu Channel, Assessment of Amount of Compensation, Judgment, I.C.J. Reports 1949, p. 244.

1950

Competence of the General Assembly for the Admission of a State to the United Nations, Advisory Opinion, I.C.J. Reports 1950, p. 4.

Protection of French Nationals and Protected Persons in Egypt, Order of 29 March 1950, I.C.J. Reports 1950, p. 59.

Interpretation of Peace Treaties with Bulgaria, Hungary and Romania, First Phase, Advisory Opinion, I.C.J. Reports 1950, p. 65.

International Status of South West Africa, Advisory Opinion, I.C.J. Reports 1950, p. 128.

Interpretation of Peace Treaties with Bulgaria, Hungary and Romania, Second Phase, Advisory Opinion, I.C.J. Reports 1950, p. 221.

Asylum, Judgment, I.C.J. Reports 1950, p. 266.

Request for Interpretation of the Judgment of 20 November 1950 in the Asylum Case, Judgment, I.C.J. Reports 1950, p. 395.

1951

Reservations to the Convention on the Prevention and Punishment of the Crime of Genocide, Advisory Opinion, I.C.J. Reports 1951, p. 15.

Haya de la Torre, Judgment, I.C.J. Reports 1951, p. 71.

Anglo-Iranian Oil Co., Interim Protection, Order of 5 July 1951, I.C.J. Reports 1951, p. 89.

Rights of Nationals of the United States of America in Morocco, Order of 31 October 1951, I.C.J. Reports 1951, p. 109.

Fisheries, Judgment, I.C.J. Reports 1951, p. 116.

1952

Ambatielos, Preliminary Objection, Judgment, I.C.J. Reports 1952, p. 28.

Anglo-Iranian Oil Co., Preliminary Objection, Judgment, I.C.J. Reports 1952, p. 93.

Rights of Nationals of the United States of America in Morocco, Judgment, I.C.J. Reports 1952, p. 176.

1953

Ambatielos, Merits, Judgment, I.C.J. Reports 1953, p. 10.

Minquiers and Ecrehos, Judgment, I.C.J. Reports 1953, p. 47.

Nottebohm, Preliminary Objection, Judgment, I.C.J. Reports 1953, p. 111.

1954

Monetary Gold Removed from Rome in 1943, Judgment, I.C.J. Reports 1954, p. 19.

Effect of Awards of Compensation Made by the United Nations Administrative Tribunal, Advisory Opinion, I.C.J. Reports 1954, p. 47.

Treatment in Hungary of Aircraft and Crew of United States of America (United States of America v. *Hungary), Order of 12 July 1954, I.C.J. Reports 1954*, p. 99.

Treatment in Hungary of Aircraft and Crew of United States of America (United States of America v. *Union of Soviet Socialist Republics), Order of 12 July 1954, I.C.J. Reports 1954*, p. 103.

Electricité de Beyrouth Company, Order of 29 July 1954, I.C.J. Reports 1954, p. 107.

1955

Nottebohm, Second Phase, Judgment, I.C.J. Reports 1955, p. 4.

Voting Procedure on Questions relating to Reports and Petitions concerning the Territory of South West Africa, Advisory Opinion, I.C.J. Reports 1955, p. 67.

1956

Aerial Incident of 10 March 1953, Order of 14 March 1956, I.C.J. Reports 1956, p. 6.

Aerial Incident of 7 October 1952, Order of 14 March 1956, I.C.J. Reports 1956, p. 9.

Antarctica (United Kingdom v. *Argentina), Order of 16 March 1956, I.C.J. Reports 1956*, p. 12.

Antarctica (United Kingdom v. *Chile), Order of 16 March 1956, I.C.J. Reports 1956*, p. 15.

Admissibility of Hearings of Petitioners by the Committee on South West Africa, Advisory Opinion, I.C.J. Reports 1956, p. 23.

Certain Norwegian Loans, Order of 28 September 1956, I.C.J. Reports 1956, p. 73.

Judgments of the Administrative Tribunal of the ILO upon Complaints Made against Unesco, Advisory Opinion, I.C.J. Reports 1956, p. 77.

1957

Certain Norwegian Loans, Judgment, I.C.J. Reports 1957, p. 9.

Interhandel, Interim Protection, Order of 24 October 1957, I.C.J. Reports 1957, p. 105.

Right of Passage over Indian Territory, Preliminary Objections, Judgment, I.C.J. Reports 1957, p. 125.

1958

Application of the Convention of 1902 Governing the Guardianship of Infants, Judgment, I.C.J. Reports 1958, p. 55.

Aerial Incident of 4 September 1954, Order of 9 December 1958, I.C.J. Reports 1958, p. 158.

1959

Interhandel, Judgment, I.C.J. Reports 1959, p. 6.

Aerial Incident of 27 July 1955 (Israel v. *Bulgaria), Judgment, I.C.J. Reports 1959*, p. 127.

Sovereignty over Certain Frontier Land, Judgment, I.C.J. Reports 1959, p. 209.

Aerial Incident of 27 July 1955 (United Kingdom v. *Bulgaria), Order of 3 August 1959, I.C.J. Reports 1959*, p. 264.

Aerial Incident of 7 November 1954, Order of 7 October 1959, I.C.J. Reports 1959, p. 276.

1960

Right of Passage over Indian Territory, Merits, Judgment, I.C.J. Reports 1960, p. 6.

Aerial Incident of 27 July 1955 (United States of America v. *Bulgaria), Order of 30 May 1960, I.C.J. Reports 1960*, p. 146.

Constitution of the Maritime Safety Committee of the Inter-Governmental Maritime Consultative Organization, Advisory Opinion, I.C.J. Reports 1960, p. 150.

Compagnie du Port, des Quais et des Entrepôts de Beyrouth and Société Radio-Orient, Order of 31 August 1960, I.C.J. Reports 1960, p. 186.

Arbitral Award Made by the King of Spain on 23 December 1906, Judgment, I.C.J. Reports 1960, p. 192.

1961

Barcelona Traction, Light and Power Company, Limited, Order of 10 April 1961, I.C.J. Reports 1961, p. 9.

South West Africa, Order of 20 May 1961, I.C.J. Reports 1961, p. 13.

Temple of Preah Vihear, Preliminary Objections, Judgment, I.C.J. Reports 1961, p. 17.

1962

Temple of Preah Vihear, Merits, Judgment, I.C.J. Reports 1962, p. 6.

Certain Expenses of the United Nations (Article 17, paragraph 2, of the Charter), Advisory Opinion, I.C.J. Reports 1962, p. 151.

South West Africa, Preliminary Objections, Judgment, I.C.J. Reports 1962, p. 319.

1963

Northern Cameroons, Judgment, I.C.J. Reports 1963, p. 15.

1964

Barcelona Traction, Light and Power Company, Limited, Preliminary Objections, Judgment, I.C.J. Reports 1964, p. 6.

1965

South West Africa, Order of 18 March 1965, I.C.J. Reports 1965, p. 3.

South West Africa, Order of 29 November 1965, I.C.J. Reports 1965, p. 9.

1966

South West Africa, Second Phase, Judgment, I.C.J. Reports 1966, p. 6.

1968

North Sea Continental Shelf, Order of 26 April 1968, I.C.J. Reports 1968, p. 9.

1969

North Sea Continental Shelf, Judgment, I.C.J. Reports 1969, p. 3.

1970

Barcelona Traction, Light and Power Company, Limited, Second Phase, Judgment, I.C.J. Reports 1970, p. 3.

1971

Legal Consequences for States of the Continued Presence of South Africa in Namibia (South West Africa) notwithstanding Security Council Resolution 276 (1970), Orders Nos. 1, 2 and 3 of 26 January 1971, I.C.J. Reports 1971, pp. 3, 6 and 9.

Legal Consequences for States of the Continued Presence of South Africa in Namibia (South West Africa) notwithstanding Security Council Resolution 276 (1970), Order of 29 January 1971, I.C.J. Reports 1971, p. 12.

Legal Consequences for States of the Continued Presence of South Africa in Namibia (South West Africa) notwithstanding Security Council Resolution 276 (1970), Advisory Opinion, I.C.J. Reports 1971, p. 16.

1972

Fisheries Jurisdiction (United Kingdom v. *Iceland), Interim Protection, Order of 17 August 1972, I.C.J. Reports 1972*, p. 12.

Fisheries Jurisdiction (Federal Republic of Germany v. *Iceland), Interim Protection, Order of 17 August 1972, I.C.J. Reports 1972*, p. 30.

Appeal Relating to the Jurisdiction of the ICAO Council, Judgment, I.C.J. Reports 1972, p. 46.

Fisheries Jurisdiction (United Kingdom v. *Iceland), Order of 18 August 1972, I.C.J. Reports 1972*, p. 181.

Fisheries Jurisdiction (Federal Republic of Germany v. *Iceland), Order of 18 August 1972, I.C.J. Reports 1972*, p. 188.

1973

Fisheries Jurisdiction (United Kingdom v. *Iceland), Jurisdiction of the Court, Judgment, I.C.J. Reports 1973*, p. 3.

Fisheries Jurisdiction (Federal Republic of Germany v. *Iceland), Jurisdiction of the Court, Judgment, I.C.J. Reports 1973*, p. 49.

Nuclear Tests (Australia v. *France), Interim Protection, Order of 22 June 1973, I.C.J. Reports 1973*, p. 99.

Nuclear Tests (New Zealand v. *France), Interim Protection, Order of 22 June 1973, I.C.J. Reports 1973*, p. 135.

Application for Review of Judgement No. 158 of the United Nations Administrative Tribunal, Advisory Opinion, I.C.J. Reports 1973, p. 166.

Fisheries Jurisdiction (United Kingdom v. *Iceland), Interim Protection, Order of 12 July 1973, I.C.J. Reports 1973*, p. 302.

Fisheries Jurisdiction (Federal Republic of Germany v. *Iceland), Interim Protection, Order of 12 July 1973, I.C.J. Reports 1973*, p. 313.

Nuclear Tests (Australia v. *France), Application for Permission to Intervene, Order of 12 July 1973, I.C.J. Reports 1973*, p. 320.

Nuclear Tests (New Zealand v. *France), Application for Permission to Intervene, Order of 12 July 1973, I.C.J. Reports 1973*, p. 324.

Trial of Pakistani Prisoners of War, Interim Protection, Order of 13 July 1973, I.C.J. Reports 1973, p. 328.

Trial of Pakistani Prisoners of War, Order of 15 December 1973, I.C.J. Reports 1973, p. 347.

1974

Fisheries Jurisdiction (United Kingdom v. *Iceland), Merits, Judgment, I.C.J. Reports 1974*, p. 3.

Fisheries Jurisdiction (Federal Republic of Germany v. *Iceland), Merits, Judgment, I.C.J. Reports 1974*, p. 175.

Nuclear Tests (Australia v. *France), Judgment, I.C.J. Reports 1974*, p. 253.

Nuclear Tests (New Zealand v. *France), Judgment, I.C.J. Reports 1974*, p. 457.

Nuclear Tests (Australia v. *France), Application for Permission to Intervene, Order of 20 December 1974, I.C.J. Reports 1974*, p. 530.

Nuclear Tests (New Zealand v. *France), Application for Permission to Intervene, Order of 20 December 1974, I.C.J. Reports 1974*, p. 535.

1975

Western Sahara, Order of 22 May 1975, I.C.J. Reports 1975, p. 6.

Western Sahara, Advisory Opinion, I.C.J. Reports 1975, p. 12.

1976

Aegean Sea Continental Shelf, Interim Protection, Order of 11 September 1976, I.C.J. Reports 1976, p. 3.

1978

Aegean Sea Continental Shelf, Judgment, I.C.J. Reports 1978, p. 3.

1979

United States Diplomatic and Consular Staff in Tehran, Provisional Measures, Order of 15 December 1979, I.C.J. Reports 1979, p. 7.

1980

United States Diplomatic and Consular Staff in Tehran, Judgment, I.C.J. Reports 1980, p. 3.

Interpretation of the Agreement of 25 March 1951 between the WHO and Egypt, Advisory Opinion, I.C.J. Reports 1980, p. 73.

1981

Continental Shelf (Tunisia/Libyan Arab Jamahiriya), Application for Permission to Intervene, Judgment, I.C.J. Reports 1981, p. 3.

United States Diplomatic and Consular Staff in Tehran, Order of 12 May 1981, I.C.J. Reports 1981, p. 45.

1982

Delimitation of the Maritime Boundary in the Gulf of Maine Area, Constitution of Chamber, Order of 20 January 1982, I.C.J. Reports 1982, p. 3.

Continental Shelf (Tunisia/Libyan Arab Jamahiriya), Judgment, I.C.J. Reports 1982, p. 18.

Application for Review of Judgement No. 273 of the United Nations Administrative Tribunal, Advisory Opinion, I.C.J. Reports 1982, p. 325.

1984

Continental Shelf (Libyan Arab Jamahiriya/Malta), Application for Permission to Intervene, Judgment, I.C.J. Reports 1984, p. 3.

Delimitation of the Maritime Boundary in the Gulf of Maine Area, Appointment of Expert, Order of 30 March 1984, I.C.J. Reports 1984, p. 165.

Military and Paramilitary Activities in and against Nicaragua (Nicaragua v. *United States of America), Provisional Measures, Order of 10 May 1984, I.C.J. Reports 1984*, p. 169.

Military and Paramilitary Activities in and against Nicaragua (Nicaragua v. *United States of America), Declaration of Intervention, Order of 4 October 1984, I.C.J. Reports 1984*, p. 215.

Delimitation of the Maritime Boundary in the Gulf of Maine Area, Judgment, I.C.J. Reports 1984, p. 246.

Military and Paramilitary Activities in and against Nicaragua (Nicaragua v. *United States of America), Jurisdiction and Admissibility, Judgment, I.C.J. Reports 1984*, p. 392.

1985

Frontier Dispute, Constitution of Chamber, Order of 3 April 1985, I.C.J. Reports 1985, p. 6.

Continental Shelf (Libyan Arab Jamahiriya/Malta), Judgment, I.C.J. Reports 1985, p. 13.

Application for Revision and Interpretation of the Judgment of 24 February 1982 in the Case concerning the Continental Shelf (Tunisia/Libyan Arab Jamahiriya) *(Tunisia* v. *Libyan Arab Jamahiriya), Judgment, I.C.J. Reports 1985*, p. 192.

1986

Frontier Dispute, Provisional Measures, Order of 10 January 1986, I.C.J. Reports 1986, p. 3.

Military and Paramilitary Activities in and against Nicaragua (Nicaragua v. *United States of America), Merits, Judgment, I.C.J. Reports 1986*, p. 14.

Frontier Dispute, Judgment, I.C.J. Reports 1986, p. 554.

1987

Elettronica Sicula S.p.A. (ELSI), Constitution of Chamber, Order of 2 March 1987, I.C.J. Reports 1987, p. 3.

Frontier Dispute, Nomination of Experts, Order of 9 April 1987, I.C.J. Reports 1987, p. 7.

Land, Island and Maritime Frontier Dispute (El Salvador/Honduras), Constitution of Chamber, Order of 8 May 1987, I.C.J. Reports 1987, p. 10.

Application for Review of Judgement No. 333 of the United Nations Administrative Tribunal, Advisory Opinion, I.C.J. Reports 1987, p. 18.

Border and Transborder Armed Actions (Nicaragua v. *Costa Rica), Order of 19 August 1987, I.C.J. Reports 1987*, p. 182.

1988

Applicability of the Obligation to Arbitrate under Section 21 of the United Nations Headquarters Agreement of 26 June 1947, Order of 9 March 1988, I.C.J. Reports 1988, p. 3.

Border and Transborder Armed Actions (Nicaragua v. *Honduras), Provisional Measures, Order of 31 March 1988, I.C.J. Reports 1988*, p. 9.

Applicability of the Obligation to Arbitrate under Section 21 of the United Nations Headquarters Agreement of 26 June 1947, Advisory Opinion, I.C.J. Reports 1988, p. 12.

Border and Transborder Armed Actions (Nicaragua v. *Honduras), Jurisdiction and Admissibility, Judgment, I.C.J. Reports 1988*, p. 69.

Elettronica Sicula S.p.A. (ELSI), Composition of Chamber, Order of 20 December 1988, I.C.J. Reports 1988, p. 158.

1989

Applicability of Article VI, Section 22, of the Convention on the Privileges and Immunities of the United Nations, Order of 14 June 1989, I.C.J. Reports 1989, p. 9.

Elettronica Sicula S.p.A. (ELSI), Judgment, I.C.J. Reports 1989, p. 15.

Land, Island and Maritime Frontier Dispute (El Salvador/Honduras), Composition of Chamber, Order of 13 December 1989, I.C.J. Reports 1989, p. 162.

Applicability of Article VI, Section 22, of the Convention on the Privileges and Immunities of the United Nations, Advisory Opinion, I.C.J. Reports 1989, p. 177.

1990

Land, Island and Maritime Frontier Dispute (El Salvador/Honduras), Application to Intervene, Order of 28 February 1990, I.C.J. Reports 1990, p. 3.

Arbitral Award of 31 July 1989, Provisional Measures, Order of 2 March 1990, I.C.J. Reports 1990, p. 64.

Land, Island and Maritime Frontier Dispute (El Salvador/Honduras), Application to Intervene, Judgment, I.C.J. Reports 1990, p. 92.

Territorial Dispute (Libyan Arab Jamahiriya/Chad), Order of 26 October 1990, I.C.J. Reports 1990, p. 149.

1991

Passage through the Great Belt (Finland v. *Denmark), Provisional Measures, Order of 29 July 1991, I.C.J. Reports 1991*, p. 12.

Military and Paramilitary Activities in and against Nicaragua (Nicaragua v. *United States of America), Order of 26 September 1991, I.C.J. Reports 1991*, p. 47.

Maritime Delimitation and Territorial Questions between Qatar and Bahrain, Order of 11 October 1991, I.C.J. Reports 1991, p. 50.

Arbitral Award of 31 July 1989, Judgment, I.C.J. Reports 1991, p. 53.

1992

Questions of Interpretation and Application of the 1971 Montreal Convention arising from the Aerial Incident at Lockerbie (Libyan Arab Jamahiriya v. *United Kingdom), Provisional Measures, Order of 14 April 1992, I.C.J. Reports 1992*, p. 3.

Questions of Interpretation and Application of the 1971 Montreal Convention arising from the Aerial Incident at Lockerbie (Libyan Arab Jamahiriya v. *United States of America), Provisional Measures, Order of 14 April 1992, I.C.J. Reports 1992*, p. 114.

Border and Transborder Armed Actions (Nicaragua v. *Honduras), Order of 27 May 1992, I.C.J. Reports 1992*, p. 222.

Certain Phosphate Lands in Nauru (Nauru v. *Australia), Preliminary Objections, Judgment, I.C.J. Reports 1992*, p. 240.

Passage through the Great Belt (Finland v. *Denmark), Order of 10 September 1992, I.C.J. Reports 1992*, p. 348.

Land, Island and Maritime Frontier Dispute (El Salvador/Honduras: Nicaragua intervening), Judgment, I.C.J. Reports 1992, p. 351.

1993

Application of the Convention on the Prevention and Punishment of the Crime of Genocide, Provisional Measures, Order of 8 April 1993, I.C.J. Reports 1993, p. 3.

Maritime Delimitation in the Area between Greenland and Jan Mayen, Judgment, I.C.J. Reports 1993, p. 38.

Certain Phosphate Lands in Nauru (Nauru v. *Australia), Order of 25 June 1993, I.C.J. Reports 1993*, p. 316.

Certain Phosphate Lands in Nauru (Nauru v. *Australia), Order of 13 September 1993, I.C.J. Reports 1993*, p. 322.

Application of the Convention on the Prevention and Punishment of the Crime of Genocide, Provisional Measures, Order of 13 September 1993, I.C.J. Reports 1993, p. 325.

1994

Territorial Dispute (Libyan Arab Jamahiriya/Chad), Judgment, I.C.J. Reports 1994, p. 6.

Land and Maritime Boundary between Cameroon and Nigeria, Order of 16 June 1994, I.C.J. Reports 1994, p. 105.

Maritime Delimitation and Territorial Questions between Qatar and Bahrain, Jurisdiction and Admissibility, Judgment, I.C.J. Reports 1994, p. 112.

1995

Legality of the Threat or Use of Nuclear Weapons, Order of 1 February 1995, I.C.J. Reports 1995, p. 3.

Maritime Delimitation and Territorial Questions between Qatar and Bahrain, Jurisdiction and Admissibility, Judgment, I.C.J. Reports 1995, p. 6.

Fisheries Jurisdiction (Spain v. *Canada), Order of 2 May 1995, I.C.J. Reports 1995*, p. 87.

East Timor (Portugal v. *Australia), Judgment, I.C.J. Reports 1995*, p. 90.

Request for an Examination of the Situation in Accordance with Paragraph 63 of the Court's Judgment of 20 December 1974 in the Nuclear Tests (New Zealand *v.* France) *Case, Order of 22 September 1995, I.C.J. Reports 1995*, p. 288.

Maritime Delimitation between Guinea-Bissau and Senegal, Order of 8 November 1995, I.C.J. Reports 1995, p. 423.

1996

Aerial Incident of 3 July 1988 (Islamic Republic of Iran v. *United States of America), Order of 22 February 1996, I.C.J. Reports 1996*, p. 9.

Land and Maritime Boundary between Cameroon and Nigeria, Provisional Measures, Order of 15 March 1996, I.C.J. Reports 1996, p. 13.

Fisheries Jurisdiction (Spain v. *Canada), Order of 8 May 1996, I.C.J. Reports 1996*, p. 58.

Legality of the Use by a State of Nuclear Weapons in Armed Conflict, Advisory Opinion, I.C.J. Reports 1996, p. 66.

Legality of the Threat or Use of Nuclear Weapons, Advisory Opinion, I.C.J. Reports 1996, p. 226.

Application of the Convention on the Prevention and Punishment of the Crime of Genocide, Preliminary Objections, Judgment, I.C.J. Reports 1996, p. 595.

III. Abbreviated References to Pleadings, Oral Arguments, Documents

In order to standardize the abbreviated references to the *Pleadings, Oral Arguments, Documents* series of the International Court of Justice and the corresponding volumes *(Series C)* of the *Permanent Court of*

International Justice, the Court decided to use the titles below, which are given in chronological order based on the date of entry of the case in the General List.

For the convenience of the reader, the names of the Parties in contentious cases (separated by a stroke if proceedings were instituted by means of a special agreement), or the name of the body which requested the advisory opinion, have been added in small type to the abbreviated references.

An asterisk indicates that a case was removed from the list before a final judgment or an advisory opinion was given, or if it failed for some other reason to reach its normal conclusion.

1. Permanent Court of International Justice

1922

Competence of the ILO in Regard to International Regulation of the Conditions of Labour of Persons Employed in Agriculture, P.C.I.J., Series C, No. 1.

L of N Council

Designation of the Workers' Delegate for the Netherlands at the Third Session of the International Labour Conference, P.C.I.J., Series C, No. 1.

L of N Council

Competence of the ILO to Examine Proposals for the Organization and Development of the Methods of Agricultural Production, P.C.I.J., Series C, No. 1.

L of N Council

Nationality Decrees Issued in Tunis and Morocco, P.C.I.J., Series C, No. 2 (and additional volume).

L of N Council

1923

S.S. "Wimbledon", P.C.I.J., Series C, No. 3, Vols. I and II (and additional volume).

France, Italy, Japan, United Kingdom *v.* Germany

German Settlers in Poland, P.C.I.J., Series C, No. 3, Vols. I, III (1) and III (2).

L of N Council

Status of Eastern Carelia, P.C.I.J., Series C, No. 3, Vols. I and II.

L of N Council

Acquisition of Polish Nationality, P.C.I.J., Series C, No. 3, Vols. I, III (1) and III (2).

L of N Council

Jaworzina, P.C.I.J., Series C, No. 4.

L of N Council

1924

Mavrommatis Concessions, P.C.I.J., Series C, No. 5, Vol. I; *No. 7,* Vol. II; *No. 13 (III).*

Greece *v.* United Kingdom

Treaty of Neuilly, Article 179, Annex, Paragraph 4 (Interpretation), P.C.I.J., Series C, No. 6 (and additional volume).

Bulgaria/Greece

Monastery of Saint-Naoum, P.C.I.J., Series C, No. 5, Vol. II.

L of N Council

Exchange of Greek and Turkish Populations, P.C.I.J., Series C, No. 7, Vol. I.

L of N Council

1925

Polish Postal Service in Danzig, P.C.I.J., Series C, No. 8.

L of N Council

**Expulsion of the Oecumenical Patriarch, P.C.I.J., Series C, No. 9 (II).*

L of N Council

Certain German Interests in Polish Upper Silesia, P.C.I.J., Series C, No. 9 (I); No. 11, Vols. I-III.

Germany *v.* Poland

Interpretation of Article 3, paragraph 2, of the Treaty of Lausanne, P.C.I.J., Series C, No. 10.

L of N Council

1926

Competence of the ILO to Regulate Incidentally the Personal Work of the Employer, P.C.I.J., Series C, No. 12.

L of N Council

**Denunciation of the Treaty of 2 November 1865 between China and Belgium, P.C.I.J., Series C, No. 16 (I).*

Belgium *v.* China

Jurisdiction of the European Commission of the Danube, P.C.I.J., Series C, No. 13 (IV), Vols. I-IV.

L of N Council

1927

"Lotus", P.C.I.J., Series C, No. 13 (II).

France/Turkey

Factory at Chorzów, P.C.I.J., Series C, No. 13 (I); No. 13 (V); No. 15 (II); No. 16 (II).

Germany *v.* Poland

Jurisdiction of the Courts of Danzig, P.C.I.J., Series C, No. 14 (I).

L of N Council

1928

Rights of Minorities in Upper Silesia (Minority Schools), P.C.I.J., Series C, No. 14 (II).

Germany *v.* Poland

Free Zones of Upper Savoy and the District of Gex, P.C.I.J., Series C, No. 17 (I), Vols. I-IV; *No. 19*, Vols. I-V; *No. 58.*

France/Switzerland

Brazilian Loans, P.C.I.J., Series C, No. 16 (IV).

Brazil/France

Serbian Loans, P.C.I.J., Series C, No. 16 (III).

France/Yugoslavia

Interpretation of the Greco-Turkish Agreement of 1 December 1926 (Final Protocol, Article IV), P.C.I.J., Series C, No. 15 (I).

L of N Council

Territorial Jurisdiction of the International Commission of the River Oder, P.C.I.J., Series C, No. 17 (II).

Czechoslovakia, Denmark, France, Germany, Sweden, United Kingdom/Poland

1930

Greco-Bulgarian "Communities", P.C.I.J., Series C, No. 18 (I).

L of N Council

Free City of Danzig and ILO, P.C.I.J., Series C, No. 18 (II).

L of N Council

1931

Railway Traffic between Lithuania and Poland, P.C.I.J., Series C, No. 54.

L of N Council

Access to German Minority Schools in Upper Silesia, P.C.I.J., Series C, No. 52.

L of N Council

Customs Régime between Germany and Austria, P.C.I.J., Series C, No. 53.

L of N Council

Treatment of Polish Nationals and Other Persons of Polish Origin or Speech in the Danzig Territory, P.C.I.J., Series C, No. 56.

L of N Council

Legal Status of Eastern Greenland, P.C.I.J., Series C, Nos. 62-67 (and table of contents and maps).

Denmark *v.* Norway

Access to, or Anchorage in, the Port of Danzig, of Polish War Vessels, P.C.I.J., Series C, No. 55.

L of N Council

Interpretation of the Greco-Bulgarian Agreement of 9 December 1927, P.C.I.J., Series C, No. 57.

L of N Council

Delimitation of the Territorial Waters between the Island of Castellorizo and the Coasts of Anatolia, P.C.I.J., Series C, No. 61.

Italy/Turkey

1932

Interpretation of the Statute of the Memel Territory, P.C.I.J., Series C, No. 59.

France, Italy, Japan, United Kingdom *v.* Lithuania

Interpretation of the Convention of 1919 concerning Employment of Women during the Night, P.C.I.J., Series C, No. 60.

L of N Council

**Prince von Pless Administration, P.C.I.J., Series C, No. 70.*

Germany *v.* Poland

**Appeals from Certain Judgments of the Hungaro/Czechoslovak Mixed Arbitral Tribunal, P.C.I.J., Series C, No. 68.*

Czechoslovakia *v.* Hungary

**Legal Status of the South-Eastern Territory of Greenland, P.C.I.J., Series C, No. 69.*

Norway *v.* Denmark; Denmark *v.* Norway

1933

Appeal from a Judgment of the Hungaro/Czechoslovak Mixed Arbitral Tribunal (The Peter Pázmány University), P.C.I.J., Series C, Nos. 72-73.

Czechoslovakia *v.* Hungary

Lighthouses case between France and Greece, P.C.I.J., Series C, No. 74.

France/Greece

**Polish Agrarian Reform and German Minority, P.C.I.J., Series C, No. 71.*

Germany *v.* Poland

1934

Oscar Chinn, P.C.I.J., Series C, No. 75.

Belgium/United Kingdom

1935

Minority Schools in Albania, P.C.I.J., Series C, No. 76.

L of N Council

Consistency of Certain Danzig Legislative Decrees with the Constitution of the Free City, P.C.I.J., Series C, No. 77.

L of N Council

**Losinger, P.C.I.J., Series C, No. 78.*

Switzerland *v.* Yugoslavia

1936

Pajzs, Csáky, Esterházy, P.C.I.J., Series C, Nos. 79-80.
Hungary *v.* Yugoslavia

Phosphates in Morocco, P.C.I.J., Series C, Nos. 84-85.
Italy *v.* France

Diversion of Water from the Meuse, P.C.I.J., Series C, No. 81.
Netherlands *v.* Belgium

Lighthouses in Crete and Samos, P.C.I.J., Series C, No. 82.
France/Greece

1937

Borchgrave, P.C.I.J., Series C, No. 83.
Belgium/Spain

Panevezys-Saldutiskis Railway, P.C.I.J., Series C, No. 86.
Estonia *v.* Lithuania

1938

Electricity Company of Sofia and Bulgaria, P.C.I.J., Series C, No. 88.
Belgium *v.* Bulgaria

Société Commerciale de Belgique, P.C.I.J., Series C, No. 87.
Belgium *v.* Greece

1939

**Gerliczy* (No volume published).
Liechtenstein *v.* Hungary

2. International Court of Justice

1947

I.C.J. Pleadings, Corfu Channel, Vols. I-VI.
United Kingdom *v.* Albania

I.C.J. Pleadings, Conditions of Admission of a State to Membership in the United Nations (Article 4 of the Charter).
UN General Assembly

1948

I.C.J. Pleadings, Reparation for Injuries Suffered in the Service of the United Nations.
UN General Assembly

1949

I.C.J. Pleadings, Fisheries, Vols. I-IV (and charts).
United Kingdom *v.* Norway

**I.C.J. Pleadings, Protection of French Nationals and Protected Persons in Egypt.*

France *v.* Egypt

I.C.J. Pleadings, Asylum, Vols. I-II.

Colombia/Peru

I.C.J. Pleadings, Interpretation of Peace Treaties with Bulgaria, Hungary and Romania.

UN General Assembly

I.C.J. Pleadings, Competence of the General Assembly for the Admission of a State to the United Nations.

UN General Assembly

I.C.J. Pleadings, International Status of South West Africa.

UN General Assembly

1950

I.C.J. Pleadings, Rights of Nationals of the United States of America in Morocco, Vols. I-II.

France *v.* USA

I.C.J. Pleadings, Reservations to the Convention on the Prevention and Punishment of the Crime of Genocide.

UN General Assembly

I.C.J. Pleadings, Haya de la Torre.

Colombia *v.* Peru

1951

I.C.J. Pleadings, Ambatielos.

Greece *v.* United Kingdom

I.C.J. Pleadings, Anglo-Iranian Oil Co.

United Kingdom *v.* Iran

I.C.J. Pleadings, Minquiers and Ecrehos, Vols. I-II.

France/United Kingdom

I.C.J. Pleadings, Nottebohm, Vols. I-II.

Liechtenstein *v.* Guatemala

1953

I.C.J. Pleadings, Monetary Gold Removed from Rome in 1943.

Italy *v.* France, United Kingdom, USA

**I.C.J. Pleadings, Electricité de Beyrouth Company.*

France *v.* Lebanon

I.C.J. Pleadings, Effect of Awards of Compensation Made by the United Nations Administrative Tribunal.

UN General Assembly

1954

**I.C.J. Pleadings, Treatment in Hungary of Aircraft and Crew of United States of America.* (starred)

USA *v.* Hungary;
USA *v.* USSR

I.C.J. Pleadings, Voting Procedure on Questions Relating to Reports and Petitions concerning the Territory of South West Africa.

UN General Assembly

1955

**I.C.J. Pleadings, Aerial Incident of 10 March 1953.*

USA *v.* Czechoslovakia

**I.C.J. Pleadings, Antarctica.*

United Kingdom *v.* Argentina;
United Kingdom *v.* Chile

**I.C.J. Pleadings, Aerial Incident of 7 October 1952.*

USA *v.* USSR

I.C.J. Pleadings, Certain Norwegian Loans, Vols. I-II.

France *v.* Norway

I.C.J. Pleadings, Judgments of the Administrative Tribunal of the ILO upon Complaints Made against Unesco.

Unesco Executive Board

I.C.J. Pleadings, Admissibility of Hearings of Petitioners by the Committee on South West Africa.

UN General Assembly

I.C.J. Pleadings, Right of Passage over Indian Territory, Vols. I-V.

Portugal *v.* India

1957

I.C.J. Pleadings, Application of the Convention of 1902 Governing the Guardianship of Infants.

Netherlands *v.* Sweden

I.C.J. Pleadings, Interhandel.

Switzerland *v.* USA

I.C.J. Pleadings, Aerial Incident of 27 July 1955.

Israel *v.* Bulgaria;
*USA *v.* Bulgaria;
*United Kingdom *v.* Bulgaria

I.C.J. Pleadings, Sovereignty over Certain Frontier Land.

Belgium/Netherlands

1958

I.C.J. Pleadings, Arbitral Award Made by the King of Spain on 23 December 1906, Vol. I (with maps) and Vol. II.

Honduras *v.* Nicaragua

**I.C.J. Pleadings, Aerial Incident of 4 September 1954.*

USA *v.* USSR

**I.C.J. Pleadings, Barcelona Traction, Light and Power Company, Limited.*

Belgium *v.* Spain

1959

**I.C.J. Pleadings, Compagnie du Port, des Quais et des Entrepôts de Beyrouth and Société Radio-Orient.*

France *v.* Lebanon

I.C.J. Pleadings, Constitution of the Maritime Safety Committee of the Inter-Governmental Maritime Consultative Organization.

IMCO Assembly

**I.C.J. Pleadings, Aerial Incident of 7 November 1954.*

USA *v.* USSR

I.C.J. Pleadings, Temple of Preah Vihear, Vols. I-II.

Cambodia *v.* Thailand

1960

I.C.J. Pleadings, South West Africa, Vols. I-XII.

Ethiopia *v.* South Africa;
Liberia *v.* South Africa

1961

I.C.J. Pleadings, Northern Cameroons.

Cameroon *v.* United Kingdom

I.C.J. Pleadings, Certain Expenses of the United Nations (Article 17, paragraph 2, of the Charter).

UN General Assembly

1962

I.C.J. Pleadings, Barcelona Traction, Light and Power Company, Limited (New Application: 1962), Vols. I-X[1].

Belgium *v.* Spain

---

[1] In this case, annexes to written pleadings, and documents submitted after the closure of the written proceedings, were not reproduced. Sets of these texts were, however, deposited in a number of public libraries, a list of which is given in the introductory pages of Volume X.

1967

I.C.J. Pleadings, North Sea Continental Shelf, Vols. I-II.

Fed. Rep. Germany/Denmark;
Fed. Rep. Germany/Netherlands

1970

I.C.J. Pleadings, Legal Consequences for States of the Continued Presence of South Africa in Namibia (South West Africa) notwithstanding Security Council Resolution 276 (1970), Vols. I-II.

UN Security Council

1971

I.C.J. Pleadings, Appeal Relating to the Jurisdiction of the ICAO Council.

India *v.* Pakistan

1972

I.C.J. Pleadings, Fisheries Jurisdiction, Vols. I-II.

United Kingdom *v.* Iceland;
Fed. Rep. Germany *v.* Iceland

I.C.J. Pleadings, Application for Review of Judgement No. 158 of the United Nations Administrative Tribunal.

Committee on Applications
for Review of UNAT Judgements

1973

I.C.J. Pleadings, Nuclear Tests, Vols. I-II.

Australia *v.* France;
New Zealand *v.* France

**I.C.J. Pleadings, Trial of Pakistani Prisoners of War.*

Pakistan *v.* India

1975

I.C.J. Pleadings, Western Sahara, Vols. I-V.

UN General Assembly

1976

I.C.J. Pleadings, Aegean Sea Continental Shelf.

Greece *v.* Turkey

1978

I.C.J. Pleadings, Continental Shelf (Tunisia/Libyan Arab Jamahiriya), Vols. I-VI (with maps).

Tunisia/Libyan Arab Jamahiriya

1979

I.C.J. Pleadings, United States Diplomatic and Consular Staff in Tehran.
USA *v.* Iran

1980

I.C.J. Pleadings, Interpretation of the Agreement of 25 March 1951 between the WHO and Egypt.
World Health Assembly

1981

I.C.J. Pleadings, Application for Review of Judgement No. 273 of the United Nations Administrative Tribunal.
Committee on Applications for Review of UNAT Judgements

I.C.J. Pleadings, Delimitation of the Maritime Boundary in the Gulf of Maine Area, Vols. I-VIII (with maps).
Canada/USA

1982

I.C.J. Pleadings, Continental Shelf (Libyan Arab Jamahiriya/Malta), Vols. I-V (with maps).
Libyan Arab Jamahiriya/Malta

1983

I.C.J. Pleadings, Frontier Dispute (not yet published).
Burkina Faso/Republic of Mali

1984

I.C.J. Pleadings, Military and Paramilitary Activities in and against Nicaragua (not yet published).
Nicaragua *v.* USA

I.C.J. Pleadings, Application for Revision and Interpretation of the Judgment of 24 February 1982 in the Case concerning the Continental Shelf (Tunisia/Libyan Arab Jamahiriya).
Tunisia *v.* Libyan Arab Jamahiriya

I.C.J. Pleadings, Application for Review of Judgement No. 333 of the United Nations Administrative Tribunal.
Committee on Applications for Review of UNAT Judgements

1986

**I.C.J. Pleadings, Border and Transborder Armed Actions (Nicaragua* v. *Costa Rica)*.

Nicaragua *v.* Costa Rica

**I.C.J. Pleadings, Border and Transborder Armed Actions (Nicaragua* v. *Honduras)* (not yet published).

Nicaragua *v.* Honduras

I.C.J. Pleadings, Land, Island and Maritime Frontier Dispute (El Salvador/Honduras: Nicaragua intervening) (not yet published).

El Salvador/Honduras

1987

I.C.J. Pleadings, Elettronica Sicula S.p.A. (ELSI), Vols. I-III.

USA *v.* Italy

1988

I.C.J. Pleadings, Applicability of the Obligation to Arbitrate under Section 21 of the United Nations Headquarters Agreement of 26 June 1947.

UN General Assembly

I.C.J. Pleadings, Maritime Delimitation in the Area between Greenland and Jan Mayen (not yet published).

Denmark *v.* Norway

1989

I.C.J. Pleadings, Aerial Incident of 3 July 1988 (Islamic Republic of Iran v. *United States of America)* (not yet published).

Iran *v.* USA

**I.C.J. Pleadings, Certain Phosphate Lands in Nauru (Nauru* v. *Australia)* (not yet published).

Nauru *v.* Australia

I.C.J. Pleadings, Applicability of Article VI, Section 22, of the Convention on the Privileges and Immunities of the United Nations.

UN Economic and Social Council

I.C.J. Pleadings, Arbitral Award of 31 July 1989 (not yet published).

Guinea-Bissau *v.* Senegal

1990

I.C.J. Pleadings, Territorial Dispute (Libyan Arab Jamahiriya/Chad) (not yet published).

Libyan Arab Jamahiriya/Chad

1991

I.C.J. Pleadings, East Timor (Portugal v. *Australia)* (not yet published).

Portugal *v.* Australia

**I.C.J. Pleadings, Maritime Delimitation between Guinea-Bissau and Senegal (Guinea-Bissau* v. *Senegal)* (not yet published).

Guinea-Bissau *v.* Senegal

**I.C.J. Pleadings, Passage through the Great Belt (Finland* v. *Denmark)* (not yet published).

Finland *v.* Denmark

1993

I.C.J. Pleadings, Legality of the Use by a State of Nuclear Weapons in Armed Conflict (not yet published).

World Health Assembly

1994

I.C.J. Pleadings, Legality of the Threat or Use of Nuclear Weapons (not yet published).

UN General Assembly

CHAPTER VIII
FINANCES OF THE COURT

I. Financial Regulations

In regard to financial matters, the International Court of Justice applies Articles 32, 33, 35 and 64 of the Statute of the Court, Article 26, paragraph 1 *(j)*, of the Rules of Court, the Staff Regulations for the Registry and the relevant resolutions of the General Assembly of the United Nations.

1. General Regulations

(a) *Method of covering expenditure*

Article 33 of the Statute of the Court provides: "The expenses of the Court shall be borne by the United Nations in such a manner as shall be decided by the General Assembly." As the budget of the Court has consequently been incorporated in the budget of the United Nations, member States participate in the expenses of both in the same proportion, in accordance with the scale of assessments determined by the General Assembly.

States which are not members of the United Nations but which are parties to the Statute pay, in accordance with the undertaking into which they entered when they became parties to the Statute (see Chap. III, pp. 64-65, above), a contribution the amount of which is fixed from time to time by the General Assembly in consultation with them. By its resolution 49/19 of 23 December 1994, the General Assembly decided that these States should contribute to the expenses of the Court for the years 1995, 1996 and 1997 in the following proportions: Nauru 0.01%; Switzerland 1.21%.

If a State which is not a party to the Statute but to which the Court is open is a party to a case, the Court will fix the amount which that party is to contribute towards the expenses of the Court (Statute, Art. 35, para. 3). Payment is then made by the State concerned to the account of the United Nations in New York.

The contributions of States which are not members of the United Nations are taken into account as miscellaneous income received by the Organization.

Under an established rule, sums derived from staff assessment, sales of publications (dealt with by the Sales Sections of the Secretariat – see Chap. VII, p. 289, above), bank interest, etc., are also recorded as United Nations income.

(b) *Drafting of the budget*

In accordance with the Instructions for the Registry (Arts. 26-30), a preliminary draft budget is prepared by the Registrar. If the Court is sitting, this preliminary draft is submitted for the consideration of the Budgetary and Administrative Committee of the Court and then, for approval, to the Court itself. If the Court is not sitting, approval must be given by the President.

When it has been approved, the draft budget is forwarded to the Secretariat of the United Nations for incorporation in the draft budget of the United Nations. It is then examined by the United Nations Advisory Committee on Administrative and Budgetary Questions and is afterwards submitted to the Fifth Committee of the General Assembly. It is finally adopted by the General Assembly in plenary meeting, within the framework of the resolutions concerning the budget of the United Nations and its unforeseen and extraordinary expenses.

Since 1974 the budget has been presented biennially.

(c) *Financing of appropriations and accounts*

The Registrar is responsible for executing the budget, with the assistance of the Accountant/Establishment Officer. He has to ensure that proper use is made of the funds voted and must see that no expenses are incurred that are not provided for in the budget (Instructions for the Registry, Art. 31). He alone is entitled to incur liabilities in the name of the Court, subject to any possible delegations of authority (Instructions for the Registry, Art. 35).

The accounts of the Court are audited every year by the auditors of the Secretariat of the United Nations and by the Board of Auditors appointed by the General Assembly. At the end of each biennium, the closed accounts are forwarded to the Secretariat of the United Nations (Instructions for the Registry, Art. 34).

2. *Salaries and Expenses of Judges*

(a) *Emoluments*

By virtue of Article 32, paragraph 5, of the Statute, the salaries, allowances and compensation paid to the judges are fixed by the General Assembly. In this connection, the General Assembly adopted resolution 19 (I) of 6 February 1946, resolution 85 (I) of 11 December 1946, resolution 474 (V) of 15 December 1950, resolution 1738 (XVI) of 20 December 1961, resolution 2366 (XXII) of 19 December 1967, resolution 2890 B (XXVI) of 22 December 1971, resolution 3193 B (XXVIII) of 18 December 1973, resolution 3537 B (XXX) of 17 December 1975, resolution 31/204 of 22 December 1976, resolution 35/220 A of 17 December 1980, resolution 40/257 of 18 December 1985, resolution 43/217 of 21 December 1988, resolution 45/250 of 21 December 1990, resolution 48/252 of 26 May 1994 and resolution 50/216 of 23 December 1995.

The emoluments of Members of the Court are made up of an annual salary which may not be decreased during the period of office (Statute of the Court, Art. 32, paras. 1 and 5). With effect from 1 January 1991, the General Assembly (resolution 45/250) has fixed the emoluments of Members of the Court at US$145,000. The General Assembly further decided that the emoluments and other conditions of service shall be reviewed every three years with the next review at its fifty-third session.

Under Article 32, paragraphs 2 and 3, of the Statute, the President of the Court and the Vice-President (for every day on which he acts as President) receive special allowances in addition, at a rate fixed by resolution 40/257 of 18 December 1985.

Finally, under Article 32, paragraph 4, of the Statute and General Assembly resolution 19 (I) of 6 February 1946, judges *ad hoc* chosen to sit in certain cases under Article 31 of the Statute receive daily fees. With effect from 1 January 1991, the daily fee of *ad hoc* judges has been fixed at US$397, being 1/365th of US$145,000.

The emoluments of the judges are thus as set out on the following scale:

	US$
President:	
Annual salary	145,000
Special allowance	15,000
Vice-President:	
Annual salary	145,000
Allowance equivalent to US$94 for every day on which he acts as President, up to an annual maximum of . .	9,400
Other Members:	
Annual salary	145,000
Judges ad hoc:	
Fee of US$397 for each day on which they exercise their functions.	

(b) *Pensions*

Article 32, paragraph 7, of the Statute provides: "Regulations made by the General Assembly shall fix the conditions under which retirement pensions may be given to Members of the Court." The General Assembly adopted the Pension Scheme Regulations for Members of the International Court of Justice which appear as an annex to resolution 86 (I) of 11 December 1946. Amendments to these regulations were made by resolution 1408 (XIV) of 1 December 1959. The General Assembly adopted new regulations by its resolution 1562 (XV) of 18 December 1960. Some provisions of the regulations were modified by resolution 1925 (XVIII) of 11 December 1963, resolution 2367 (XXII) of 19 December 1967, resolution 2890 A (XXVI) of 22 December 1971, resolution 3193 A (XXVIII) of 18 December 1973, resolution 3537 A (XXX) of 17 December 1975, resolution 35/220 B of 17 December 1980. The General Assembly effected further modifications by resolution 38/239 of 20 December

1983, resolution 40/257 of 18 December 1985 and resolution 45/250 of 21 December 1990.

According to the regulations which came into operation on 1 January 1984, any Member of the Court who has ceased to hold office and who has reached the age of 60 years is entitled, if he has completed at least three years of service, to a retirement pension during the remainder of his life.

With effect from 1 January 1991 (resolution 45/250), if a Member of the Court has served a full term of nine years, the amount of the annual pension is US$50,000. If he has served for more than nine years, the amount of the pension is increased up to a maximum of US$75,000. It is reduced if he has served for less than nine years.

Furthermore, a Member of the Court who ceases to hold office before the age of 60 and who would be entitled to a retirement pension when he reached that age, may elect to receive a pension from any date after the date on which he ceases to hold office. The amount of such pension would be that amount which has the same actuarial value as the pension which would have been paid to him at the age of 60.

Provision is made also for disability pensions and pensions for widows and children.

By its resolution 31/204 of 22 December 1976, the General Assembly decided that the retirement pensions given to Members of the Court should be reviewed concurrently with the periodic revision of their annual salary.

(c) *Conditions of service*

In Section C of resolution 40/257 of 18 December 1985, the General Assembly laid down certain conditions of service applicable to Members of the Court. The text of the relevant portion of this resolution is as follows:

> "*The General Assembly,*
>
> *Recalling* its resolutions 37/237, section XIV, of 21 December 1982, 38/234, section XVII, of 20 December 1983, and 39/236, section V, of 18 December 1984, on conditions of service and compensation for officials other than Secretariat officials,
>
> *Having considered* the report of the Secretary-General and the related report of the Advisory Committee on Administrative and Budgetary Questions,
>
> 1. *Decides* that, with effect from 1 January 1986, the President and members of the Court who have taken up primary residence in The Hague, shall be reimbursed, up to a ceiling of $4,500, for the actual cost of educating their children in respect of each child each year up to the award of the first recognized degree and that provision shall be made for one related travel per year in respect of each child from the place of scholastic attendance, when outside the Netherlands, to The Hague;

2. *Decides* that, with effect from 1 January 1986, those members of the Court, who have taken up and maintained a *bona fide* primary residence at The Hague for at least five continuous years during service with the Court, shall be eligible to receive a lump sum equivalent to eighteen weeks of annual net base salary upon completion of their appointment and resettlement outside the Netherlands, and that those members of the Court, who have taken up and maintained a *bona fide* primary residence at The Hague for nine continuous years or more during service with the Court, shall receive the equivalent of twenty-four weeks of annual net base salary upon completion of service and relocation outside the Netherlands;

3. *Decides* that, with effect from 1 January 1986, in the event of the death of a member of the Court during his service, compensation shall be provided to the survivors in the form of a lump-sum payment equivalent to one month of base salary per year of service, subject to a minimum of three months and a maximum of nine months."

With effect from 1 January 1995, the ceiling for reimbursement for the actual cost of education, referred to in paragraph 1 of the above resolution, was fixed at US$12,675.

(d) *Travelling expenses*

By virtue of Article 32, paragraph 7, of the Statute, regulations made by the General Assembly fix the conditions under which Members of the Court have their travelling expenses refunded. The General Assembly adopted the Travel and Subsistence Regulations of the International Court of Justice which appear in the annex to resolution 85 (I) of 11 December 1946. On 21 December 1982, by resolution 37/240, it adopted new Travel and Subsistence Regulations of the International Court of Justice (set out in *I.C.J. Yearbook 1982-1983*, pp. 164-167).

3. Salaries, Allowances and Expenses of the Registrar and Officials of the Registry

(a) *Emoluments*

By virtue of Article 32, paragraph 6, of the Statute, the salary of the Registrar is fixed by the General Assembly on the proposal of the Court. By resolution 85 (I) of 11 December 1946 confirmed by resolution 474 (V) of 15 December 1950, the General Assembly decided that "the annual salary of the Registrar of the International Court of Justice shall be assimilated to that of a top-ranking director of the Secretariat of the United Nations". In the existing structure, the Registrar has the rank of an Assistant Secretary-General and the Deputy-Registrar that of a Director.

Officials of the Registry in the professional category, both permanent and temporary, receive the same salary and the same allowances as officials of the United Nations belonging to the same category.

For the purposes of the schedule of post adjustments applicable to the permanent staff of the professional category, The Hague was in Class 8/+3.5 as from 1 July 1995. For temporary staff of the professional category, the subsistence allowance is fixed at 347 guilders a day.

Salaries and allowances of permanent and temporary staff members in the general service category are based on the best prevailing local rates.

The figures given in the budget estimates and accounts in respect of salaries are net figures, after deduction of staff assessment.

(b) *Pensions*

By virtue of Article 12 of the Staff Regulations for the Registry, the Registrar and the officials of the Registry are participants in the United Nations Joint Staff Pension Fund. They participate on the same conditions as all other officials of the United Nations.

(c) *Travelling expenses*

Under Article 5 of the regulations concerning the travel and subsistence allowances of the Members of the International Court of Justice, dated 21 December 1982 (*I.C.J. Yearbook 1982-1983*, p. 167), the travel and subsistence provisions applicable to the Registrar of the Court are as set out in the Staff Regulations of the United Nations for officials of comparable rank, subject to any exceptions authorized by the President of the Court.

The travelling expenses of officials of the Registry are paid under conditions similar to those applied in the Secretariat of the United Nations (Staff Regulations for the Registry, Art. 12).

4. *Common Services*

The common services of the Court and of the Registry and the capital expenditure of the Court come under special items in the budget.

In particular, the Court pays to the Carnegie Foundation an annual contribution for the premises it occupies at the Peace Palace and in the new wing (see Chap. V, p. 140, above). The amount of the contribution was first fixed by the General Assembly in resolution 84 (I) of 11 December 1946 and has subsequently undergone successive alterations. It was increased to 1,157,100 guilders as from 1 January 1995 and to 1,209,170 guilders as from 1 January 1996.

II. Budget for the Biennium 1996-1997

1. *Ordinary Expenses*

The Budget of the Court for the biennium 1996-1997, which forms Part III, Section 5, of the Budget of the United Nations, was adopted by the General Assembly on 23 December 1995 (resolution 50/215).

	US$	US$
PROGRAMME UN-N-08-181. MEMBERS OF THE COURT		
Salaries and allowances	4,398,800	
Pensions	2,003,600	
Travelling expenses	577,200	
Education grants	209,300	
		7,188,900
PROGRAMME UN-N-08-182. THE REGISTRY		
Salaries – established posts	6,275,300	
Salaries – temporary posts	251,400	
Common staff costs	2,181,200	
Salaries and travel costs of temporary assistance	1,206,900	
Consultants	50,400	
Travelling on official business	46,400	
Overtime	86,800	
Representation allowance	7,200	
Hospitality	11,600	
		10,117,200
PROGRAMME UN-N-08-800. COMMON SERVICES		
Contribution to the Carnegie Foundation	1,853,600	
General operating expenses	475,500	
Contractual printing	617,800	
Contracts – external translation	242,300	
Data processing services	102,600	
Supplies and materials	205,000	
Library	127,700	
Furniture and equipment	61,900	
Miscellaneous expenses	27,500	
Acquisition/replacement office automation equipment	560,600	
		4,274,500
		21,580,600

2. *Unforeseen and Extraordinary Expenses*

On 23 December 1995 the General Assembly, in accordance with previous practice, adopted resolution 50/217, containing the following provisions:

"*The General Assembly*

1. *Authorizes* the Secretary-General, with the prior concurrence of the Advisory Committee on Administrative and Budgetary Questions and subject to the Financial Regulations of the United Nations and the provisions of paragraph 3 below, to enter into commitments in the biennium 1996-1997 to meet unforeseen and extraordinary expenses arising either during or subsequent to that biennium, provided that the concurrence of the Advisory Committee shall not be necessary for:

. . . .

(b) Such commitments as the President of the International Court of Justice certifies relate to expenses occasioned by:

(i) The designation of *ad hoc* judges (Statute of the International Court of Justice, Article 31), not exceeding a total of $300,000;
(ii) The appointment of assessors (Statute, Article 30), or the calling of witnesses and the appointment of experts (Statute, Article 50), not exceeding a total of $50,000;
(iii) The maintenance in office for completion of the cases of judges who have not been re-elected (Statute, Article 13, paragraph 3), not exceeding a total of $40,000;
(iv) The payment of pensions and travel and removal expenses of retiring judges, and travel and removal expenses and installation grant of members of the Court (Statute, Article 32, paragraph 7) not exceeding a total of $180,000;
(v) The holding of sessions of the Court away from The Hague (Statute, Article 22), not exceeding a total of $50,000."

III. Accounts for the Biennium 1994-1995

1. Budget Accounts

The Court's accounts are presented in the *I.C.J. Yearbook* in relation to the biennial period concerned and not on the basis of the single financial year.

The table on page 325 gives a summary of the budget accounts for the biennium 1994-1995.

2. Audit of Accounts

The accounts were audited by the competent authorities from 27 February to 10 March 1995 and from 26 February to 1 March 1996.

Budget Accounts for the Biennium 1994-1995

	Appropriation after modifications and transfers US$		*Expenditure* US$	
Programme UN-N-08-181. Members of the Court				
Salaries and allowances	4,463,800		4,484,230	
Pensions	2,044,100		1,951,186	
Travelling and removal expenses	954,600		1,079,784	
Education grants	134,300		123,717	
		7,596,800		7,638,917
Programme UN-N-08-182. The Registry				
Salaries and overtime	8,680,900		8,677,377	
Common staff costs	2,046,300		2,101,164	
Travelling expenses	67,700		72,597	
Representation allowance	7,200		7,200	
Hospitality	7,900		8,007	
		10,810,000		10,866,345
Programme UN-N-08-800. Common Services				
Contribution to the Carnegie Foundation	1,320,200		1,326,760	
General operating expenses	503,900		501,311	
Contractual services	558,000		550,926	
Supplies and materials	212,800		215,696	
Library	115,300		113,587	
Furniture and equipment	213,300		207,662	
Miscellaneous expenses	27,300		27,589	
		2,950,800		2,943,531
		21,357,600		21,448,793